D1105795

Unity
Games
by Tutorials

By the raywenderlich.com Tutorial Team

Mike Berg, Sean Duffy, Brian Moakley, Eric Van de Kerckhove, & Anthony Uccello

Unity Games by Tutorials

Mike Berg, Sean Duffy, Brian Moakley, Eric Van de Kerckhove, and Anthony Uccello

Copyright ©2016 Razeware LLC.

ISBN: 978-1-942878-32-2

Dedications

"To the experimenters, learners and creators. To those taking on the monumental task of making games, and learning to create art on top of that. To the creation of something no one has seen before."

— *Mike Berg*

"To my wife Carmen, and my son Braeden, who provide me inspiration every day to achieve more than I would ever think possible."

— *Sean Duffy*

"To Lizzie, Fiora, and Rowen — these words exist only from your sacrifice and blessings. My others find joy in them as I find joy in you."

— *Brian Moakley*

"To my loving girlfriend who has always been patient with me and respects the time I spend making and playing games."

— *Eric Van de Kerckhove*

"To my loving wife Carrie Oglestone, and our two dogs, Bowser and Daisy, and our three cats, Jack, Ripper, and Boo."

— *Anthony Uccello*

About the authors

 **Mike Berg** is a full-time game artist who is fortunate enough to work with many indie game developers from all over the world. When he's not manipulating pixel colors, he loves to eat good food, spend time with his family, play games and be happy. You can check out his work at www.weheartgames.com

 Sean Duffy is a software engineer by day, and hobbyist game and tools developer by night. He loves working with Unity, and is also a Unity Asset Store developer with a special focus on 2D tools to help other game developers. Some of Sean's more popular Unity Assets include his 2D Shooter Bullet and Weapon System and 2D Homing Missiles assets. You can find Sean on Twitter at @shogan85.

 **Brian Moakley** leads the Unity team at raywenderlich.com and also produces video tutorials on iOS, Unity, and various other topics. When not writing or coding, Brian enjoys story driven first person shooters, reading genre fiction, and epic board game sessions with friends.

 **Eric Van de Kerckhove** is a belgian hobbyist game dev and has been so for more than 10 years. He started with DarkBasic, RPG Maker, Game Maker & XNA and now he makes games using Unity. Eric also takes interest in 3D modelling, vector art and playing video games.

 **Anthony Uccello** Anthony Uccello is a hardcore gamer and has been playing games since the Atari. The only thing he loves more than playing games is making them with Unity. He has contributed to 2 published video games on both iOS and Android. Anthony is a Senior Consultant at Infusion and is working on his own dungeon-crawling-tactical-RPG video game during his off hours. AnthonyUccello.com

About the editors

Adrian Strahan is a tech editor of this book. He is a freelance iOS developer and Project Manager living in the South West of England. He's worked on iPhone and iPad apps since 2010 (iOS3) and specializes in mobile- and web-based application development.

Mitch Allen is a tech editor of this book. Mitch is an indie developer, maker and tech writer. You can find his games on iTunes and his modules on npmjs. mitchallen.com

Chris Belanger is an editor of this book. Chris Belanger is the Book Team Lead and Lead Editor for raywenderlich.com. If there are words to wrangle or a paragraph to ponder, he's on the case. When he kicks back, you can usually find Chris with guitar in hand, looking for the nearest beach, or exploring the lakes and rivers in his part of the world in a canoe.

Wendy Lincoln is an editor of this book. She is a full-time project manager (PMP, actually) specializing in IT marketing and content development. She has an unusual background that involves a culinary degree, cooking show, writing and activism. Occasionally, she logs off help her husband with home improvement projects or enjoy beach life.

Brian Moakley is a final pass editor of this book. Brian leads the Unity team at raywenderlich.com and also produces video tutorials on iOS, Unity, and various other topics. When not writing or coding, Brian enjoys story driven first person shooters, reading genre fiction, and epic board game sessions with friends.

Ray Wenderlich is a final pass editor of this book. Ray is part of a great team - the raywenderlich.com team, a group of over 100 developers and editors from across the world. He and the rest of the team are passionate both about making apps and teaching others the techniques to make them. When Ray's not programming, he's probably playing video games, role playing games, or board games.

About the artists

 **Mike Berg** made all of the 3D models, animations, and textures for this book. He is a full-time game artist who is fortunate enough to work with many indie game developers from all over the world. When he's not manipulating pixel colors, he loves to eat good food, spend time with his family, play games and be happy. You can check out his work at: www.weheartgames.com

 **Vinnie Prabhu** created all of the music and sounds for the games in this book. Vinnie is a music composer/software engineer from Northern Virginia who has done music and sound work for concerts, plays and video games. He's also a staff member on OverClocked ReMix, an online community for music and video game fans. You can find Vinnie on Twitter as @palpablevt.

Table of Contents:

Introduction

If you're reading this book, chances are that you have a dream of making your own video game. But if you're like I was a few years ago, you might be worried that this is too difficult, or something that's out of your reach.

Don't worry! The Unity development platform makes that dream a reality for aspiring game developers everywhere. Unity's aim is to "democratize" game development, by providing a AAA-level engine to independent game developers in a way that is both affordable and accessible.

And with this book, we'll show you how to make your own games with Unity step-by-step — even if you're a complete beginner.

You'll learn by doing. Through this book, you will develop four complete games from scratch:

- A twin-stick shooter

- A first-person shooter

- A 2D platfomer

- A tower defense game (with VR support!)

By the time you're done reading this book, not only will you have created four kick-ass games, but you'll be ready to create that dream game of your own!

Why Unity?

Unity is one of the most powerful and popular game frameworks used today. But why use it rather than other frameworks?

Well, here are a few good reasons:

- **It's free to use.** If you're an indie game developer, you can download and start using Unity for free, which is great when you're just learning. You do have to pay once your company earns $100K or more in a year or in certain other situations, but a lot of the time the free version is just fine. For example, the free version is all you need for this book!

- **It's cross-platform.** With Unity, you can make your game once and build it for a variety of platforms, including Windows, macOS, Linux, iOS, and more.

- **It's powerful.** Unity isn't just for indie games — it has been used by AAA game developers in popular games such as City Skylines, the Long Dark, Hearthstone, and more.

- **It has a visual editor.** Unlike other game platforms where you have to type tons of code before you see anything on the screen, with Unity you can simply import an asset and drag and drop. This visual style of development is great for beginners and professionals alike, and makes game development fast and fun.

- **Live debugging.** With Unity you can click a button to preview your game instantly in the editor, and you can even modify game objects on the fly. For example, you can drag new enemies onto the level as you play it, tweak gameplay values and more, allowing for an iterative game design process.

- **Asset store.** Need some functionality Unity doesn't provide on its own? Chances are somebody has provided the functionality through the Asset Store — a place where you can buy scripts, models, sounds, and more for your games.

- **Unity is fun!** You can think of Unity like a box of LEGO: the only limits are those of your own imagination.

Note that Unity has some cons to consider as well:

- **Learning curve.** It's not hard to learn Unity itself — this book has you covered in that department. :] But if you want to make a game, in addition to knowing how to build it in Unity, you'll also need 3D models, textures, and sounds. These are all made in different tools like Blender, Photoshop, and Audacity, and each of these are subjects of their own books. If you're lucky enough to work with a team of artists that specialize in these tools, then you're set — but if you're an indie developer trying to learn them all, it can be a challenge.

- **Can be expensive.** Although Unity starts out free, eventually you'll have to move to the paid version (such as if your company earns enough money, or if you want to get rid of the splash screen, or access certain other features). When you do move to the paid tier, it can get expensive quickly, especially as your team size grows.

Unity vs. Apple Game Frameworks

Note: If you are not an iOS developer, feel free to skip this section.

If you are familiar with our website, raywenderlich.com, you may know that we have released two other books on game development as well:

1. 2D iOS & tvOS Games by Tutorials, which covers making 2D games using Apple's built-in 2D game framework, Sprite Kit.

2. 3D iOS Games by Tutorials, which covers making 3D games using Apple's built in 3D game framework, Scene Kit.

If you are an iOS developer, you may be wondering which you should use: Unity, or one of the Apple game frameworks.

Here's our recommendation:

- **If you are an experienced iOS developer making a simple game and want to target iOS devices only**, you may want to consider using one of Apple's game frameworks. They are very easy to learn and leverage much of your existing iOS development experience.

- **If you want to target non-iOS devices, or if you want to make games at a professional level**, you may want to consider using Unity. Unity is much more powerful than the Apple game frameworks, and does not lock you into the iOS ecosystem. That's well worth the increased learning curve.

What you need

To follow along with the tutorials in this book, you'll need the following:

- **A PC running Windows 7 or later or a Mac running Mountain Lion or later**. You'll need this to install the latest version of Unity. Note this book will work fine whether you prefer to develop on Windows or on the Mac, since Unity is cross-platform.

- **Unity 5.5 or later**. You'll need Unity 5.5 or later for all tasks in this book. You can download the latest version of Unity for free here: https://store.unity.com/

- **Blender 2.70 or later**. A lot of the assets in this book are Blender files which requires the software to be installed on your computer. Don't worry, it's free! You can download the latest version of Blender for free here: https://www.blender.org/download/

- **(Optional) One or more iOS devices running iOS 7 or later or Android version OS 2.3.1 or later**. This is required for the chapter on publishing your game. If you choose not to read that chapter, you can ignore this requirement.

- **(Optional) A virtual reality headset such as the Occulus Rift or HTC Vive**. If you want to try the chapter on Virtual Reality, you'll need a headset to test the game with. If you don't have a headset don't worry, you can skip this chapter.

- **(Optional) A GPU with DX9 or DX11 capabilites**. For most of the chapters, you should be able to run all the examples on an older video card — except for the virtual reality chapter, for which you'll need a relatively new card with some processing power behind it.

Once you have these items in place, you'll be able to follow along with every chapter in this book.

Who this book is for

This book is for complete beginners to Unity, or for those who'd like to bring their Unity skills to a professional level. The book assumes you have some prior programming experience (in a language of your choice).

If you are a complete beginner programming, we recommend you learn some basic programming skills first. A great way to do that is to watch our free Beginning C# with Unity series, which will get you familiar with programming in the context of Unity. You can watch it for free here:

- https://www.raywenderlich.com/category/unity

The games in the book are made with C#. If you have prior programming experience but are new to C#, we recommend you read through the appendix on C# to get you up to speed with the language before starting the book.

How to use this book

This book is designed to teach you Unity from the ground up. The following chapters, included with this early release, are designed to give you a solid foundation in Unity:

- Chapter 1, "Hello Unity"

- Chapter 2, "GameObjects"

- Chapter 3, "Components"

- Chapter 4, "Physics"

- Chapter 5, "Managers and Pathfinding"

- Chapter 6, "Animation"

- Chapter 7, "Sound"

- Chapter 8, "Finishing Touches"

That covers the most important features of Unity; from there you can dig into the rest of the book and other topics of particular interest to you.

Book source code and forums

You can get the source code for the book here:

www.raywenderlich.com/store/unity-games-by-tutorials/source-code

You'll find all the code from the chapters, as well as solutions to the challenges for your reference.

We've also set up an official forum for the book at www.raywenderlich.com/forums. This is a great place to ask any questions you have about the book, or to submit any errors you might find.

PDF Version

We also have a PDF version of this book available, which can be handy if you want a soft copy to take with you, or you want to quickly search for a specific term within the book.

Buying the PDF version of the book also has a few extra benefits: free PDF updates each time we update the book, access to older PDF versions of the book, and you can download the PDF from anywhere, at anytime.

Visit the book store page here: https://www.raywenderlich.com/store/unity-games-by-tutorials.

License

By purchasing *Unity Games by Tutorials*, you have the following license:

- You are allowed to use and/or modify the source code in *Unity Games by Tutorials* in as many games as you want, with no attribution required.

- You are allowed to use and/or modify all art, images, or designs that are included in *Unity Games by Tutorials* in as many games as you want, but must include this attribution line somewhere inside your game: "Artwork/images/designs: from the *Unity Games by Tutorials* book, available at www.raywenderlich.com".

- The source code included in *Unity Games by Tutorials* is for your own personal use only. You are NOT allowed to distribute or sell the source code in *Unity Games by Tutorials* without prior authorization.

- This book is for your own personal use only. You are NOT allowed to sell this book without prior authorization, or distribute it to friends, co-workers, or students; they must to purchase their own copy instead.

All materials provided with this book are provided on an "as is" basis, without warranty of any kind, express or implied, including but not limited to the warranties of merchantability, fitness for a particular purpose and noninfringement. In no event shall the authors or copyright holders be liable for any claim, damages or other liability, whether in an action of contract, tort or otherwise, arising from, out of or in connection with the software or the use or other dealings in the software.

All trademarks and registered trademarks appearing in this guide are the property of their respective owners.

Acknowledgments

We would like to thank many people for their assistance in making this possible:

- **Our families:** For bearing with us in this crazy time as we worked all hours of the night to get this book ready for publication!

- **Everyone at Unity Technologies:** For developing an amazing platform, for constantly inspiring us to improve our games and skill sets and for making it possible for many developers to make a living doing what they love!

- **And most importantly, the readers of raywenderlich.com — especially you!** Thank you so much for reading our site and purchasing this book. Your continued readership and support is what makes all of this possible!

Section I: Getting Started

This section covers the basics of making 3D games with Unity. These are the most important techniques, the ones you'll use in almost every game you make. When you reach the end of this section, you'll be ready to make your own simple game. Throughout this section, you will create a 3D action game called **Bobblehead Wars**, where you take the role of a space marine blasting hordes of aliens!

Chapter 1, "Hello Unity"

Chapter 2, "GameObjects"

Chapter 3, "Components"

Chapter 4, "Physics"

Chapter 5, "Managers and Pathfinding"

Chapter 6, "Animation"

Chapter 7, "Sound"

Chapter 8, "Finishing Touches"

Chapter 1: Hello Unity

By Brian Moakley

To say game development is a challenge would be the understatement of the year.

Until recently, making 3D games required low-level programming skills and advanced math knowledge. It was akin to a black art reserved only for super developers that never saw the sunlight.

That all changed with Unity. Unity has made this game programming into a craft that's now accessible to mere mortals. Yet, Unity still contains those complicated AAA features, so as you grow as a developer you can begin to leverage them in your games.

Just like every game has a beginning, so does your learning journey — and this one will be hands-on. Sure, you *could* pore over pages and pages of brain-numbing documentation until a lightbulb appears above your head, or you can learn by creating a game.

You obviously would prefer the latter, so you'll build a game named **Bobblehead Wars**.

In this game, you take the role of a kickass space marine, who just finished obliterating an alien ship. You may have seen him before; he also starred in our book *2D iOS & tvOS Games* in a game called Drop Charge.

After destroying the enemy ship, our space marine decides to vacation on a desolate alien planet. However, the aliens manage to interrupt his sun tan — and they are out for blood. After all, space marines are delicacies in this parts of the galaxy!

This game is a twin-stick shooter, where you blast hordes of hungry aliens that relentlessly attack:

You'll toss in some random powerups to keep gameplay interesting, but success lies in fast footwork and a happy trigger finger.

You'll build the game across the next eight chapters, in stages:

1. **Chapter 1, Hello Unity**: You are here! You'll start by exploring the Unity interface and you'll learn how to import assets into your project.

2. **Chapter 2, GameObjects**: Learn about two critical concepts in Unity – GameObjects and Prefabs – by adding and laying out the initial objects for Bobblehead Wars.

3. **Chapter 3, Components**: In Unity, you build up your game objects by combining a set of components. In this chapter, you'll use components to give your hero the ability to walk and blast away at the oncoming horde.

4. **Chapter 4, Physics**: Learn the basics of game physics by adding collision detection and giving the hero the ability to turn on a dime.

5. **Chapter 5, GameManager and Pathfinding**: This is where it gets rough for the space marine. In this chapter, you'll create the tools that spawn the aliens, and then enable them to chase after the hero.

6. **Chapter 6, Animations**: It's time for some shooting and chomping! Learn how to add animations to the marine and the aliens.

7. **Chapter 7, Sounds**: Bring your game game to life by adding background music and a variety of sound effects.

8. **Chapter 8, Finishing Touches**: Games are pointless without winners and losers. In this chapter, you'll add a winning and losing condition, and wrap up the game with some classy touches.

Installing and running Unity

Before you can take on aliens, you need to download the Unity engine itself. Head over to the following URL: http://unity3d.com/get-unity. You'll see a page with many options from which to choose:

You can go Pro if you'd like, but it's excessive at this stage of your journey. For this book, you only need the free version. In fact, you can even release a complete game and sell it on Steam with the free version.

Previously, certain engine features were disabled in the free version. With the release of Unity 5, all those closed-off features are now available to **everybody** who uses the personal version.

In case you are curious, here are what the three options mean:

- **Unity Personal:** This edition allows you to create a complete game and distribute it without paying Unity anything. However, your company must make less than $100,000/year. The other catch is that each game will present a *Made by Unity* splash screen that you can't remove.

- **Unity Plus:** This edition costs $35/month. It comes with performance reporting tools, the Unity Pro skin and some additional features. This version requires your company make less than $200,000/year, and allows you to either disable or customize the "Made by Unity" splash screen.

- **Unity Pro:** This is the highest tier available. It costs $125 per month and comes with useful Unity services, professional iOS and Android add-ons, and has no splash screen. There is no revenue cap either.

There's also an enterprise edition for large organizations that want access to the source code and enterprise support.

> **Note:** Recently Unity switched from a "perpetual" model, where you paid a one-time fee, to a subscription-based model. If you prefer the perpetual model, note that Unity will offer this payment option until the end of 2017.

Under **Unity Personal**, click **Download Now**.

Give it a moment to download then double-click it to start the installation.

Click through the installer until you reach the following screen where you select components.

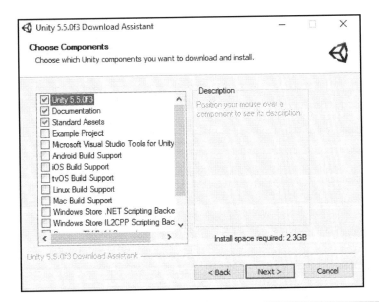

Note: You can develop with Unity equally well on a Windows or Mac machine.

The screenshots in this book are made on Windows, because that is what the majority of Unity developers use (mainly because Windows is a more popular gaming platform).

If you are developing on the Mac, your screenshots may look slightly different, but don't worry — you should still be able to follow along with this book fine. Several of our tech editors are Mac users and have done exactly that while reviewing this book! :]

By default, you should select the **Unity engine**, **Documentation** and **Standard Assets**. Here's why they are significant:

- **Unity Engine:** This is the powerhouse that will drive all your games. When you update the engine, keep this — and only this — selected to avoid downloading unnecessary files.

  Don't worry if your version number is slightly different than what we've shown — Unity is constantly updating.

- **Documentation**: This is your lifeline when your run into issues you don't understand. Downloading the documentation frees you from reliance on the internet. Having it on hand is particularly helpful when traveling or dealing with unstable networks.

- **Standard Assets**: These are additional objects that help you build games such as first-person and third-person character controllers, anti-aliasing and other useful items.

If you plan on reading the chapter about publishing your game, then make sure to check **Android build support** and **iOS build support**.

> **Note:** iOS build support will only work on macOS. For Android build support, You'll need to download Android Studio. The chapter on publishing will cover all of this in detail.
>
> After you finish reading this book, you may find that you need additional platform support, such as tvOS build support.
>
> In that case, you just run the installer again, uncheck everything then check the required platforms. Follow the installer to completion to install those components.

Run the program once installation completes. The first thing you'll see is a dialog box asking for your Unity credentials.

If you don't have an account, click **create one** and follow the steps. Unity accounts are free. You'll have to log in every time you fire it up, but the engine does have an offline mode for those times when you have no network.

Once you're logged in, you'll be presented with a project list that provides an easy place to access all of your projects. Since you don't have any projects, click the **New** button.

You should be looking at the project creation dialog. You'll notice that you have a few options, so fill them in as follows:

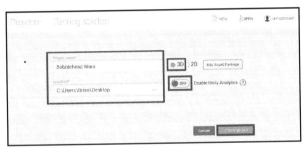

Here's what everything on this screen means:

- The **Project name** represents the internal name of the game. It's not published with your final game, so you can name your projects whatever you like. Give this one the name **Bobblehead Wars**.

- The **Location** field is where you'll save the project and related items. **Click the three dots** in the **Location field** to choose a location on your computer.

- The **3D** option determines whether the game is 3D or 2D — it just configures the editor for that mode. You can switch between the two without starting a new project. For Bobblehead Wars, you want **3D**.

- The **Add Asset Package** button allows you to include additional assets in your game or any others you download from the Unity Asset Store. You don't need to do anything with this for now.

- Finally, you have the option to **Enable Unity Analytics**, which give you insight into your players' experiences. By reading the data, you can determine areas where players struggle and make changes based on the feedback. This book will not delve into analytics, so set the switch to set it to **off**.

Once you're ready, click the **Create project** button. Welcome to the world of Unity!

Learning the interface

When your project loads, you'll see a screen packed full of information. It's perfectly normal to feel a little overwhelmed at first, but don't worry — you'll get comfortable with everything as you work through the first few chapters.

Your layout will probably look like this:

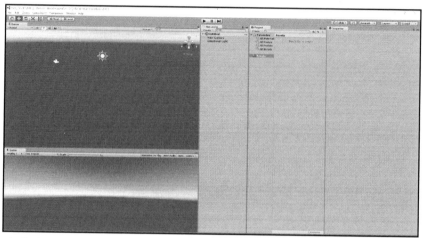

If not, click the Layout button in the top-right and select **2 by 3** from the dropdown.

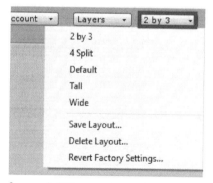

Each layout is composed of several different views. A **view** is simply a panel of information that you use to manipulate the engine. For instance, there's a view made for placing objects in your world. There's another view for you to play the game.

Here's what the interface looks like when broken down into individual views:

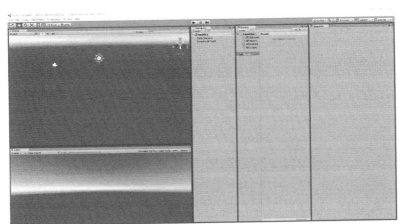

Each red rectangle outlines a view that has its own purpose, interface and ways that you interact with it. Throughout this book, you'll learn about many of these views.

To see a list of all views, click the **Window** option on the menu bar.

The Unity user interface is completely customizable so you can add, remove, and rearrange views as you see fit.

When working with Unity, you'll typically want to rearrange views into a **Layout** that's ideal for a given task. Unity allows you to save layouts for future use.

In the Editor, look for the **Game tab** (the view to the lower left) and **right-click** it. From the drop-down, select **Add Tab** then choose **Profiler**.

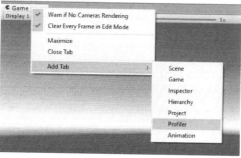

The Profiler view lets you analyze your game while it's running. Unfortunately, the profiler is also blocking the Game view, so you won't be able to play the game while you profile it — not so helpful.

Click and hold the **Profiler tab** and **drag it** to the **Scene tab** above.

As you see, views can be moved, docked and arranged. They can also exist outside the editor as floating windows.

To save the layout, select **Window\Layouts\Save Layout...** and name it **Debugging**.

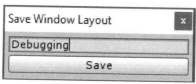

Whenever you need to access this particular layout, you can select the Layout button and choose Debugging.

When clicked, you'll see a listing of all your views.

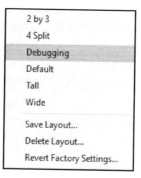

You can also delete layouts. If you ever accidentally trash a stock layout, you can restore the default layouts.

Organizing your assets

Beginners to Unity might imagine that you develop your game from start to finish in Unity, including writing code, creating 3D models and textures, and so on.

In reality, a better way of thinking about Unity is as an integration tool. Typically you will write code or create 3D models or textures in a separate program, and use Unity to wire everything together.

For Bobblehead Wars, we've created some 3D models for you, because learning how to model things in Blender would take an entire book on its own!

In this chapter, you will learn how to import models into your game.

But before you do, it pays to be organized. In this game, you're going to have a lot of assets, so it's critical to organize them in way that makes them easy to find.

The view where you import and organize assets is called the **Project Browser**. It mimics the organization of your file system.

In the Project Browser, select the **Assets** folder and click the **Create** button. Select **Folder** from the drop-down and name it **Models**.

This will be home to all your models. You may feel tempted to create folders and manipulate files in your file system instead of the Project Browser. That's a bad idea — do not do that, Sam I Am!

Unity creates metadata for each asset. Creating, altering or deleting assets on the file system can break this metadata and your game.

Create the following folders: **Animations**, **Materials**, **Prefabs**, **Scenes**, **Scripts** and **Textures**.

Your Project Browser should look like this:

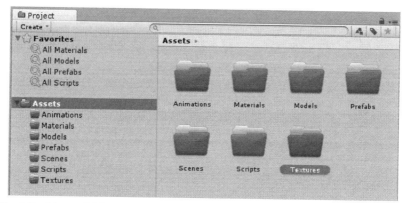

Personally, I find large folder icons to be distracting. If you also have a preference, you can increase or decrease the size by using the slider at the bottom of the Project Browser.

> **Note:** All the screenshots in this book will show the smallest setting.

Importing Assets

Now that you've organized your folders, you're ready to import the assets for the game. First, you'll import the star of the show: the space marine.

In the folder for this chapter, open the **resources** folder and look for 3 files:

1. **BobbleMarine-Head.fbx**

2. **BobbleMarine-Body.fbx**

3. **Bobble Wars Marine texture.psd**

Drag these three files into the Models folder. Don't copy BobbleWars.unitypackage: that comes later.

> **What is an FBX file?** FBX files typically contain 3D models, but they can also include textures and animations. 3D programs, such as Maya and Blender, allow you to export your models for import into programs such as Unity using this file format.

Select the **Models** folder and you'll see that you have a bunch of new files. Unity imported and configured the models for you and created a folder named Materials.

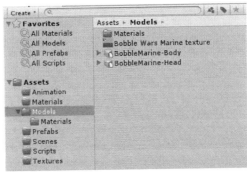

To keep things tidy, move **Bobble Wars Marine texture** from the Models folder to the **Textures** folder. Also move the **contents** of the newly generated **Materials** folder (in the Models folder) into the **parent-level Materials** folder, and then **delete** that new **Materials** folder by pressing **delete** (or command-delete on the Mac).

What are materials? Materials provide your models with color and texture based upon lighting conditions. Materials use what are known as shaders that ultimately determines what appears on screen. Shaders are small programs written in a specific shader language which is far beyond the score of this intro book. You can learn more about materials through Unity's included documentation.

Switch back to the Models folder and select **BobbleMarine-Body**. The Inspector view will now display information specific to that model as well as a preview.

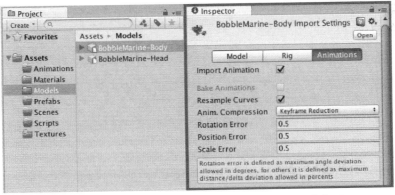

If you see no preview, then its window is closed. At the bottom of the Inspector, find a **gray bar** then **drag it upwards** with your mouse to expand the preview.

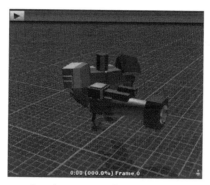

The Inspector allows you to make changes to the model's configuration, and it allows changes to any selected object's properties. Since objects can be vastly different from one another, the Inspector will change context based on the object selected.

Installing Blender

At this point, you've imported the models and texture for the space marine. The models were in FBX format, and the texture was in PSD format.

We supplied the space marine models to you in the FBX format, as this is a popular format for artists to deliver assets. But there's another popular format you should understand how to use as well: Blender files.

Unlike FBX, Blender files contain the source model data. This means you can actually edit these files inside Blender, and the changes will immediately take effect in Unity, unlike an FBX file.

With an FBX, you'd need to export and re-import the model into Unity *every time you change it*.

There is a small tradeoff for all this delicious functionality. For Unity to work with Blender files, you need Blender installed on your computer. Blender is free, and you'll be happy to know that you'll use it to make your own models in a few chapters.

Download and install Blender at the following URL: https://www.blender.org/download/

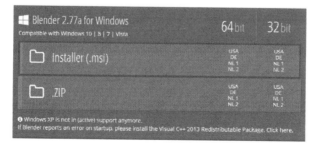

> **Note**: Blender evolves at a rapid pace, so the version you see on your desktop will probably be different than this screenshot.

After you install Blender, run the app and then quit. That's it — you can now use Blender files with Unity.

Importing Packages

Now that you've installed Blender, you can now import the rest of the assets.

The rest of the assets are combined into a single bundle called a **Unity package**. This is a common way that artists deliver assets for Unity, especially when you purchase them from the Unity store.

Let's try importing a package. Select **Assets\Import Package\Custom Package...**, navigate to your resources folder and select **BobbleheadWars.unitypackage** then click **Open**.

You'll be presented with a list of assets included in that package, all of which are selected by default. Note that some of these are Blender files, but there are also other files like textures and sounds as well. Click the **Import** button to import them into Unity.

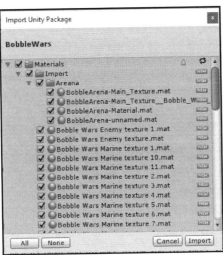

The import will add a bunch of additional assets to your project. If you get a warning, just dismiss it.

As you did before, to keep things tidy, **single click** the newly generated **Materials** folder (in the Models folder) and rename it to **Models**. Drag this new folder into the **parent-level Materials** folder.

Add models to the Scene view

At this point, you have imported everything into Unity. It's time to start putting your game together, and you'll kick it off by adding your models to the Scene view.

The Scene view is where game creation happens. It's a 3D window where you'll place, move, scale and rotate objects.

First, make sure to select the **Scene** view tab. Then, in the Project Browser, select **BobbleArena** from the **Models** subfolder and drag it into the **Scene** view.

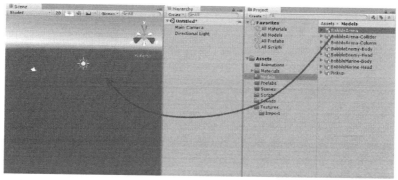

Check out the arena in the Scene view:

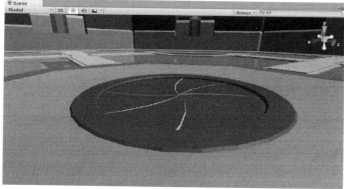

Pretty cool, eh?

The Scene view gives you a way to navigate your game in 3D space:

• **Right-click** and **rotate your mouse** to look around.

• Hold down the **right mouse button** and use the **WASD keys** to actually move through the scene.

• Moving too slow? Give it some juice by holding down the **Shift** key.

- **Scroll** with your **mouse wheel** to zoom.

- **Press** your **mouse wheel** and **move** your mouse to pan.

By default, the view displays everything with textures in a shaded mode. You can switch to other viewing modes such as wireframes or shaded wireframe.

Let's try this out. Just underneath the Scene tab, click the **Shaded dropdown** and select **Wireframe**. Now you'll see all your meshes without any textures, which is useful when you're placing meshes by eye.

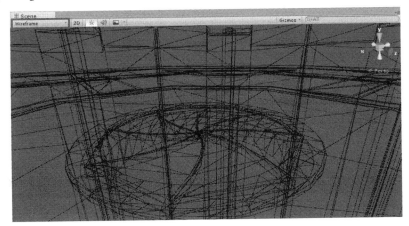

Switch the Scene view back to Shaded textures.

In the Scene view, you'll notice a gizmo in the right-hand corner with the word **Persp** underneath it. This means the Scene view is in perspective mode; objects that are closer to you appear larger than those that are farther away.

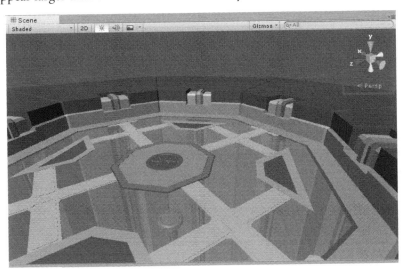

Clicking on a colored axis will change your perspective of the scene. For example, click the green axis and the Scene view will look down from the Y-axis. In this case, the Persp will read **Top** because you're looking at the world from that perspective.

How's it feel to be on top of the world? :]

Clicking the center box will switch the view into **Isometric mode** aka Orthographic mode. Essentially, objects are the same size regardless of their proximity to you.

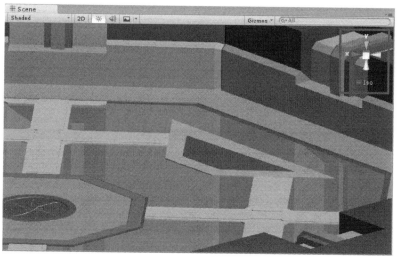

To return to Perspective mode, simply click the center box again. You'll learn more about Isometric mode later in this book.

Adding the hero

At this point, you have the arena set up, but it's missing the guest of honor!

To fix this, in the Project Browser find and open the Models folder then drag **BobbleMarine-Body** into the Hierarchy view.

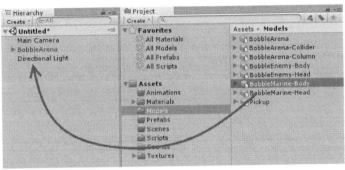

In Unity, games are organized by scenes. For now, you can think of a scene as a level of your game. The Hierarchy view is a list of all objects that are currently present in the scene.

Note that your scene already contains several objects. At this point, it contains your arena, the space marine, and two default objects: the main camera and a directional light.

With the marine body still selected, **hover the mouse** over the Scene view and press the **F** key to zoom to the marine. This shortcut is useful when you have many objects in your scene, and you need to quickly get to one of them.

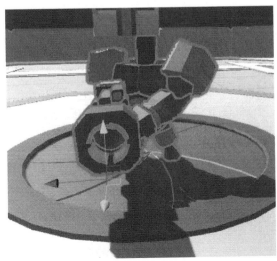

Don't worry if your space marine isn't placed at this exact position. You'll fix that later.

While the space marine's dismembered body is pretty intimidating, he's going to have a hard time seeing and bobbling without a head!

Drag the **BobbleMarine-Head** from the Project Browser into the Hierarchy. Chances are, the head will not go exactly where you'd hope.

Select the head in the **Hierarchy** to see its navigation gizmos. By selecting and dragging the colored arrows, you can move the head in various directions.

The colored faces of the cube in the middle of the head allow you to move the object along two axes at the same time. For example, selecting and dragging the red face — the x-axis — allows you to move the head along the y- and z-axes.

You can use the toolbar to make other adjustments to an object. The first item is the hand tool. This allows you to pan the Scene and is equivalent to holding down the middle mouse button.

Select the position tool to see the position gizmo that lets you reposition the selected object.

Use the rotate tool to rotate the selected object.

The scale tool allows you to increase and decrease the size of an object.

The rect tool lets you rotate, scale and reposition sprites. You'll be using this when working with the user interface and Unity 2D.

Using the aforementioned tools, tweak the position of the helmet so it sits on the neck. Also, see if you can move the space marine so he's centered in the arena. In the next chapter, you'll position these precisely with the Inspector. When done, the marine should look like this:

After positioning the space marine's head, select **File\Save Scene**. Unity will present you with a save dialog. Name the scene **Main**, and after you finish creating it drag the file to the **Scenes** folder.

> **Note:** Unity does not autosave and unfortunately can be a little bit "crashy" at times. Make sure to save early and often. Otherwise, you will lose work (and possibly sanity).

Where to go from here?

Congratulations! You now have a space marine at the ready to kill all the alien monsters, and you've learned a lot about the Unity user interface and importing assets along the way.

Specifically, in this chapter you've learned:

- **How to configure the Unity layout**, including customizing it for specific tasks.

- **How to import assets** and organize them within Unity.

- **How to add assets to a scene** and position them manually.

In the next chapter, the aliens will finally catch up with the space marine — and you'll learn about GameObjects and Prefabs along the way!

Chapter 2: GameObjects

By Brian Moakley

In the last chapter, our brave hero was left alone with fantasies of seeing some aliens to blast running through his barely attached bobblehead.

In this chapter, you'll make his dreams come true. But first, you must understand one crucial concept: **GameObjects**.

> **Note:** This chapter's project continues from the previous chapter. If you didn't follow along or want to start fresh, please use the starter project from this chapter.

Introducing GameObjects

In Unity, game scenes contain objects with a name you'll never guess: GameObjects. :] There are GameObjects for your player, the aliens, bullets on the screen, the actual level geometry — basically, everything in the game itself.

Just like the Project Browser contains all assets, the Hierarchy contains a list of GameObjects in your scene.

To see this, you'll need to have your project open, so if it isn't open already, do so now.

> **Note:** Unity's way of opening project files is a bit strange. You can navigate your file system and look for a scene file. Double-click the scene then Unity will open your project with the current scene selected.

> Or, if you start Unity or click **File\Open Project**, you'll see a project list. Select the desired project and Unity will take care of the rest.
>
> If your project isn't listed, click the **Open** button to bring up a system dialog box. Instead of searching for a particular file, try navigating to the top-level directory of your Unity project and click **Select Folder**. The engine will detect the Unity project within the folder and open it.

Once your project is open, take a look at your Hierarchy and count the GameObjects.

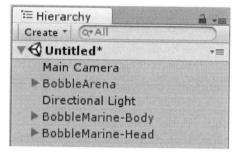

Your first thought may be *three* because you added three GameObjects in the last chapter: arena, space marine body and space marine head.

However, there are two other GameObjects: **Main Camera** and **Directional Light**. Remember how Unity creates these by default? Yes, these are also GameObjects.

Yet, there are even more GameObjects. You'll notice that there are disclosure triangles to the left of the GameObjects you imported.

Holding down the **Alt button** on PC or Option on Mac, **click** each **disclosure triangle**.

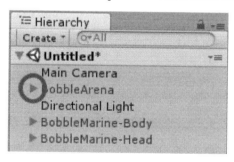

As you can see, you have *so* many GameObjects:

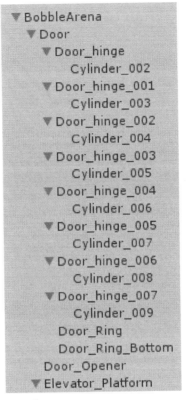

Three important points to remember:

- **GameObjects can contain other GameObjects**. On a base level, this useful behavior allows organizing and parenting of GameObjects that are related to each other. More importantly, changes to parent GameObjects may affect their children — more on this in just a moment.

- **Models are converted into GameObjects**. Unity creates GameObjects for the various pieces of your model that you can alter like any other GameObject.

- **Everything contained in the Hierarchy is a GameObject**. Even things such as cameras and lights are GameObjects. If it's in the Hierarchy, it's a GameObject that's subject to your command.

Our hero is so bored that he's picking his nose with his gun. You need to get him moving, but first, you need to reposition your GameObjects.

Moving GameObjects

Before starting, **collapse** all the GameObject trees by clicking the disclosure triangles.

Select **BobbleArena** in the Hierarchy and take a moment to observe the **Inspector**, which provides information about the selected GameObject.

GameObjects contain a number of components, which you can think of as small units of functionality. There is one component that all GameObjects contain: the **Transform** component.

The Transform component contains the position, rotation, and scale of the GameObject. Using the inspector, you can set these to specific numbers instead of having to rely upon your eyeballs. When hovering the mouse over the axis name, you'll see arrows appear next to the pointer.

Press the **left mouse button** and **drag** the mouse either left or right to adjust those numbers. This trick is an easy way to adjust the values by small increments.

With **BobbleArena** selected, set **Position** to (**-6.624, 13.622, 6.35**). As I developed this game, the arena ended up in this position. You could just as well place it in the center of the game of the game world. Set the **Scale** to (**2.0, 2.0, 2.0**). This gives the player more room to navigate the arena.

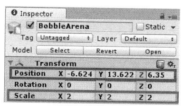

If you zoom out of the Scene view, you'll probably notice the space marine is suspended in the void; mostly likely, he's questioning his assumptions about gravity. You could move his head and then his body, but your life will be much easier if you group his body parts into one GameObject.

In the Hierarchy, click the **Create** button and select **Create Empty**.

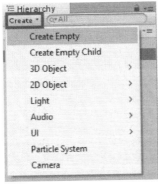

An **empty** is a GameObject that only has only the one required component that all GameObjects have — the Transform component, as you learned earlier.

> **Note**: You can also create an empty GameObject by clicking **GameObject\Create Empty**. This goes for other things such as components. There is no "preferred" way to do things — go with whatever works best for your workflow.

Parenting the space marine

In the Hierarchy, you'll see your new GameObject creatively named: GameObject. **Single-click** the **GameObject** and name it **SpaceMarine**.

You can insert spaces in GameObjects' names, e.g., *Space Marine*. However, for the sake of consistency, you'll use camel casing for names in this book.

Drag **BobbleMarine-Body** and **BobbleMarine-Head** into the **SpaceMarine** GameObject.

A few things happen when you parent GameObjects. In particular, the position values for the children change even though the GameObjects don't move. This modification happens because GameObject positions are always relative to the parent GameObject.

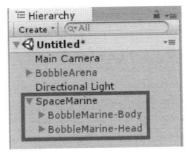

Select the **SpaceMarine** in the Hierarchy. Go to the **Scene** view and press **F** to focus on it. Chances are, the arena is blocking your view.

Thankfully, you don't need to get Dumbledore on speed dial. You can make it disappear! Select **BobbleArena** in the Hierarchy, and in the **Inspector, uncheck** the box to the left of the GameObject's name. This will make the arena disappear.

You only should see the hero now. Select the **SpaceMarine** GameObject. In the Inspector, **mouse over** the **X position label** until you see the scrubber arrows. Hold the **left mouse button** and move your mouse **left or right**. Notice how all the GameObjects move relative to the parent.

As you can see, having parents does have its advantages. No offense to any parentless deities out there.

When you parent a GameObject in another, the position of the child GameObject won't change. The difference is that of the child GameObject is now positioned relative to the parent. That is, setting the child to (0, 0, 0) will move the child to the center of the parent versus the center of the game world.

You'll do this now to assemble your marine.

Select **BobbleMarine-Body**, and in the **Inspector**, set **Position** to (0, 0, 0). Go select **BobbleMarine-Head** and set **Position** to `(-1.38, 6.16, 1.05)` in the Inspector.

Congratulations! Your hero is assembled.

Positioning the marine

Now to it's time to place the space marine in his proper starting position. Select **BobbleArena**, and in the Inspector, **check** the box next to the name to reenable it.

Select **SpaceMarine**, and in the Inspector, set its **position** to (**-4.9, 12.54, 5.87**). Also, set the **rotation** to (**0, 0, 0**). Your marine should end up directly over the hatch. If this isn't the case, then feel free to tweak the values until that is the case.

Once the hero is in place, press **F** in the Scene view so you can see him standing proud.

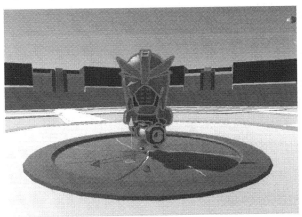

The hero should now be positioned precisely over the elevator, ready to rock. Unfortunately for him, his grandiose rock party will soon degrade into a bug hunt.

Creating a prefab

This game features creepy crawly bugs, and like the hero, they're composed of many pieces. Some assembly is required.

In the Hierarchy, click the **Create** button and select **Create Empty** from the drop-down. **Single-click** the GameObject to name it **Alien**.

Select **Alien** in the Hierarchy, and in the Inspector, set the **position** to: (**2.9, 13.6, 8.41**).

From the Project Browser, drag **BobbleEnemy-Body** from the **Models** folder into the **Alien GameObject**.

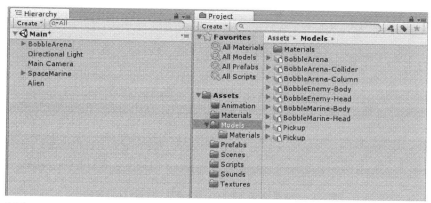

Set **BobbleEnemy-Body Position** to **(0, 0, 0)**. Now the alien and hero should be side by side in the arena.

As creepy as the alien is without a head, the hero needs more to shoot at than that spindly little frame. From the Project Browser, drag **BobbleEnemy-Head** into the **Alien GameObject**. Set **Position** to **(0.26, 1.74, 0.31)**, **Rotation** to **(-89.96, 0, 0)** and **Scale** to **(100, 100, 100)**.

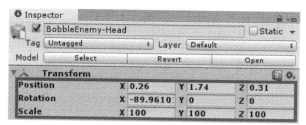

That's one fierce little bug. They go together so well that you could mistake them for the next superstar crime-fighting duo.

At this point, you have one parent GameObject for the hero and another for the alien. For the hero, this works great because you need only one. For the alien, you're going to need many — so, so many.

You could copy and paste the alien to make clones, but they'd all be individuals. If you needed to make a change to the alien's behavior, you'd have to change each instance.

For this situation, it's best to use a **prefab**, which is a master copy that you use to make as many individual copies as you want. Prefabs are your friend because when you change anything about them, you can apply the same to the rest of the instances.

Making a prefab is simple. Select the **Alien GameObject** and **drag** it into the **Prefabs folder** in the Project Browser.

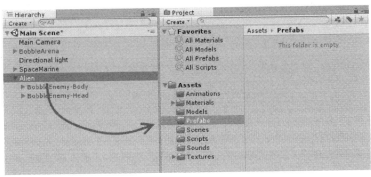

A few things have changed. There's a new entry in your Prefabs folder with an icon beside it. You'll also note the name of the GameObject in the Hierarchy is now blue.

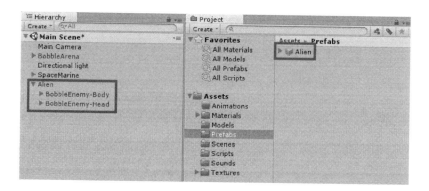

Note: You don't have to drag your model into that specific folder to create a prefab — all that's required is dragging a GameObject into *any* folder in the Project Browser. Having a Prefabs folder is simply good housekeeping.

The blue indicates the GameObject has been either instanced from a prefab or a model, such as the BobbleArena. Select the **Alien** GameObject in the Hierarchy and look at the Inspector; you'll notice some additional buttons:

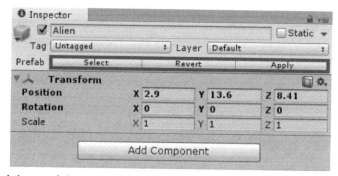

Here's the breakdown of these new buttons:

- **Select** will select the prefab inside the Project Browser. This is useful when you have lots of files and want easy access to the prefab to make changes.

- **Revert** will undo changes you've made to your instance. For example, you might play around with size or color but end up with something horrible, like a viciously pink spider. You'd click the Revert button to restore sanity.

- **Apply** will apply any changes you made to that instance to its prefab. All instances of that prefab will be updated as well.

Creating a prefab instance is quite easy. Select the **Alien** prefab in the Project Browser and **drag it** next to your other Alien in the Scene view.

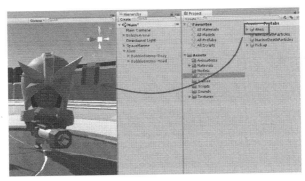

You can also drag an instance to the Hierarchy. As you can see, creating more aliens is as easy as dragging the `Alien prefab` from the Project Browser. But you don't need droves of aliens yet, so **delete** all the Aliens from the Hierarchy. You delete a GameObject by selecting it in the Hierarchy, and pressing Delete on your keyboard, (Command–Delete on a Mac), or you can right-click it and select **Delete**.

Fixing the models

The next to-do is fixing some of your models. In this case, Unity imported your models but lost references to the textures.

In the **Models** folder of your Project Browser, drag a **BobbleArena-Column** into the Scene view. You'll find a dull white material.

If a material name or texture name changes in the source package, Unity will lose connection to that material. It tries to fix this by creating a new material for you but with no textures attached to it.

To fix this, you have to assign a new texture to the material. In the Project Browser, select the **Models** subfolder and then, expand the **BobbleArena-Column** to see all the child objects.

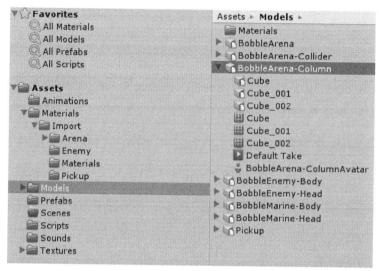

Next, select **Cube_001** in the Project Browser, and in the Inspector, **click the disclosure triangle** for the **Main_Material** shader.

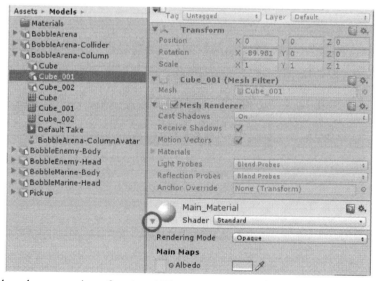

You'll see that there are a lot of options! These options configure how this material will look.

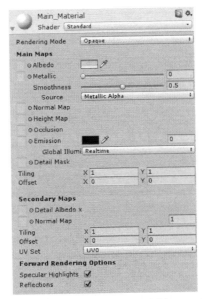

For example, the Metallic slider determines the metal-like quality of the material. A high value metallic value means the texture will reflect light much like metal. You'll notice a grey box to the left of most of the properties. These boxes are meant for textures.

In this case, all you want is a an image on your model. In the Project Browser, select the Textures folder. **Click and drag** the **Bobble Wars Marine texture** to the **Albedo** property box located in the shader properties.

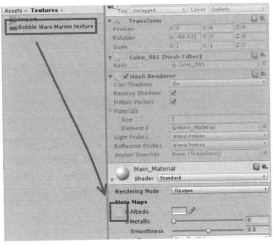

The Albedo property is for textures, but you can put colors there are well. Once you do this, your columns will now have a texture.

The arena also suffered a texture issue.

In the Hierarchy, expand the **BobbleArena** and then expand **Floor**. Select the **Floor Piece**.

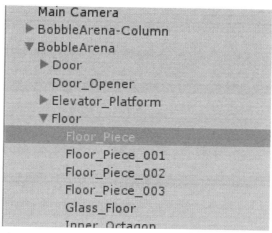

In the Inspector, you'll notice two materials attached to the floor piece. The **BobbleArena-Main_Texture** material does not have a texture assigned to it. You can tell because the material preview is all white.

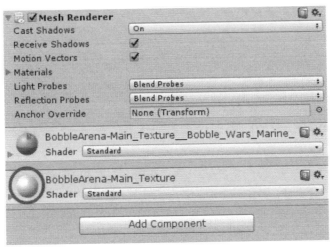

Like you did for the column, select the **Textures** folder in the Project Browser. **Click and drag** the **Bobble Wars Marine texture** to the **Albedo** property box located in the shader properties.

Your floor will now acquire borders. How stylish!

You'll also notice that not just one, but all the floor sections acquired borders. This is because they all use the same material.

Adding obstacles

Now, that you have your models fixed, it's time add a bunch of columns to the arena. You'll make a total of seven columns, and you'll use prefabs for this task.

> **Note:** Whenever it seems like you should make a duplicate of a GameObject, use a prefab instead — it's another best practice. Some Unity developers insist on using prefabs for everything, even unique objects.
>
> The thinking is that it's much easier to create a prefab and make duplicates than it is to turn a group of existing GameObjects into prefab instance. The former

> method requires minimal work whereas the latter requires you to extract the
> commonalities into a prefab while maintaing any unique changes for each
> instance. This results a lot of work.

In the Hierarchy, drag the **BobbleArena-Column** into your **Prefabs** folder to turn it into
a prefab.

With **BobbleArena-Column** instance still selected in the Hierarchy View, go to the
Inspector and set **position** to (**1.66**, **12.83**, **-54.48**). Set **scale** to (**3.5**, **3.5**, **3.5**). You *do*
want all the prefabs to be the same scale, so click the **Apply** button.

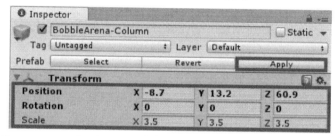

Now it's time for you to make the rest of the columns.

Dragging one column at a time from project to project in the Scene view can be a little
tedious, especially when there are several instances. Duplicate a column by selecting one
in the Hierarchy and pressing **Ctrl–D** on PC or **Command–D** on Mac.

Create a total of six duplicates and give them following positions:

- **Column 1**: (44.69, 12.83, -28.25)

- **Column 2**: (42.10, 12.83, 30.14)

- **Column 3**: (-8.29, 12.83, 63.04)

- **Column 4**: (80.40, 12.83, -13.65)

- **Column 5**: (-91.79, 12.83, -13.65)

- **Column 6**: (-48.69, 12.83, 33.74)

You should now have seven columns in the arena.

The arena looks good, but the Hierarchy is a bit messy. Tidy it up by clicking the **Create button** and select **Create Empty**. Rename the GameObject to **Columns** and drag each column into it.

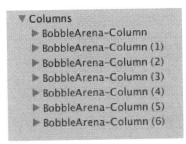

You'll notice the columns have a similar name with unique numbers appended to them. Since they essentially act as one entity, it's fine for them to share a name. Hold the **Shift** key and **select all the columns** in the Hierarchy. In the Inspector, **change the name** to **Column**.

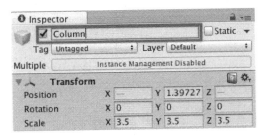

Note: As you can see, it's possible to change a common property for a bunch of GameObjects at once.

Creating spawn points

What good are bloodthirsty aliens unless they spawn in mass quantities? In this section, you'll set up spawn points to produce enemies to keep our hero on his toes.

So far, you've assembled the game with GameObjects that you want the player to see. When it comes to spawn points, you don't want anybody to see them. Yet, it's important that *you* know where they lay.

You could create a 3D cube and place it in your scene to represent a spawn point, then remove it when the game starts, but that's a clunky approach. Unity provides a simpler mechanism called **labels**, which are GameObjects visible in the Scene view, but invisible during gameplay. To see them in action, you'll create a bunch of different spawn points similar to how you created the columns.

Click the **Create** button in the Hierarchy and select **Create Empty**. Give it the name **Spawn** and set **position** to (**-5.44, 13.69, 90.30**).

In the Inspector, **click** the **colored cube** next to the checkmark. A flyout with all the different label styles will appear. Click **blue capsule**.

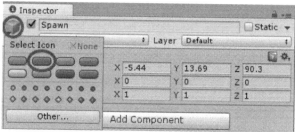

Look at your Scene view; you'll see it's been annotated with the Spawn point.

You need to create ten more spawn points. Make placement easier by doing the following:

1. In the Scene view, **click** on the **center cube** of the **scene gizmo** to switch the Scene view to Isometric mode.

2. Click the **green y-axis arrow** so that you look down on the scene.

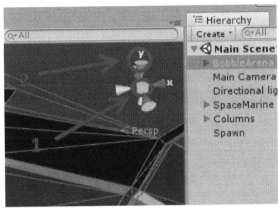

Now go ahead with duplicating and repositioning ten more spawn points, according to the following image:

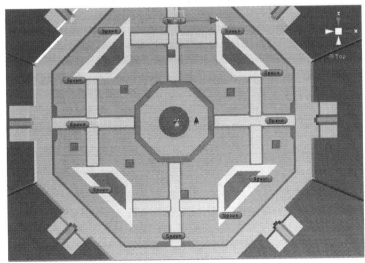

Don't worry if you don't get them exactly the same — game design is more of an art than a science!

Once you're done, click the **Create** button in the Hierarchy, select **Create Empty** and name it **SpawnPoints**. Drag all the spawn points into it. **Batch rename** them like you did with the columns to **Spawn**.

Congratulations! Your game is now properly set up. Make sure to **save**!

Where to go from here?

At this point, you have your hero, his enemy the alien, and the arena in which they will battle to the death. You've even created spawn points for the little buggers. As you set things up, you learned about:

- **GameObjects** and why they are so important when working with Unity.

- **Prefabs** for when you want to create many instances of a single GameObject.

- **Labels** to help you annotate game development without interfering with the game.

There's still not any action in your game, but that's fine. You're ready to learn how to give your game the breath of life and take it away (via the space marine's magnificent machine gun).

Chapter 3: Components

By Brian Moakley

At this point, you've accomplished your goal of having all the main actors ready, but it's essentially an empty stage. Sure, you might win some avante-garde awards for a poignant play on the lack of free will, but that's not going to pay the bills.

In this chapter, you'll add some interactivity to your game through the use of **Components**, which are fundamental to Unity game development. If you were to think of a GameObject as a noun, then a component would be a verb; a component does something on behalf of a GameObject.

You've learned a bit about components already. In previous chapters, you learned how each GameObject has one required component: the **Transform** component, which stores the GameObject's position, rotation, and scale.

But Unity comes with far more components than that. For instance, there's a **light** component that will illuminate anything near it. There's an **audio source** component that will produce sound. There's even a **particle system** component that will generate some impressive visual effects. And of course, if there isn't a component that does what you want, you can write your own.

In this chapter, you'll learn about several types of components, including the **Rigidbody** component, the **script** component, and more. By the end of this chapter, your marine will be running and gunning!

Getting started

If you completed the last chapter, **open** your current **Bobblehead Wars** project to pick up where you left off. If you got stuck or skipped ahead, open the **Bobblehead Wars** starter project from this chapter's resources.

Currently, the space marine only knows how to stand like a statue. He needs to move around if he's going to avoid being some alien's snack.

The first thing you'll add is a **Rigidbody** component, which opts the GameObject into the physics engine. By adding it, you'll enable the GameObject to collide with other GameObjects.

You'll learn much more about rigidbodies and collisions when you reach the chapter on physics. For now, just take it at face value and move forward.

Adding the rigidbody component

In the Hierarchy, select the **SpaceMarine** GameObject and click the **Add Component** button in the Inspector.

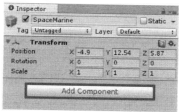

You'll see many different categories. When you know which component you need, simply search by name. Otherwise, select one of the categories and pick the best option.

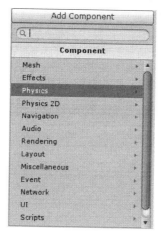

Click the **Physics category** then select **Rigidbody**.

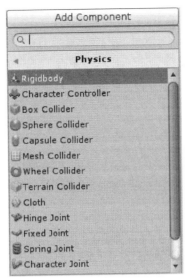

You'll see that a Rigidbody component was attached to the GameObject. Congratulations! You've added your first component.

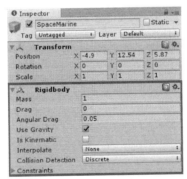

Each component has its own set of properties, values and so forth. These properties can be changed in the Inspector or in code. Components also have their own icon to make it easy to determine their type at a glance.

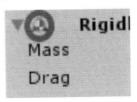

You'll notice a couple of icons in the right-hand corner of each component, like this:

The first icon is the **Reference** icon. **Click it**. It'll open another window with the documentation page for that component. If you installed the documentation, this page is on your computer, and yes, the search bar works.

You'll also see a gear icon. **Click it**. This dialog will appear:

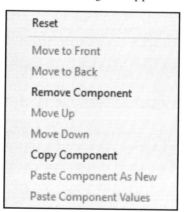

Here are the most important options listed here:

- **Reset** will reset the component to its default values.

- **Move to Front** and **Move to Back** adjust the ordering of sprites in 2D games.

- **Remove Component** will delete the component from the GameObject — you can undo this action.

- **Copy Component** allows you to copy a component from one GameObject and paste it onto another.

- **Paste Component as New** will paste a copied component to a GameObject.

- **Paste Component Values** allows you to overwrite the values of the current component from a copied component. Specifically, you can copy the values of a component while your game is being played. When you stop the game, you can paste those values onto another component. This is quite useful because sometimes it's useful to tweak things as you play to see what works in practice.

By adding the Rigidbody component to the space marine, you've made it so that he now can respond to collision events and respond to gravity. However, you don't want him bouncing off enemies or walls. You definitely want to know about those collisions events, but you don't want the hero to fly out of control just because he bumped into a column.

In the **Rigidbody** component, check the **IsKinematic** checkbox. Also, **uncheck** the **Use Gravity** option.

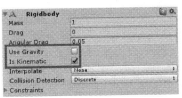

The `isKinematic` property tells the physics engine that you're manually controlling the marine, rather than letting the physics engine move the marine for you. But the physics engine is still aware of where the marine is and when it collides with something. This is helpful so that when the marine collides with an alien, the physics engine will notify you so you can make something happen — like the space marine getting chomped!

By unchecking the `Use Gravity` option, the space marine won't be affected by gravity. Again — you don't need this because you'll be moving the marine manually and are only using the Rigidbody for collision detection.

Now comes the fun part: it's time to make that marine dance! Or move. That's fine too.

Unity provides some built-in components to make movement easy, and you'll use them in the next chapter. But for learning purposes, in this chapter you'll do everything manually through the power of scripting.

Introducing scripting

For the non-programmer, at best, scripting is a small barrier to entry. At worst, scripting is the devil that never sleeps.

Coming from an arts background, I can say that scripting is not as hard as you might imagine. Like anything, it just requires some time and patience to understand how it works.

In this book, you'll write scripts in C#, which is a popular language developed by Microsoft that works for both mobile and desktop apps. It's feature-rich and fully versatile. Unfortunately, I can't teach it all within the covers of this book.

Thankfully, you can learn C# at raywenderlich.com where there's a free course that teaches the language from the ground up, for complete beginners.

It's designed for non-programmers and taught within the context of Unity.

If you're a beginner to programming, definitely check that out first. If you're an experienced developer, or a particularly brave beginner feel free to continue along, since everything in this book is step-by-step; just understand that there may be some gaps in your understanding without C# knowledge.

Why not Javascript?

Believe it or not, Unity supports other programming languages such as Javascript and Boo. Some people consider Javascript to be "easy" to learn, so you may wonder why we elected to use C#.

The truth of the matter is that Unity's implementation of Javascript IS NOT JavaScript. It's actually called UnityScript and considerably different than the Javascript widely used on the web. While you can certainly be productive with it in Unity, there are no viable use cases for it outside of the engine.

C#, on the other hand, is completely compatible with the outside world. Skills that you learn in Unity can easily be applied outside of game development. For instance, if you find yourself disliking game development (or having a hard time making a living) but enjoying the language, you can transition those skills into a C# development job, creating desktop or mobile apps, or even developing backend server apps.

Finally, most professional Unity developers write in C#, so by taking the time to learn it, you'll be in a better position to take advantage of game development opportunities as they come up.

The way coding works in Unity is that you create **scripts**. Scripts are simply another type of component that you attach to GameObjects, that you get to write the code for.

A script derives from a class called **MonoBehaviour**, and you can override several methods to get notified upon certain events:

- **Update**(): This event occurs at every single frame. If your game runs at sixty frames per second, `Update()` is called sixty times. Needless to say, you don't want to do any heavy processing in this method.

- **OnEnable**(): This is called when a GameObject is enabled, and also when an inactive GameObject suddenly reactivates. Typically, you deactivate GameObjects when you don't need them for a while but will have a need at a later point in time.

- **Start**(): This is called once in the script's lifetime and before Update() is called. It's a good place to do set up and initalization.

- **Destroy**(): This is called right before the object goes to the GameObject afterlife. It's is a good place to do clean up such as shutting down network connections.

There are many other events that you'll discover throughout this book. To see a complete listing, head to the `MonoBehavior` reference on Unity's site:

- https://docs.unity3d.com/ScriptReference/MonoBehaviour.html

Creating your first script

It's showtime!

You have many options for creating a script. You could click the Add Component button and then select New Script.

But I'd like you to try it this way: select the **Scripts** folder in the **Project Browser**, and then click the **Create** button. Select **C# Script** from the drop-down and name it **PlayerController**.

You'll see your new script in the Scripts folder. **Drag it** from the **Scripts** folder onto the **SpaceMarine GameObject**.

You should now see the script listed as one of the components on the Space Marine:

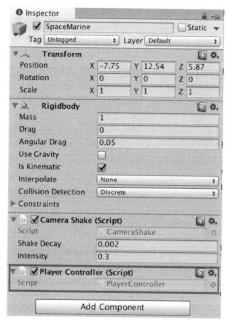

You've added your first custom component! Granted, it doesn't do anything...yet.

You'll change that in just a moment, but before you do, you need to learn about the Input Manager.

Managing Input

Inputs are the game's controls, and if you're developing a game for a desktop computer, your users will expect the ability to rebind keys. Unity's **Input Manager** makes this easy, and is the preferred way for your game to deal with user input.

To get access to the Input Manager, click **Edit\Project Settings\Input**.

The Inspector will look pretty empty. Click the **disclosure triangle** next to the word **Axes**.

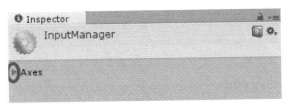

Once expanded, you'll see all the pre-configured inputs that are available to you.

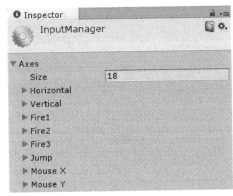

The first property is **Size**, and it's the number of inputs your game uses. You can decrease the number to decrease the amount and increase it if you want more inputs. The current amount of inputs is more than enough for this game.

Click the **disclosure triangle** next to **Horizontal**. Here you can configure the input for the horizontal axis, i.e., left or right.

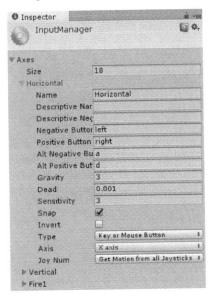

Here's a breakdown of the key fields:

- **Horizontal** is the name Unity gives the input, but you can name it anything. This is also the name you reference in code, which you'll see in a moment.

- **Descriptive Name and Negative Name** are the names presented to the user in the Unity game launcher if they want to remap the keys. You can disable the Unity game launch and provide your own key mapping interface if you'd like, so these aren't required properties.

- **Negative and Positive Buttons** are the actual keys being used. Unity allows buttons to have negative or opposite keys. For instance, the `right` arrow key is positive while the `left` arrow key is negative. You don't need to provide a negative for all keys — it wouldn't make sense to provide a negative key for a use action.

- **Alt Negative and Alt Positive Buttons** are alternative keys. In this case, instead of left and right arrow keys, you enable the `a` and `d` keys.

The other fields mostly relate to the functionality of analog sticks. For simplicity, this game will only use keyboard input. If you wanted to make the game a bonafide twin stick shooter, these are the options you'd tweak to create a tight control scheme.

Accessing input from code

Now to actually implement the control scheme. In the Project Browser, **double-click** the **PlayerController** script to launch the editor.

> **Note:** If you've never set up or used a code editor before, prepare to see MonoDevelop launch. MonoDevelop is part of Unity's default installation and allows you to edit code.
>
> However, you can use other editors. For instance, uf you're running Unity on Windows, you can opt to use Visual Studio instead. To learn more about Visual Studio and MonoDevelop, check out the Appendix chapter, "Code Editors".

When the code editor opens, you'll see your first script. Every new script contains empty implementations for `Start()` and `Update()`.

Look for a blank line below the first { (aka "curly bracket") — that's the class definition. Add the following code there:

```
public float moveSpeed = 50.0f;
```

Note: If you are new to programming languages, it's critical that you copy everything exactly as it is written. Any deviation will produce errors. Programming languages are very precise and become grumpy when you use the incorrect case or syntax.

If your script throws an error, carefully review the code to make sure you didn't miss, forget or mess up something.

moveSpeed is a variable that determines how fast the hero moves around in the arena. You set it to a default value of 50 that you can change later in Unity's interface.

Now, to write the actual moving code. In Update(), add the following:

```
Vector3 pos = transform.position;
```

This bit of code simply gets the current position of the current GameObject — in this case the space marine since that is what this script is attached to — and stores it in a variable named pos. In Unity, a Vector3 encapsulates the x, y and z of a GameObject, i.e., the object's point in 3D space.

Now comes the tricky part. Add the following after the previous line:

```
pos.x += moveSpeed * Input.GetAxis("Horizontal")
    * Time.deltaTime;
pos.z += moveSpeed * Input.GetAxis("Vertical")
    * Time.deltaTime;
```

When you move the object, it'll only be on z- and x-axes because y represents up and down. Because there are two different input sources ("Horizontal" for left and right, and "Vertical" for up and down), you need to calculate values for each axis separately.

Input.GetAxis("Horizontal") retrieves a value from the Horizontal component of the Input Manager. The value returned is either 1 or −1, with 1 indicating that a positive button in the Input Manager is being pressed. According to the settings you saw defined earlier, this is either the right arrow or d keys. Similarly, a value of −1 indicates that a negative button is being pressed, meaning it was either the left arrow or the a key.

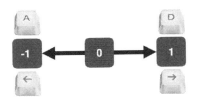

Whatever the returned value may be, it's then multiplied by the moveSpeed and added to the current x position of the GameObject, effectively moving it in the desired direction.

The same thing happens with Input.GetAxis("Vertical"), except it retrieves a value from the vertical component of the Input Manager (indicating the s, down, w or up keys), multiplies this (1 or −1) value by the moveSpeed and adds it to the z position of the GameObject.

So what's with Time.deltaTime? That value indicates how much time has passed since the last Update(). Remember, Update() is called with every frame, so that time difference must be taken into account or the space marine would move too fast to be seen.

TL/DR: Time.deltaTime ensures movement is in sync with the frame rate.

What do these numbers mean?

By default, Unity considers 1 point to be equal to 1 meter, but you don't have to follow this logic. For instance, you may be making a game about planets, and that scale would be way too small. For the purposes of simplicity in this book, we have sized our models to follow Unity's default of one point per meter.

Now that you've altered the location, you have to apply it to the SpaceMarine. Add the following after the previous line:

```
transform.position = pos;
```

This updates the SpaceMarine's position with the new position.

Save the script and switch back to Unity. You may be tempted to run your game, but there's a slight problem. The camera is not positioned correctly.

In the Hierarchy, select the **Main Camera**, and in the Inspector, set **Position** to (-9.7, 53.6, -56.1) and **Rotation** to (30, 0, 0). I got these values by moving the camera around manually and looking at the Camera preview in the lower right until I was happy with the result.

In the **Camera** component, set **Field of View** to **31**. This effectively "zooms in" the view a bit.

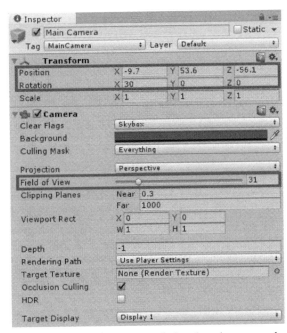

Now it's time to give your game a test run. Look for the play controls at the center-top of the editor. Click the **play** button.

Note: You'll notice the controls give you two more options: **pause** and **pause stepper**. Pause allows you to, well, pause your game in motion. The stepper allows you to step through the animation one frame at a time and is especially useful for debugging animation issues.

Now, look at the Game window and move your character by pressing the arrow keys or WASD keys. Behold...life!

The Game Window

The Game window is where you actually play the game. There are two life-and-death details to keep in mind as you play.

First, when you start playing, the interface becomes darker to give a visual queue that you're in play mode.

Second, when you play your game you can change anything about it (including changing values on components in the inspector), but when you stop playing the game, **ALL YOUR CHANGES WILL BE LOST**. This is both a blessing and a curse. The blessing is that you have the ability to tweak the game without consequence. The curse is that sometimes you forget you're in play mode, continue working on your game, then for some reason the game stops. *Poof! Buh-bye changes!*

Thankfully, you can (and should) make play mode really obvious. Select **Edit\Preferences** on PC or **Unity\Preferences** on Mac to bring up a list of options.

Select the **Colors** section. Here you can change the colors used throughout the editor. Look for **Playmode tint**. Click the **color box** next to it, and then give it an unmistakable color — I prefer red. Now play your game to see if it's conspicuous enough.

Camera movement

There's only one problem with the space marine's movement: he will slip off screen. You want the camera to follow the hero around the arena, so he doesn't get away from you.

With a little scripting, you can keep the marine in focus.

In the Hierarchy, click the Create button and select **Create Empty**. Name it **CameraMount**.

The basic idea is you want CameraMount to represent the position the camera should focus on, and have the camera be relative to this position.

Initially you want the camera to focus where the space marine is, so let's configure the CameraMount to be at the exact same position as the space marine.

To do this, select the **space marine**, click on the gear button to the upper right of the Transform component, and select **Copy Component**.

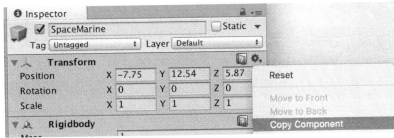

Then select the **CameraMount**, click on the gear button to the upper right of the Transform component, and select **Paste Component Values**:

Next, drag the **Main Camera** GameObject into the **CameraMount** GameObject.

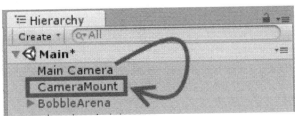

Great! Now as you move the player around, you can move the CameraMount to move with the player, and the camera will track the player. You just need to write a script to do this.

With the CameraMount selected, click the **Add Component** button in the Inspector and select **New Script**. Call it **CameraMovement** and set the language to **C Sharp**.

> **Note:** When you make a new script by clicking the Add Component button, Unity will create the script in the top level of your assets folder. Get into the habit of moving assets into their respective folders the moment you make or see them.

Drag your new file from the top level of the assets folder into the **Scripts** folder.

Double-click the **CameraMovement** script to open it in your code editor. Underneath the class definition, add the following variables:

```
public GameObject followTarget;
public float moveSpeed;
```

followTarget is what you want the camera to follow and moveSpeed is the speed at which it should move. By creating these as public variables, Unity will allow you to set these within the Unity editor itself, so you can set the followTarget to the space marine and fiddle with the moveSpeed to your heart's content, as you'll see shortly.

Now add the following to `Update()`:

```
if (followTarget != null) {
    transform.position = Vector3.Lerp(transform.position,
        followTarget.transform.position, Time.deltaTime *
    moveSpeed);
    }
```

This code checks to see if there is a target available. If not, the camera doesn't follow.

Next, `Vector3.Lerp()` is called to calculate the required position of the CameraMount.

`Lerp()` takes three parameters: a start position in 3D space, an end position in 3D space, and a value between 0 and 1 that represents a point between the starting and ending positions. `Lerp()` returns a point in 3D space between the start and end positions that's determined by the last value.

For example, if the last value is set to `0` then `Lerp()` will return the start position. If the last value is `1`, it returns the end position. If the last value is `0.5`, then it returns a point half-way between the start and end positions.

In this case, you will supply the camera mount position as the start and the player position as the end. Finally, you multiply the time since the last frame rate by a speed multiplier to get a suitable value for the last parameter. Effectively, this makes the camera mount position smoothly move to where the player is over time.

Save your code and return to Unity. If you look in the Inspector now, you'll see two new fields named **Follow Target** and **Move Speed**. As mentioned earlier, these were automatically derived by Unity from the `public` variables you just added to the script. These variables need some values.

With the CameraMount still selected in the Hierarchy, drag **SpaceMarine** to the **Follow Target** field and set the **Move Speed** to **20**.

Play your game to see what's changed.

The marine is a real superstar now, complete with a personal camera crew. Granted, he can't turn, and he walks right through objects just like Kitty Pryde, but these are easily solvable issues that you'll tackle in the next chapter.

> **Note**: The bigger the move speed, the faster the camera mount will move to the player. The smaller, the more the camera will "lag" behind the player's position, letting the player "jump ahead" of the camera. Try changing the move speed to a smaller value like 2 and see what happens for yourself!

Adding Gunplay

Unfortunately, the finer parts of diplomacy are lost on the flesh-eating antagonists of this game. It's best you give the hero some firepower so he can protect himself on his terribly relaxing (terrible?) vacation.

First, you need to create a bullet. In the Hierarchy, click the **Create** button. From the drop-down, select **3D Object\Sphere** to create a sphere in the Scene view.

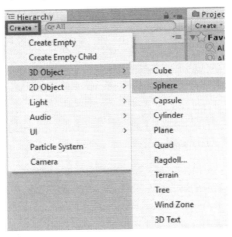

Give it the name **Projectile**. With it still selected, check out the Inspector. You'll notice a bunch of new components.

The three new components are:

1. The **Mesh Filter** is a component that contains data about your model's mesh and passes it to a renderer.

2. The **Mesh Renderer** displays the mesh. It contains a lot of information about lighting, such as casting and receiving shadows.

3. Finally, you'll notice the sphere contains a **Sphere Collider**. This component serves as the GameObject's boundaries. You'll learn cover colliders in the next chapter.

Since you want the bullet to participate in Unity's physics, it needs a rigidbody.

Luckily, you've done this before. Click the **Add Component** button, and select **Rigidbody** from the **Physics** category. Make sure to **uncheck** Use Gravity.

Since the marine will burn through lots of projectiles, **drag it** from the Hierarchy to the **Prefabs** folder in the **Project Browser**. **Delete** the **projectile** from the **Hierarchy** because you don't need it now that it's gone on to be a prefab.

At this point, you need to create a script to launch the projectile. In the Project Browser, select the **Scripts** folder then click the **Create** button. Choose **C# Script** and name it **Gun**. Double-click the file to launch the code editor.

This file needs a few properties underneath the class definition. Add the following:

```
public GameObject bulletPrefab;
public Transform launchPosition;
```

Again when you create a public variable on a script, Unity exposes these variables in the editor. You will set the bulletPrefab to the bullet prefab you just created, and you will set the launchPosition to the position of the barrel of the Space Marine's gun.

Next, add the following method:

```
void fireBullet() {
  // 1
  GameObject bullet = Instantiate(bulletPrefab) as GameObject;
  // 2
  bullet.transform.position = launchPosition.position;
  // 3
  bullet.GetComponent<Rigidbody>().velocity =
    transform.parent.forward * 100;
}
```

Let's review this section by section:

1. Instantiate() is a built-in method that creates a GameObject instance for a particular prefab. In this case, this will create a bullet based on the bullet prefab. Since Instantiate() returns a type of Object, the result must be cast into a GameObject.

2. The bullet's position is set to the launcher's position — you'll set the launcher as the barrel of the gun in just a moment.

3. Being that the bullet has a rigidbody attached to it, you can specify its velocity to make the bullet move at a constant rate. Direction is determined by the transform of the object to which this script is attached — you'll soon attach it to the body of the space marine, thus ensuring the bullet travels in same the direction as the marine is facing.

Save and switch back to Unity. In the Hierarchy, expand the SpaceMarine GameObject and **select** the **BobbleMarine-Body** GameObject.

In the Inspector, click the **Add Component** button and near the bottom of the list of components, select **Scripts**. From the list of scripts, choose **Gun**.

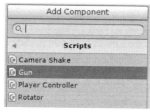

You'll see that your Gun script component has been added to the body of the marine. You'll also notice there are two new fields: **Bullet Prefab** and **Launch Position**. Do those sound familiar?

Click the circle next to **Bullet Prefab**. Select **Projectile** from the resulting asset list. Now you have loaded the bullet and just need to set the launch position.

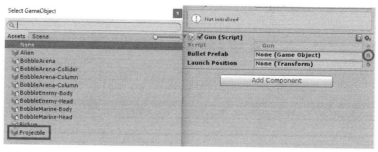

In the Hierarchy, hold the **Alt** key on PC or **Option** on Mac and click the **disclosure triangle** next to the **BobbleMarine-Body**. You'll see a large list of child GameObjects. Look for **Gun**.

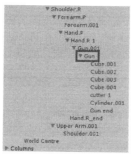

Select that GameObject and click the **Create** button. Choose **Create Empty Child** and rename it to **Launcher**. This new GameObject lives in the center of the gun's barrel and represents where bullets will spawn from — feel free to move it around in the scene editor if you'd like to tweak the spawn position.

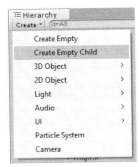

Keep all the GameObjects expanded and select **BobbleMarine-Body** so that the Inspector shows all the components. Drag the new **Launcher** GameObject into the Gun component's **Launch Position** field.

Notice that when you add the GameObject to a transform field, Unity finds and references the attached transform.

It's official! The marine's gun is locked and loaded. All that's left is the firing code. Thankfully, it's pretty easy.

Switch back to your code editor and open **Gun.cs**.

The gun should fire when the user presses the mouse button and stop when the user releases it.

You could simply check to see if the button is pressed in Update() and call fireBullet() if so, but since Update() is called every frame, that would mean your space marine would shoot up to 60 times per second! Our space marine can shoot fast, but not *that* fast.

What you need is a slight delay between when you shoot bullets. To do this, add the following to Update():

```
if (Input.GetMouseButtonDown(0)) {
  if (!IsInvoking("fireBullet")) {
```

```
        InvokeRepeating("fireBullet", 0f, 0.1f);
    }
}
```

First, you check with the Input Manager to see if the left mouse button is held down.

> **Note:** If you wanted to check the right mouse button, you'd pass in 1, and for the middle mouse button, you'd pass in 2.

If the mouse is being held down, you check if `fireBullet()` is being invoked. If not, you call `InvokeRepeating()`, which repeatedly calls a method until you call `CancelInvoke()`.

`InvokeRepeating()` needs a method name, a time to start and the repeat rate. `InvokeRepeating()` is a method of `MonoBehaviour`.

After that bit of code, add the following:

```
if (Input.GetMouseButtonUp(0)) {
    CancelInvoke("fireBullet");
}
```

This code makes it so the gun stops firing once the user releases the mouse button. **Save** your work and return to Unity, then **play** the game.

Hold down the mouse button. You have bullets for days!

Where to go from here?

At this point, you should be feeling more comfortable with Unity. You have a walking space marine with a functioning weapon. You've learned the following:

- **Components** and how they give your GameObjects behavior.
- **Scripting** and how to use scripts to create custom behavior.

- The **Input Manager** and how to access it from code.

- The **Game window** and how to test your games.

This was a thick, heavy chapter and you made it to the end. Congratulations! You've come a long way.

There's still a lot more to do. Your poor marine is a sitting duck because he can't turn around to see what's sneaking up behind him. At the same time, he has nothing to worry about because there are no aliens hordes attacking him.

You'll solve these issues and more in the next chapter when you learn about the laws of game physics and how you can bend them to your own will!

Chapter 4: Physics

By Brian Moakley

Physics is one of those subjects that triggers nightmare flashbacks of my high school days when rolling toy cars down slopes was the peak of intellectual pursuit. If you're like me, then the notion of learning physics is about as exciting as watching a download progress meter.

Don't worry: Unity makes physics great again. Its built in physics engine allows you to easily create games with explosions, guns, and bodies smashing into beautiful walls — *without* having to study a boring textbook.

In this chapter, you'll learn how Unity's physics engine works, and use it to add collision detection, raycasts, and even bobbleheads into the game. Let's get started!

Getting started

Open your existing project, or you can open the starter project for this chapter.

Currently, the space marine can run around the arena and shoot things. However, with no targets and the no ability to turn around, he's bored and prone to sneak attack. He also has the superhero ability of walking through walls. You're going to solve these problems with physics!

Giving the marine something to shoot

First, you need to add a target for the marine. In the Project Browser, drag an **Alien** from the **Prefabs** folder and place it in front of the marine. In the Inspector, set the Alien's **position** to (-27.67, **13.57**, **74.53**).

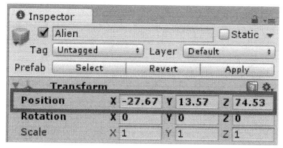

Play the game and shoot the alien.

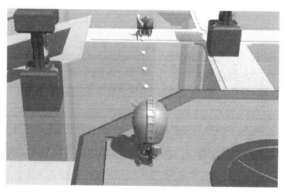

Haha! The bullets pass right through without inflicting any harm, which is the default behavior for all GameObjects. You have to opt your GameObjects into receiving collisions. Sound familiar? Can you guess what component you'll use?

That's right; you need another Rigidbody! In the previous chapters, you used this component to opt objects into the physics engine. With the Rigidbody in place, not only can the GameObject respond to forces like gravity, but it can get a notification when another object, such as a bullet, collides with it. Then you can define what happens after such a collision, e.g., the alien explodes or vanishes.

Your alien has no Rigidbody, which is why it's impervious to our hero's attack. Select the **Alien** in the Hierarchy. In the Inspector, click the **Add Component** button. Select the **Physics** category and select **Rigidbody**.

Play your game.

Um, ok, the alien falls through the floor. Funny, but not ideal. To fix this, you can either turn off the gravity for the alien or use a collider.

Adding colliders

Colliders perform a variety of functions. They allow you to define the bounds of a GameObject for the purpose of collisions and are also useful for keeping your GameObjects from falling through the floor.

Usually for colliders, you want to use primitive shapes such as spheres and boxes. For example, you'll make a sphere that's about the same size of the alien. It won't match the shape of the alien exactly, but this is usually "good enough" for collision detection purposes, and results in a much faster game. If you need more precise collision detection, you can use a mesh collider instead — more on that in just a minute.

First, let's stop that alien from dropping through the floor.

Select the **Alien** GameObject in the Hierarchy and click the **Add Component** button in the Inspector. Select the **Physics** category, and from the components listing, select **Sphere collider**.

You'll see the collider, complete with many options, appear in the Inspector.

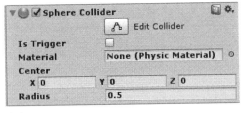

Here's the breakdown of the options:

- The **Edit Collider** button allows you to move and resize a collider visually in the Unity scene editor. Right now if you zoom in, you'll notice that the sphere is much smaller than the alien, and this option would allow you to move and resize it to better represent the alien's shape.

Alternatively, you can set the center and radius properties manually, as you will do shortly.

- The **Is Trigger** checkbox means that the collider can pass through other colliders. Although the collider doesn't act like a hard surface, you'll still get collision notifications.

  A good use case for a trigger is to open a door when a player steps on a certain area.

- The **Material** option allows you to apply something known as a **Physics Material**, which are materials that have physical properties. For instance, you could create a surface that causes players to slide and assign it to ice models to make a skating rink.

- The **Center** is a sphere collider's center point.

- The **Radius** determines the size of the collider.

With all that mind, you can fix the collider for the alien to make it behave.

If the alien isn't already selected in the Hierarchy, select it now. In the Inspector for the sphere collider, set the **Center** to **(0.34, 2.54, 0.57)** and the **Radius** to **2.52**. Check out the Scene view now.

You'll see a green outline around the alien — it's the radius of the collider.

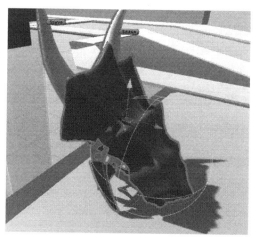

Click the **Edit Collider** button to see control points along the collider.

You can select those points and drag to either increase or decrease the size of the collider. This is how I came up with the radius and position values you entered a second ago originally — just sizing it until it was an approximation of the alien's size. Feel free to play around with the placement of the collider, and then undo to get back to the original size.

After you're done, play the game to see what happens. Make sure to **Apply** your changes to the prefab.

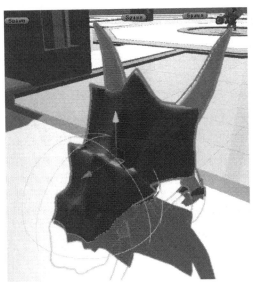

Unfortunately, the alien still falls through the floor. This is because there's no collider for the floor — you need to create one for that as well.

As mentioned, there are many colliders at your disposal and you're not restricted to just one. Any GameObject may have multiple colliders, giving you the ability to create complex shapes and reactions to collisions.

You could add a bunch of colliders to the arena to approximate its shape, but the arena is quite complicated and that would take a lot of work. So in this case, you'll use a mesh collider instead.

A **mesh collider** creates the collider boundaries from an actual mesh object, i.e., the geometry used to create the model. It's a great option when you have a complicated model. The problem with mesh colliders is they can be "expensive" — it takes a lot of resources to maintain the collider and determine if it's involved in collisions. In such cases, it helps to have a very low-poly collider.

To create a low-poly collider, you just take the original model and strip it of extraneous detail until you're down to the shape. Mike Berg, the artist for Bobblehead Wars, has done that for you.

In the Hierarchy, expand the **BobbleArena** GameObject and select the **World_Center** GameObject. In the Inspector, click the **Add Component** button. Select **Physics**, and in the component listing, click **Mesh Collider**.

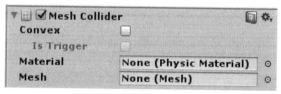

Find the **BobbleArena-Collider** in the **Models** folder, expand it by clicking the disclosure triangle, and then drag the **Inner_Octagon** mesh to the collider's **Mesh** property.

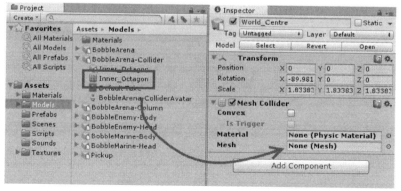

Initially, the mesh is a little too large and misaligned.

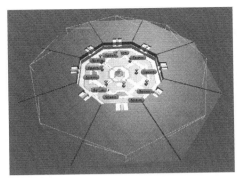

In the transform component, set the **Rotation** to (**-89.98, 0, -22.26**) and the **Scale** to (**0.949, 0.949, 0.949**). The collider will now match the arena.

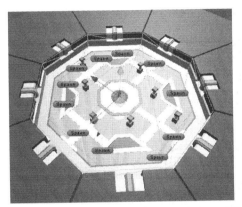

Play your game! Unfortunately for the hero, the bug no longer falls through the floor.

Blast that bugger away!

Introducing character controllers

The hero, not to be forgotten, needs some upgrades.

In the last chapter, you learned how to make the character move by adding a Rigidbody, adding colliders, and writing a script to make your character move. This was great for learning purposes, but there's a simpler way: the character controller.

A **character controller** is a built-in component that makes it easier to make characters in your game move based on user input. It combines all of the components that you added manually last chapter into one, and provides a simple API to use it.

Sorry to do this to you after all that work in the last chapter, but you need to strip the marine of his Rigidbody. Select the SpaceMarine in the Hierarchy, and in the Inspector, click the Rigidbody's **gear icon** and select **Remove Component**.

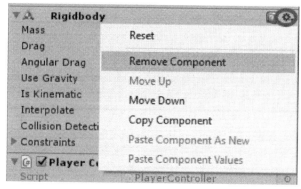

Click the **Add Component** button, go to the **Physics** category and choose **Character Controller**.

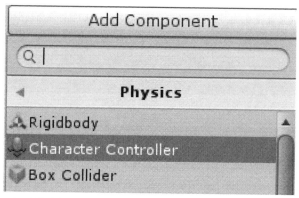

You'll notice a bunch of fields that influence the character's movement.

Set **Center** to (-1.82, 6.53, 0.7), **Radius** to 2.5 and **Height** to 11.08. These properties affect the size of the collider.

▼ 🔧 ✔ Character Controller				
Slope Limit	45			
Step Offset	0.3			
Skin Width	0.08			
Min Move Distance	0.001			
Center	X -1.82	Y 6.53	Z 0.7	
Radius	2.5			
Height	11.08			

In the Scene view, you'll see a fine green capsule around the marine.

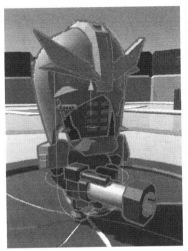

Now that you've added a character controller, you need to make a few tweaks to your PlayerController script. Start by double-clicking the **PlayerController** script to open it in your editor.

First, you need to get a reference to `CharacterController`. You could get this in `Update()`, but it's best to store it in an instance variable during `Start()`. That way, the game doesn't spend unnecessary time fetching components.

Add the following beneath the `moveSpeed` variable declaration:

```
private CharacterController characterController;
```

This creates an instance variable to store the `CharacterController`.

In `Start()`, add the following to get a reference to the component:

```
characterController = GetComponent<CharacterController>();
```

`GetComponent()` gets a reference to current component passed into the script. Replace all the code in `Update()` with the following:

```
Vector3 moveDirection = new Vector3(Input.GetAxis("Horizontal"),
    0, Input.GetAxis("Vertical"));
characterController.SimpleMove(moveDirection * moveSpeed);
```

First, the above code creates a new `Vector3` to store the movement direction then it calls `SimpleMove()` and passes in `moveDirection` multiplied by `moveSpeed`. `SimpleMove()` is a built-in method that automatically moves the character in the given direction, but not allowing the character to move through obstacles.

Save your changes and play the game.

You'll see the hero move much like before but with simpler code. In addition, your hero stops when he collides with the wall of the arena.

Unfortunately, you still have the problem of a character that runs through columns, which is easy to fix with colliders. Go ahead and make the fix now.

Stop your game. In the Project Browser, select the **BobbleArena-Column** in the **Prefabs** folder then click the **Add Component** button. In the **Physics** category, add a **Box Collider**. In the Inspector, set **Center** to (0, 2.7, 0) and **Size** to (2.07, 4.27, 2).

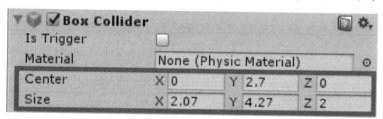

Once you make changes to the column, your next thought is probably that you need to apply those changes to the rest of the prefabs. You don't have to because you've modified the source prefab. Those changes are added automatically to all the instances!

Now play your game and charge at a column. You're now blocked!

Take a moment to shoot at the alien.

Two things will happen: The alien will get pushed around, and the arena floor will be littered with bullets. In fact, if you look at the Hierarchy, you'll see a boatload of bullets.

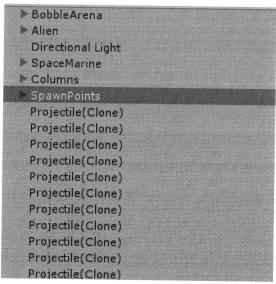

The best way to handle these issues is with collisions and layers.

Destroying old objects

As you can see, you create a lot of GameObjects when firing bullets. They're novel, but if you don't take action, your game will have serious performance issues.

You need to delete unused bullets as soon as they are out of play to keep the Hierarchy clean and the game performing.

What's the best way to manage used-up bullets?

Here's the problem: the game creates a new GameObjects every time the gun fires and over time. Since the player can fire continually, this will result in more and more bullets, until eventually your game runs out of memory and crashes. Creating unbounded objects by mistake is a common problem in game design.

You can delete the bullets, or you can reuse them by using **pools**. For example, after the GameObject exits the play area, it's put into a pool of objects to use in the future, rather than deleting it.

When the player fires again, the game checks if there are any available bullets in the pool. If not, the game creates a new bullet. Otherwise, it reuses an existing one. After a while, the game reuses bullets instead of squandering processing time on the creation and deletion of bullets.

In this chapter, for simplicity's sake you will delete the object, but you may want to investigate pools if performance becomes an issue.

In the Project Browser, open the **Prefabs** folder and select the **Projectile** prefab. Click the **Add Component** button and select **New Script** at the bottom. Give it the name **Projectile**, choose **C Sharp** as the language then click **Create and Add**.

Double-click the script to open it in the editor and add these two methods:

```
void OnBecameInvisible() {
   Destroy(gameObject);
}

void OnCollisionEnter(Collision collision) {
   Destroy(gameObject);
}
```

OnBecameInvisible() is a useful method that is called when the object is no longer visible by any camera. In this case, this is called when the bullet goes off the screen. This is a perfect time to destroy the bullet, as it's no longer needed.

Note: There are two important things to understand about this.

First, for this to work the GameObject must have a renderer component attached to it. Otherwise, Unity has no idea if the GameObject is visible or not.

Second, Unity considers a GameObject invisible if it's invisible from *all* cameras. For instance, the GameObject may not be visible in the Game window but if it's visible in your **Scene view**, then it's still considered visible.

Weird? Yes, but that's how Unity rolls. :]

OnCollisionEnter() is called during a collision event. The Collision object contains information about the actual collision as well as the target object. For example, this will be called when a bullet hits an alien or a wall. When this occurs, you simply destroy the bullet.

Now play your game and fire. Your bullets disappear as they collide into objects. How about another test?

With the game still running, select the **SpaceMarine**. In the Character Controller component, set **Radius** to **5.17**.

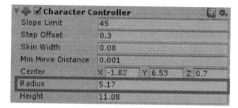

Now, fire your gun. Believe it or not, the gun is firing, but the bullets are hitting the marine's collider, and then being instantly destroyed, so it looks as though nothing is happening. You can solve this problem with selective collisions that you set up with layers.

Collisions and layers

By default, all GameObjects exist on one physics layer. This means that all GameObjects with Rigidbodies will collide with one another.

As you can see from how the bullets collide with the space marine, the default isn't ideal. You need the bullets to ignore the marine — and to do this, you need to create a new layer.

First, **stop** the game and navigate to **Edit\Project Settings\Tags and Layers**. The Inspector will show the Tags and Layers view with the layers section expanded. The first eight layers are controlled by Unity but the rest are wide open.

Label User Layer 8 and onwards as follows: **Player, Head, Wall, Bullet, Alien Head, Floor, Alien** and **Upgrade**.

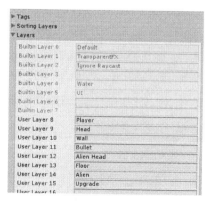

Yes, you'll use all those physics layers in your game. Notice how they correspond with the GameObjects.

In the Hierarchy, select the **SpaceMarine**. In the Inspector set the **Layer** drop-down to **Player**.

You'll see a prompt that asks if you want to set the layer for all the child objects. Click **No, this object only**.

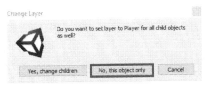

> **Note:** GameObjects can only belong to one layer, but their children can belong to different layers, as you'll see later in this book.

Next, in the **Prefabs** folder, select the **Projectile** prefab, and in the layer drop-down, select **Bullet**.

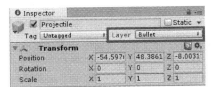

By default, all layers interact with each other, and you have to opt them out of collisions. To do this, click **Edit\Project Settings\Physics**, scroll to the bottom and look for a matrix of layers.

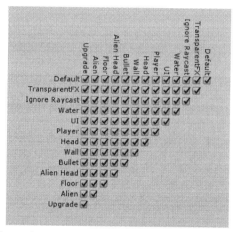

The y-axis shows the subject layers, and the x-axis shows the collision target layers. The checkmark indicates whether the subject layer will interact with the target layer.

In the **Player row**, **uncheck** the **Bullet column**. Now, the Player layer will ignore all interactions with the Bullet layer.

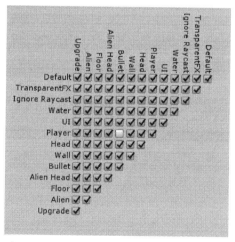

Play your game and run that same test while it's live — select the **SpaceMarine** and set the **Radius** to 5.17 in the Inspector. Fire your gun. This time, you get bullets galore!

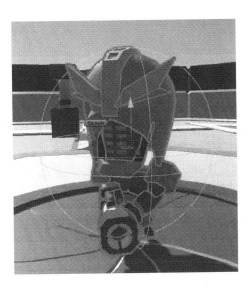

Joints

When you first started making this game, you called it `Bobblehead Wars` but so far, it's been all wars and no bobble. Thankfully, Unity physics comes to the rescue with **joints**.

These aren't the kinds of joints that would require you to be in Amsterdam, Oregon, Colorado or Washington, nor are they the kinds of joints made by the filmmaker Spike Lee.

These are *physics* joints with a more conventional purpose: connecting two GameObjects together in a relationship defined by the physics engine.

Think about a wrecking ball for a moment, specifically, the chain. Each link would be a GameObject, and you'd need to join them together with joints to allow each link to move individually but affect its neighbors, and in turn, the whole group is influenced by the ball.

There are many joints available to you:

- A **Hinge Joint** ties the movement of one GameObject to another — for instance, a door hinge.

- A **Spring Joint** acts like an invisible spring between two GameObjects.

- A **Fixed Joint** restricts a GameObject's movement with an unrelated GameObject. A good example (from the documentation, even) is a sticky grenade.

- A **Character Joint** allows you to constrain motion to create rag doll effects.

- A **Configurable Joint** incorporates the features of the other joints and more. In essence, you use it to modify existing joints or create your own.

You'll use a **Hinge Joint** to make the head bobble back and forth.

Playing off the example above, the space marine's body is the doorframe, and his head is the door. Every time the marine moves, you'll add force to his head to make it bounce back and forth.

Adding joints

In the Hierarchy, expand **SpaceMarine** and select the **BobbleMarine-Head**. Then from the main menu, click **Component\Physics\Hinge Joint**. (As you can see, there's more than one way to add a component.)

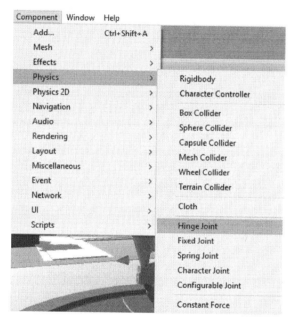

Check the Inspector. You'll see the hinge joint in there now.

For the hinge joint to work, the connected GameObjects must have Rigidbodies attached to them; Unity automatically adds these for you when you create a hinge joint.

In the Rigidbody component, **uncheck** the **Use Gravity** property.

In the Hierarchy, select **BobbleMarine-Body** and in the Inspector, click the **Add Component** button. From the component listings, select **Physics** and then **Rigidbody**. **Uncheck** the **Use Gravity** property and **check** the **Is Kinematic** property.

Now, select **BobbleMarine-Head** in the Hierarchy, and look at the hinge joint in the Inspector. You'll see many options!

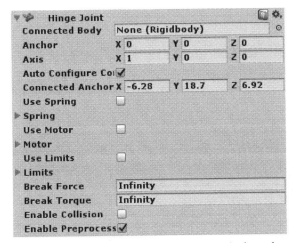

The first option is the **Connected Body**, and in this case, it's the other GameObject that the head will be "hinged" to.

In the Hierarchy, drag the **BobbleMarine-Body** to the **Connected Body** property. Now, the GameObjects are connected by physics.

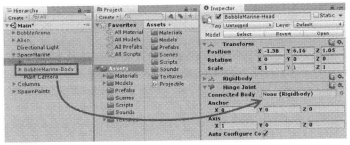

The **Anchor** indicates where the end point of the joint attaches to the GameObject as specified in the object's **local coordinate space**. (0, 0, 0) within the head's local coordinate space represents the neck area, so leaving the value at (0, 0, 0) is fine.

The **Axis** determines what direction the body will swing. You want this to move on the z-axis, i.e., up and down. Set the **Axis** to (**0, 0, 1**).

The **Connected Anchor** parameter specifies the anchor point of the other end of the joint. If the Connected Rigid Body field is empty, this value is in the scene's coordinate system. However, when Connected Rigid Body is set, as it is now to the Space Marine's body, the Connected Anchor coordinates refer to the connected rigid body's local coordinate space.

By default, Unity sets the **Connected Anchor** point to the same position as the **Anchor** point. For this game, you want these to be slightly different, so **Uncheck** the **Auto Configure Connected Anchor** checkbox.

Figuring out the connected anchor's best settings tends to involve some trial and error. Thankfully, Unity shows you the anchor point's location that you can use as a starting point.

Switch the Scene view to **Wireframe** mode to show a small orange line. This represents the anchor's position, and it'll update as you alter the Connect Anchor values.

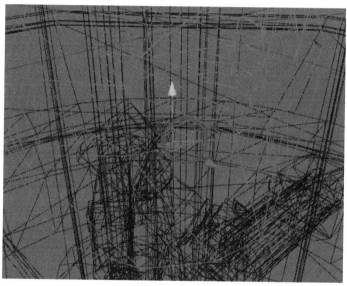

Set the **Connected Anchor** to (**-2.06**, **6.16**, **0.16**) to pin the anchor to the marine's neck.

The spring properties will add "springy" behavior to the joint and the motor property will move the joint without any external force. To illustrate motor values, think of a door mysteriously opening on its own.

The **Limits** properties control how far the joint should swing.

Check the **Use Limits** checkbox and **expand** the **Limits** property. In the **Min** property, put −25 and set the **Max** to 25 — this represents that the head should bounce at most 25 degrees in either way. To make it bounce like a proper bobble head, set **Bounciness** to 1 — that's the max value.

Keep the rest of the values as they are, but take note of **Break Force** and **Break Torque**. You'd use these if you wanted the hinge to snap under a certain threshold, e.g., create the effect of a door being blown off its hinges.

Here's the configured joint:

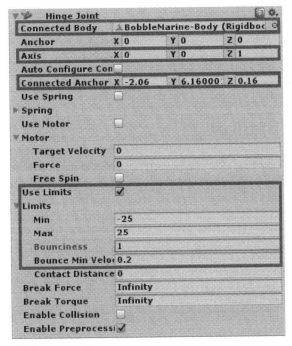

The hinge needs a collider to work.

Click the **Add Component** button, and from the **Physics** category, select **Sphere Collider**. Set **Center** to (**0.41, 2.7, -0.21**) and **Radius** to **2.36**. This closely matches the width of the head.

The last thing this effect needs is some force to make the head bob.

Open **PlayerController.cs** in your code editor. You need a reference to the connected head Rigidbody, so add the following instance variable:

```
public Rigidbody head;
```

You might ask why you're using a Rigidbody instead of a GameObject.

Remember, a Rigidbody deals with physics. You're adding the head to apply force to it, and there's no way to apply force to a regular GameObject. Hence, you need a Rigidbody.

So how do you assign a Rigidbody to a public field?

Just like you did with the transform. Save your change and switch back to Unity.

Select the **SpaceMarine** in the Hierarchy. In the Inspector, look for a property named **Head** that can accept a rigidbody. **Drag the BobbleMarine-Head** to it.

Much like it does with the transform, Unity uses the Rigidbody component attached to the GameObject to assign to the head field.

Switch back to **PlayerController.cs**. Add the following underneath `Update()`:

```
void FixedUpdate() {

}
```

As you know, `Update()` runs with every frame and it's called as often as the frame changes, so 40 fps means it's called 40 times per second.

`FixedUpdate()` is an entirely different beast. Because it handles physics, it's called at consistent intervals and not subject to frame rate. If you were to check the `deltaTime` between each call to `FixedUpdate()`, you'd see it doesn't change.

Anything that affects a Rigidbody should be updated in `FixedUpdate()`. Given that you are applying force to a rigidbody to move the Bobblehead, you need to use `FixedUpdate()` instead of `Update()`.

Add the following to `FixedUpdate()`:

```
Vector3 moveDirection = new Vector3(Input.GetAxis("Horizontal"),
   0, Input.GetAxis("Vertical"));
if (moveDirection == Vector3.zero) {
   // TODO
} else {
   head.AddForce(transform.right * 150, ForceMode.Acceleration);
}
```

This code moves the head when the marine moves. First, you calculate the movement direction. If the value equals `Vector3.zero`, then the marine is standing still.

`AddForce()` is how you get the head to move. You provide a direction then multiply it by the force amount.

There are different force types, and you're using `ForceMode.Acceleration`, which gives a continuous amount of force that ignores the mass.

> **Note:** If you wanted to use the mass, you'd use `ForceMode.Force`. For more detail about the other options, search the documentation for `ForceMode`.

Now play your game and move. Uh-oh, by the looks of the marine's head, he needs an exorcist. Based on everything you've learned so far, can you guess what's going wrong?

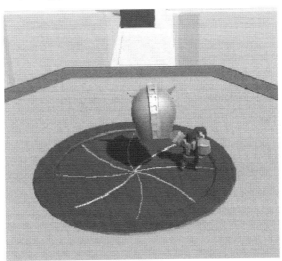

You added a sphere collider to the head, but the character controller added another collider, and there's interference between them. Layers to the rescue!

> **Note:** If the head is not moving, make sure that the head's `Rigidbody` component has `IsKinematic` unchecked.

Select **BobbleMarine-Head** in the Hierarchy. In the Inspector, assign it the **Head** layer and select the **Yes, change children** option in the confirmation dialog.

Finally, click **Edit\Project Settings\Physics**, and in the physics matrix, uncheck the **Head column** in the **Player row**.

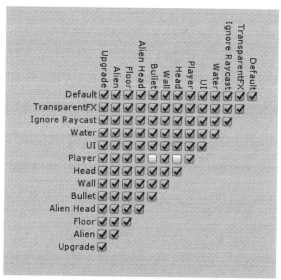

Play your game. Begun, these Bobblehead wars have.

Raycasting

At this point, you can fire a weapon and push the alien around. Unfortunately, our hero still can't turn. Considering that these aliens love to chew on back hair (they truly are alien), the space marine needs to duck, spin and weave.

During gameplay, you also want the marine to shoot in the direction of the mouse pointer. Seems simple enough, right?

Fundamentally, it's a tricky problem; the game exists in 3D space but the mouse exists in 2D.

The solution is to convert the mouse pointer to 3D space, then determine where it's pointing. It sounds like a complicated process, but it's quite easy with **raycasting**.

Raycasting shoots an invisible ray from a target to a destination, and it sends a notification when it hits a GameObject. You'll likely encounter a lot of GameObjects that intersect with a ray. Using a mask lets you filter out unwanted objects.

Raycasts are incredibly useful and serve a variety of purposes. They're commonly used to test if another player was struck by a projectile, but they can help you test if there's geometry underneath a mouse pointer, as you'll soon see.

The following image shows a raycast from a cube to a cone. Since the ray has a cone mask on it, it ignores the iconsphere layer and reports a hit to the cone.

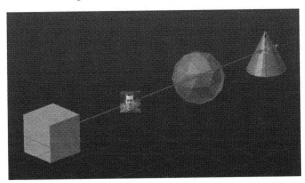

You'll cast a ray from the camera to the mouse pointer. Then the space marine will turn to wherever the ray hits the floor, essentially following the mouse.

Open **PlayerController.cs** and add the following instance variables:

```
public LayerMask layerMask;
private Vector3 currentLookTarget = Vector3.zero;
```

The LayerMask lets you indicate what layers the ray should hit. currentLookTarget is where you want the marine to stare. Since you don't know where to look at the start of the game, you set the value to zero.

> **Note**: As you add instance variables, you'll see that public and private variables become jumbled together. It's for the sake of brevity. A best practice is to group them by access modifier and keep public and private variables together.

Next, add the following to `FixedUpdate()` underneath the existing code:

```
RaycastHit hit;
Ray ray = Camera.main.ScreenPointToRay(Input.mousePosition);
```

First, this creates an empty `RaycastHit`. If you get a hit, it'll be populated with an object. Second, you actually cast the ray from the main camera to the mouse position.

Rays are invisible, so they are hard to debug. You might *think* they will hit an object, but you won't *know* until you actually see it hit something. Add the following code:

```
Debug.DrawRay(ray.origin, ray.direction * 1000, Color.green);
```

This will draw a ray in the Scene view while you're playing the game.

Return to Unity and run your game. Look in the Scene view while moving your mouse in the Game window. You should see the ray as a green line.

Return to PlayerController.cs, and add this code where you left off in `FixedUpdate()`:

```
if (Physics.Raycast(ray, out hit, 1000, layerMask,
    QueryTriggerInteraction.Ignore)) {
}
```

These two lines of code do quite a bit:

- `Physics.Raycast` actually casts the ray.

- First you pass in the `ray` that you generated along with the `hit`. Since the `hit` variable is marked as `out`, it can be populated by `Physics.Raycast()`.

- `1000` indicates the length of the ray. In this case, it's a thousand meters.

- The `layerMask` lets the cast know what you are trying to hit.

- `QueryTriggerInteraction.Ignore` tells the physics engine not to activate triggers.

Add the following code inside the braces:

```
if (hit.point != currentLookTarget) {
   currentLookTarget = hit.point;
}
```

The `hit.point` comprises the coordinates of the raycast hit — it's the point where the hero should look. If it's different, perhaps because the player moved the mouse, then `currentLookTarget` will be updated.

Add the following after the previous bit of code:

```
// 1
Vector3 targetPosition = new Vector3(hit.point.x,
   transform.position.y, hit.point.z);
// 2
Quaternion rotation = Quaternion.LookRotation(targetPosition -
   transform.position);
// 3
transform.rotation = Quaternion.Lerp(transform.rotation,
   rotation, Time.deltaTime * 10.0f);
```

This is where the actual rotation comes into play.

1. You get the target position. Notice that the y axis is derived from the marine's position, because you want the marine to look straight ahead instead of the floor. If you used the floor, then the marine would rotate downwards.

2. You calculate the current `Quaterion`, which is used to determine rotation. (You can learn all about Quaterions in the Unity API appendix chapter.) To find the target quaternion, you subtract the `targetPosition` from the current position. Then you call `LookRotation()`, which returns the quaterion for where the marine should turn.

3. Finally, you do the actual turn by using `Lerp()`. Remember, `Lerp()` is used to change a value (such as rotation in this place) smoothly over time. To learn more about `Lerp()`, check out the Unity API appendix chapter.

Save your changes and go back to Unity. In the Hierarchy, select the **SpaceMarine**. Look for the Player Controller script in the Inspector, and select **Floor** in the drop-down.

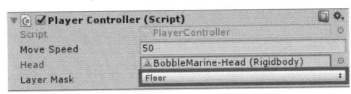

The last thing to do is assign the floor physics layer to the, er, floor. In the Hierarchy, expand the **BobbleArena** and select **World_Centre**. In the layer dropdown, select **floor**.

Play your game like you mean it.

Now the marine follows your mouse cursor and turns on a dime. Now you're playing with power! :]

Where to go from here?

Wow! That was quite a chapter! As you can see, the physics engine has a stockpile of features and does a lot of cool stuff. In this chapter, you learned about:

- **Character Controllers** and how they help simplify your code.
- **Collisions and Layers** for when you want to collide with another object or opt out of collisions entirely.
- **Joints** and how to put them in practice.
- **Raycasting** and how to use rays to increase interactivity.

There's a lot more to do in Bobblehead Wars. So far, you have just one alien, and he's little more than a creepy-crawly couch potato.

In the next chapter, you'll make a horde of aliens and unleash them upon the marine. He better stay sharp and hope that raycast is working right!

Chapter 5: Managers and Pathfinding

By Brian Moakley

Bobblehead Wars is coming along handsomely! At this point, you have a feisty space marine who can turn, shoot, and gun down aliens. Also, through the use of a hinge joint, his head can wobble back and forth so he can do so in style.

Nevertheless, Bobblehead Wars isn't ready for release. First, there is just one alien when the space marine was expecting a horde. And second, the alien currently isn't that scary — he just stands around!

To fix this, you'll learn how to spawn enemies over time and make them chase after the space marine, through the power of the Game Manager and pathfinding. Let the battle begin!

Introducing the GameManager

Unity refers to an object that handles a specific subsystem as a **manager**. Given your experience in the workplace, you might think this means they do nothing and leave all the work for their underlings, but in Unity managers actually lend a hand. ;]

For instance, an input manager is an object that lets you adjust all the controls for your game. There's also a settings manager that handles all your project settings, and a network manager for managing the state of a networked game.

In this chapter, you'll create your own kind of manager. Specifically, you'll create a game manager so that you can easily tweak your game setting while it's being played. This will make it much easier to balance your game during play testing.

Imagine that you're playing and there are just too many enemies. The space marine has no chance. You could make an adjustment to your game manager to dial back the aliens hordes in real time.

Remember, any changes you make while your game is played will be lost, right? There's an exception to this rule that you'll try out in this chapter.

Creating the game manager

Open your project from Chapter 4. If you need to start fresh, please find the starter project that's included with the resources for this chapter.

In the Hierarchy, click the **Create** button, select **Create Empty** from the drop-down and name it **GameManager**.

Congratulations! You've made your game manager. That's it for this chapter.

Ok, ok, you're right. That wasn't very nice. You have *much* more to do. :]

Unity doesn't provide a "stock" game manager component — it would be silly because each game is unique. You need to write your own.

Select the **GameManager** in the Hierarchy and click the **Add Component** button in the Inspector. Pick **New Script** and name it **GameManager**. Set the language to **C Sharp** then click **Create and Add**.

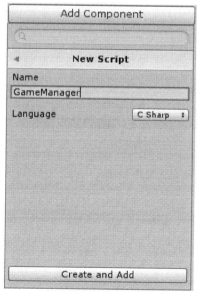

Don't forget to move the script into your scripts folder!

Double-click the **GameManager script** to open it in your code editor. Get ready to spend some time in here; this script will manage all aspects of your game, and you have many variables to add.

Add this code underneath the opening brace:

```
public GameObject player;
public GameObject[] spawnPoints;
public GameObject alien;
```

These three variables are critical to the manger's function. Here's a breakdown:

- `player` represents the hero's GameObject. `GameManager` will use this to determine its current location.

- `spawnPoints` are locations from which aliens will spawn in the arena. You declare it as an array because you have multiple locations — remember those capsules you laid out across the arena floor?

- `alien` represents the prefab for the alien. The GameManger will create an instance of this object when it's time to spawn.

Save your script and switch back to Unity. Select the **GameManager** in the Hierarchy to see three new fields.

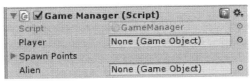

Notice that **Spawn Points** has an adjacent disclosure triangle, indicating that it takes multiple values.

First, you'll populate the **player** field. **Select** the **SpaceMarine** in the Hierarchy. You'll notice the Inspector switches from the **GameManager** to the **SpaceMarine**, which isn't what you actually want the engine to do. There are a three ways to work around this behavior:

1. As you've done in previous chapters, you could click and drag the object to the property (rather than clicking without dragging). When you click and drag, the Inspector doesn't select the given object.

2. A second option is to click the round circle to the right of a property to bring up a popup to select the approrpiate object.

3. A third option is to lock the GameManager to the Inspector. This prevents you from accidentally selecting another GameObject.

Locking the GameManager is the best option of the two since you've got quite a few changes to make. To do this, select the **GameManager** in the hierarchy, and click the **lock icon** at the top of the Inspector.

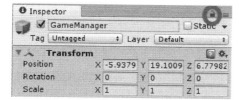

Select the **SpaceMarine** in the Hierarchy; the Inspector doesn't change anymore. In fact, the Inspector will remain locked to the GameManager until you click the lock again.

Drag the **SpaceMarine** to the **Player** field. **Expand** the **SpawnPoints** GameObject in the Hierarchy.

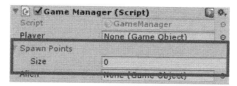

Select all the spawn points by pressing **Shift** and **selecting** the top and bottom **Spawn** objects.

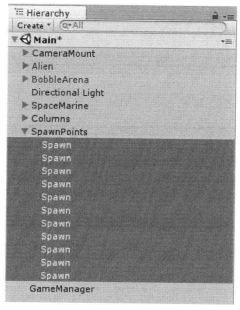

Drag all the spawn points to the **Spawn Points** property in the GameManager. You'll know you're in the right spot when a green plus icon appears.

Next, **Drag** the **Alien prefab** from the Prefabs folder (**not** the Hierarchy) to the **Alien** field.

The GameManager should now look like this:

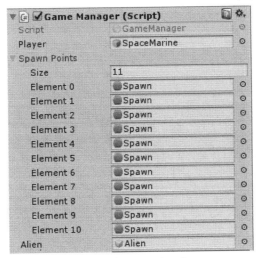

Unlock the Inspector and switch back to your code editor.

Add the following beneath the previous variables:

```
public int maxAliensOnScreen;
public int totalAliens;
public float minSpawnTime;
public float maxSpawnTime;
public int aliensPerSpawn;
```

These are some variables that you will use to configure gameplay for Bobblehead Wars:

- maxAliensOnScreen: will determine how many aliens appear on the screen at once.

- totalAliens: will represent the total number of aliens the player must vanquish to claim victory.

- minSpawnTime and maxSpawnTime: will control the rate at which aliens appear.

- aliensPerSpawn: will determine how many aliens appear during a spawning event.

Next you need to add a few private variables that the game manager will need for recordkeeping. Place the following underneath the public variables:

```
private int aliensOnScreen = 0;
private float generatedSpawnTime = 0;
private float currentSpawnTime = 0;
```

Here's what these will manage:

- `aliensOnScreen`: will track the total number of aliens currently displayed. You'll use it to tell the game manager whether to spawn or wait.

- `generatedSpawnTime`: will track the time between spawn events. You'll randomize this to keep the player on their toes.

- `currentSpawnTime`: will track the milliseconds since the last spawn.

Finally, this script needs some C# generics. Add the following at the top of the script underneath all the other `using` statements:

```
using System.Collections.Generic;
```

This allows the use of generic arrays, which you'll use in just a moment.

Spawning the aliens

Next up is writing the spawning code. With the `GameManager` script still open, add the following to `Update()`:

```
currentSpawnTime += Time.deltaTime;
```

`currentSpawnTime` accumulates the amount of time that's passed between each frame update. Next, add the following:

```
if (currentSpawnTime > generatedSpawnTime) {

}
```

The entirety of the spawning code exists between the parentheses. Once `currentSpawnTime` exceeds `generatedSpawnTime`, you get new aliens.

Between the braces, add the following:

```
currentSpawnTime = 0;
```

This bit of code resets the timer after a spawn occurs — no reset means no more enemies.

Next, add the following:

```
generatedSpawnTime = Random.Range(minSpawnTime, maxSpawnTime);
```

This is your spawn time randomizer. It creates a time between `minSpawnTime` and `maxSpawnTime`. You'll see it come into play during the next change to `Update()`.

Now, add the following:

```
if (aliensPerSpawn > 0 && aliensOnScreen < totalAliens) {

}
```

Here's the logic that determines whether to spawn. First, `aliensPerSpawn` should be greater than zero, and `aliensOnScreen` can't be higher than `totalAliens`. This code is a preventative measure that stops spawning when the maximum number of aliens are present.

Between the braces, add the following:

```
List<int> previousSpawnLocations = new List<int>();
```

This creates an array you will use to keep track of where you spawn aliens each wave. This will be handy so you make sure not to spawn more than one alien from the same spot each wave.

Next, add the following:

```
if (aliensPerSpawn > spawnPoints.Length) {
   aliensPerSpawn = spawnPoints.Length - 1;
}
```

This limits the number of aliens you can spawn by the number of spawn points.

Add the following:

```
aliensPerSpawn = (aliensPerSpawn > totalAliens) ? aliensPerSpawn
- totalAliens : aliensPerSpawn;
```

This is another chunk of preventive code. If `aliensPerSpawn` exceeds the maximum, then the amount of spawns will reduce. This means a spawning event will never create more aliens than the maximum amount that you've configured.

Now comes the actual spawning code. Add the following:

```
for (int i = 0; i < aliensPerSpawn; i++) {

}
```

This loop iterates once for each spawned alien. Add the following between the braces:

```
if (aliensOnScreen < maxAliensOnScreen) {
   aliensOnScreen += 1;
   // code goes here
}
```

This code checks if `aliensOnScreen` is less than the maximum, and then it increments the total screen amount.

After the comment, add the following:

```
// 1
int spawnPoint = -1;
// 2
while (spawnPoint == -1) {
  // 3
  int randomNumber = Random.Range(0, spawnPoints.Length - 1);
  // 4
  if (!previousSpawnLocations.Contains(randomNumber)) {
    previousSpawnLocations.Add(randomNumber);
    spawnPoint = randomNumber;
  }
}
```

This code is responsible for finding a spawn point.

1. `spawnPoint` is the generated spawn point number. Because it references an array index, it's set to -1 to indicate that a spawn point hasn't been selected yet.

2. This loop runs until it finds a spawn point or the spawn point is no longer -1.

3. This line produces a random number as a possible spawn point.

4. Next, it checks the `previousSpawnLocations` array to see if that random number is an active spawn point. If there's no match, then you have your spawn point. The number is added to the array and the `spawnPoint` is set, breaking the loop. If it finds a match, the loop iterates again with a new random number.

Now that you have the spawn point index, you need to get the actual spawn point GameObject. Hang in there for a few more steps! You're close to unlocking an achievement.

Add the following after the closing brace of the `while` statement:

```
GameObject spawnLocation = spawnPoints[spawnPoint];
```

Since there are already assigned spawn points in the Inspector, this grabs the spawn point based on the index that you generated in the last code.

Now, to spawn the actual alien. Add the following:

```
GameObject newAlien = Instantiate(alien) as GameObject;
```

`Instantiate()` will create an instance of any prefab passed into it. It'll create an object that is the type `Object`, so you must cast it into a `GameObject`. Now add the following:

```
newAlien.transform.position = spawnLocation.transform.position;
```

This positions the alien at the spawn point. Save your code and switch back to Unity.

Select the GameManager and go to the Inspector. Set the **Max Aliens on Screen** to 10, **Total Aliens** to 10, **Min Spawn Time** to 0, **Max Spawn Time** to 3, and **Aliens Per Spawn** to 1.

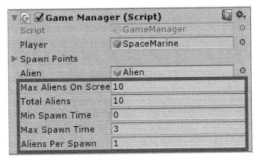

Play your game and watch the Scene view. Glorious! Look at all those creepy critters. Achievement unlocked!

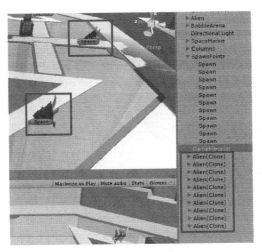

Pathfinding in Unity

The aliens have arrived, but they're little more than decorations at this point. They need to get moving!

Seems like an easy enough task, yes? You could set a target for the aliens, and in each frame move them towards the target. Problem solved. End of chapter!

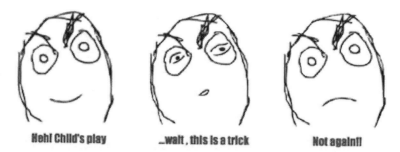

Of course it's not that easy. First, you'd have to rotate the alien constantly so it faces the space marine. Second, a real problem occurs when an alien runs into a column.

The aliens will keep walking into the column until something causes them to move in a different direction. It's pretty ridiculous when a single column can block an entire mob.

Perhaps you could get away with this behavior 20 years ago, but modern gamers expect better than this.

So what do you do?

Your first inclination may be to write the pathfinding. For instance, you could write code that makes the aliens turn and move until they are free of the column, then redirect them towards the hero.

It's not that it wouldn't work, but you'd be treating a fundamental problem like an edge case. What would happen if you added another floor to the mix? You'd have to apply similar fixes, and then your code quickly becomes an unreadable pile of spaghetti.

Thankfully, there's a better way.

Unity's navigation system

It turns out Unity has pathfinding solutions you can use right out of the box, through its navigation system. Four objects comprise the navigation system:

1. **NavMesh:** Represents walkable areas. This works on flat and dimensional terrain such as stairs.

2. **NavMesh Agent**: The actor or agent using the NavMesh. You give your agent a goal and it will find its way using the NavMesh.

3. **Off-Mesh Link**: A shortcut that can't be represented on the map, such as a gap that characters can actually cross.

4. **NavMesh Obstacle**: Obstacles that the agent should avoid. Your agents will use pathfinding to figure a way around them.

To get the aliens to chase the hero, you first need a NavMesh over the entire floor to designate it as a walkable area. To get started, click **Window\Navigation**.

Unity will display the Navigation window (it appears in the right panel where the Inspector usually is by default). Take note of the tabs:

• **Object**: Lists the GameObjects you've added to the NavMesh.

• **Bake**: Configures the NavMesh's properties.

• **Areas**: Defines an area mask, much like a physics layer.

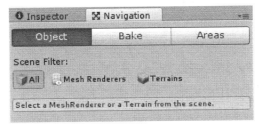

Select the **Object** tab and in it, select the **Mesh Renderers** icon to apply a filter to the Hierarchy. Now it'll only display GameObjects that have renderers attached to them. You can see it in the search field:

You can filter the Hierarchy by other types. To remove the filter, you can simply click the small clear button (but don't do that right now).

Press **Control** on PC or **Command** on Mac and select **Floor_Piece, Floor_Piece_001, Floor_Piece_002, Floor_Piece_003, Glass_Floor**.

Some options will appear in the Navigation window. **Check** the **Navigation Static** checkbox to tell your selected meshes not to move.

Leave the **Generate OffMeshLinks** option **unchecked**. Otherwise, you'll get links between selected GameObjects.

Finally, you'll see a Navigation Area option — this is the navigation mesh you're currently building. Right now, you're working on the **Walkable mask** but can switch to **Not Walkable** or **Jump**. Your custom masks also appear in this drop-down as you create them in the Areas tab.

Click **Bake** at the bottom of the Navigation view to save the mesh. Now you have a place for aliens to walk! After clicking the Bake button, the arena will turn a lighter blue. This indicates you've got a walkable NavMesh mask.

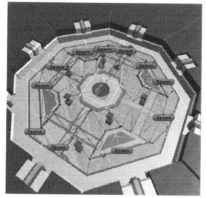

If you don't see the blue nav mesh, check the **Show NavMesh** checkbox in the Scene view.

If you selected a different navigation area, such as Jumpable, then the color would have been orange.

Click the Areas tab to see all the areas and colors that are available to you:

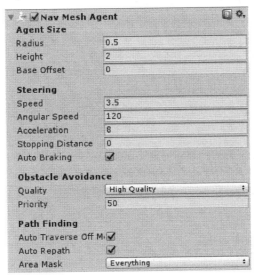

The pretty colors will "vanish" when you switch from the Navigation window, and you'll learn about the Bake tab in just a bit.

Clear the search in the Hierarchy at this point, as you are done with it.

Creating agents

You have the mesh, so now you need agents. Select the **Alien** in the Hierarchy (you should clear the Hierarchy filter to easily find this), and in the Inspector tab click the **Apply** button at the top. As previously mentioned, this is how you push changes to the GameObject back up to the corresponding prefab.

Select the **Alien** prefab in the Prefabs folder. Click **Add Component** then click **Nav Mesh Agent** in the **Navigation** category. You have many options here:

Start by configuring the size of the agent. In the Agent Size section, set **Radius** to `1.45`, **Height** to `6.2` and **Base Offset** to `0`.

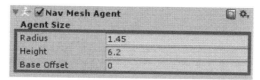

Radius determines the collision distance between other agents. **Height** is the clearance to pass below an overhang, and **Base offset** is the difference between the center of the agent and the center of the GameObject.

You can see visual representations of these figures in the Scene view where a green cylinder defines the agent's bounds.

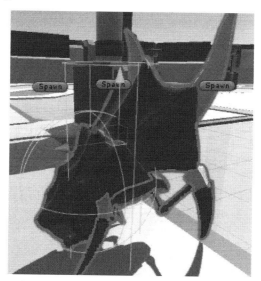

At this point, you've configured the NavMesh Agent, and this new component will drive your GameObject. However, there's a rigidbody attached. Since the rigidbody won't be controlled by physics, **check** the **Is Kinematic** checkbox.

Now you need to set the agent's goal. Click the **Add Component** button then click **New Script** and name it **Alien**. Open it in your code editor.

First you need access to the `NavMeshAgent` classes. Underneath the `using` statements, add the following:

```
using UnityEngine.AI;
```

Add the following variables underneath the opening class brace.

```
public Transform target;
private NavMeshAgent agent;
```

The `target` is where the alien should go — notice the variable name doesn't reference the hero. You don't always want the aliens to chase the hero down. For instance, the hero might throw a noise-maker to attract aliens to a certain area and then mow them down, or maybe he'll get a powerup that makes the aliens turn on each other.

By making the enemies' goal a target instead a certain character, you leave yourself open to more game design opportunities.

Next, add the following to `Start()`:

```
agent = GetComponent<NavMeshAgent>();
```

This gets a reference to the `NavMeshAgent` so you can access it in code. Now, in `Update()`, add the following code:

```
agent.destination = target.position;
```

Save the file and switch over to **GameManager.cs** to set the target for the alien.

Return to where you left off in `Update()`, and add the following code just after the line that sets `newAlien.transform.position`:

```
Alien alienScript = newAlien.GetComponent<Alien>();
```

This gets a reference to the `Alien` script. Now, add:

```
alienScript.target = player.transform;
```

This sets the target to the player's current position.

Finally, the alien should rotate towards the hero right after being spawned. Otherwise, it'll squander time by rotating instead of attacking. Add this:

```
Vector3 targetRotation = new
Vector3(player.transform.position.x,
    newAlien.transform.position.y, player.transform.position.z);
newAlien.transform.LookAt(targetRotation);
```

The code rotates the alien towards the hero using the alien's y-position so that it doesn't look upwards and stares straight ahead.

Save and play your game.

You'll notice a bunch of things, none of which will bring you immediate joy:

1. There are a ton of errors in the console.

2. The aliens move crazy slow.

3. The aliens walk through the columns.

Start with the first issue. You should see the following in the console:

It states that no variable target was assigned to the alien, i.e. one of the aliens doesn't have a reference to the space marine. This is an easy fix. Open **Alien.cs** in your code editor, and then change Update() to match the following:

```
if (target != null) {
    agent.destination = target.position;
}
```

Now run your game and check if the console is clear. If not, make sure to click the **Clear On Play** option.

You successfully resolved the console errors, but you merely addressed the symptoms. Why did you get console errors in the first place?

Play the game again and watch the aliens carefully. You'll see all but one of them milling about. You dragged this non-moving alien into the Scene a while back — it wasn't created by the GameManager. Hence, it has no target and the GameManager doesn't know about it.

This seemingly small issue has potential to break the balance of your game. To fix this, find the alien in the hierarchy and delete it. Buh-bye little orphan alien!

Move on to the second issue: slow-moving aliens. Thankfully, this is an easy fix. It's part of the NavMeshAgent properties.

In the Project browser, select the **Alien** from the **Prefabs** folder. You'll see that the NavMeshAgent component has a section called **Steering**. Here's the breakdown:

• **Speed**: how fast the agent moves in world units per second. **Set this to 20.**

- **Angular Speed**: determines rotation speed in angles per second. **Set** this to **120** (the default value).

- **Acceleration**: how fast the agent increases speed per second. **Set** this to **15.5**.

- **Stopping Distance**: how close the agent stops near its goal. **Set** this to **0** (the default value).

- **Auto Braking**: slows the agent as it approaches its goal. **Uncheck** this.

Steering	
Speed	20
Angular Speed	120
Acceleration	15.5
Stopping Distance	0
Auto Braking	☐

Underneath that section, you'll notice an **Obstacle Avoidance** section. **Quality** determines how the path will be defined. At the highest quality, the path will be determined according to obstacles and other agents. At the lowest quality — none — the path will ignore agents and merely try to avoid immediate collisions.

Since there are many agents in play, set the **Quality** to **Low Quality** to reduce CPU time for calculating the paths.

Play your game. Now the aliens will move with purpose.

Now for the last problem: the little buggers can't just walk through the columns. In the Project browser, select the **BobbleArena-Column** in the Prefabs folder. Click the **Add Component** button. Select **Nav Mesh Obstacle** in the **Navigation** category.

This works just like a plain old collider. Set the **Shape** to **Box** then **Center** to (**0, 2.3, 0**) and **Size** to (**2.07, 4.27, 2**).

You'll notice your columns gain a green wireframe that indicates the NavMeshObstacle.

Play your game, but don't move this time.

Although you resolved the last three problems, now you have a new one: a cluster of aliens in the wrong part of the map.

The root cause is that they're blocked by other renderers. You added only a few pieces of geometry whereas the bugs are getting stuck on the rest of them.

Open the **Navigation** window, and at the bottom of the window, click the **Clear** button.

This will reset the Walkable NavMesh. Add the following renderers to it:

- **Cylinder_xxx**

- **Door_Ring_Bottom**

- **Floor_Piece_xxx**

- **Glass Floor**

- **Inner_Octagon**

- **Outer_Octagon**

Check the **Navigation Static** checkbox and click the **Bake** button — at the bottom, not in the Bake tab — and play your game.

Thankfully, the aliens can make it to the space marine, although some may get stuck. You're getting closer to perfection but not there yet!

The problem now is that the NavMesh's default properties expect smaller agents. In the Navigation window, click the **Bake tab** — not the Bake button.

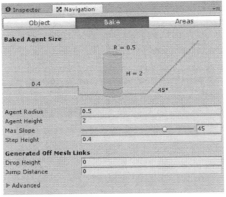

The Bake tab is where you configure the NavMesh. Here's a rundown of the most important properties and how to set them:

- **Agent Radius**: determines how close an agent can get to an obstacle. **Set** it to 1.45.

- **Agent Height**: determines minimum height of a ceiling for the agent to pass beneath. **Set** it to 6.2.

- **Max Slope**: determines the angle at which a slope becomes impassable for the agent. Leave as-is.

- **Step Height**: determines the minimum height at which a step becomes impassable for the agent. **Set** to 0.73.

Where did you get those magic numbers? They are from your NavMesh agent's settings, i.e., your alien. Unity recommends you set the values to the **smallest** agent that's in use.

Click the **Bake** button. Play your game once it's fully baked. The space marine will promptly find that he's the center of attention.

Tuning the pathfinding

Although the pathfinding appears to work without any issue, you actually have a significant problem to solve. Every time you assign a destination to a NavMeshAgent, Unity goes through the process of a calculating a route to that destination.

It wouldn't be a big deal if it happened here and there, but consider that the game will spawn many aliens and perform this calculation each time. Review your implementation with that fact in mind. You'll see that you're calculating the pathfinding once per frame.

This isn't scalable — there will be more pathfinding calculations when aliens spawn. Eventually, your frame rate will tank and it'll kickoff a tragic chain of events for your player.

Open **Alien.cs** in your code editor. Under the public variables, add the following:

```
public float navigationUpdate;
private float navigationTime = 0;
```

navigationUpdate is the amount of time, in milliseconds, for when the alien should update its path. navigationTime is a private variable that tracks how much time has passed since the previous update.

In Update(), replace agent.destination = target.position with the following:

```
navigationTime += Time.deltaTime;
if (navigationTime > navigationUpdate) {
  agent.destination = target.position;
  navigationTime = 0;
}
```

This code checks to see if a certain amount of time has passed then updates the path.

Switch back to Unity. In the Project view, select the **Alien** prefab in the **Prefabs** folder. In the Alien script, set the **Navigation Update** field to 0.5.

Now play your game. You'll notice the aliens are a little slower to dial in on the marine, but for the most part, they will get to him.

At this point, you'd want to play around with the variables that affect play and performance to find that balance point. Testing and profiling your game is the only way to find the right config!

Final touches

You have now hordes of aliens chasing a marine. There's just one thing left to be done — you need something to happen when the marine blows them to bits.

Switch back to **Alien.cs** in your code editor and add the following code before the last closing brace:

```
void OnTriggerEnter(Collider other) {
   Destroy(gameObject);
}
```

This code works like a typical collision code, except that it makes the collision event into a trigger.

Why a trigger? Remember, you set the Alien's rigidbody to Is Kinematic, so the rigidbody won't respond to collision events because the Navigation system is in control.

That said, you can still be informed when a rigidbody crosses a collider through trigger events. That way, you can still respond to them.

In this case, you call Destroy() and pass in the gameObject, which will delete the alien instance. Save the file and switch back to Unity.

Select the **Alien** in the Prefabs folder, and in the Inspector, look for the **Sphere Collider**. **Check** the **Is Trigger** checkbox.

At this point, anything that collides with the alien will kill it — walls, columns, the marine, etc. You need to opt out of some collisions.

With the Alien prefab still selected, assign it to the **Alien layer**. When prompted to apply the layer to all child objects as well, select **No, this object only**. Next, in the Project browser, select the **BobbleArena-Column** in the Prefabs folder.

In the Layer drop-down, assign it to the **Wall** layer and, again, select **No, this object only** in the subsequent prompt dialog.

Next, click **Edit\Project Settings\Physics**. In the collision matrix, uncheck the following in the Alien column: **Wall, Alien Head, Floor, Alien.**

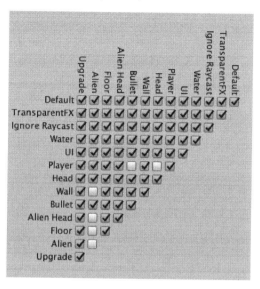

Play your game.

Now you can shoot Aliens to your heart's content, and when you collide with them, they'll despawn. In a later chapter, you'll give the aliens a more fitting death. But as it is now, you can get a good feel for your game. Take this moment to do a little more tuning.

Restart your game, and pause right as it starts.

Select the **GameManager** in the Hierarchy, and in the Inspector, set the following values:

• **Max Aliens On Screen**: 50

• **Total Aliens**: 50

• **Min Spawn Time**: 0

• **Max Spawn Time**: 3

• **Aliens Per Spawn**: 3

Now **unpause** the game, and prepare to be confronted by a lot of aliens. If you experience a slowdown, dial back the numbers until you find what works best for your system.

Once you find the right amount, **pause** the game one more time. **Do not stop the game.** You need to copy the GameManager values. You could write them down, but there's a better way.

Select **GameManager** in the Hierarchy (if it isn't already), and in the Inspector, **click the gear icon** over the Game Manager script component. From the drop-down, select **Copy Component.**

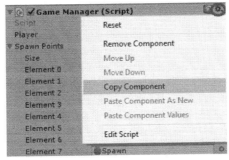

Now **stop** your game. Pay no attention to the fact that the Game Manager reverts the values. **Click the gear icon** again and select **Paste Component Values**.

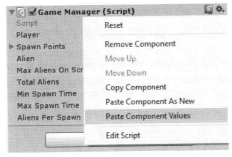

The component will update with all the values you added during run time. Pretty awesome, eh? The downside is that you can only do this with one component at a time.

Where to go from here?

It's hard to believe that one little chapter on pathfinding could bring a relatively static game to life. As you worked through the process of pathfinding, you learned about:

- **Creating Managers**, such as a Game Manager to manage the gameplay and allow you to tweak settings in real time.

- **NavMeshes** and how they define movable areas for GameObjects.

- **NavAgents** and how to build them and give them targets.

- **NavObstacles** to have your agents avoid various parts of your level geometry.

Not surprisingly, there's much more to learn. Have you noticed that everybody moves without moving their legs? Curious. In the next chapter, you'll give your models a little spring in their step and learn all about Unity's animation system in the process.

Chapter 6: Animation

By Brian Moakley

At this point, you've learned how to move GameObjects in Unity in a variety of ways, including:

1. **Writing scripts to manually change the position**. You learned this in Chapter 3, "Components", when you wrote scripts to move the player, camera, and bullets.

2. **Using the Character Controller**. You learned this in Chapter 4, "Physics", when you replaced the player movement script with the built-in Character Controller, which has powerful functionality and is often easier than writing movement scripts on your own.

3. **Letting the Unity physics engine move objects for you**. You learned this in Chapter 4, "Physics" when configured the space marine's bobblehead by attaching it to the body with a joint and periodically applying a force to make it bobble.

4. **Employing the Navigation System to move objects on your behalf**. You learned this in Chapter 5, "Pathfinding", when you configured the aliens as a NavMesh agent and gave it a target so they could pathfind their way to the space marine.

There's another important way to move GameObjects in Unity that you haven't explored yet: the animation system, otherwise known as Mecanim.

Mecanim is a powerful system that allows you to animate models as well as *every single exposed property* in Unity.

That's right, if you can set a value in the Inspector, you can animate that value over time! Powerful stuff.

Getting started

The first animation that you will create is a simple animation to make the arena walls go up and down.

This is because currently there's an issue. As the space marine moves towards the camera, the wall blocks your view of him. This is *bad* mojo; not can you not see what you're shooting, but the spawning aliens can attack instantly.

Causing people to lose because their view was blocked is no way to win gamers' hearts and minds!

One technique to solve the problem is to make the wall transparent, but that doesn't solve the problem of the partially obscured play area. For slow-paced games, it wouldn't be a serious problem, but fast reaction times are required to win Bobblehead Wars.

To solve the problem, you'll lower the walls of the arena when the player gets close and raise them when the player walks away.

The animation window

Open your project from the last chapter, or if you're reading this chapter out of order, feel free to open the starter project that's located in the resources for this chapter.

You're going to animate various child GameObjects of the BobbleArena. You could animate them individually, but this technique will have you grouping child GameObjects together, which is far more efficient.

In the Hierarchy, select the **BobbleArena** GameObject. Click **Window\Animation** to open the Animation window.

The window has several sections, and you'll spend quite a bit of time here in this chapter.

On the left, you have a **Property List** where you select the properties you intend to animate. On the right, you have the **Dope Sheet** where you create **keyframes** — more on this in a moment.

Above the dope sheet is the **Timeline** where you scrub back and forth on the animation to preview how it looks. Finally, above the property list, you'll see **Frame Navigation** where you control playback and add animation events.

Animation events allow you to run code at certain frames in an animation.

Introducing keyframe animations

Unity animates objects through the use of **keyframe animation**.

In keyframe animation, you set up a series of (time, value) pairs to indicate how you want an object to animate over time. You don't need to specify every single second; the beauty is the game engine will automatically calculate the values in-between your **key frames**.

For example, say have a cube at (0, 0, 0) that you want to move to (0, 10, 0) two seconds later. Then you would set up two keyframes:

• Time 0 seconds: Position (0, 0, 0)

• Time 2 seconds: Posttion (0, 10, 0)

Where would the cube be at time 1 second? Unity would automatically calculate this for you through interpolation — for example (0, 5, 0).

Keyframe animation makes creating animations easy. You just have to specify the important points — again, the key frames, and Unity takes care of the rest!

Your first animation

In the dope sheet, click the **Create** button.

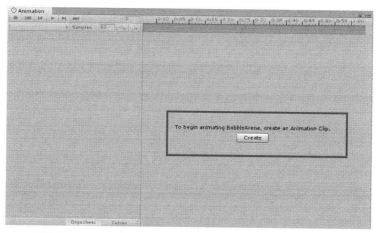

Give it the name **Walls.anim** and save it in the Animations folder. While you were busy saving, Unity was busy behind the scenes:

• Created a new animation clip

• Created a new animation controller

In the Hierarchy, select **BobbleArena** and see it for yourself in the Inspector.

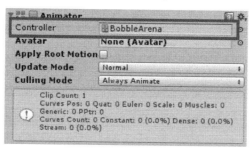

That new animator controller was assigned to the `Controller` property. Note that Unity only does these things when you create a *new animation* on a GameObject *without an animator controller.*

Unity attaches an animator controller on the GameObject but it also creates an animator controller file in the same folder as your animation clips. This file keeps track of all your states which you'll learn in just a bit.

Now to the part where you actually make the animation!

Click the **Add Property** button in the Animation window.

You're in the place where you select the GameObject or property that you wish to animate. You'll see each component listed as well as the child GameObjects.

Expand the **Floor** disclosure triangle then expand the **Outer_Wall_003** GameObject. Next, expand the **Transform** component and click the **plus sign** next to the **Position** property.

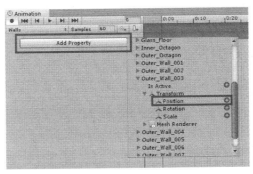

Do the same thing for **Outer_Wall_004** and **Outer_Wall_006**.

At this point, you're technically ready to start recording the animation. Do you feel ready? Huh? Do you?

Good! Click the little red record button in the Animation window with authority.

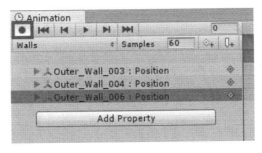

By pressing the button, you've also caused the Unity's player controls to have turned red. It's go time now!

If you select one of the GameObjects that you're animating, you'll also notice that its position properties turn red.

These are all visual reminders that you're currently animating. It's surprisingly easy to forget that you're in animation mode.

Many developers suffer from this acute condition, aptly named *animanesia*. It's what happens when you're working in animation mode but start making changes to your game; you get deep into it then realize — in one terrible flash — that you've just made a bunch of useless animation clips.

The unpleasant discovery usually triggers a storm of curses to flow from your mouth, which is then followed by begrudgingly redoing all your work.

Go to the Dope Sheet and **Click the timeline** above the keyframes at the 1:00 mark.

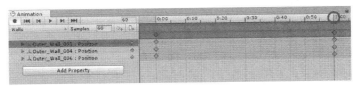

Since you are in animation mode, you can think of this as "time traveling" to what the animation will look like at the 1:00 mark. You can see what it will look like in the Unity editor, and modify the values.

Note that if you don't move the scrubber exactly over the keyframes at the 1:00 mark, Unity will create new keyframes at the scrubber's current position.

Make sure that just **Outer_Wall_003** is selected, and in the Inspector, set the **y position** to −0.48. In the Scene view, you'll see the wall drop down.

Do the same for **Outer_Wall_004** and **Outer_Wall_006**. The walls should look as follows:

Now, **click** the animation **play** button (in the animation window, not the normal play button). Just like that, you have moving walls!

Hit the animation **play** button again to stop the looping animation. Note you can also move the scrubber on the timeline to see the interpolated values at any point.

When you finish, **click** the **recording button** to stop recording mode.

Animation states

As you start creating animations, you'll accrue many clips. Some GameObjects are going to have many animations, so you'll need a way to control which animations run when. It's possible to do this via through code, but why would you go to the hassle when Unity provides a tool that makes this easy?

Meet the **Animator**.

You can think of the animator as the director in a movie. It runs around giving orders of which animations to play when.

For instance, when a character stands idle, the animator could order an animation to move the head and portray breathing and fidgeting. When a character's horizontal speed increases, the animator could order a walking animation; once speed surpasses a defined threshold, the animator could order a running animation.

With the animator, you define the conditions and their animation relationships. Then, in essence, the game takes care of itself.

Click **Window\Animator** to open the Animator window.

> **Note:** When you first start working with Unity, you may confuse the *Animation* and *Animator* windows.
>
> Try a little memory trick: the anima-*tion* window is where you do crea-*tion*. The animat-*or* window is where you're an organiz-*er*.

You'll probably see an empty window because you didn't select a GameObject that has an animator component attached to it.

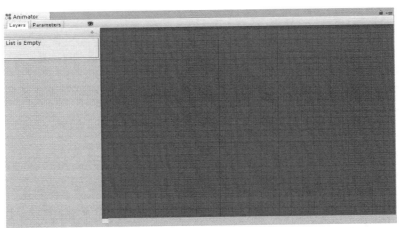

In the Hierarchy, click **BobbleArena** and check if you see the following in the Animator:

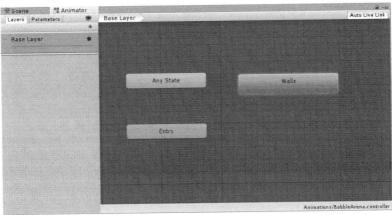

You'll see the Walls animation is already present in the controller. Any new animation clips are added the current animator controller automatically.

Each rectangle indicates an animation state:

- The green rectangle is the entry point of the animator.
- The orange rectangle indicates the default state; it's always played first.
- The arrows indicate transitions between states.

Play your game and move the hero until you can see the lower walls. The animation loops endlessly.

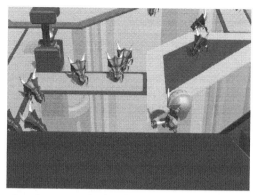

The `Walls` animation plays because it's the designated default state. It loops because that's the default behavior.

Watch the animator as it plays to see the animation's progress.

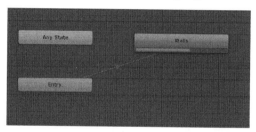

In the Project browser, click the **Animations** folder and **select** the **Walls** animation. In the Inspector, **uncheck Loop Time**.

That's how you override the default — no loop for you!

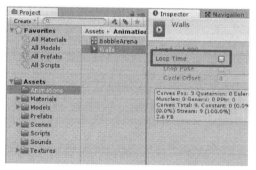

Unfortunately, "Walls" isn't a very descriptive name. Click the **Walls** state in the Animator and move your eyes to the Inspector to see all the available properties. You'll learn and change a bunch of these throughout this book.

For now, change the name from **Walls** to **WallsLower**. That's it in here.

Notice that the state reflects the updated name.

Being that you have a WallsLower state, you need a WallsRaise state. You could create a new animation, but since this animation is very similar to the WallsLower animation (just reversed), I'll show you a shortcut.

Right-click in the Animator, select **Create State** and then **Empty**.

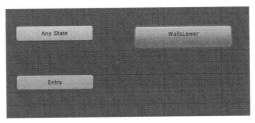

You'll now have a new empty state.

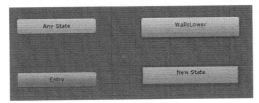

Select this new state and name it **WallsRaise** in the Inspector. Next, drag the **Walls** animation from the Animations folder to the **Motion** property. Finally, set the **speed** to −1.

The Motion property references the actual animation clip. In this case, you're using the same animation clip that you used in WallsLower. The Speed property lets you designate how fast the clip will play. Setting the speed to 1 indicates that it will play at normal speed. Higher numbers make the clip run slower, whereas lower numbers make it run faster.

Why -1? Negative numbers play the clip in reverse. In this case, you're using the same clip, but playing it in reverse at normal speed.

You need one more state: an idle state. Open the **Animation** window, making sure the **BobbleArena** is selected in the Hierarchy. You'll see the name of the currently displayed animation in the property list, which should be walls.

Click **Walls** and select **Create New Clip...** from the drop-down.

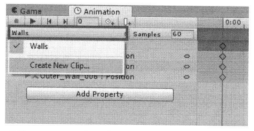

Give it the name **ArenaIdle.anim** and make sure to **stop recording**. That's right — your animation clip comprises an empty animation. Although you can create a state with no associated animation, Unity will do weird things that might ruin your plans. At times, it helps to play it safe and make an animation clip for the idle state, even if it's empty.

Your animator should look something like this:

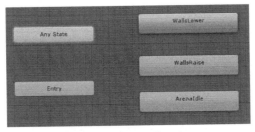

You need to organize it, and you'll do that through transitions.

Animation state transitions

Transitions perform a variety of functions. They let you know the flow of animations, but more importantly, you can gate them according to certain conditions.

The first part of a transition is a condition, so that's the next thing you'll set up.

In the Animator window, **right-click** the **ArenaIdle** state and select **Make Transition**.

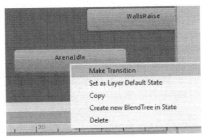

A line will now follow your mouse cursor. Click the **WallsLower** state to create that **new transition**.

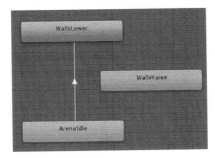

> **Note:** You might find that a state is out of view. By holding down the middle mouse button, you can pan around inside the animator and find it.

Create a **new transition** from **WallsLower** to **WallsRaise**, and then another from **WallsRaise** to **ArenaIdle**. Your states should look like this:

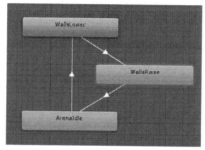

This depicts the entire animation flow.

Play your game while watching the animator.

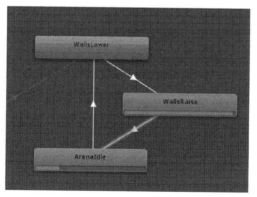

Select BobbleArena in the Hierarchy if you don't see any motion.

You'll notice the animation moves in an endless loop and that some states start before others finish; the Animator is blending the states.

Animation state transition conditions

Looping isn't ideal in this case; you need a condition to prevent it. Also, blending is helpful, but you might want to make it more or less subtle. In some cases, you may not want it at all.

Go to the animator window and **click** the **Parameters** tab. It will currently read *List is Empty* because there are no parameters.

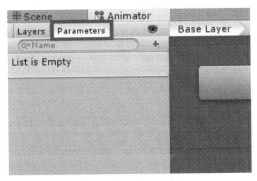

Click the **plus sign** and select **Bool** from the drop-down.

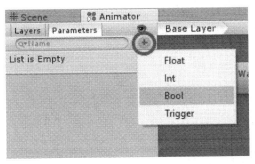

Give it the name **IsLowered**.

Although you chose **Bool** in this case, note that the menu has 4 options to choose from: **Float**, **Int**, **Bool**, and **Trigger**. Except for the Trigger, all of them correspond to the types used in C# . The `trigger` is a distinctive Unity condition type that behaves like a `bool`, except it resets itself after an animation.

Select the **transition arrow** between `ArenaIdle` and `WallsLower` to see your blending options in the Inspector.

Uncheck Has Exit Time to tell Unity you want the animation to conclude immediately instead of waiting until the end of the animation. Otherwise, Unity will take additional time to blend the animation with the next animation.

In the Conditions section, **click** the **plus sign**. Since you have only one parameter, the `IsLowered` property will populate the field; set its condition to **true**.

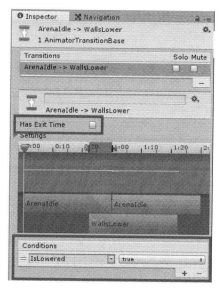

The reason you did this is because you will set the `IsLowered` boolean in code when you want the animation to trigger. By setting the condition that `IsLowered` must be true for this animation to run, once you set it in code the animation will play.

You need to make one more small adjustment before playing the game. In the Animator window, **right-click ArenaIdle** and elect **Set as Layer Default State** from the options.

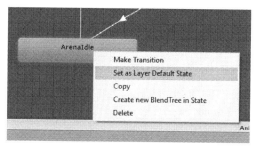

This change indicates that `ArenaIdle` is the entry state for the animator controller. To make the relationships easier to understand at a glance, organize them like so:

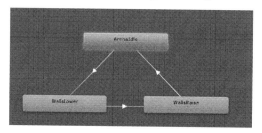

Play your game again while keeping the Animator open. You'll see the wall doesn't drop because the condition hasn't been met. With the game still playing, **check IsLowered** in the Animator.

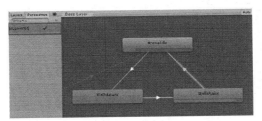

Now the wall lowers, raises and loops unless you uncheck IsLowered.

You need one more condition.

Stop your game and select the **transition arrow** from **WallsLower** to **WallsRaise**. In the Inspector, **uncheck Has Exit Time**. Click the **plus sign** in the Conditions section and set **IsLowered** to **false**.

Play it again and **click** the **IsLowered** checkbox. This time, the walls will lower, but they stop there due to the new condition. **Uncheck IsLowered** to raise the walls again.

You now have animations in place. Time to call them in code!

Triggering animations in code

At this point, you have animation clips, animation states and conditions in place to activate your animations.

Next, you'll use a collider trigger to put everything together in code.

Select **BobbleArena** in the Hierarchy then click the **Create** button. From the drop-down, select **Create Empty Child** and name it **Wall Trigger**. Set **Position** to (**0, 0, 0**) and **Scale** to (**0.5, 0.5, 0.5**). Next, click the **Add Component button** and from the **Physics** category, select **Box Collider**.

In the Box Collider component, **check** the **Is Trigger** checkbox, set Center to (**0, 6.72, -90.6**) and **Size** to (**250.55, 17.14, 66.7**).

You should see a large trigger in the Scene view toward the back walls. When the space marine walks into this area, you want to lower the walls.

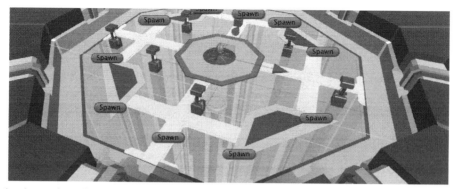

To do this, select the **WallTrigger** then click the **Add Component** button and select **New Script**. Name it **ArenaWall**, make sure **language** is **C Sharp** and click the **Create and Add** button.

Double-click the new script to edit it, and add this variable inside the class:

```
private Animator arenaAnimator;
```

You could make it a public variable so you can set this in the inspector, but this isn't necessary.

This is because `WallTrigger` is a child of the `BobbleArena`, so you can get a reference to the animator by accessing the `WallTrigger`'s `parent` property, and gettng the appropriate component.

To do this, add this to `Start()`:

```
GameObject arena = transform.parent.gameObject;
arenaAnimator = arena.GetComponent<Animator>();
```

First, this gets the parent GameObject by accessing the `parent` property on the transform. Once it has a reference to the `arena` GameObject, it calls `GetComponent()` for a reference to the animator.

Again, the above script works because it assumes the caller is a child of `BobbleArena`. It would fail if the caller were moved to a different GameObject.

Next add the following:

```
void OnTriggerEnter(Collider other) {
  arenaAnimator.SetBool("IsLowered", true);
}
```

When the trigger is activated, the code sets `IsLowered` to `true`. You do this by calling `SetBool()`.

> **Note:** There are similar methods for other types. For example, for a `float`, you'd use `SetFloat()`.

Now you need logic to raise the walls. Add the following:

```
void OnTriggerExit(Collider other) {
    arenaAnimator.SetBool("IsLowered", false);
}
```

When the hero leaves the trigger, this code tells the animator to set `IsLowered` to `false` to raise the walls.

There's one outstanding detail for this script. Currently, any GameObject that enters the trigger lowers the walls. You need a filter so it only applies to the space marine.

Save the file and go back to Unity. With **WallTrigger** still selected, assign it the **Wall** layer. Navigate to **Edit\Project Settings\Physics**.

Uncheck all the checkboxes in the **Wall** row.

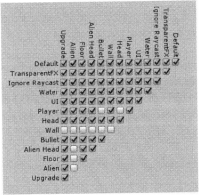

Play your game. Just as you intended, the walls lower when the marine walks down the screen, allowing you to see the action. How's that for convenience?

Animating models

At some point, you may want to add animations for your models. Unity provides this power; unfortunately, it's not always the right tool for the job. As mentioned in Chapter 1, "Hello, Unity", Unity is more of an integration tool than it is a creation tool.

Although Unity shares many features with popular 3D modeling and animation programs, it's not well-equipped to handle advanced tasks. Many developers prefer to create animations in an external program then import them into Unity.

That said, making simple animations is fine. After all, animating a custom model is no different from what you just did with the walls.

Take the alien for an example. Like the space marine, it has a large head that's begging to bobble. For learning purposes, rather than create this effect with physics, you'll use animation to create the effect.

So you can easily preview the animation as you work on it, select the **Alien** in the Hierarchy, or drag an instance of the **Alien** into the Scene view if it's not there.

Last time you created an animation, Unity made the animator controller. This time, you'll do that for yourself.

Expand the Alien in the Hierarchy to reveal its child GameObjects. Select **BobbleEnemy-Head** and click the **Add Component** button. Select **Animator** from the **Miscellaneous** section.

In the Project view, select the **Animations** folder and click the **Create** button. From the drop-down, select the **Animator Controller** and name it **AlienHead**.

Drag the **AlienHead** animator controller to the **Controller** property of the animator component.

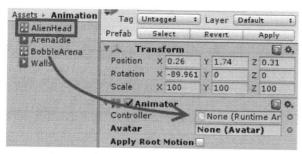

Open the animations window, make sure you've selected BobbleEnemy-Head and click the **Create** button. Call it **HeadBob.anim** and save it in the **Animations** folder.

Click the **Add Property** button. From the flyout menu, expand the Transform component and click the **plus sign** next to **Rotation**.

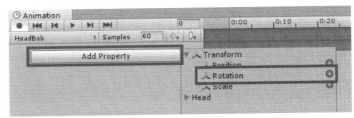

You'll use three keyframes in this animation. But first, you need to make the animation smaller. Select the **last keyframe** and drag it to **frame 0:10**.

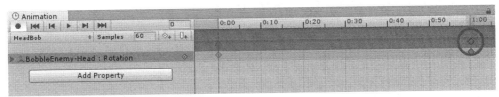

Next, move the **red scrubber** to **frame 0:5** then **right-click** and select **Add Key**.

With the middle keyframe still selected, go to the Inspector. Set **Rotation** to (**-61, 0, 0**) — now play the animation.

Watch your alien do a little head banging. You'll notice that changing one middle keyframe value resulted in a difference that's causing the head to move up and down.

You'll notice that the animation runs somewhat fast. In the **Samples** field, set the value to **20**. For perspective, keep in mind that the last animation you made ran at the default 60 frames per second — this one will run slower.

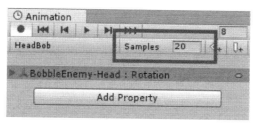

Click the **red record button** in the animation window to stop recording mode. In the Inspector, **apply the changes** to the prefab so all the instances bobble, and delete the temporary alien from the hierarchy.

Play the game again to see if the aliens all belong to headbanging club.

Imported animations

Unity provides a number of tools for animating GameObjects, and as you know, you can import animations with models. In fact, you've already imported some with the space marine and alien! All you need to do is incorporate them into your game, which is pretty easy.

In the Project view, select the **BobbleEnemy-Body** GameObject from the Models folder. You'll see three tabs in the Inspector: **Model**, **Rig** and **Animations**.

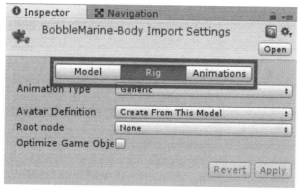

The **Model** and **Rig** tabs deal with the actual model structure.

Avatars and Rigs

Typically, models are **rigged**, which means Unity creates a system that acts as a virtual skeleton to helps your models move naturally.

For instance, when you move an arm of a model, all the child GameObjects that comprise the arm will move in accordance with the rig's limitations as well as any that you dictate.

Rigs in Unity are called **avatars** and they can share animations. Unity provides a library of free motion capture animations, and with a proper rig, you can incorporate these motions with minimal work.

The **Animations** tab is where you configure your imported animations. You're about to get a crash course in all this...starting now!

Animating the alien

Click the **Animations** tab. Here's the animations you imported with the model.

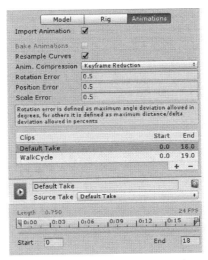

You have many options. The first deals with compressing the animation and addressing any resulting errors. Under the Clips section are your imported animation clips.

Select the **Default Take** animation.

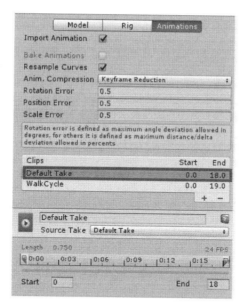

Beneath the animation are all tools for tweaking it. The timing bar allows you to edit the length of animation; a common use case is making a seamless loop effect.

Check the box for **Loop Time**.

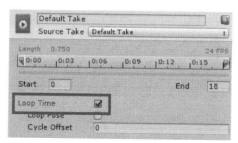

Look a little further down to find the preview pane. If you don't see a preview, look for a black bar at the bottom and drag it upwards.

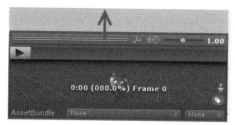

Click the **play** button and the model will show the selected animation.

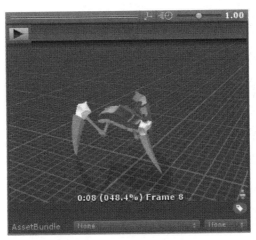

Once you're satisfied with the preview you'll need to save it. At the bottom of the Inspector, just above the preview window, click the **Apply** button.

In the Project browser, select the **Animations** folder and click the **Create** button. From the drop-down, select **Animator Controller** and call it **AlienBody**. With the animation controller selected in the Project browser, open the **Animator window**.

Next, **right-click** in the Animator window and select **Create State\Empty**.

Select the new empty and name it **Walking** in the Inspector. Next, **click** the circle beside the **Motion** property.

You're looking for **Default Take** but, in the list of animations, there are many clones. Select the **top-most Default Take**. Check the footer to see which model owns the animation.

Click through the Default Takes to find the one that belongs to **Assets/Models/BobbleEnemy-Body.blend**. Double-click it to select it.

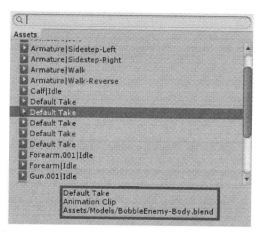

Go to the Prefabs folder in the Project browser and expand **Alien's** disclosure triangle. Select **BobbleEnemy-Body**. You'll see that it already has an animator component attached.

In the Project browser, drag the **AlienBody** animation controller to the **Controller** property in the Inspector.

Play your game. Congrats! You officially have creepy-crawly aliens!

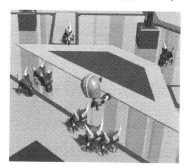

Animating the space marine

Now that the aliens mobilized, it's time to summon the space marine.

In the **Models** folder in the Project view, select the **BobbleMarine-Body** and click the **Animations** tab in the Inspector.

You'll see many unused animations that were imported with the model. This may have been the result of the export to FBX, but in future projects you may have animations you don't need.

Delete all of them *except* **Armature|Walk animation** and **Armature|Idle** by selecting and clicking the **minus sign**. Unfortunately you must do this one at a time.

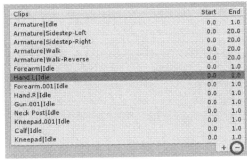

If you mistakenly delete the wrong animation, just click the **Revert** button at the bottom of the Inspector.

Breathe a sigh of relief now that you have a tidy workspace. Select the **Armature|Walk** animation and check the **Loop Time** box beneath to loop the animation indefinitely.

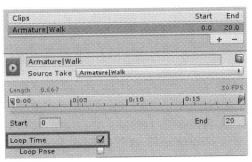

Click Apply at the bottom to save changes.

You'll need to create a transition between the two different states. In the Project browser, select the **Animations** folder and click the **Create** button. From the drop-down, select **Animator Controller**. Give it the name **SpaceMarine**.

In the Hierarchy, expand the SpaceMarine and select **BobbleMarine-Body**. There is already an animator attached to it — you can see it in the Inspector. **Drag** the **SpaceMarine animation controller** from the Project browser to the **Controller** property on the Animator.

With the BobbleMarine-Body still selected in the Hierarchy, switch to the Animator. Create two different states: **MarineIdle** and **MarineWalk**. Assign **Armature|Idle** to the **MarineIdle** and **Armature|Walk** animation to the **MarineWalk** state.

Set **MarineIdle** as the default state.

Now, you need to add some transitions. Right-click **MarineIdle** and select **Make Transition**. Drag it to **MarineWalk**. Do the same from **MarineWalk** to **MarineIdle**. Your animator controller should look like the following:

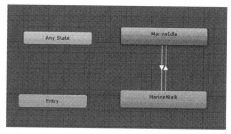

Click the **Parameters** tab then click the **plus sign**. Select **Bool** from the drop-down and name it: **IsMoving**.

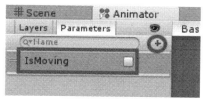

Now click the transition from **MarineIdle** to **MarineWalk**, and in the Inspector, **uncheck Has Exit Time**. Also, click the **plus sign** under Conditions, and set the value to **true**.

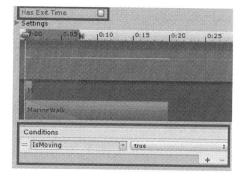

Do the same for the transition from **MarineWalk** to **MarineIdle**, but set the Condition to **false**. When `IsMoving` is true, the walking animation will play. Otherwise, the marine will stand still.

To make this work, you need to write a little code. Open the **PlayerController** script in your code editor and add the following instance variable underneath the others:

```
public Animator bodyAnimator;
```

Next, in `FixedUpdate()`, find the `\\ TODO` comment (inside the if statement that checks if `moveDirection == Vector3.zero`). Replace it with the following:

```
bodyAnimator.SetBool("IsMoving", false);
```

In the `else` branch, add the following before the closing brace:

```
bodyAnimator.SetBool("IsMoving", true);
```

This simply sets the appropriate values on the Animator.

Save the code and switch back to Unity.

In the Hierarchy, drag the **BobbleMarine-Body** into the **Body Animator** property of the **SpaceMarine**.

Finally, play your game. Now your SpaceMarine can do the moonwalk! :]

Where to go from here?

Bobblehead Wars is really coming along. You have bobbling heads and moving characters. In the process of making all these animations, you thoroughly explored Unity's animation engine, Mecanim. In the process you learned:

- **Keyframe animation**: The basics of creating an animation clip.
- **Animator**: How to use it and manage animations within it.
- **Triggering animations**: How to do this in code (like a boss).
- **Outside animations**: How to use animations created outside of Unity.

Although the game is coming together, it feels like there's something missing. How can you have a game without sound?!

You'll fix that in the next chapter, where you'll bring Bobblehead Wars to life with some kickass sound effects and groovy tunes.

Chapter 7: Sound

By Brian Moakley

Graphics are always top of your mind when you're creating games, largely because we're visual creatures. That said, graphics can only take a game so far.

Sound gives depth to the visuals and can trigger powerful emotions. For example, graphics can adeptly depict a large cavernous structure, but echoing footsteps and the sound of dripping water make it an immersive experience.

In this chapter, you'll take Bobblehead Wars from good to great, throught the power of Unity's audio engine!

Getting started

Open your Bobblehead Wars project that's in progress, or start fresh with the starter project from the resources for this chapter.

The first thing you need to hear sounds in Unity is an **Audio Listener**. This is a component that you attach to a GameObject so the engine knows where the listener is. This is important because some audio depends on location — for example if you're near a humming generator, the noise will be loud, but if you move far away you might not even be able to hear it.

By default, every new scene includes an audio listener that's attached to the Main Camera.

Click on the camera to see it for yourself:

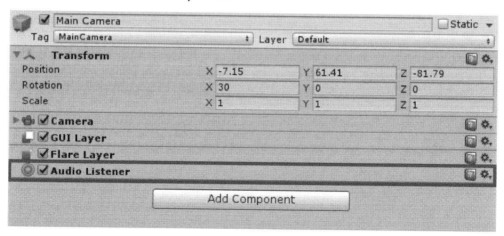

> **Note:** This default listener can trigger an error when you import a first person character controller, like you will do later in this book. You'll receive a message that states:
>
> *"There are 2 audio listeners in the scene. Please ensure there is always exactly one listener in the scene."*
>
> Unity's a bit like the Highlander when it comes to listeners: "There can be only one". Add the AudioListener to the single GameObject that most accurately represents the listener.

The second thing you need to play sounds in Unity is an **Audio Source**. As you might guess, this is an object that emits a sound, such as a sound effect or background music.

You already have an Audio Listener set up, so let's add your first Audio Source — one for background music in the game. As Corinne Bailey Rae would say, it's time to put your records on!

Playing background music

Select **Main Camera** in the Hierarchy. Click the **Add Component** button and select **Audio Source** in the Audio category.

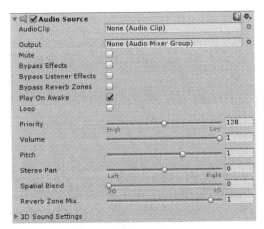

You're adding the audio source for the background music to the camera, since that's the same place the audio listener is. This way, the volume of the background music will always stay the same; think of it like carrying around your own boom box!

As you can see, you have an array of options. Here's the breakdown:

- **AudioClip**: The actual sound file. You create a clip by dragging a sound file into Unity, and then the engine converts it to an audio clip. In your case, you imported the sounds when you imported the models in Chapter 1, "Hello, Unity".

> **Pro tip**: Avoid formats such as MP3 because Unity sometimes re-encodes compressed files to a lower quality when it exports the game. To avoid these, we have provided the audio as ogg files.

- **Output**: This represents the Audio Mixer to use. You'll learn what this means later in this chapter.

- **Mute**: Check this if you'd like to mute the audio. This can be useful to programatically mute sounds mid-game, or to disable sounds while testing.

- **Bypass Effects/Listener Effects/Reverb Zones**: Turns off any additional effects you might add to a sound. Effects can add depth and increase realism. For instance, consider the difference between footsteps in that cavernous structure with and without an echo. By the way, you used to have to buy a paid Unity license to access these features — but they are free for all to use now.

- **Play on Awake**: Plays the sound as soon as the GameObject is activated. Note that this is checked, which is great: it means that the background music will start playing automatically as soon as the game begins.

- **Sound Sliders**: Adjusts the current sound's properties, such as volume and pan location.

- **3D Sound Settings**: Changes how a sound plays in 3D space. For instance, you can adjust the doppler level here. That can be used to create the pitch and frequency of the sound for a fast-moving object, such as a bullet whizzing past your player.

It's important to understand that Unity doesn't factor in level geometry when playing sounds. Here's a case where level geometry matters: imagine that two players, each with a large ray gun, stand on opposite sides of a 2-meter thick concrete wall. If player one fires, in Unity player two would hear the shot as if player 1 was right next to him (rather than it being muffled as you might expect).

Let's look at the audio clip for the background music. In the Project browser, open the **Sounds** folder and select **bw_bg**. The Inspector shows you all the properties for this audio clip.

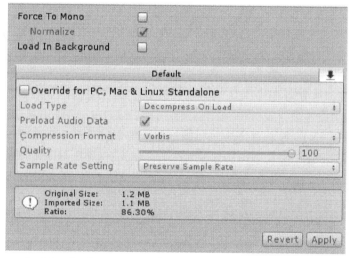

In here, you can decide whether to go with stereo or mono, load the clip in a background thread or normalize.

You also have the ability to change how the audio clip plays, which can have a ripple effect on performance. By default, audio clips are decompressed in memory when loaded. Ogg files expand ten times when decompressed, so 1 MB file requires 10 MB when it's loaded. It's not ideal.

Check the **Override for PC, Mac, & Linux** standalone option. From the **Load Type** option, select **Compressed in Memory**. Instead of hogging memory space, the audio will decompress as it plays. This setting does increase CPU usage, but it's a fair trade-off in this case.

Note that you have the option to stream the file too, but you can try that out another time.

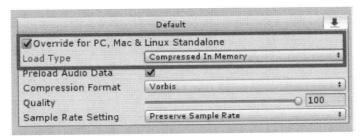

Click **Apply** to save changes.

Next, select the **Main Camera** and drag **bw_bg** from the Project browser to the **AudioClip** property on the Main Camera's audio source. **Check** the **Loop** checkbox to make it repeat continuously.

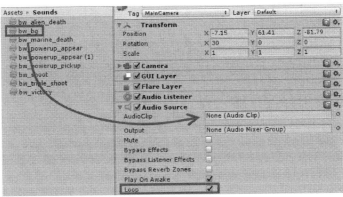

Play your game and listen to those sweet, sweet tunes. Don't worry about volume for the moment. You've got a sound manager to build.

Building a sound manager

Sounds stack up quickly when you're building a game. I bet you're already thinking about audio you'd like in Bobblehead Wars — like a sound effect for when the marine fires his gun, or perhaps a battle cry for the aliens.

You could create AudioClip properties throughout your scripts, but it's hard to keep things organized. It's actually easier to build and use a sound manager as an audio library for your game.

In the Hierarchy, click the **Create** button and from the drop-down, select **Create Empty**. Give it the name **SoundManager**.

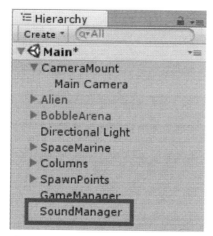

Click the **Add Component** button, and from the Audio category, select **Audio Source**. SoundManager will provide audio clips when asked most of the time, but sometimes it iwll play sounds directly too.

Now that you have a sound manager, you should move the background audio source to the sound manager, to keep all the audio in one place. To do this, select **Main Camera** and expand the Audio Source component in the Inspector. **Click** the **gear icon** and select **Copy Component** from the options.

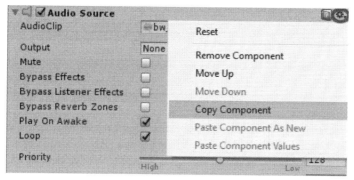

Click the **gear icon** again, and this time, select **Remove Component**. Finally, select the **SoundManager** in the Hierarchy and find the Transform component in the Inspector.

Click the **gear icon** and choose **Paste Component as New**.

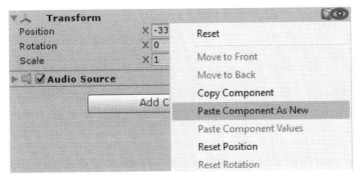

Now you have two audio sources. The first plays sound effects while the second plays the background music.

Click the **Add Component** button and select **New Script**. Name it **SoundManager**, make sure the language is **C Sharp**, and then click **Create and Add**. Open the script in your code editor.

You want to be able to access this script anywhere in your game. After the opening brace, add the following:

```
public static SoundManager Instance = null;
private AudioSource soundEffectAudio;
```

`Instance` will store a static reference to the single instance of `SoundManager`. This will be handy so you can quickly get a reference to the `SoundManager` anywhere in your scripts, without having to go through the normal process of making a public variable that you set in the Unity editor.

`soundEffectAudio` refers to the audio source you added to the `SoundManager` earlier that will be used to play sound effects. Since you won't need to adjust the second audio source that plays background music in code, there's no reason to create a reference for it.

Next, add the following to `Start()`:

```
if (Instance == null) {
  Instance = this;
} else if (Instance != this) {
  Destroy(gameObject);
}
```

This is a simple coding design pattern, known as a Singleton pattern, that ensures that there is always only one copy of this object in existence. If this is the first `SoundManager` created, it sets the static `Instance` variable to the current object. If for some reason a second `SoundManager` is created, it automatically destroys itself to make sure that one and only one `SoundManager` exists.

Next, add the following after the last bit of code:

```
AudioSource[] sources = GetComponents<AudioSource>();
foreach (AudioSource source in sources) {
  if (source.clip == null) {
    soundEffectAudio = source;
  }
}
```

You need to get a handle to the AudioSource you added to the SoundManager that you'll use to play sound, but currently you have two AudioSources on the GameManager. How can you find the correct one?

Well, one way is to search through all the AudioSource components for the one you're looking for. `GetComponents()` returns all of the components of a particular type. Although Unity tends to return components in the same order as they are the Inspector, you shouldn't count on that as that behavior may change. Instead you should look for something that distinguishes the one you're looking for. In this case, since you added music to one of the sources, this checks for the audio source that has no music before setting `soundEffectAudio`.

Now you're going to build out your sound effect library.

Add the following instance variables after the class definition:

```
public AudioClip gunFire;
public AudioClip upgradedGunFire;
public AudioClip hurt;
public AudioClip alienDeath;
public AudioClip marineDeath;
public AudioClip victory;
public AudioClip elevatorArrived;
public AudioClip powerUpPickup;
public AudioClip powerUpAppear;
```

These variables represent the clips for each sound effect in the game. You've made them all public so you can set them to the correct clips in the Unity editor.

Save and return to Unity. Select **SoundManager** in the Hierarchy, open the **Sounds** folder, and then assign the following sounds to the SoundManager:

- Gun Fire: **bw_shoot**

- Upgraded Gun Fire: **bw_triple_shoot**

- Hurt: **bw_marine_hurt**

- Alien Death: **bw_alien_death**

- Marine Death: **bw_marine_death**

- Victory: **bw_victory**

- Elevator Arrived: **bw_elevator**

- PowerUp Pickup: **bw_powerup_pickup**

- PowerUp Appear: **bw_powerup_appear**

The component should look as follows:

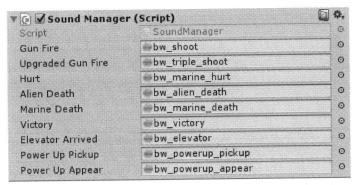

Good work! You've got a sound library nicely organized in one spot, and are ready to integrate the rest of the audio into the game.

Playing sounds

In the Hierarchy, expand the **SpaceMarine** and select **BobbleMarine-Body**. In the Inspector, click the **Add Component** button, and select **Audio Source** from the Audio category.

Next, **double-click** the **Gun** script to edit it and add the following instance variable:

```
private AudioSource audioSource;
```

Add the following to Start():

```
audioSource = GetComponent<AudioSource>();
```

This just gets a reference to the attached audio source — you'll be using this a lot. In fireBullet(), add the following before the closing brace:

```
audioSource.PlayOneShot(SoundManager.Instance.gunFire);
```

This code plays the shooting sound.

Note that there are two ways to play sound effects via code in Unity:

- `PlayOneShot()`, as you've used here, allows the same sound effect to play muliple times at once, effectively overlapping the sound. For example, the space marine could shoot one bullet and while the sound effect for that was still playing, the space marine could quickly fire another bullet, and you'd hear both sound effects at once. The space marine fires quickly, so this is what we want here.

- `Play()` only allows the sound effect to play a single time at once. If you play a sound effect, and then call `Play()` again, it will restart the sound effect, making the first effect sound like it was cut off. The advantage of `Play()` over `PlayOneShot()` is that `Play()` can be stopped in progress where `PlayOneShot()` cannot.

Save the file and go back to Unity. Play your game and fire that gun to hear the shooting sounds.

It's sounding awesome, but it is a bit disappointing that you don't hear the aliens die when you blast them away. So let's add the sound for that next.

Note that you can't make the alien play its own sound as you did for the bullet, because when an alien dies, you destroy the alien GameObject. When you destroy a GameObject, any sounds playing on an AudioSource stop instantly.

So instead, you'll make the GameManager play the death sounds. Although it's tempting to use the SoundManager for all the sounds, doing so would narrow your options. You'll learn more about this when you dive into the mixer.

Open the **SoundManager** script in your code editor, and add the following method:

```
public void PlayOneShot(AudioClip clip) {
    soundEffectAudio.PlayOneShot(clip);
}
```

This is a simple a wrapper call to `PlayOneShot()`.

Save and close the **SoundManager** script, then open the **Alien** script. In `OnTriggerEnter()`, add the following before the closing brace:

```
SoundManager.Instance.PlayOneShot(SoundManager.Instance.alienDea
th);
```

Save the script and head back to Unity. Play the game and obliterate some aliens. Explosions abound!

Adding power-ups

You've made it pretty difficult for the poor space marine. In Chapter 4, "Physics", you added an excessive amount of aliens. In Chapter 5, "Pathfinding", you've taught the aliens how to chase after the space marine, out for blood.

Worst of all, you've been making him work without theme music. Who does that? That's cruel!

Now's a good time to give our hero a boost — something to level playing field. You'll create a powerup that'll sound really cool and temporarily triple the rate of fire.

First, you need to create the triple-shot gun. Open the **Gun** script, and add the following under the instance variables:

```
public bool isUpgraded;
public float upgradeTime = 10.0f;
private float currentTime;
```

- isUpgraded is a flag that lets the script know whether to fire one bullet or three.

- upgradeTime is how long the upgrade will last (in seconds).

- currentTime keeps track of how long it's been since the gun was upgraded.

Take a look at fireBullet(). Note how it creates each bullet on one line and sets its position on the following line. Instead of copying these lines multiple times, you'll refactor it into a method.

Add the following method:

```
private Rigidbody createBullet() {
  GameObject bullet = Instantiate(bulletPrefab) as GameObject;
  bullet.transform.position = launchPosition.position;
  return bullet.GetComponent<Rigidbody>();
}
```

As you can see, this method simply encapsulates the bullet creation process. It returns a Rigidbody after you create the bullet, all you need to do is set its velocity.

Next, replace fireBullet() with the following:

```
void fireBullet() {
  Rigidbody bullet = createBullet ();
  bullet.velocity =  transform.parent.forward * 100;
}
```

This code creates the bullet just like the previous version of the script. Now add the following to modify how the upgraded gun fires bullets (before the final curly brace):

```
if (isUpgraded) {
  Rigidbody bullet2 = createBullet();
  bullet2.velocity =
    (transform.right + transform.forward / 0.5f) * 100;
  Rigidbody bullet3 = createBullet();
  bullet3.velocity =
    ((transform.right * -1) + transform.forward / 0.5f) * 100;
}
```

This bit of code fires the next two bullets at angles. It calculates the angle by adding the forward direction to either the right- or left-hand direction and dividing in half. Since there is no explicit left property, you multiply the value of `right` by –1 to negate it.

Now to integrate the sound. Add the following before the closing brace:

```
if (isUpgraded) {
  audioSource.PlayOneShot(SoundManager.Instance.
    upgradedGunFire);
} else {
  audioSource.PlayOneShot(SoundManager.Instance.gunFire);
}
```

This provides the shooting sound. Now you can see how working with `SoundManager` makes playing sounds relatively easy.

Next, you need a way to initiate the upgrade. Add the following new method:

```
public void UpgradeGun() {
  isUpgraded = true;
  currentTime = 0;
}
```

This method lets the gun know it's been upgraded and sets the counter timer to zero.

Save the file and switch back to Unity. Since you're firing three bullets at once, there's a chance they'll collide with each other, so you need to disable bullet collisions. Do you remember how to do this?

Click **Edit\Project Settings\Physics** and scroll down to the collision matrix. **Uncheck** the box where the Bullet column and Bullet row intersect.

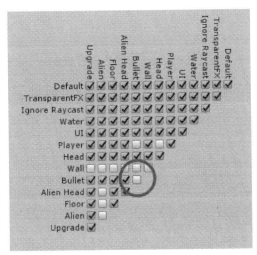

Believe it or not, you can test your power-up already, thanks to the power of live-editing values in the Unity editor.

Play the game and select the **BobbleMarine-Body**. In the Inspector, **check** the **Is Upgraded** checkbox and blast away!

A power-up pick-up

It's great that you can test the power-up while debugging, but let's add a way for the space marine to get his awesome new gun without cheating.

But first, let's make it so the power-up expires. After all, our hero will get spoiled if you leave it like this!

To do this, switch back to the **Gun** script and add the following to Update():

```
currentTime += Time.deltaTime;
if (currentTime > upgradeTime && isUpgraded == true) {
  isUpgraded = false;
}
```

This increments the time. If the time here is greater than the time the player has been upgraded, this code takes the upgrade away.

Excellent work! You've successfully coded the powerup and just need to add it to your game. **Save** the file and switch back to Unity.

In the Project view, open the **Prefabs** folder and select the **Pickup prefab**. You'll see it has some configuration already.

Click the **Add Component** button and select **New Script**. Name it **Upgrade**, set the language to **C Sharp** and click **Create and Add**.

Open the script in your code editor. Replace the contents of the class with the following:

```
public Gun gun;

void OnTriggerEnter(Collider other) {
  gun.UpgradeGun();
  Destroy(gameObject);
  SoundManager.Instance.
    PlayOneShot(SoundManager.Instance.powerUpPickup);
}
```

When the player collides with the powerup, this sets the gun to upgrade mode, and then it will destroy itself (each pickup is good for one upgrade only). Also, a sound plays when the player picks up the upgrade.

Since the powerup should only be available to the space marine, you need to adjust the physics layers. The pickup is already set to the Upgrade layer. You just need to adjust the collision matrix. **Save** and switch back to Unity.

Click **Edit\Project Settings\Physics**. In the layers matrix, **uncheck** the following from the **Upgrade column**: **Bullet, Alien Head, Alien**.

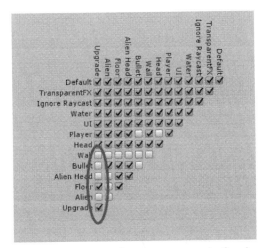

With all that set up, you're clear to write the spawning code for the powerup — yes, it spawns like the aliens. Open the **GameManager** script in your code editor and add the following instance variables:

```
public GameObject upgradePrefab;
public Gun gun;
public float upgradeMaxTimeSpawn = 7.5f;

private bool spawnedUpgrade = false;
private float actualUpgradeTime = 0;
private float currentUpgradeTime = 0;
```

Here you've defined several new variables:

- `upgradePrefab` refers to the GameObject the player must collide with to get the update — you already imported this into your project.

- `gun` is a reference to Gun script because the gun needs to associate it with the upgrade.

- `upgradeMaxTimeSpawn` is the maximum time that will pass before the upgrade spawns.

- `spawnedUpgrade` tracks whether the upgrade has spawned or not since it can only spawn once.

- `actualUpgradeTime` and `currentUpgradeTime` track the current time until the upgrade spawns.

Now to determine the actual upgrade time. Add the following to `Start()`:

```
actualUpgradeTime = Random.Range(upgradeMaxTimeSpawn - 3.0f,
    upgradeMaxTimeSpawn);
actualUpgradeTime = Mathf.Abs(actualUpgradeTime);
```

The upgrade time is a random number generated from `Random.Range()`. The minimum value is the maximum value minus 3, and `Mathf.Abs` makes sure it's a positive number.

Add the following to the start of `Update()`:

```
currentUpgradeTime += Time.deltaTime;
```

This adds the amount of time from the past frame. Now, add the following:

```
if (currentUpgradeTime > actualUpgradeTime) {
  if (!spawnedUpgrade) { // 1
    // 2
    int randomNumber = Random.Range(0, spawnPoints.Length - 1);
    GameObject spawnLocation = spawnPoints[randomNumber];
    // 3
    GameObject upgrade = Instantiate(upgradePrefab)
      as GameObject;
    Upgrade upgradeScript = upgrade.GetComponent<Upgrade>();
    upgradeScript.gun = gun;
    upgrade.transform.position =
      spawnLocation.transform.position;
    // 4
    spawnedUpgrade = true;
  }
}
```

Here's the breakdown:

1. After the random time period passes, this checks if the upgrade has already spawned.

2. The upgrade will appear in one of the alien spawn points. This ups the risk and reward dynamic for the player because the sides of the arena are the most dangerous.

3. This section handles the business of spawning the upgrade and associating the gun with it.

4. This informs the code that an upgrade has been spawned.

Now back to the business of sound! The player needs an auditory queue when the powerup is available. Add the following after `spawnedUpgrade = true`:

```
SoundManager.Instance.PlayOneShot(SoundManager.Instance.
  powerUpAppear);
```

Save the game and switch to Unity. Select the **GameManager** in the Hierarchy. In the Inspector, drag the **Pickup** from the **Prefabs** folder to the **upgradePrefab** field. Also, drag **BobbleMarine-Body** from the Hierarchy to **Gun**.

Since the SpaceMarine has a Gun script attached, Unity will reference the Gun component like it has done for Transforms and Rigidbodies.

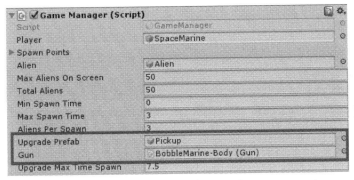

Save your work and play the game. Check out that working powerup!

Introducing the Audio Mixer

While playing your game, you might notice that the sounds are a little out of whack. For example, the music is a bit too loud, the death sounds are a tad too soft and the bullets are lacking pizzazz!

You could tweak each sound individually, but you have better things to do, such as killing aliens and designing an epic game.

Think about it; you'd have to play the game and keep track of the individual sound levels then make adjustments. While you could copy some of the changes, most of the work would be done by hand.

Before Unity 5, the painful one-at-a-time process would have been your only option, but Unity 5 puts an audio mixer in your hands.

Go to the Project browser and select the **Sounds** folder. Click the **Create button** and select **Audio Mixer** in the drop-down. Name it **MasterMix**.

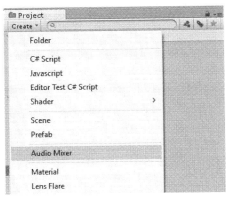

Click **Window\Audio Mixer** and drag the view to a place in the UI where it can expand horizontally instead of vertically.

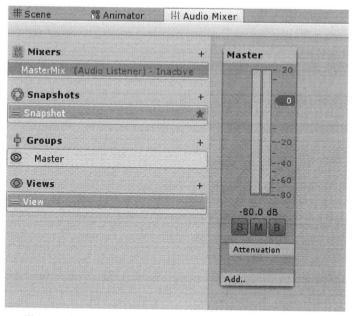

In the mixer, you'll see only one group named Master. This group will affect anything that's assigned to the mixer. Right now, you have assigned nothing, so the mixer is sitting idle.

Expand **MasterMix** in the Project browser, and you'll see the group **Master**. Select **SoundManager**, and in the Inspector, find the audio source that controls the background music. Drag the **Master group** into the **Output** property.

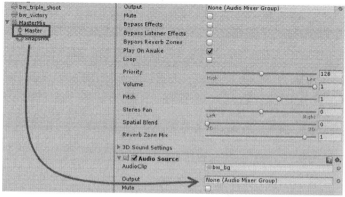

Play the game again.

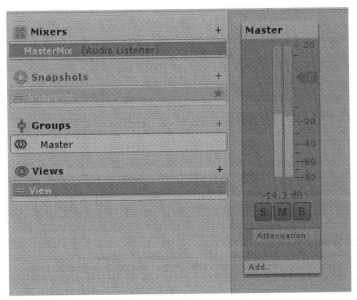

You'll see a cool bar chart showing the sound levels of the Master group. By default, you can't adjust the levels while your game is being played — but you can when you click the **Edit in Playmode** button, so do that now.

The **Edit in Playmode** button will appear when you play your game.

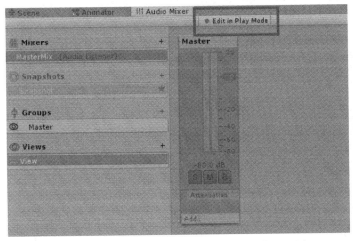

It'll turn red and allow you to adjust levels while you're in play mode. Lower the **volume** to -**20** and stop the game. You'll notice that the group stays at that level.

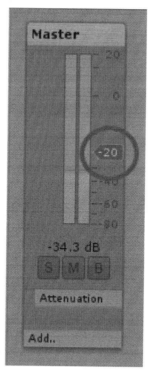

The mixer's capabilities shine when you create subgroups.

Stop the game. Click the **plus sign** in the **groups** section and name it **Music**.

In the Hierarchy, select the **Sound Manager**, and in the Inspector, drag the **Music** group from the MasterMix to the background music AudioSource's **Output field** (overwriting the existing Master setting).

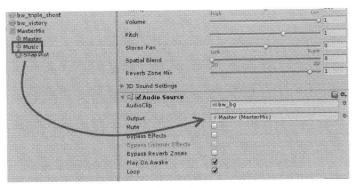

Play your game again. You'll see two levels in the mixer.

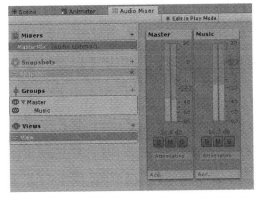

The Master group now controls overall volume, whereas the Music group controls background music.

In the Audio Mixer window, select the **Master** group and click the **plus sign** again. Call this new group **Sound Effects**. Under this new group, create the following groups: **Gun**, **SoundManager**.

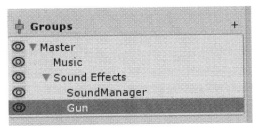

Assign the **SoundManager** group to the non-background music AudioSource's **SoundManger output** properties. For the Gun group, select **BobbleMarine-Body** in the Hierarchy, and in the Inspector, set the Audio Source's **Output** property to the **Gun** mixer group. When you play the game, you'll see all the levels in action.

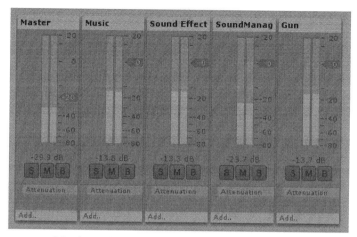

At this point, you could adjust the volume of each of the types of audio easily and independently.

Isolating sounds

Sometimes, you want to only listen to certain sound effects while you're testing your game. For example, imagine you want to isolate the sound of the gun shooting so you can tweak that effect.

You could lower the volume for each, but that's a bad idea because it's easy to forget the original settings.

Notice that each group has three buttons on it. S is for **Solo** and it lets you isolate a certain group. M is for **Mute** and it works how you'd expect. B is for **Bypass** and it lets you bypass the effects in the group.

In the **Music** group, click the **M** button to mute the background music.

Play your game if you aren't already, and you'll notice that the background music is now muted, however you can still hear the other sounds.

To fix this, in the **Music** group click the **M** button again to unmute the background, and then in the **Gun** group, click the **S** button to hear the gunfire — and only the gunfire.

Ah, sweet beautiful gunfire — music to a space marine's ears!

Adding audio effects

Another cool thing the Sound Manager can do is add special effects to audio files. **Click the Gun** group to see the effect properties in the Inspector. Click the **Add Effect** button at the bottom.

Then choose **Chorus**. Set the **Depth** to `0.93` and fire that gun.

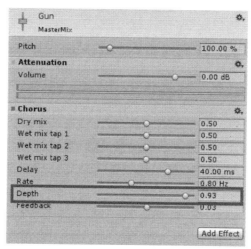

The chorus makes it sounds like rapid fire. Feel free to play around with more effects — the mixer comes with plenty of them.

To hear the group without effects, **click** the **B** button.

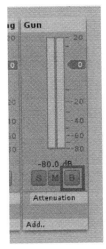

Click **B** again to put the effects back. **Click** the **S** button to re-enable the rest of the sounds.

At this point, hopefully you see that the using the Audio Mixer is much better than trying to adjust sounds manually through the SoundManager. If you'd gone that route, you'd lose the ability to easily set levels on individual sounds, group souns, add effects, and more. By creating a small subset of sounds, you can leverage the mixer while also enjoying the convenience of a single source.

Set the final values as follows:

- **Music** to −9
- **Sound Effects** to 0
- **Sound Manager** to −3
- **Gun** to −8

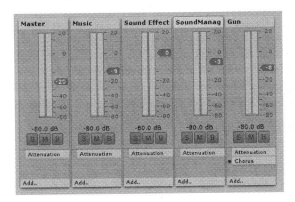

So far, you've only scratched the surface of the possibilities with the audio mixer. You can also do things like hiding groups and saving them as views to aid your focus during various editing tasks. It's also possible to take Snapshots to save different groups of settings — either for the sake of comparison or just for different situations.

Where to go from here?

Wow! You've got sound now. With the addition of a few lines of code, your game should feel much more awesome.

In doing so, you've learned:

- The basics of Unity sound, such as the difference between **audio listeners** and **audio sources**

- The import settings for new audio files and how they can affect performance

- How to call your sounds in code

- How to balance all your sounds with the mixer

- **Bonus**: How to create a powerup, complete with sound effects!

What's left to do? You've got aliens. You've got lots of bullets. Sounds like you're all set!

What you're missing is an ending. In the next and final chapter for Bobblehead Wars, you'll put the finishing touches on the game, e.g., lots of exploding aliens and a marine who can't keep his head on straight. Lastly, you'll provide a winning condition.

Exciting things are ahead: stay tuned!

Chapter 8: Finishing Touches

By Brian Moakley

It's funny to think that only seven chapters ago, you might have fired up Unity for the first time, and now you're about to put final touches on your first game!

At this point, gameplay is pretty much set, sounds are properly mixed and the assets are pretty much launched.

What's left to do? Ship it!

Actually, no. This game isn't early access! We're going to ship this completed. (Followed by a massive Day One patch. ;])

Currently, Bobblehead Wars doesn't provide a winning or losing condition. After a bit of time, the aliens stop spawning, leaving the space marine to ponder existence with nothing more than a loaded weapon in an empty arena.

In this chapter, you'll provide a winning and losing condition and add some realism. In the process, you'll learn about Unity Events, the Unity particle system, and some additional animation features.

Of course, before you even think about game endings, you need to squash a rather big bug that you might not have noticed.

Fixing the game manager

As the hero shoots aliens, the game takes them off the screen, but the GameManager knows nothing of their deaths.

Why is this important?

For one thing, the GameManager may want to send condolence cards to the families. :]

Secondly, the manager must know how many aliens are on the screen and when to end the game. Without that information, the space marine enjoys too much down time.

Thankfully, it's not an insurmountable problem. Instead of counting the alien population, you'll make it so that the GameManager gets notification of each death.

You'll do this by using Unity events. C# also has an event system, but Unity events are built right into the engine.

Open the **Alien** script in your code editor. Add the following underneath the existing `using` statements:

```
using UnityEngine.Events;
```

This allows you to access UnityEvents in code. Next, add the following instance variable inside the class:

```
public UnityEvent OnDestroy;
```

The `UnityEvent` is a custom event type that you can configure in the Inspector. In this case, you're creating an `OnDestroy` event. The `OnDestroy` event will occur with each call to an alien.

Defining an event is only part of the equation. It's kind of like planning a party. No matter how well you plan, it's not a party if there are no guests.

Just as parties need guests, events need listeners, which do the job of taking notifications when something has happened. In the case of Bobblehead Wars, the GameManager needs to know when an alien dies. Hence, the GameManager needs to subscribe to the `OnDestroy` event.

Save and head back to Unity. In the Project browser, select the **Alien** in the **Prefabs** folder. The Inspector for the Alien component now displays the `OnDestroy` event.

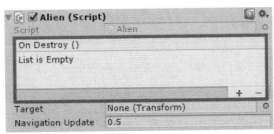

Before you can add GameManager to this list, you need to create a public method to subscribe to the event. Open the **GameManager** script and add the following at the bottom of the file, just before the closing brace:

```
public void AlienDestroyed() {
    Debug.Log("dead alien");
}
```

This prints a simple message to the console to let you know the GameManager got a notification. **Save** and switch to Unity.

In the Project browser, select the **Alien** in the **Prefabs** folder again. Find and select **OnDestroy** in the Inspector and click the **plus sign** to add a new event.

This is where you add event listeners. You'll notice a drop-down that reads **Runtime Only**, which means the events will run in play mode.

Click the circle next to where it says **None**, and a **Select Object** popup will appear. Scroll through, and you'll notice that the **GameManager** GameObject does not appear in the list (the script does, but not the GameManager object itself). What gives?

There's a logical explanation for this: A prefab can't contain a reference to a GameObject in the Hierarchy because that object may not be around when the game instantiates the prefab.

When you link the two together, you're introducing a potential error. For example, you could create another scene with aliens in it, but that scene may not have a GameManager in the other scene.

You can workaround this restriction with scripting.

Click the minus button to remove the entry in the OnDestroy() list you added a second ago, then open the **GameManager** script, and find newAlien.transform.LookAt(targetRotation); in **Update**(). Add the following after it:

```
alienScript.OnDestroy.AddListener(AlienDestroyed);
```

Here you call AddListener on the event and pass in the method to call whenever that event occurs — in this case, AlienDestroyed. In short, every time this event occurs, the GameManager gets a notification.

Now you need to generate the event. **Save** your changes and open the **Alien** script in the editor. Add the following method:

```
public void Die() {
    Destroy(gameObject);
}
```

This destroys the alien.

In OnTriggerEnter(), replace the line Destroy(gameObject); with:

```
Die();
```

Here you've refactored the destroy code into another method. It allows other objects to trigger the death behavior.

In Die(), add the following before the Destroy() statement:

```
OnDestroy.Invoke();
```

This notifies all listeners, including the GameManager, of the alien's tragic death.

Save, play the game and shoot some aliens. You'll see a barrage of log messages.

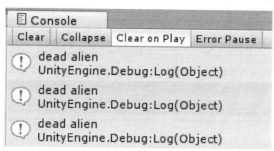

When an object that has an event is destroyed, the best practice is to remove all listeners from that event. Otherwise, you may create a memory leak by having a reference cycle.

After `OnDestroy.Invoke();` add the following:

```
OnDestroy.RemoveAllListeners();
```

This removes any listeners that are listening to the event.

Now you need to update the GameManager. Open **GameManager** in your code editor, and replace `AlienDestroyed()` with the following:

```
public void AlienDestroyed() {
    aliensOnScreen -= 1;
    totalAliens -= 1;
}
```

This officially decreases the number of aliens on screen. **Save** your work and review how what you just did works:

1. The Alien script contains a UnityEvent called `OnDestroy`.

2. The GameManager script periodically spawns aliens. Each time it spawns an alien, it adds itself as a listener to the `OnDestroy` event.

3. When the alien collides with something and is about to die, it invokes its `OnDestroy` event. This has the effect of notifying the GameManager.

4. The GameManager updates the count of aliens on the screen, and the total aliens.

5. The alien removes all listeners and destroys itself.

Now take a breather — you just squashed that bug with a mega-size fly swatter. On to more important matters.

Killing the hero

So far life is a little bit too easy on the hero. The marine is impervious to death!

Let's put our Doctor Evil hats on, and talk about how we'll kill our hero (mwuahaha). Death in Bobble Wars will work in this fashion:

• Once the marine gets hurt, the camera will shake and you'll hear grunting to indicate the marine's agony.

• The more hits, the harder the shake.

• Finally, when the marine suffers that final blow, he'll emit a blood-curdling cry to signal his inglorious death and his head will pop off. I mean, why wouldn't it?

You'll start with the camera shake effect; this script is pre-included with the project for convenience.

In the Project view, select the **CameraShake** script and drag it to **Main Camera** in the Hierarchy.

This script works by providing a shake intensity then it calls Shake().

Select **Main Camera** in the Hierarchy, and in the Inspector, change **Shake Decay** to 0.02 to set the shake's duration.

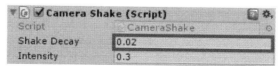

Next up is providing intensity values. Open **PlayerController** in your code editor and add the following instance variable:

```
public float[] hitForce;
```

This provides an array of force values for the camera.

Save and switch to Unity. Select **SpaceMarine** in the Hierarchy, and find the **Player Controller** component in the Inspector. Click the disclosure triangle next to **Hit Force** and set the **Size** to 3. Add the following values for the elements: 0.1, 0.2, 0.3:

At this point, you could call CameraShake() each time an alien collides with the hero, but it'll be a little problematic. When the hero is swarmed by aliens, he could die in a matter of seconds, and the game would cease to be fun.

To avoid this frustration, you'll add a delay between each hit to give the player time to react and escape a bad situation.

Open **PlayerController** in your code editor and add the following instance variables:

```
public float timeBetweenHits = 2.5f;
private bool isHit = false;
private float timeSinceHit = 0;
private int hitNumber = -1;
```

- `timeBetweenHits` is the grace period after the hero sustains damage.

- `isHit` is a flag that indicates the hero took a hit.

- The above variables mean the hero won't accrue damage for a period of time after taking a hit.

- `timeSinceHit` tracks of the amount of time in the grace period.

- `hitNumber` references the number of times the hero took a hit. It's also used to get the shake intensity for the camera shake.

Add the following method:

```
void OnTriggerEnter(Collider other) {
    Alien alien = other.gameObject.GetComponent<Alien>();
    if (alien != null) { // 1
        if (!isHit) {
            hitNumber += 1; // 2
            CameraShake cameraShake =
                Camera.main.GetComponent<CameraShake>();
            if (hitNumber < hitForce.Length) { // 3
                cameraShake.intensity = hitForce[hitNumber];
                cameraShake.Shake();
            } else {
                // death todo
            }
            isHit = true; // 4
            SoundManager.Instance
                .PlayOneShot(SoundManager.Instance.hurt);
        }
        alien.Die();
    }
}
```

Here's the breakdown:

1. First, you check if the colliding object has an `Alien` script attached to it. If it's an alien and the player hasn't been hit, then the player is officially considered hit.

2. The `hitNumber` increases by one, after which you get a reference to `CameraShake()`.

3. If the current `hitNumber` is less than the number of force values for the camera shake, then the hero is still alive. From there, you set force for the shaking effect and then shake the camera. (You'll come back to the death todo in a moment.)

4. This sets `isHit` to true, plays the grunt and kills the alien.

You're getting closer to making the hero's day, but not quite there yet. Once `isHit` is set to true, there's no unsetting it and the hero becomes invincible — the opposite of what you want to do here.

Add the following code to `Update()` to strip away those divine powers:

```
if (isHit) {
  timeSinceHit += Time.deltaTime;
  if (timeSinceHit > timeBetweenHits) {
    isHit = false;
    timeSinceHit = 0;
  }
}
```

This tabulates time since the last hit to the hero. If that time exceeds `timeBetweenHits`, the player can take more hits.

Play your game and charge those aliens. Resistance is futile.

The hero will now react to each hit until the maximum number of hits. At that point, nothing will happen - but you'll fix that next, in a dramatic way!

Removing the bobblehead

There's nothing more terrifying to a bobblehead then losing its precious head. Your space marine is no different. It's only fitting that the head rolls off the body to make the game's end spectacular and undeniable.

Time for a little more scripting. Open **PlayerController** in your editor and add the following instance variables:

```
public Rigidbody marineBody;
private bool isDead = false;
```

`marineBody` is, well, the marine's body. You're adding this because you'll make some physics alterations when the hero dies. And of course, `isDead` keeps track of the player's current death state.

Together, they let the script know if the space marine is dead.

Now you need a method that manages the death, so add the following:

```
public void Die() {
    bodyAnimator.SetBool("IsMoving", false);
    marineBody.transform.parent = null;
    marineBody.isKinematic = false;
    marineBody.useGravity = true;
    marineBody.gameObject
        .GetComponent<CapsuleCollider>().enabled = true;
    marineBody.gameObject.GetComponent<Gun>().enabled = false;
}
```

You set `IsMoving` to `false` since the marine is dead and you don't want a zombie running around. Next, you set the parent to `null` to remove the current GameObject from its parent. Then by enabling `Use Gravity` and disabling `IsKinematic`, the body will drop and roll, and you enable a collider to make this all work. Disabling the gun prevents the player from firing after death.

At this point, the head and body still share a joint. You need to destroy the hinge joint to enable the hero's inevitable disembodiment.

Add the following code beneath the previous block:

```
Destroy(head.gameObject.GetComponent<HingeJoint>());
head.transform.parent = null;
head.useGravity = true;
SoundManager.Instance
    .PlayOneShot(SoundManager.Instance.marineDeath);
Destroy(gameObject);
```

First, this destroys the joint to release the head from the body. Then, like the body, you remove the parent and enable gravity. Now that head can roll!

Finally, you destroy the current GameObject while playing the death sound.

Now to trigger the death. In `OnTriggerEnter()`, replace the `death todo` with the following:

```
Die();
```

Save the file and go back to Unity.

Select **SpaceMarine** in the Hierarchy. In the Inspector, drag the **BobbleMarine-Body** to the new **Marine Body** property.

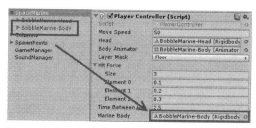

The space marine's body can fall now, but you need to attach a collider to it. Select **BobbleMarine-Body** and click the **Add Component** button. Select the **Physics** category and choose **Capsule Collider**.

Set **Center** to (**-1.61, 3.58, 0**), **Radius** to **2.08** and **Height** to **0.24**. Make sure the **Direction** is set to **Y-Axis**. Finally, **disable** the collider by unchecking the checkbox in the upper left of the component.

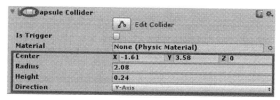

Currently, the GameManager may spawn more aliens after the space marine dies. There's no need to subject the player to an inevitable feeding frenzy!

Open **GameManager** in your code editor, and add the following before any of the existing code in Update():

```
if (player == null) {
    return;
}
```

If there's no player, the GameManager won't spawn enemies. **Save** and switch to Unity.

Play your game and charge the aliens. After a bit of time, the marine successfully loses that head. Why is the marine's body still standing around?

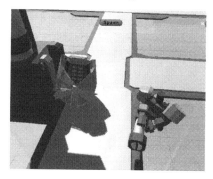

This strange behavior is due to gravity and scaling. The typical gravity level is set to -9.81. If you scaled the models to one meter per unit, then they'd play well with gravity. However, your models are somewhat larger. You can fix this by scaling down the models or scaling up the gravity — you'll scale up the gravity in this book.

Click **Edit\Project Settings\Physics** and set **Gravity** to **(0, -900, 0)**.

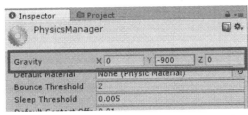

Now the player's death makes both head and body fall like you'd see in a good episode of Game of Thrones.

Decapitating the alien

Aliens have bobbleheads too, so they should die the same way, but you'll have a little fun with the poor alien's head.

Open the **Alien** script and add the following instance variables:

```
public Rigidbody head;
public bool isAlive = true;
```

head will help you launch the head, and isAlive will track the alien's state.

Replace Die() with the following:

```
public void Die() {
   isAlive = false;
   head.GetComponent<Animator>().enabled = false;
   head.isKinematic = false;
   head.useGravity = true;
   head.GetComponent<SphereCollider>().enabled = true;
   head.gameObject.transform.parent = null;
   head.velocity = new Vector3(0, 26.0f, 3.0f);
   }
```

This code works similarly to the marine's death, but you disable the animator for the alien. In addition, this code launches the head off the body.

Add this code before the closing brace:

```
OnDestroy.Invoke();
OnDestroy.RemoveAllListeners();
SoundManager.Instance.PlayOneShot(SoundManager.Instance.
  alienDeath);
Destroy(gameObject);
```

This block notifies the listeners, removes them, and then it deletes the GameObject.

You want to make sure that you don't call `Die()` more than once, so modify `OnTriggerEnter()` as follows:

```
void OnTriggerEnter(Collider other) {
  if (isAlive) {
    Die();
    SoundManager.Instance.PlayOneShot(SoundManager.Instance.
      alienDeath);
  }
}
```

Here you check `isAlive` first.

Finally, in `Update()`, surround the existing navigation code with a similar check to see if the alien is alive.

```
if (isAlive) {
  ...
}
```

Save and switch to Unity. In the Project view, click the down arrow next to the Alien prefab to reveal is children, and select **BobbleEnemy-Head**. Click the **Add Component** button and select **Rigidbody** from the physics category. **Uncheck** the **Use Gravity** option and **check** the **Is Kinematic** option.

Click **Add Component** once again, and select **Sphere Collider** from the physics category. Set **Center** to (**0, 0, 0.02**) and **Radius** to **0.03**. Disable the component by **unchecking** the **component** checkbox.

Finally, assign it to the layer **Alien Head** and select **Yes, change children** when prompted.

Select the **Alien** prefab in the Project view. In the Inspector, drag the **BobbleEnemy-Head** to the **head** property.

Finally, select **Edit\Projects Settings\Physics**. In the **Alien Head** row, **uncheck the Alien** column if you haven't already.

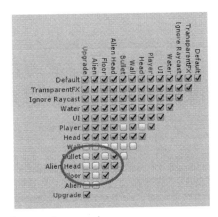

Play the game. It's getting interesting now!

You'll notice that sometimes the aliens are immune from bullets, and their heads can fly right through the columns. The reason is that you have colliders in conflict with one another.

In the Project browser, select the **Alien** prefab. Set the **Radius** to 2.63 in the **Sphere Collider** to give the alien plenty of collider space.

You'll need a new layer to resolve the issue of heads flying through columns. Select the **BobbleArena-Column** prefab in the Project browser. In the **Layer** drop-down, select **Add Layer**, name it **Column** and assign it to the **BobbleArena-Column** prefab. Select **Yes, change children** when prompted.

Finally, select **Edit\Projects Settings\Physics**. In the **Column** column, **uncheck** the **Alien** row.

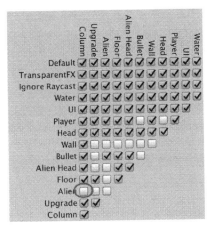

Play your game.

It won't take long to accumulate an excess of disembodied alien heads. After a while, the space marine will struggle to differentiate the dead aliens from the living.

Stop your game and select the **BobbleEnemy-Head** prefab. In the Inspector, click the **Add Component** button and select **New Script**.

Name it **SelfDestruct** and click the **Create and Add** button. Open it in your editor. Inside the class, replace the contents of the script with the following:

```
public float destructTime = 3.0f;

public void Initiate() {
  Invoke("selfDestruct", destructTime);
}

private void selfDestruct() {
  Destroy(gameObject);
}
```

This deletes the attached GameObject after a given amount of time. You could have named it `AlienHead`, but its general name makes it available throughout the game.

Open **Alien** and add the following to `Die()` before the `Destroy(gameObject);` line:

```
head.GetComponent<SelfDestruct>().Initiate();
```

Now play the game and watch those heads disappear after three seconds.

Adding particles

Are you having a little trouble believing that the process of dismembering characters is so clean? Normally, beheading makes a big mess — this game should be no exception. You'll use particles to increase the, um, realism a bit.

Particles are small bits of geometry created by a game engine that you can use to create effects such as fire, water and other chaotic systems.

Ever play a game that featured snow? In most cases, the effect was produced by a particle emitter directly over the character. It probably seemed like it was snowing in the entire game world, but the particle emitter was most likely following you around like a little dark cloud.

Particles are a deep topic that you should cover in more depth on your own. For convenience, you'll use pre-made particles.

> **Note:** If you'd like to explore Unity's particle system in depth, please check out our free detailed introduction at https://www.raywenderlich.com/introduction-unity-particle-systems.

In the Project browser, drag an instance of the **AlienDeathParticles** prefab into the scene. You'll see an instant splash of alien blood. Ew!

Select it in the Hierarchy; you'll see a dialog in the Scene view with a few options.

This control panel lets you tweak settings in real time when building particle effects.

Press the **Simulate** button. You'll see the blood fly once again and notice that the button becomes a pause button. You also have a stop button to end the particle effect.

Temporarily drag an **Alien** prefab into the scene, and make **AlienDeathParticles** to make it a child of **Alien**. With **AlienDeathParticles** selected, set **Position** to (0, 1.07, -1.7) and **Rotation** to (-90, 0, 0). Click the **Apply** button to apply the changes to the AlienDeathParticle prefab.

Also apply the changes to all the instances of the Alien prefab by selecting the **Alien** in the Hierarchy and **clicking** the **Apply** button in the Inspector.

Now, click **AlienDeathParticles** in the Hierarchy and click on the **Simulate** button to see the alien bathed in green blood.

They're working, but they fall through the floor, so clearly you need special treatment for the particles. You could have the particles collide with the world, but in this case, a death floor makes more sense.

In the Hierarchy, select **BobbleArena**. Click the **Create** button, select **3D Object** and choose **Plane**. Name it **DeathFloor** and drag it to be a child of **BobbleArena**. Set **Position** to (8.66, -0.16, 12.15) and **Scale** to (-14.9, 0.5, 15.6). **Uncheck** the **Mesh Collider** and **Mesh Renderer** to disable them.

In the Hierarchy, select **AlienDeathParticles**. You'll see there are many options for particles.

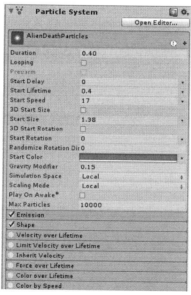

Expand the **Collision** section by clicking on it — scroll down if you don't see it. Drag the **DeathFloor** to the **Planes** property.

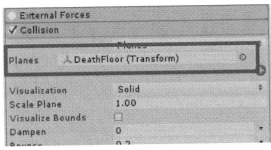

Click the **Simulate** button. The blood will pool on the new floor!

Now you have to address a small rendering issue. In this case, Unity renders the particles underneath the floor because it draws the floor *after* it draws the particles.

To avoid this, you need to assign the particles to a **Sorting Layer**, which will determine the order in which Unity renders objects. Typically, you use these with Unity 2D, but there are use cases for sorting layers in 3D games too.

Expand the **Renderer** section of the particle system. In the **Sorting Layer** property, select **Add Sorting Layer....** The Inspector will change to **Tags & Layers**. Click the **plus** sign and name the sorting layer **Foreground**.

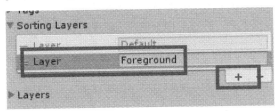

Return to the **Renderer** module, and in the **Sorting Layer**, select the **Foreground** property. Keep in mind you'll need to do the same thing for the space marine.

Now click the **Apply** button to apply the changes to the prefab.

You've unveiled a new problem: the death floor isn't added to the prefab because it's an instance in the scene and your alien prefabs don't know about it. You'll address this in a moment.

Meanwhile, give your hero some blood too. Drag the **MarineDeathParticles** prefab to be a child of the **BobbleMarine-Body**. Set **Position** to (**-1.68, 5.29, 0.63**) and **Rotation** to (**-90, 0, 0**).

In the Particle System, expand the **Collision** section and drag the **DeathFloor** to the **Planes** property. In the **Renderer** section, set the **Sorting Layer** to **Foreground**.

Click the **Simulate** button to see the marine gush like a fountain.

The particle systems are ready to go for the alien and space marine; you just need to activate them in code.

Activating particles in code

Unity allows for all sorts of adjustments to particle systems in code. In your case, you just need to know if the particle system is running or not.

In the Project view, select the **Scripts** folder and click the **Create** button. Choose **C# Script** and name it **DeathParticles**. Open the script in your editor.

Add the following instance variables:

```
private ParticleSystem deathParticles;
private bool didStart = false;
```

`deathParticles` refers to the current particle system and `didStart` lets you know the particle system has started to play.

You need to get a reference to the particle system, so add the following to `Start()`:

```
deathParticles = GetComponent<ParticleSystem>();
```

Add the following method:

```
public void Activate() {
   didStart = true;
   deathParticles.Play();
}
```

This starts in the particle system and informs the script that it started. In `Update()`, add the following:

```
if (didStart && deathParticles.isStopped) {
   Destroy(gameObject);
}
```

Once the particle system stops playing, the script deletes the death particles because they are meant to play only once.

Finally, to address the need for a collision plane that's set in code, add the following method:

```
public void SetDeathFloor(GameObject deathFloor) {
   if (deathParticles == null) {
      deathParticles = GetComponent<ParticleSystem>();
   }
   deathParticles.collision.SetPlane(0, deathFloor.transform);
}
```

The script first checks to see if a particle system has been loaded, which is necessary because the alien prefab is instanced and used immediately.

In case `Start()` hasn't been called and `deathParticles` isn't populated, this line populates it. Then it sets the collision plane.

Now to activate the particles — it's a similar process for the alien and the marine, but the alien requires a little set up work.

First, you need to get a reference to the particle system, and it's a child of the Alien GameObject, so you need code to get it.

Open **Alien** in your code editor, and add the following instance variable:

```
private DeathParticles deathParticles;
```

Then create the following method:

```
public DeathParticles GetDeathParticles() {
  if (deathParticles == null) {
    deathParticles = GetComponentInChildren<DeathParticles>();
  }
  return deathParticles;
}
```

The magic occurs in `GetComponentInChildren()`. It returns the first death particle script that it finds. There's only one script so there's no possibility of grabbing the wrong one.

In `Die()`, add the following before `Destroy(gameObject)`:

```
if (deathParticles) {
  deathParticles.transform.parent = null;
  deathParticles.Activate();
}
```

This makes the blood splatter when an alien dies. You have to remove the parent. Otherwise, the particles are destroyed along with the GameObject.

Open **GameManager** and add this instance variable:

```
public GameObject deathFloor;
```

This contains a reference to the death floor.

Add the following after `alienScript.OnDestroy.AddListener(AlienDestroyed);` in `Update()`:

```
alienScript.GetDeathParticles().SetDeathFloor(deathFloor);
```

Finally **save** all your files and switch to Unity.

In the Project view, expand the Alien prefab and select the **AlienDeathParticles** GameObject. Click **Add Component** and under scripts, choose **DeathParticles**.

Next, select the **GameManager** in the Hierarchy and drag the **DeathFloor** to the **DeathFloor property** in the Inspector.

Delete the **Alien** from the hierarchy as that was only a temporary copy and you don't need it anymore.

Now play your game and shoot some aliens — you might need a mop.

Now for the marine. Select **MarineDeathParticles** in the Hierarchy and click **Add Component**. Under scripts, choose **DeathParticles**. Next, open the **PlayerController** in your editor.

Add the following instance variable:

```
private DeathParticles deathParticles;
```

In `Start()`, add the following:

```
deathParticles =
  gameObject.GetComponentInChildren<DeathParticles>();
```

Finally, in `Die()`, add the following before `Destroy()`:

```
deathParticles.Activate();
```

Play your game and charge those aliens. You'll get a satisfying splatter when the marine dies.

Congratulations! You've lost the game!

Winning the game

Thankfully, you have an alternative to losing your head.

The winning sequence will run as follows:

- When the marine kills all the aliens, the hatch opens and the elevator rises.

- Once the space marine steps on the elevator, it ascends to the ceiling — perhaps to elevate the marine to an immortal or the next level. Who knows?

Take a deep breath, and grab your favorite caffeinated beverage — you're in the home stretch!

This section will be a great review for everything you've learned so far.

First, you need to create a collider for the elevator hatch so that it knows when the player steps on it.

In the Hierarchy, select the **BobbleArena** and click **Add Component**. From the Physics category, select **Sphere Collider**.

First, **check** the **Is Trigger** checkbox. Next set **Center** to (**0, 0.22, 0**) and **Radius** to **1.65**. Make sure to **uncheck the component** to make it inactive. It only needs to be active when the marine clears the arena.

Next, click **Add Component** and select **New Script**. Name it **Arena**, set the language to **C Sharp** and click **Create and Add**. Open the script in your code editor.

Add the following instance variables:

```
public GameObject player;
public Transform elevator;
private Animator arenaAnimator;
private SphereCollider sphereCollider;
```

You need each of these to win the game:

- You need to access both the player and the elevator to raise the marine to the top of the arena.

- The arenaAnimator will kick off the animation.

- The sphereCollider will initiate the entire sequence.

In `Start()`, add the following:

```
arenaAnimator = GetComponent<Animator>();
sphereCollider = GetComponent<SphereCollider>();
```

You should be used to this by now; in here, you're getting access to the components.

There needs to be a chain of events to specify what happens after the marine steps onto the trigger.

You want the hero to ride the elevator towards the ceiling. Animating the player is one approach that might work, but it's easier to make the marine a child of the elevator. As it goes up, the marine has no choice but to follow. Additionally, the camera will try to follow, so you need to disable it.

Add the following:

```
void OnTriggerEnter(Collider other) {
  Camera.main.transform.parent.gameObject.
    GetComponent<CameraMovement>().enabled = false;
  player.transform.parent = elevator.transform;
}
```

The first line gets the camera then disables the movement. Then the player is made into a child of the platform.

You need to disable the player's ability to control the marine. Add the following to `OnTriggerEnter()`:

```
player.GetComponent<PlayerController>().enabled = false;
```

This stops the player from turning, shooting or doing anything with the marine.

Now you need an audio cue to alert the player to the elevator's arrival:

```
SoundManager.Instance.PlayOneShot(SoundManager.Instance.
  elevatorArrived);
```

You also need to kick off the animation, so add this line after the previous code you entered:

```
arenaAnimator.SetBool("OnElevator", true);
```

This will start the animation state and work when the player enters the sphere collider, but remember that the collider is disabled. It should be active when the platform arrives but not before. **Save** and switch to Unity.

Select **BobbleArena** in the Hierarchy. In the Inspector, drag the **SpaceMarine** to the **player** property. Expand the **BobbleArena** and look for a child GameObject named **Elevator_Platform**. Drag it to the **Elevator** property in BobbbleArena.

You're down to the last step of calling your code. Thankfully, animation events can do this. How cool is that?

Animation events

An animation event is very much like a keyframe. You determine a point in the animation at which to run the code, and then you assign it a method. This approach allows precision control over when the code runs.

> **Note:** Remember, you can animate all properties, including the collider you've enabled.

You imported the animations for summoning and rising in Chapter 1 and just need to associate them with the Animator.

With **BobbleArena** selected in the Hierarchy, open the **Animator** window. You'll see the wall states you set up in Chapter 6, "Animation".

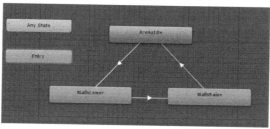

You need a new state to summon the elevator, and it should be accessible from all the states because a win may occur at any time. You could create a transition from each state, but Unity has you covered with the "Any State" state.

In the Animator, **right-click** anywhere and select **Create State\Empty**. Select **New State**, and name it **ElevatorSummon** in the Inspector. Set **Motion** to be the **ElevatorSummon** animation clip and **Speed** to `0.5` to slow the elevator to half its normal speed. As-is, it runs a little fast and stops before its audio clip ends. Slowing it down keeps the elevator in sync with its audio.

Create another empty state, call it **ElevatorRise** and assign the **ElevatorRise** animation clip to it.

The animator should look as follows:

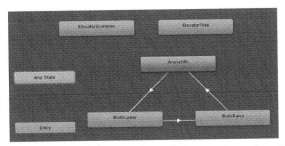

Create a transition from **AnyState** to **ElevatorSummon** and another from **ElevatorSummon** to **ElevatorRise**. It should look like the following:

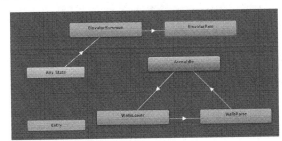

Now you need a condition. Click the **parameters** tab then **+**, choose **Trigger** and name it **PlayerWon**.

Select the transition from **AnyState to ElevatorSummon**. In the Inspector, add a condition and set it to **PlayerWon**. You don't have to set a value for the condition because it's a trigger.

Why use a trigger? By creating a transition from Any State, then any state can reach the condition, including the destination of that transition.

If you were to use a boolean condition like you did before, once you transition from Any State to ElevatorSummon, the animator would repeat the transition until the bool value switches to false. It would creates an infinite loop, but using a trigger means the transition only occurs once.

Next, create a new **Bool** parameter and name it **OnElevator**.

Select the transition between **ElevatorSummon** and **ElevatorRise**. In the Inspector, **uncheck Has Exit Time** and give it a new condition: **OnElevator** is equal to **true**.

Open **Arena** in your code editor and add the following method:

```
public void ActivatePlatform() {
  sphereCollider.enabled = true;
}
```

Save and switch back to Unity. Select **BobbleArena** in the Hierarchy and open the **Animation** window. From the animation drop-down, select **Elevator Summon**.

Over the last keyframe (which is at 0:28), **right-click** the gray bar above the frame counters and select **Add Animation Event**. You'll see a white pip appear over that frame, and this is where you call your code. You'll also see a dialog. From the drop-down, select **ActivatePlatform()**.

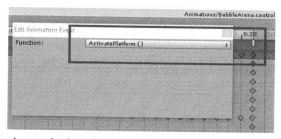

All the public methods attached to the current GameObject show in this dialog. Remember, you just wrote `ActivatePlatform` to enable the sphere collider on top of the elevator once the player has won the game, so you can detect when the player enters that area.

You're down to writing your last bit of code for Bobblehead Wars! Whoa!

Open the **GameManager** in your code editor and add a public reference for the arena animator:

```
public Animator arenaAnimator;
```

Add the following to initiate the game's end:

```
private void endGame() {
  SoundManager.Instance.PlayOneShot(SoundManager.Instance.
    elevatorArrived);
  arenaAnimator.SetTrigger("PlayerWon");
}
```

This kicks off the entire process and you just need to call it. In `AlienDestroyed()`, add the following before the closing brace:

```
if (totalAliens == 0) {
  Invoke("endGame", 2.0f);
}
```

You've done a lot here, so let's review how the entire end-game process works:

1. Once the count of aliens hits 0, you schedule the `endGame()` method to be called after 2 seconds.

2. This fires the "PlayerWon" trigger on the arena animator.

3. Once the arena animator detects this trigger, it plays the elevator summon animation.

4. You configured the elevator summon animation to fire an animation event when the animation completes, to call the `ActivatePlatform()` method.

5. This enables a collider on the elevator.

6. When the player hits the collider, `OnTriggerEnter()` is called on the arena. This attaches the player to the elevator and sets the "OnElevator" boolean on the arena animator.

7. This causes the arena animator to play the elevator rise animation.

8. Phew! If you understand this sequence, pat yourself on the back - you've learned a lot about Unity!

Save the code and head back to Unity. Select **GameManager** in the Hierarchy and drag the **BobbleArena** to the **arenaAnimator** property.

Now for the final play test. Kill all the aliens then step on the elevator. Victory is yours!

Where to go from here?

Congratulations on completing your first Unity game! It's no small feat, but now you can see that building games is fun and probably easier than you thought when you decided to pick up this book.

In the process of finishing Bobblehead Wars, you learned some new concepts, including:

- **Unity Events** and how to use them inside your code.

- **Particle System** and how it can make some cool effects.

- **Animation Events** and how they can be used to call code from your animation clips.

Believe it or not, you've barely explored Unity's capabilities and have a lot more to look forward to in this book.

In the next section, you'll put your skills to use to create a first-person shooter that features some rather angry robots. Pick up your gun and get blasting. You're in for a fun ride!

Section II: First-Person Shooters

In this section, you'll learn how to create one of the most popular types of games: a first-person shooter.

In the process, you'll create a game called **Robot Rampage**, where you'll blast waves of enemy robots using a variety of weapons and power-ups. Get your boom stick ready!

Chapter 9, "Making a First Person Shooter"

Chapter 10, "Adding Enemies"

Chapter 11, "Unity UI"

Chapter 9: The Player and Environment

By Anthony Uccello

In the next few chapters, you'll create a first-person shooter, or FPS as it's more commonly known. Some well-known FPS titles include *Halo*, *Call of Duty*, and *Doom*.

The game you'll create is **Robot Rampage**; you'll control a player who has to mow down robots to survive. The robots will spawn in waves and the player must collect health, ammunition, and armor pickups in order to stave off the robots as long as possible. The longer the player survives, and the more robots they kill, the higher their score.

This game is broken down into three parts. In this part you'll set up the weapons, add sounds, and the code to handle all the firing.

In the next chapter, you'll add the robot bad guys, some powerups, and lots of flying projectiles.

In the final chapter, you'll add the all the user interface elements to keep track of the score, ammo, and even a menu to restart the game when it's over.

In short, you'll have a completed first person shooter game.

Getting started

To get started, open up the Starter project in Unity. In the Project Browser, open the **Scenes** folder and double-click the **Battle** scene to open it.

Believe it or not, the map is mostly setup for you. The map itself consists of a floor, surrounded by a series of walls. After you complete the tutorial, feel free to create other configurations for the game by adjusting the wall positions.

To get started, you'll need to setup the wall GameObjects so the robots can avoid them. So far in this book you've been using Layers, but Unity has another tool known as **tags**. A tag is just a bit of text used to identify GameObjects. Each GameObject can have only one tag, and thankfully, they're easy to use. By assigning a tag to each wall GameObject you'll be able to setup some pathfinding rules for the robots to follow so they can move around walls.

In the Hierarchy, click on the **Inner Walls** GameObject. In the Inspector, click the **Tag** dropdown and click **Add Tag**.

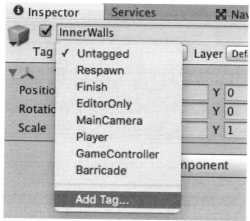

Click the plus button in the **Tag Window** and type **Wall** in the first slot:

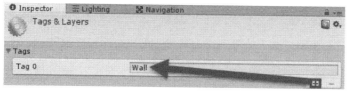

Expand the `InnerWalls` GameObject by clicking the arrow next to it in the Hierarchy. Select all the child GameObjects (named **Wall** and **WallPost**); a quick way to do this is select the first GameObject then hold **Shift** and click the last item.

With all the child GameObjects selected, click the the **Tag dropdown** and select the **Wall** tag you just created:

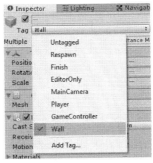

All the walls are properly tagged. Now you can make your NavMesh for your robots.

Note: Forgot how to make a NavMesh or you skipped ahead to this chapter? If so, check out Chapter 5, "Managers and Pathfinding" which covers NavMeshes in depth.

Open the **Navigation** window by going to **Window/Navigation**. Ensure the **Wall** and **WallPost** GameObjects are selected, and make sure that the **Navigation Static** checkbox in the **Object tab** is checked.

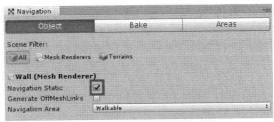

Click the **Bake** button at the bottom of the **Navigation** window and you should see the ground turn light blue in the scene:

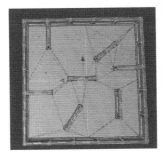

The robots now have a walkable area in the map. Pretty cool, eh? You can now click the mini arrow next to **InnerWalls** to hide the list of Wall and WallPost GameObjects.

With the NavMesh taken care of, it's time to create the player.

Adding the player

The first step for adding the player ... is to add the player! :]

In the Hierarchy, create an empty GameObject and name it **Player**. You are going to use Unity's **Character Controller** with a few modifications. Click **Assets\ImportPackage\Characters**.

If you don't see the Character Controller option, then you didn't import the Standard Assets when you installed Unity. To fix this, re-rerun the Unity installer and only check Standard Assets for the install. A standard Unity Asset is like any regular package. It's just a collection of files.

Click **Import** on the menu to import the character assets. When the import is completed, you'll notice a new folder in the Project Browser called Standard Assets. This contains everything that you imported.

The first modification is to remove jumping and a few other actions you won't need such as footsteps and headbobbing. Robot Rampage doesn't have jump obstacles, and by default the Unity **Character Controller** uses the spacebar to jump.

In the Project browser, open the **FirstPersonController** in your code editor located in **Assets/Standard Assets/Characters/FirstPersonCharacter/Scripts**.

Comment out lines **39**, **50**, **112 to 127**, **165-176**, and **182-200**. To comment out a line, simply place **//** in front of the line.

Save the file and switch back in Unity. Drag the **FirstPersonController** script on top of the **Player** GameObject. Click the **Player** GameObject, and use the Inspector to set **Position** to (**23.7, 2.68, 24.11**), **Rotation** to (**0, -88.18, 0**).

This puts the player in the one of the corners and rotates the player facing the open hallway as opposed to staring at a wall.

The `FirstPersonController` script also has values for run speed and walk speed. Set the **Player Walk Speed** to **10**, and **Run** to **20**.

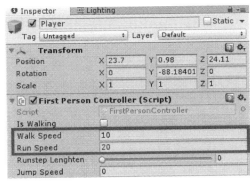

Those run and walk values worked best for this game. When you make your games, play around with these values to see what works for you.

Adding the camera

Currently, the camera is divorced from the player when you want them to be a happy couple, frolicking together through the robot wasteland. Thankfully, you don't have to play matchmaker.

Click the the **Camera** GameObject and drag it onto the **Player** GameObject to make it a child of **Player**. The camera will now move with the player.

Set the **Camera** position as: **(0, 0.8, 0)** and **Rotation** to **(0,0,0)**.

Click Play; use the WASD keys to move around and the mouse to look around as you move. You can also hold the Shift key to run.

Unfortunately, stopping the game can be a little difficult when using the first person character controller since the mouse pointer is not available. Thankfully there are shortcuts. Press **Control-P** (or **Command-P** on the Mac) to exit play mode.

With first person controller added, you just need to configure the capsule collider. A first person character controller comes with a plain old regular character controller which already contains a capsule collider. You can learn more about character controllers in Chapter 4, "Physics".

With the Player GameObject still selected, find the **Character Controller** in the Inspector and set the **Center** property to (**-1.5, 0, 0**), the **Radius** to **1**, and the **Height** to **3.13**.

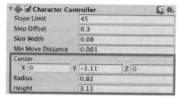

Next is the fun part where you get to add three weapons and start shooting them!

Creating weapons

In Unity, a gun is just another GameObject. The big difference is the perspective. Putting it close to to the camera gives you the perspective of a first person shooter that we all love.

Select the **Camera** GameObject, then right-click on it and select **Create Empty** to create an empty GameObject under the **Camera**. Name your new GameObject **1Pistol**. The number in front of the name refers to the equip key the player will use.

Drag the **RobotRampage_Pistol** model from inside the Models folder in the Project browser onto the **1Pistol** GameObject. By parenting the model to a GameObject, the animations you'll create later will occur in local space.

Set the **Position** of the **1Pistol** GameObject to (**0.69, -0.72, 1.26**) and the **rotation** to (**0, 0, 0**).

This gives you the perspective of the gun directly in front of you. In the Inspector, **deactivate** the pistol by **unchecking** the checkbox next to the gun name. This makes it disappear so you can add another gun.

Create another empty GameObject under the **Camera** and name it **2AssaultRifle**. You'll usually need to adjust the scale of imported models to fit your game, and this is no exception. Drag the **RobotRampage_AssaultRifle** model underneath your new GameObject. Set the **2AssaultRifle position** to (**0.54, -0.67, 0.913**), the **rotation** to (**0, 0, 0**), and set the **scale** to (**0.01, 0.01, 0.01**).

Deactivate the assault rifle like you did with the pistol.

Do the same again for the Shotgun, name it **3Shotgun** and use the **RobotRampage_Shotgun** model. Set the **3Shotgun** position to (**0.3, -0.36, 0.65**), the **rotation** to (**0, 0, 0**), and set its **scale** to (**0.01, 0.01, 0.01**).

At this point, you now have your three weapons added to your game. Leave the **1Pistol** GameObject active and deactivate the **2AssaultRifle** and **3Shotgun** GameObjects.

The code will work this way as well: As the player switches guns, you will turn on the active gun and turn off the other ones.

Click Play and walk around with one of the weapons. Feels good, doesn't it? :]

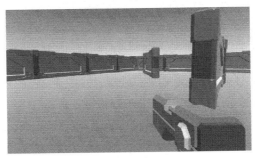

Now is a good time to set the tags on each weapon.

Adding tags to GameObjects

Select the **1Pistol** GameObject, click the **Tag** dropdown and click **Add Tag**. Click the + button under **Tags** and type **Pistol**. Click the + again and type in **AssaultRifle**, then finally click the + one more time and type in **Shotgun**.

Now to assign the appropriate tag to its weapon.

Click the **1Pistol**, then click the **Tags** dropdown and set it to the **Pistol** tag you just created. Do the same for the **2AssaultRifle** and **3Shotgun**, setting their tags appropriately:

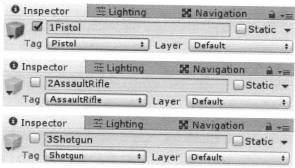

With everything tagged and ready to go, it's time to jump into the code editor.

Creating the Constants file

The very first thing you'll do is create a Constants file. This makes life easier by having common name references all other scripts can use. Whenever you create a new C# script in this section, you'll do it in a generic **Scripts** folder.

Right-click the **Assets** folder in the Project browser, select **Create\Folder** and name the new folder **Scripts**. In the new **Scripts** folder, create a **C# Script** and name it **Constants**.

Open your new **Constants** script in your script editor and replace the contents of the file with the following:

```
public class Constants {
  // Scenes
  public const string SceneBattle = "Battle";
  public const string SceneMenu = "MainMenu";

  // Gun Types
  public const string Pistol = "Pistol";
  public const string Shotgun = "Shotgun";
  public const string AssaultRifle = "AssaultRifle";

  // Robot Types
```

```
    public const string RedRobot = "RedRobot";
    public const string BlueRobot = "BlueRobot";
    public const string YellowRobot = "YellowRobot";

    // Pickup Types
    public const int PickUpPistolAmmo = 1;
    public const int PickUpAssaultRifleAmmo = 2;
    public const int PickUpShotgunAmmo = 3;
    public const int PickUpHealth = 4;
    public const int PickUpArmor = 5;

    // Misc
    public const string Game = "Game";
    public const float CameraDefaultZoom = 60f;
}
```

Each commented section represents the type data you'll use in upcoming scripts. You don't need to know what each constant does right now; you'll learn that as you work through the next few sections.

To start, you'll use the gun types to create the weapon switching logic.

Add the following before the closing brace:

```
public static readonly int[] AllPickupTypes = new int[5] {
    PickUpPistolAmmo,
    PickUpAssaultRifleAmmo,
    PickUpShotgunAmmo,
    PickUpHealth,
    PickUpArmor
};
```

This keeps track of all possible pickup types.

Weapon logic

Save your work and switch back to Unity. Create a C# script in the **Scripts** folder, name it **GunEquipper** and add the following variables to the class:

```
public static string activeWeaponType;

public GameObject pistol;
public GameObject assaultRifle;
public GameObject shotgun;

GameObject activeGun;
```

The GameObject variables reference each gun, and `activeGun` keeps track of the currently equipped gun.

Add the following method below `activeGun`, replacing the original `Start()`:

```
void Start () {
    activeWeaponType = Constants.Pistol;
    activeGun = pistol;
}
```

Here you initialize the starting gun as the pistol.

You now need to load the appropriate gun when the player switches weapons. Add the following method:

```
private void loadWeapon(GameObject weapon) {
  pistol.SetActive(false);
  assaultRifle.SetActive(false);
  shotgun.SetActive(false);

  weapon.SetActive(true);
  activeGun = weapon;
}
```

This method will turn off all gun GameObjects, set the passed-in GameObject as active, then update the `activeGun` reference. You'll call this code from `Update()`. Update that method so it looks like the following:

```
void Update () {
  if (Input.GetKeyDown("1")) {
    loadWeapon(pistol);
    activeWeaponType = Constants.Pistol;
  } else if (Input.GetKeyDown("2")) {
    loadWeapon(assaultRifle);
    activeWeaponType = Constants.AssaultRifle;
  } else if (Input.GetKeyDown("3")) {
    loadWeapon(shotgun);
    activeWeaponType = Constants.Shotgun;
  }
}
```

The code each in each `if` statement checking whether the pressed key is 1, 2, or 3. Checking for input in every frame like this is known as **polling**. If one of those number keys is hit, the appropriate block calls `loadWeapon()` and passes it the appropriate weapon to activate. It then sets **activeWeaponType** as a static. This makes it easy for other scripts to query which gun is the player has equipped.

Finally, add the following convenience method:

```
public GameObject GetActiveWeapon() {
  return activeGun;
}
```

This simply returns the `activeGun` so other scripts can read that piece of information.

Save your work, switch back to Unity, and attach the **GunEquipper** script to the **Player** GameObject:

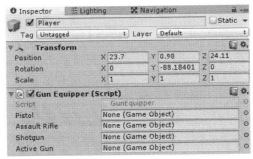

Select the **Player** GameObject and drag the **1Pistol** GameObject from the Hierarchy to the respective field in the **GunEquipper** script component. Repeat this for **2AssaultRifle** and **3Shotgun**.

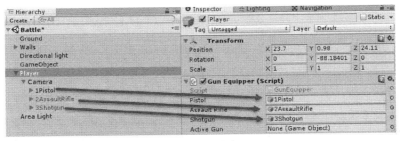

Click Play and press the 1, 2, or 3 key to change the weapon.

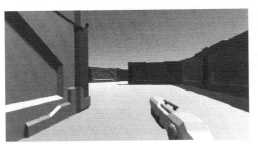

What use is a great-looking weapon without ammunition?

Ammunition logic

To get the gun firing, you have determine a fire rate. When the player fires a gun, you want there to be a pause between each bullet. This means you must keep track of when the last bullet has fired so you can fire the next bullet.

Create a C# script, name it **Gun** and add to it the following variables:

```
public float fireRate;
protected float lastFireTime;
```

`fireRate` is the speed at which the gun will fire, and `lastFireTime` tracks the last time the gun was fired.

Update `Start()` in **Gun** to:

```
void Start() {
    lastFireTime = Time.time - 10;
}
```

This sets `lastFireTime` to 10 seconds ago. When the game starts, the player will be able to fire the gun immediately.

Finally, replace `Update()` with the following:

```
protected virtual void Update() {

}

protected void Fire() {

}
```

You will subclass these later on, as each weapon will have its own slight variation on these methods.

Save your work and switch back to Unity. Create a C# script, name it **Pistol** and replace its contents with the following:

```
using UnityEngine;

public class Pistol : Gun {
    override protected void Update() {
        base.Update();
        // Shotgun & Pistol have semi-auto fire rate
        if (Input.GetMouseButtonDown(0) && (Time.time -
lastFireTime)
            > fireRate) {
            lastFireTime = Time.time;
            Fire();
        }
    }
}
```

This checks whether enough time has elapsed between shots to allow another one. If so, it will trigger the gun firing animation — you'll be adding that in just a moment.

Save your work, switch back to Unity and attach your **Pistol** script to the **1Pistol** GameObject.

Note that the **fireRate** hasn't been set yet. Click on the **1Pistol** GameObject and set the **fireRate** to **0.6**.

Excellent. Now, it's time for the shotgun. Select the **Pistol** script and press **Control-D** (or **Command-D** on the mac). This will duplicate the script. Change the name to **Shotgun**. Open the script in your code editor. Replace this:

```
public class Pistol : Gun {
```

with this:

```
public class Shotgun : Gun
```

As with the pistol, this will be a semi-automatic weapon, but since it's a shotgun it needs a longer time between shots. Save your work, switch back to Unity, attach the **Shotgun** script to the **3Shotgun** GameObject and set the **fireRate** to **1**.

Finally, you need to do the same with assault rifle. Create a script named **AssaultRifle**, attach it to the **2AssaultRifle** GameObject, and replace its contents with the following:

```
using UnityEngine;

public class AssaultRifle : Gun {

    override protected void Update() {
        base.Update();
        // Automatic Fire
        if (Input.GetMouseButton(0) && Time.time - lastFireTime >
fireRate) {
            lastFireTime = Time.time;
            Fire();
        }
    }
}
```

This looks almost the same as the code you added to the **Pistol** script, but there's one key difference: Instead of `GetMouseButtonDown`, this script uses `GetMouseButton` to see if the player is holding down the left mouse button to auto-fire.

Save and switch back Unity. Set the **fireRate** of the **AssaultRifle** script to **0.1**.

With the firing in place, you now need to apply your animations. You'll write the actual firing code itself in just a moment.

Working with animation states

Now to add the animation. If you've jumped directly to this chapter without reading any of the others or you still feel shaky with Unity's animation in general, then definitely read Chapter 5, "Animation".

Right-click on the **Animations** folder, select **Create\Animator Controller** and name it **Pistol**. Right-click on your new **AnimatorController** and click **open** to bring up the **Animator** window.

Right-click in the grid area and select **Create State\Empty**. Click on the new state and in the Inspector, rename it to **Fire**. Click on the control to the right of the **Motion** box and enter **Fire** in the Search pop-up. Find **Assets/Models/RobotRampage_Pistol.fbx** in the list and double-click it.

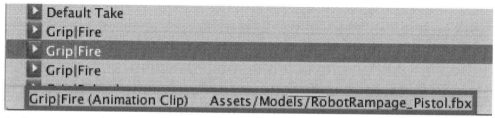

At this point you have a controller with one job: to fire the gun.

You need a default state for this animation. In the Animator window create another empty state as you did above and name it **Base**.

Right-click **Fire**, then click **Make Transition**. Drag from **Fire** to **Base** like so:

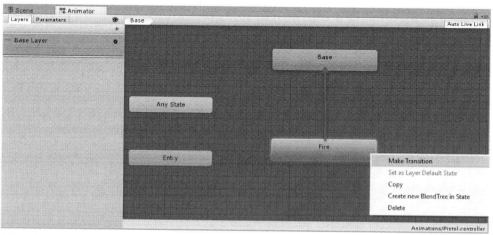

After the Fire animation plays, the animation will change to the Base state, where the gun is at rest.

Right-click the **Base** state and select **Set as Layer Default State** to make it the base animation:

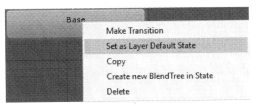

Theres only one thing left to do: Hook up this animation to the code! Open the **Gun** script and add the following line to **Fire()**:

```
GetComponentInChildren<Animator>().Play("Fire");
```

This fetches the animator controller and tells it to play the Fire animation. But before the animation can play, you'll need to add that component to your GameObjects.

Of course, by creating a animator controller for the pistol, you need one for the shotgun and assault rifle. In the Project Browser, select the **Pistol animator controller** in the Animations folder. **Duplicate it twice** by pressing **Control-D** (or **Command-D** on a Mac). Name one **Shotgun** and the other **AssaultRifle**.

Open the **Shotgun** animator controller, and select the **Fire** state. In the Inspector, set the **Motion** to **Grip|Fire**, making sure it originates from the **Assets/Models/RobotRampage_Shotgun.fbx** model.

Finally, open the **AssaultRifle** animator controller in the animator, and select the **Fire** state. In the Inspector, set the **Motion** to **Grip|Fire**, making sure it originates from the **Assets/Models/RobotRampage_AssaultRifle.fbx** model.

With all your animations in place, you just need to add them to the weapons.

Adding Animator components

Head back to Unity, click on the **1Pistol** GameObject, click **Add Component**, type in **Animator** and select the **Animator** component. Click the **Controller** box on the **Animator** you just added and select the **Pistol** animator controller from the pop-up:

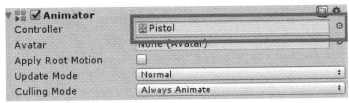

Next click the **Avatar** box on the **Animator** and select the **RobotRampage_PistolAvatar**.

An **Avatar** tells the animation system how to animate the transforms of the model. When you import a model, you need to configure the avatar. For the sake of simplicity, we've done this for you as such configuration goes well beyond the scope of the book.

Click Play and click the left mouse button to fire the pistol.

For the assault rifle, select the **2AssaultRifle** GameObject and this time, drag the **AssaultRifle** animator controller on to the Inspector, beneath all the existing components. Unity will automatically add the animator to the GameObjet. Set the **Avatar** to **RobotRampage_AssaultRifleAvatar**.

Do the same with **3Shotgun**, dragging the **Shotgun** animator controller on it and setting the **Avatar** to **RobotRampage_ShotgunAvatar**

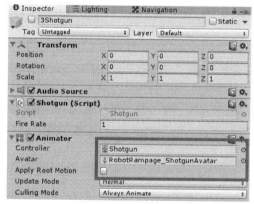

Click Play and test your weapons, switching between them with 1, 2, or 3:

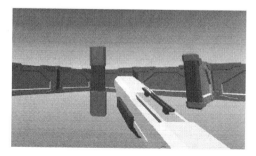

Adding the reticle

It's time to add the reticle each gun will use. The reticle is just a simple 2D image placed in front of the camera. This is the equivalent of pasting a target over the lens of your cell phone camera! It's not very technical, but it gets the job done.

You'll do this using Unity's user interface tools. In a few more chapters, you'll really learn about them in depth. For this chapter, consider this section a warm-up!

To get started placing user interface elements, you need a canvas. Unity provides several types of canvases. For this game, you'll use an overlay canvas. This works as an overlay on top of the screen. Elements added to the overlay will cover the game behind it, but you can minimize the effect through transparency.

In the Hierarchy, click Create and select **UI\Canvas**. Right-click on the **Canvas**, select **UI\Image** and rename the **Image** to **Reticle**. In the Inspector, click the control to the right of the **Source Image** box and select **reticleRed** from the dialog.

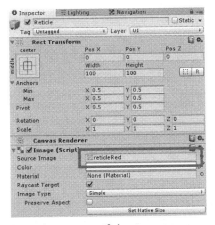

You'll now see the red reticle in the center of the screen.

The shotgun and assault rifle have coordinating colored reticles, so the reticle should update when you switch guns.

To do this, create a new script and name it **GameUI**. Then create a new GameObject in the Hierarchy and name it **GameUI** as well. Attach the **GameUI** script to the **GameUI** GameObject.

Open **GameUI** in your code editor and add the following to the top of the script:

```
using UnityEngine.UI;
```

This lets you access the base Unity UI classes. Next, add the following variables inside the class:

```
[SerializeField]
Sprite redReticle;
[SerializeField]
Sprite yellowReticle;
[SerializeField]
Sprite blueReticle;
[SerializeField]
Image reticle;
```

There's a few things going on in this code block. First, you'll notice the `SerializeField` attribute. Attributes allow you to convey information to the C# runtime about particular classes. In this case, you are declaring that variables are accessible from the Unity Inspector but not from other scripts.

You'll notice there is both a **Sprite** and an **Image**. A sprite represents an imported texture meant to be used with a 2D game or the user interface (UI). These are your JPG and PNG files that you have imported into Unity. By setting the texture type to a Sprite in the Inspector, you can add them to the user interface.

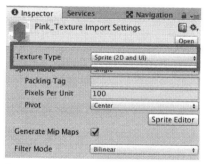

An Image is what displays the Sprite to the screen. You can think of it like so: the Sprite is a film reel whereas the Image is the film projector.

In this case, you have three Sprites acting as source image data for the reticle. Since only one will be displayed, there is only one Image.

Add the following method below the last variable:

```
public void UpdateReticle() {
  switch (GunEquipper.activeWeaponType) {
    case Constants.Pistol:
      reticle.sprite = redReticle;
      break;
    case Constants.Shotgun:
      reticle.sprite = yellowReticle;
      break;
    case Constants.AssaultRifle:
      reticle.sprite = blueReticle;
      break;
    default:
      return;
  }
}
```

This will change the sprite to reflect the active gun.

Save your work and switch back to Unity.

Click the **GameUI** GameObject, click on each [**ColorName**]**Reticle** box and add the appropriate Sprite. For example, you'd add the **redReticle** Sprite to **Red Reticle**. When you've added all three, drag the **Reticle** GameObject to the **ReticleField** like so:

You'll need to call `UpdateReticle()` from somewhere to change the reticles. The **GunEquipper** script looks like the perfect spot.

Open the **GunEquipper** script in your code editor. Create a reference to the **GameUI** by creating a `GameUI` variable at the top of the script, just below the opening brace:

```
[SerializeField]
GameUI gameUI;
```

Save the script and go back to Unity. Select the **Player** GameObject in the Hierarchy and drag the **GameUI** GameObject to the **Game UI** field in the **Gun Equipper** component:

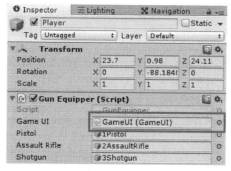

Now open the **GunEquipper** script in the code editor and add the following line to the end of each `if` statement in **Update()**:

```
gameUI.UpdateReticle();
```

Update() should now look like the following:

```
void Update() {
    if (Input.GetKeyDown("1")) {
        loadWeapon(pistol);
        activeWeaponType = Constants.Pistol;
        gameUI.UpdateReticle();
    } else if (Input.GetKeyDown("2")) {
        loadWeapon(assaultRifle);
        activeWeaponType = Constants.AssaultRifle;
        gameUI.UpdateReticle();
    } else if (Input.GetKeyDown("3")) {
        loadWeapon(shotgun);
        activeWeaponType = Constants.Shotgun;
        gameUI.UpdateReticle();
    }
}
```

This will update the reticle every time the player changes weapons.

Click Play and switch between weapons to see the reticle change:

Now the player can see exactly where their shots will go.

Managing ammunition

Since the player has to manage their ammunition in Robot Rampage, you should provide some audible feedback so the player knows when they've run dry. If the player has sufficient ammunition, play a "fire" sound along with the fire animation. If the player is out of ammunition, play an empty chamber "click" sound and don't run the fire animation.

You've probably guessed you simply need a variable to track the amount of ammunition. That would work, but in Robot Rampage you need to worry about the type of ammunition as well. In this case, it makes sense to have an **Ammo** class.

Create a C# script, name it **Ammo**. Open it in your code editor and add the add the following import to the top:

```
using System.Collections.Generic;
```

This lets you use the `Dictionary` type. In the body of the class at the top, add the following variables:

```
[SerializeField]
GameUI gameUI;

[SerializeField]
private int pistolAmmo = 20;
[SerializeField]
private int shotgunAmmo = 10;
[SerializeField]
private int assaultRifleAmmo = 50;

public Dictionary<string, int> tagToAmmo;
```

The variables `pistolAmmo`, `shotgunAmmo`, `assaultRifleAmmo` track their respective ammunition counts. `tagToAmmo` is a dictionary of type `string` and `int`, which lets you map a gun's type to its ammunition count.

You need to initialize the Dictionary at game start, so add the following method below where you declare the Dictionary:

```
void Awake() {
   tagToAmmo = new Dictionary<string, int> {
      { Constants.Pistol , pistolAmmo},
      { Constants.Shotgun , shotgunAmmo},
```

```
        { Constants.AssaultRifle , assaultRifleAmmo},
      };
    }
```

`Awake()` is a special method called before `Start()`. In this case, you want the dictionary to initialize before any `Start()` methods to prevent null access errors. This method simply makes each gun type a key in the dictionary and sets that key's value to the appropriate ammunition type. If you ever wanted to add another ammunition type, you can simply extend the dictionary.

Add the following method:

```
public void AddAmmo(string tag, int ammo) {
  if (!tagToAmmo.ContainsKey(tag)) {
    Debug.LogError("Unrecognized gun type passed: " + tag);
  }

  tagToAmmo[tag] += ammo;
}
```

This will add ammunition to the appropriate gun type. If you've passed in an unrecognized bad gun type, you log it as an error.

Next add the following method:

```
// Returns true if gun has ammo
public bool HasAmmo(string tag) {
  if (!tagToAmmo.ContainsKey(tag)) {
    Debug.LogError("Unrecognized gun type passed: " + tag);
  }

  return tagToAmmo[tag] > 0;
}
```

This will return `true` if the gun type has at least 1 bullet left, or `false` if it has no more bullets.

Add the following method as well:

```
public int GetAmmo(string tag) {
  if (!tagToAmmo.ContainsKey(tag)) {
    Debug.LogError("Unrecognized gun type passed:" + tag);
  }

  return tagToAmmo[tag];
}
```

This simply returns the bullet count for a gun type.

Finally, you need a method to actually consume ammunition. Add the following:

```
public void ConsumeAmmo(string tag) {
  if (!tagToAmmo.ContainsKey(tag)) {
    Debug.LogError("Unrecognized gun type passed:" + tag);
  }

  tagToAmmo[tag]--;
}
```

Like all the other methods, this checks for the correct tag. If it finds the appropriate ammunition, it subtracts a bullet.

At first glance, this code might seem like overkill, since you could simply access each ammunition type directly instead of using a dictionary. The problem with that approach is that when you add new ammunition types, you end up with redundant code along with getters and setters for every type of ammunition! With a dictionary, you can simply map it out once and fetch the corresponding ammunition by its tag, rather than having to worry about calling a specific method.

Save your work, switch back to Unity, and attach the **Ammo** script to the **Player** GameObject. Click on the **Player** GameObject and drag the **GameUI** GameObject to the **GameUI** field in the **Ammo (Script)** component.

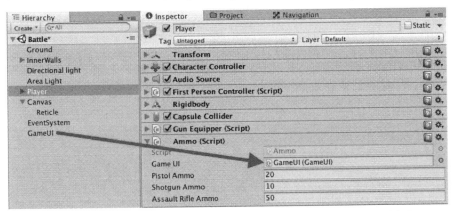

All that's missing is sound. Open the **Gun** script in the code editor and add the following just below where you declared `fireRate`:

```
public Ammo ammo;
public AudioClip liveFire;
public AudioClip dryFire;
```

This tracks the gun's ammunition and stores references to the fire and dry-fire sound effects.

Next change `Fire()` to the following:

```
protected void Fire() {
   if (ammo.HasAmmo(tag)) {
     GetComponent<AudioSource>().PlayOneShot(liveFire);
     ammo.ConsumeAmmo(tag);
   } else {
     GetComponent<AudioSource>().PlayOneShot(dryFire);
   }
   GetComponentInChildren<Animator>().Play("Fire");
}
```

This checks if the player has any remaining ammunition. If so, you play the `liveFire` sound; otherwise, play the `dryFire` sound. Of course, if you fire the gun, then you should expend one bullet.

You now need to set the Ammo and AudioClips for each gun.

Click the **1Pistol** GameObject and drag the **Player** GameObject to the **Ammo** field to create a reference to the players **Ammo** script. Click the control to the right of the **LiveFire** field and select the **pistolShot** audio file. Next, click the control to the right of the **dryFire** field and add the **dryFire** audio.

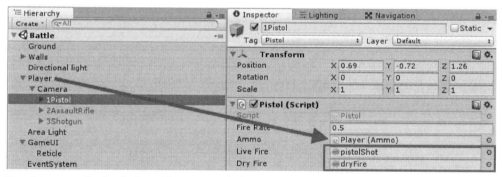

Do this again for both the **3Shotgun** and the **2Assaultrifle** using their respective sounds.

All that's left is to add an **AudioSource** component. Select the **1Pistol**, **2AssaultRifle**, and **3Shotgun** GameObjects. In the Inspector click **AddComponent**, type **AudioSource** and select the AudioSource component.

Click Play and fire away with each gun in turn; as long as you have ammunition, you should hear the fire sound. Once you run out of ammunition, you should hear the dry-fire sound instead and the fire animation should not play.

There is one issue with the assault rifle. The gun fires faster than the animations. This makes the motion out of sync with the action. To fix this, you need to return to the animator. If your animator window is closed, make sure to reopen it by clicking **Window\Animator**. In the Hierarchy, select the **2AssaultRifle** GameObject and you'll see its animation states in the animator.

By default, animations blend into each other during a transition. This blending is referred to as exit time. **Select** the **transition** from **Fire** to **Base**. In the Inspector, you'll the visual depiction of the exit time under the **Settings** category.

There are two ways to remove exit time. You can uncheck the `Has Exit Time` property, but you can only do this when you have a condition. Since you don't have a condition, you can set the duration of the transition to zero. This does the same thing.

To do this, drag the right blue arrow in the timeline all the way to the left and hit enter to save it.

252 Unity Games by Tutorials

When done, it will like like this:

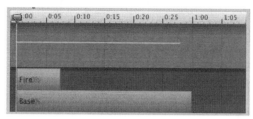

This causes new animations to interrupt any playing animations. Play your game and switch to the assault rifle. Hold down the fire button and channel your inner Rambo!

Where to go from here?

That does it for this chapter. In the next chapter, you'll add enemies to feel the wrath of your weapons — and some pickups so you can replenish your ammunition and health, among other things. You'll also get to use the NavMesh you've created and add the damage mechanics for the player and the robots.

Chapter 10: Adding Enemies

By Anthony Uccello

In the last chapter you added the first person controls, let the player switch guns, and added visual and audio effects. But what good is firing a gun if you don't have something to shoot at — and what fun is it if they can't shoot back? :]

In this chapter, you'll add some robots to the mix, but to make things interesting, these will be evil robots. Evil robots that will try to kill you. You'll add lots of them, give them the ability to fire, but to make things fair, you'll also add some pickups as well. In short, by the end of this chapter, you'll have yourself a first person shooter.

Creating the robots

Open the current project in progress, or you can start fresh by opening the starter project for this chapter included with the resources folder. Open the **Battle** scene to pick up where you left off.

Click on the **Resources** folder and drag **RedRobot, YellowRobot, and BlueRobot** onto the scene in front of the player, somewhere above ground level:

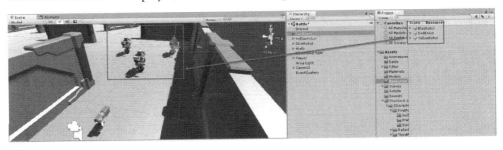

You'll now configure them all together, instead of separately as you've done.

Click on the **RedRobot** GameObject, and hold Control, or Command on a Mac, while selecting the **YellowRobot** and the **BlueRobot** GameObjects.

> **Note:** Whenever you're asked to select the robots in future, select all three of these robot GameObjects in this way.

Select all the Click **Add Component** and select the **New Script** option. Name the script **Robot**, and ensure **C Sharp** is the chosen Language. This creates a new script in the **Assets** folder.

To keep things organized, move the **Robot** script from the **Assets** folder to the **Scripts** folder. Open the **Robot** script in your code editor.

Add the following variables to your new **Robot** script inside the class:

```
[SerializeField]
private string robotType;

public int health;
public int range;
public float fireRate;

public Transform missileFireSpot;
UnityEngine.AI.NavMeshAgent agent;

private Transform player;
private float timeLastFired;

private bool isDead;
```

robotType is the type of robot: RedRobot, BlueRobot, or YellowRobot. Notice that you are serializing the variable. Again, this is so you can access it in the Inspector but not from other scripts. The value of this field matches a constant defined in the Constants script.

health is how much damage this robot can take before dying, range is the distance the gun can fire, and fireRate is how fast it can fire.

agent is a reference to the Nav Mesh Agent component, player is what the robot should track, and isDead tracks whether the robot is alive or dead.

Save your work and switch back to Unity. Click the **RedRobot** GameObject and enter **RedRobot** in the **robotType** field. Set **Health** to 14, the **Range** value to 150, and the **Fire Rate** to 2. Click **Apply** when done to apply those changes to the prefab.

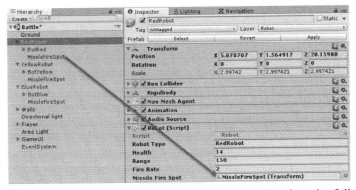

Do the same for the **YellowBot** with the following values: **Robot Type YellowRobot, Health 20, Range 300, Fire Rate 3**. Click **Apply** when done.

And of course, do the same for the **BlueRobot** with the following values: **Robot Type BlueRobot, Health 10, Range 200, Fire Rate 1**. Click **Apply** when done.

The **Missile Fire Spot** parameter is a coordinate on the robot model from which the missiles fire.

Click the arrow next to robot GameObject to display its children. Select each robot GameObject, one at a time, and drag its child GameObject **MissileFireSpot** to the **Missile Fire Spot** field on the **Robot** Component. Make sure to **apply** the change.

Now open the **Robot** script in your code editor and add and update the following methods:

```
void Start() {
  // 1
  isDead = false;
  agent = GetComponent<UnityEngine.AI.NavMeshAgent>();
  player = GameObject.FindGameObjectWithTag("Player").transform;
}

// Update is called once per frame
void Update() {
  // 2
  if (isDead) {
    return;
  }
```

```
   // 3
   transform.LookAt(player);

   // 4
   agent.SetDestination(player.position);

   // 5
   if (Vector3.Distance(transform.position, player.position) <
range
       && Time.time - timeLastFired > fireRate) {
     // 6
     timeLastFired = Time.time;
     fire();
   }
 }

 private void fire() {
   Debug.Log("Fire");
 }
```

Looking at the numbered comments, here's what this code is doing:

1. By default, all robots are alive. You then set the `agent` and `player` values to the NavMesh Agent and Player components respectively.

2. Check if the robot is dead before continuing. There are no zombie robots in this game!

3. Make the robot face the player.

4. Tell the robot to use the NavMesh to find the player.

5. Check to see if the robot is within firing range and there's been enough time between shots to fire again.

6. Update `timeLastFired` to the current time and call `Fire()`, which simply logs a message to the console for the time being.

You need to assign an appropriate tag to the Player GameObject so the robots can find it.

Save your script and switch back to Unity. Click the **Player** GameObject, and as you did before with the guns, click the **Tag** dropdown and select the **Player** tag.

Click Play; you'll see the robots move towards the player and the "Fire" log should appear in the Console.

Animating robots

Right now the robots move statically towards the player; it would look much better if they actually rolled on their ball foot. As well, the robots should make a firing motion when they fire at the player.

Click a **RobotRampage_BotBall_v1** GameObject on any Robot (expand the arrows on its children to find it), then go to **Window\Animation** to open the **Animation** window. Click the **Create** button:

Enter **Ball** for the name, set the path to the **Animations** folder, then click Save. Click **AddProperty**, click the arrow beside **Transform** then click the + next to **Rotation**:

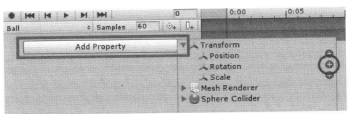

A pair of keyframes (grey diamonds) will appear 1 second apart on the timeline

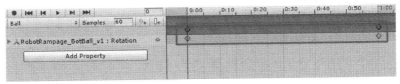

Click the last keyframe and notice that the **Rotation** fields for the GameObject have turned red in the Transform component in the Inspector. Set the **Rotation X** value to **-360**. This will cause the ball to rotate 360 degrees.

Select the other two **RobotRampage_BotBall_v1** GameObjects at the same time. You can find these by expanding the child GameObjects **BotRed**, **BotYellow**, and **BotBlue**. With all the **RobotRampage_BotBall_v1** GameObjects selected, drag the **RobotRampage_BotBall_v1** into the Inspector.

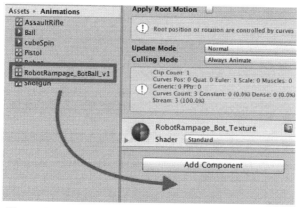

Click Play and you'll see the robot's ball spin:

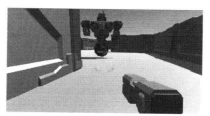

Now to add the firing animation. Select all three **RobotRampage_Bot** GameObjects and set their **Animator**'s **Controller** to **Robot** by clicking the circle beside the **Controller** field and selecting **Robot**:

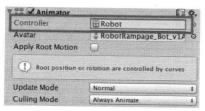

Select each **RobotRampage_Bot** individually and hit **Apply** on each one to apply the changes to the prefabs. Now open the **Robot** script. Add the following instance variable:

```
public Animator robot;
```

Then update `Fire()` to the following:

```
private void fire() {
    robot.Play("Fire");
}
```

Save and switch back to Unity. Select the **YellowRobot** and drag the child **RobotRampage_Bot** into the **Robot** property. **Apply** the change to the prefab.

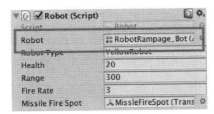

This plays the **Fire** animation when the robot fires a missile — this is one of the states inside the **Robot** animator controller. Save your work and switch back to Unity.

Do this for the **RedRobot** and the **BlueRobot**, making sure to **apply** your changes when finished.

Click Play and you'll see the fire animation run when the robot fires.

That looks good, but it's missing something. Oh, right — an actual missile! :]

Firing robot missiles

Create a C# script and name it **Missile**. Drag a copy of each of the **RobotMissile[Color]** prefabs from the **Resources** folder onto the Hierarchy. It doesn't matter where they end up on screen because you'll be removing them soon.

Select each of the **RobotMissile[Color]** GameObjects you just dragged into the Hierarchy in turn, and drag the **Missile** script on to each of them.

Open the **Missile** script in the code editor add the following variables:

```
public float speed = 30f;
public int damage = 10;
```

speed is how fast the missile should travel. damage is how much damage this missile will cause when it hits the player.

Now add the following methods just below the damage variable:

```
//1
void Start() {
```

```
      StartCoroutine("deathTimer");
   }

   // 2
   void Update() {
      transform.Translate(Vector3.forward * speed * Time.deltaTime);
   }

   // 3
   IEnumerator deathTimer() {
      yield return new WaitForSeconds(10);
      Destroy(gameObject);
   }
```

Welcome to coroutines! In computer jargon, you'll often hear the word `threading` tossed around a bit. This is just a way of having the computer do multiple things at once. In a game, this would mean calculating your artificial intelligence in one thread while playing sound in another.

Threads are a gnarly topic and while you can use them in Unity, you can simulate threading without all the pain and suffering through the use of coroutines. A coroutine will run code at a certain designated time. They run on the main thread and work pretty much like regular code, except they run in intervals. Because they run in the main thread, you don't get any of the nasty concurrency headaches from regular threading.

Coroutines take methods that return `IEnumerator`. These determine the duration of the coroutine. Here's the breakdown of what you just wrote:

1. When you instantiate a Missile, you start a coroutine called **deathTimer**(). This is name of the method that the coroutine will call.

2. Move the missile forward at `speed` multiplied by the time between frames.

3. You'll notice that the method immediately returns a `WaitForSeconds`, set to 10. Once those ten seconds have passed, the method will resume after the `yield` statement. If the missile doesn't hit the player, it should auto-destruct.

See? Coroutines aren't so bad at all! :]

Save your work and switch back to Unity. Click each **RobotMissile[Color]** one at a time and click **Apply** to set the changes on the prefabs.

Open the **Robot** script. At the top of the file, add the following just below the opening brace of the class:

```
[SerializeField]
GameObject missileprefab;
```

`missilePrefab` is the prefab for the missile.

Update the `fire()` method to the following:

```
private void fire() {
   GameObject missile = Instantiate(missileprefab);
   missile.transform.position =
missileFireSpot.transform.position;
   missile.transform.rotation =
missileFireSpot.transform.rotation;
   robot.Play("Fire");
}
```

This creates a new `missilePrefab` and sets its position and rotation to the robot's firing spot. Save your work and switch back to Unity.

Delete the three **RobotMissile[Color]** GameObjects from the Hierarchy.

Click the **RedRobot** GameObject and drag the **RobotMissileRed** prefab from the **Resources** folder to the **Missile prefab** field on the **Robot** Component and click Apply.

Do the same for the **YellowRobot** and **BlueRobot** GameObjects using their respective colored missiles, making sure to **apply** your changes.

Click Play and — duck! Watch those missiles fly!

Adding damage effects

Now is the perfect time to add damage logic to the game. The missiles should damage the player, and the player's gun shots should damage the robots.

Create a new C# script, name it **Player** and add the following variables:

```
public int health;
public int armor;
public GameUI gameUI;
private GunEquipper gunEquipper;
private Ammo ammo;
```

`health` is the remaining life of the player. When this hits zero, it's time to grab another quarter! :]

`armor` is a special health layer for the player that results in 50% reduced damage. Once `armor` reaches 0, then player receives full damage.

`gameUI` and `gunEquipper` are simply references to their respective script types. `ammo` is a reference to the **Ammo** class you created earlier to track weapon ammo.

Add the following to `Start()`:

```
void Start () {
    ammo = GetComponent<Ammo>();
    gunEquipper = GetComponent<GunEquipper>();
}
```

This just gets the `Ammo` and `GunEquipper` component attached to the player GameObject.

Add the following method:

```
public void TakeDamage(int amount) {
  int healthDamage = amount;

  if (armor > 0) {
    int effectiveArmor = armor * 2;
    effectiveArmor -= healthDamage;

    // If there is still armor, don't need to process
    // health damage
    if (effectiveArmor > 0) {
      armor = effectiveArmor / 2;
      return;
    }

    armor = 0;
  }

  health -= healthDamage;
  Debug.Log("Health is " + health);

  if (health <= 0) {
    Debug.Log("GameOver");
```

```
    }
  }
```

`TakeDamage()` takes the incoming damage and reduces its amount based on how much armor the player has remaining. If the player has no armor, then you apply the total damage to the player's health.

If `health` reaches 0, it's game over for the player; for now, you just log this to the console.

Save your work and switch back to Unity. Add the **Player** script to the **Player** GameObject. Set **Health** to **100**, **Armor** to **20**, and add the drag the **GameUI** GameObject over the **GameUI** field. You'll be incorporating armor later in the game.

Next you need to update the **Missile** script to actually tell the player to take damage.

When the **Missile** GameObject collides with the **Player Capsule Collider**, it will damage the player via **OnCollisionEnter()**. Open the **Missile** script in the code editor and add the following method:

```
void OnCollisionEnter(Collision collider) {
  if (collider.gameObject.GetComponent<Player>() != null
      && collider.gameObject.tag == "Player") {

collider.gameObject.GetComponent<Player>().TakeDamage(damage);
  }

  Destroy(gameObject);
}
```

The missile checks if it collided with the **Player** GameObject based on its tag. It also checks to see if if the player is still active, since the **Player** Component will be disabled later in the game over state. If so, it tells the `Player` script to take damage and passes along its damage value. Once the missile hits the player it destroys itself.

Save your work and switch back to Unity.

Click Play and stand in the line of missile fire. Watch as the console logs out the health of the player. In the next chapter, you'll add a UI so the health will be clearly visible on screen, but the console will do just fine for now.

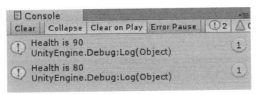

Your game logs GameOver when the player's health hits 0. Later on, you'll code a proper game over screen.

Those pesky robots are still invincible. It's time for them to take some damage, too.

Open the **Robot** script and add the following methods:

```
// 1
public void TakeDamage(int amount) {
  if (isDead) {
    return;
  }

  health -= amount;

  if (health <= 0) {
    isDead = true;
    robot.Play("Die");
    StartCoroutine("DestroyRobot");
  }
}

// 2
IEnumerator DestroyRobot() {
  yield return new WaitForSeconds(1.5f);
  Destroy(gameObject);
}
```

1. This has roughly the same logic as the player TakeDamage() method, except when health hits 0 it plays a death animation before calling DestroyRobot().

2. This adds a delay before destroying the robot. This lets the **Die** animation finish.

Save your work.

Now comes the fun part — actually shooting back. There's two things you need to do: deal damage to the robots but also implement zooming (otherwise known as iron sights).

Open **Gun** and add the following variables:

```
public float zoomFactor;
public int range;
public int damage;

private float zoomFOV;
private float zoomSpeed = 6;
```

zoomFactor controls the zoom level when the player hits the right mouse button. zoomFOV is the field of view based on the zoom factor. range is how far the gun can effectively hit its target. The shotgun has the shortest range, and the pistol has the longest. damage is how much damage the gun causes.

Save your work and switch to Unity.

Click the **1Pistol** GameObject and set its **Zoom Factor** to **1.3**, its **Range** to **60** and its **Damage** to **3**.

Click the **2AssaultRifle** GameObject and its **Zoom Factor** to **1.4**, its **Range** to **30** and its **Damage** to **1**.

Click the **3Shotgun** GameObject and set its **Zoom Factor** to **1.1**, its **Range** to **10** and its **Damage** to **10**.

Open the **Gun** script and update `Start()` to the following:

```
void Start() {
   zoomFOV = Constants.CameraDefaultZoom / zoomFactor;
   lastFireTime = Time.time - 10;
}
```

This simply initializes the zoom factor.

Modify `Update()` to the following:

```
protected virtual void Update() {
   // Right Click (Zoom)
   if (Input.GetMouseButton(1)) {
     Camera.main.fieldOfView =
Mathf.Lerp(Camera.main.fieldOfView, zoomFOV, zoomSpeed *
Time.deltaTime);
   } else {
     Camera.main.fieldOfView = Constants.CameraDefaultZoom;
   }
}
```

If the player hits the right mouse button, this smoothly animates the zoom effect via `Mathf.Lerp()`.

To determine if the robot was hit, you'll use raycasting. Raycasting is when you fire an invisible ray to check for collisions. First, you must define the damage method. Add the following:

```
private void processHit(GameObject hitObject) {
   if (hitObject.GetComponent<Player>() != null) {
     hitObject.GetComponent<Player>().TakeDamage(damage);
   }

   if (hitObject.GetComponent<Robot>() != null) {
     hitObject.GetComponent<Robot>().TakeDamage(damage);
   }
}
```

This passes the damage to the correct GameObject. Now for the actual raycasting. You can review raycasting by reading Chapter 4, "Physics". To implement the raycasting, add the following to the bottom of `Fire()`:

```
Ray ray = Camera.main.ViewportPointToRay(new Vector3(0.5f, 0.5f, 0));
RaycastHit hit;
if (Physics.Raycast(ray, out hit, range)) {
  processHit(hit.collider.gameObject);
}
```

This creates a ray and checks what that ray hits. It's that simple — a ray fires out at the range of the gun, and if it collides with a GameObject it calls `processHit()`. This determines if the GameObject hit was a robot; if so, it passes on the damage.

Save your work and switch back to Unity. Press Play and press the right mouse button to zoom, then blast those bad robots until they die.

Creating pickups

The player needs a way to gain back health, armor, and ammo. You'll do this by adding floating pickups the player can grab along the way.

Open the **Player** script in the code editor and add the following:

```
// 1
private void pickupHealth() {
  health += 50;
  if (health > 200) {
    health = 200;
  }
}

private void pickupArmor() {
  armor += 15;
}

// 2
private void pickupAssaultRifleAmmo() {
  ammo.AddAmmo(Constants.AssaultRifle, 50);
}

private void pickupPisolAmmo() {
  ammo.AddAmmo(Constants.Pistol, 20);
}

private void pickupShotgunAmmo() {
```

```
    ammo.AddAmmo(Constants.Shotgun, 10);
}
```

1. This adds to the players health and armor respectively.

2. This adds ammunition for that gun type.

Now add the following:

```
public void PickUpItem(int pickupType) {
  switch (pickupType) {
    case Constants.PickUpArmor:
      pickupArmor();
      break;
    case Constants.PickUpHealth:
      pickupHealth();
      break;
    case Constants.PickUpAssaultRifleAmmo:
      pickupAssaultRifleAmmo();
      break;
    case Constants.PickUpPistolAmmo:
      pickupPisolAmmo();
      break;
    case Constants.PickUpShotgunAmmo:
      pickupShotgunAmmo();
      break;
    default:
      Debug.LogError("Bad pickup type passed" + pickupType);
      break;
  }
}
```

`PickUpItem()` takes an `int` that represents the type of item being picked up. Now that the **Player** script can process picking up an item, it's time to create the pickup prefabs.

The `Constants` file references the IDs of all the pickups. These IDs correspond to the five types of pickups. The `int` passed into the `PickUpItem()` will be one of these values.

Save you work and switch back to Unity. Create a C# script, name it **Pickup** and add the following inside the class:

```
public int type;
```

This represents the type of the pickup. Now add the following:

```
void OnTriggerEnter(Collider collider) {
  if (collider.gameObject.GetComponent<Player>() != null
    && collider.gameObject.tag == "Player") {

    collider.gameObject.GetComponent<Player>().PickUpItem(type);
```

```
      Destroy(gameObject);
   }
}
```

This listens for a collision with the **Player** GameObject, calls `PickUpItem()` on it, passes along its item type, and then destroys itself. You will add the respawn mechanics shortly.

Save your work and switch back to Unity.

In the **Resources** folder, select the **PickupAmmoAssaultRifle**, **PickupAmmoPistol**, **PickupAmmoShotgun**, **PickupHealth**, and **PickupArmor** prefabs. With all of those selected, click the **Add Component** button from the scripts category, select the **Pickup** script.

Next, add a **Rigidbody**. Check the **Is Kinematic** box. Finally, add a **Box Collider**. **Check the Is Trigger** checkbox and set the **Size** to **(1.5, 1.5, 1.5)**.

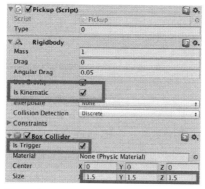

Now to configure each of the pickups. Select the **PickupAmmoPistol** prefab in the **Resources** folder and set its **Type** to **1**, set the **PickupAmmoAssaultRifle** to **2**, the **PickupAmmoShotgun** to **3**, the **PickupHealth** to **4**, and finally, the **PickupArmor** to **5**.

The last thing to do is add the spinning and bobbing animation to the pickup. The animation has been created for you, just need to create the animator. In the Project Browser, select the **Animations** folder and click the **Create** button. Select **Animator Controller** and name it **Pickup**.

Double click the **Pickup** animator controller to open the animator. Right click in the empty grid and select **Create State\Empty**. In the Inspector, name it **Spin** and set the **Motion** to **cubeSpin**.

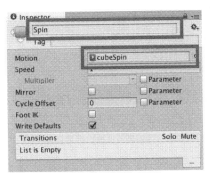

Excellent! Your pickups are ready to spin! Next, return back to the Project Browser and select the **Resources** folder. Click the arrow next to each of the the **Pickup[Type]** prefabs and select the only child prefab in each:

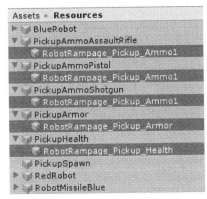

Lock the Inspector and in the Project Browser, select the **Animations** folder. Drag the **Pickup** Animator to the Inspector.

Once added, make sure to **unlock** the Inspector.

By adding the animation here, instead of the parent, the animation plays in local space.

Now drag a copy of each **Pickup[Type]** onto the scene, just slightly above the ground:

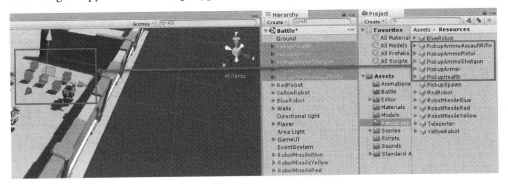

Click Play and move the player over each pickup; it should destroy itself when you make contact. You'll add a UI shortly to see the effects of these pickups on screen, but for now if the pickup GameObjects are floating and spinning, and disappear when you walk into them, you've got it all right so far!

More spawning logic

Instead of having the robots and pickups exist in the scene at the start of the game, you'll have them spawn at specific locations.

Select all the **Pickup**[Type] GameObjects and [**Color**]**Robot** GameObjects in the Hierarchy and press Delete.

You will now code the the pickups and robots to spawn at specific locations around the map.

Create a new C# script, name it **PickupSpawn**, and replace the contents of the file with the following:

```
[SerializeField]
private GameObject[] pickups;
```

pickups will store all the possible pickup types.

Now add the following methods:

```
// 1
void spawnPickup() {
  // Instantiate a random pickup
  GameObject pickup = Instantiate(pickups[Random.Range(0,
pickups.Length)]);
  pickup.transform.position = transform.position;
  pickup.transform.parent = transform;
```

```
}

// 2
IEnumerator respawnPickup() {
  yield return new WaitForSeconds(20);
  spawnPickup();
}

// 3
void Start() {
  spawnPickup();
}

// 4
public void PickupWasPickedUp() {
  StartCoroutine("respawnPickup");
}
```

Here's what each method does:

1. Instantiates a random pickup and sets its position to that of the **PickupSpawn** GameObject, which you will make in a moment.

2. Waits 20 seconds before calling `spawnPickup()`.

3. Spawns a pickup as soon as the game beings.

4. Starts the Coroutine to respawn when the player has picked up.

Save your work. Open the **Pickup** script and add the following line just above `Destroy(gameObject)`:

```
GetComponentInParent<PickupSpawn>().PickupWasPickedUp();
```

Now when the pickup collides with the player, it will signal the **PickupSpawn** script to start the spawn timer.

Save your work and switch back to Unity.

Create an empty GameObject, name it **PickupSpawn** and add the **PickupSpawn** script.

With the **PickupSpawn** GameObject selected, **lock** the Inspector.

In the Resources folder, select the **PickupAmmoAssaultRifle**, **PickupAmmoPistol**, **PickupAmmoShotgun**, **PickupHealth**, and **PickupArmor** prefabs and drag them to the **Pickups** property to add them to the array.

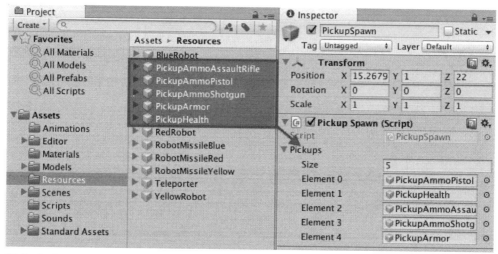

Unlock the Inspector.

Now drag the **PickupSpawn** GameObject into to the **Resources** folder to create a prefab of it.

Create an empty GameObject and name it **PickupSpawns**. Set its **position** all to **(0, 0, 0)**. Drag the **PickupSpawn** GameObject underneath the **PickupSpawns** and **duplicate** it **six** times by press Control-D (or Command D, on the Mac).

To stay organized, change the each of the names to: **PickupSpawn**.

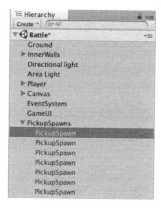

Starting from the top most **PickupSpawn** GameObject and moving down, set the following positions:

- (-26.0, 0.5, 3)

- (26.0, 0.5, -17)

- (7.0, 0.5, 3.0)

- (-27.0, 0.5, 3.0)

- (28, 0.5, -10.0)

- (-9.5, 0.5, 27.0)

- (-1.5, 0.5, 29.0)

Press Play and you'll see seven pickups spawn in the scene. Feel free to walk around and pick them up.

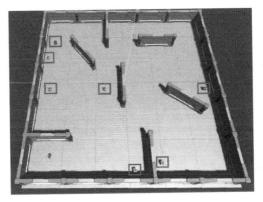

Robot spawning

Now that the pickups are spawning, you can work on the robots. Drag the **Teleporter** prefab from the **Resources** folder into the scene at ground level.

Create a C# script, name it **RobotSpawn**. Open it in your code editor and add the following variables after the opening brace of the class:

```
[SerializeField]
GameObject[] robots;

private int timesSpawned;
private int healthBonus = 0;
```

274 Unity Games by Tutorials

robots is an array of robot GameObjects to instantiate; these will be the red, yellow, and blue robots. healthBonus is how much health each robot gains each wave to make the game get harder as you go along. timesSpawned tracks the spawn cycle of the robots.

Next add the following method:

```
public void SpawnRobot() {
   timesSpawned++;
   healthBonus += 1 * timesSpawned;
   GameObject robot = Instantiate(robots[Random.Range(0,
robots.Length)]);
   robot.transform.position = transform.position;
   robot.GetComponent<Robot>().health += healthBonus;
}
```

SpawnRobot() spawns a robot, sets its health, then sets the robot's position. Save your work and switch back to Unity.

Drag the **RobotSpawn** script on to the **Teleporter** GameObject. Select the **Teleporter** GameObject in the Hierarchy, **lock** the Inspector, and drag the **RedRobot**, **YellowRobot**, and **BlueRobot** prefabs from the **Resource** folder onto the **Robots** field in the Inspector.

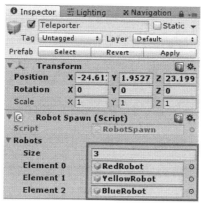

Hit **Apply** and **unlock** the inspector.

In the Hierarchy, create an **empty GameObject**, name it **RobotSpawns** and set its **position** to (**0, 0, 0**). Drag the **Teleporter** into the **RobotSpawns** and **duplicate** it three times by pressing Control-D (or Command-D on the Mac). Rename each of them **Teleporter**.

Starting from the top most **Teleporter** GameObject, set their positions to the following:

- **(-25.0, 0, -25.0)**

- **(25.0, 0, -25.0)**

- **(-25.0, 0, 28.0)**

- **(25.0, 0, 15.0)**

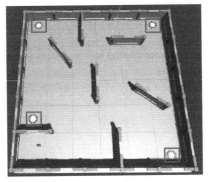

Want to make things challenging? Then add four more spawners!

In the next chapter you will add the logic to continually change waves. For now, you will simply spawn robots when you hit Play.

Create a C# script, name it **Game** and replace the contents of the file with the following:

```
private static Game singleton;

[SerializeField]
RobotSpawn[] spawns;

public int enemiesLeft;
```

This uses the **Singleton** pattern to have one and only one item; hence, a `singleton` GameObject reference. You only want one `Game` to track everything such as the score, the robots remaining and the current wave.

You'll add all that in the next chapter; for now, you'll spawn the robots just once.

`spawns` is the array of teleporters that spawn robots each wave, and `enemiesLeft` is a counter which tracks how many robots are still alive.

Now add the following methods below the final variable:

```
// 1
void Start() {
  singleton = this;
  SpawnRobots();
}

// 2
private void SpawnRobots() {
  foreach (RobotSpawn spawn in spawns) {
    spawn.SpawnRobot();
    enemiesLeft++;
  }
}
```

Here, you're doing the following:

1. Initialize the `singleton` and call `SpawnRobots()`.

2. Go through each **RobotSpawn** in the array and call `SpawnRobot()` to actually spawn a robot. You will see a warning that the singleton is 'initialized but not used'. Ignore this for now; it will be used shortly in the next chapter.

Save your work and switch back to Unity.

Create an **empty GameObject** and call it **Game**. Drag the **Game** script onto this GameObject.

Select the **Game** GameObject and **lock** the Inspector. Drag the **Teleporter** GameObjects on to the **Spawns** field. When done, **unlock** the Inspector.

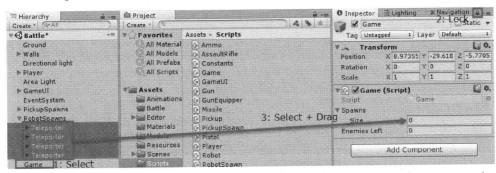

Click Play and you'll see four robots spawn. Feel free to blast them out of existence and grab some pickups while you're at it!

Adding sound

With the game mostly set up, it just needs a little sound.

Open the **Robot** script and add the following at the top:

```
[SerializeField]
private AudioClip deathSound;
[SerializeField]
private AudioClip fireSound;
[SerializeField]
private AudioClip weakHitSound;
```

Save your changes and head back to Unity. Select the **YellowRobot**, **RedRobot**, and **BlueRobot** Prefabs in the **Resources** folder by Shift-clicking (or Command-clicking on a Mac) and set the **Fire Sound** to **missile**, the **Death Sound** to **deadRobot**, and the **Weak Hit Sound** to **weakHitSound**.

Open **Robot** and add the following before the closing brace of **Fire()** to play the missile firing sound:

```
GetComponent<AudioSource>().PlayOneShot(fireSound);
```

Now, update `TakeDamage()` to play some sounds. Replace `if (health <= 0) {` with the following:

```
if (health <= 0) {
    isDead = true;
    robot.Play("Die");
    StartCoroutine("DestroyRobot");
    GetComponent<AudioSource>().PlayOneShot(deathSound);
} else {
    GetComponent<AudioSource>().PlayOneShot(weakHitSound);
}
```

Save the file and return back to Unity. Fire away and you'll hear lots of sounds!

Where to go from here?

That's it for this chapter; great job getting this far! If you ran into issues along the way you can always use the starter project in the next chapter, but it's always instructive to try and solve problems yourself first.

In the next chapter, you'll add the final layer of polish to the game with UI, more sounds, more animations, and some tweaked game mechanics like wave spawning.

Chapter 11: Introducing the UI

By Anthony Uccello

In the last chapter you got the pickups, robots spawning, and even some bullets flying. Now it's time to add the UI, wave spawning mechanics, enhanced sound and music, and doing extra damage by using the right gun for the right robot.

More importantly, you'll get an introduction into Unity's user interface system or otherwise known as the UI. This isn't the actual program itself, but rather, the tools used to create user interfaces in your games.

Pre-Unity 4.0, the UI tools were a disaster. For the most part, you had to write everything inside of `OnGui()` and as your UI grew in complexity, so did your code. Thankfully, Unity listened to developers and after many years, they released their new UI in Unity 4.6.

Getting started

In Chapter 9, "Making a First Person Shooter" you created a **Canvas** named **GameUI**. A Canvas is the root object for all UI elements. You used an overlay canvas, but there other options. For instance, a **world space** canvas allows you to create interfaces that can be accessed in your own game! Think of the computer terminals from Doom 3.

For a canvas to be useful, you needs control and Unity comes with plenty of them. The most common UI elements are **Image**, **Button**, and **Text**.

The canvas is indicated by a giant white box — and you'll notice it's huge!

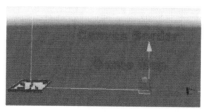

This is because the canvas is assuming 1 pixel of screen space to be 1 unit inside of Unity. The canvas pixel density can be changed using the **canvas scaler**.

The scalar has a property called **UI Scale Mode** with some interesting options.

- **Constant Pixel Size** means the UI elements are the same size, regardless of screen size.

- **Scale with Screen Size** means UI elements grow bigger with the screen.

- **Constant Physical Size** means the UI elements will always be the same size, regardless of screen size or resolution.

This one component determines how your UI will look on different screen sizes and resolutions. For the purposes of this chapter, you'll be using the default values. Although the canvas shares the same space, you can effectively ignore it. Like any other GameObject, you can always deactivate it to maintain a clear "desk space" so to speak.

An Image is a UI class of objects that lets you render an image on the screen via a **Sprite**. **Text**, quite logically, lets you render text on the screen. **Button** lets you configure hover and click events. You'll be using these throughout this tutorial.

So you may be wondering, how are controls placed? Unity uses **anchors** and they look like arrows pointing at each other.

An anchor acts like an anchor in real life: it keeps something in place. If wanted to position a UI element in the top left corner and always stay relative to that top left corner, then you would simply set its Anchor to **top left**.

Anchors also can stretch an control. This is useful if you want a control expand or contract based on the screen size. The anchor breaks into individual arrows to form a rectangle. This allows you to define the size of the stretching.

When talking about anchors it's important to understand what a **pivot** is. The pivot is the point on the Image that position is applied to, and it's what the Anchors use for keeping it locked in the right place. The pivot point is also the rotation point.

Having the pivot at the top left corner is the most common, but it can be useful to have the pivot set in various positions. For example, if you want something to be positioned in the top middle of the screen, setting the pivot to the top middle can make things a lot easier.

The pivot is set in normalized coordinates. This means that it goes from 0 to 1 for both height and width where (0,0) is the bottom left corner and (1,1) is the top right corner.

The pivot point is represented by a blue circle:

Through this chapter, you'll be setting the position and pivot points of various UI controls through the Inspector.

If you ever want to manually position controls, you can use the **Rect Tool**.

The Rect Tool is the Swiss Army knife of working with 2D. It allows you to scale, rotate, and even reset points. It even works with 3D objects as well although the tool was designed with 2D in mind.

You're about to create the UI, so the above theory will make perfect sense after you complete the section below. Load the **Battle** scene to start. If you need to start fresh, open the starter project in the resources.

Adding UI elements

You are going to create a bunch of Image and TextView UIGameObjects to go under the GameUI you created earlier.

Select the **GameUI** GameObject and in the Hierarchy, right-click, select **UI\Image** and rename it **BottomBar**. Select the image and look at the Inspector. You'll notice it has changed:

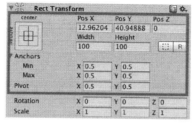

The position property has been replaced by a whole new set of properties that are specifically designed for the UI. This is called the **Rect Transform**.

Whenever you want to set the position of a control in code, you use the Rect Transfrom instead of the regular Transform.

To set this image at the bottom left of the screen, click the **anchor presets** box.

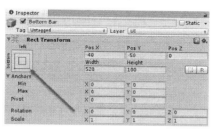

You'll get a whole bunch of options that corresponds to positions on the screen. Along the bottom and right hand side, you'll see stretching presets as well.

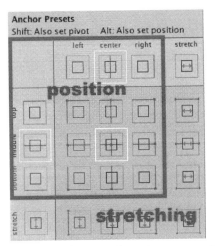

The keyword being: presets. You can do everything here manually by moving the anchor.

Time to get started. To set the position, click the **bottom left** preset.

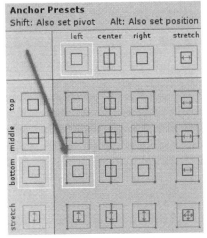

Set **Pivot** to (0, 0), **Pos** to (-40, -50, 0), **Width** to 520, **Height** to 100, and **Source Image** to Pink_Grey_Text.

You'll end up with an image in the lower left hand side of the Canvas like so:

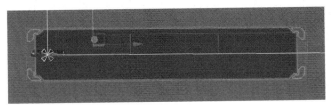

> **Note:** Since this is an overlay UI, it's helpful to switch the Scene view to isometric mode. In the Scene view, simply click the center cube in the gizmo to change modes, then click it again to return back to perspective mode.

The `Pos` fields work in relation to the anchor. In your case, you set the `PosY` to −50. This has the affect of lowering the image from the lower left hand corner of the canvas by −50.

At a later point you may switch presets. You can do this, but the control won't change its on-screen placement although the position numbers change. This is due to Unity calculating the control's new position relative to the new anchor point.

At this point, you'll have a lot of new elements to place to create the UI. First start with the images.

Here's the breakdown:

Type	Name	Anchor Preset	Pivot	Pos	Width	Height	Source Image
Image	TopRightBar	top right	(1, 1)	(40, 50, 0)	220	100	Pink_Grey_Texture
Image	TopLeftBar	top left	(0, 0)	(-40, -50, 0)	260	100	Pink_Grey_Texture

Once done, your UI should look like the following:

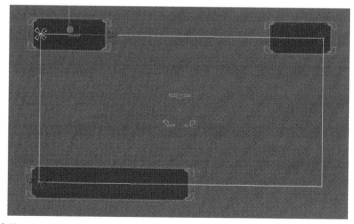

Now create following text items. To speed things up, use the duplicate key (Control-D or Command-D on the Mac).

Type	Name	Anchor Preset	Pivot	Pos	Width	Height	Text	Font	Font Style	Font Size	Color
Text	Ammo	bottom left	(0, 0.5)	(16.2, 19, 0)	138	37	Ammo: 0	heavy_data	Bold	25	White
Text	Health	bottom left	(0, 0.5)	(153.9, 19, 0)	162	37	Health: 100	heavy_data	Bold	25	White
Text	Armor	bottom left	(0, 0.5)	(315.9, 19, 0)	168	37	Armor: 20	heavy_data	Bold	25	White
Text	Score	top center	(0, 0.5)	(-105, -48, 0)	208	75.3	0	heavy_data	Bold	62	White
Text	PickupText	bottom right	(0, 0.5)	(-292.1, 44.9, 0)	288.4	77.5	Pickup Text	heavy_data	Bold	25	White
Text	WaveText	top left	(0, 0.5)	(15, -32, 0)	317	47	Next Wave: 30	heavy_data	Bold	25	White
Text	EnemyText	top right	(0, 0)	(-141, -55.5, 0)	317	47	Enemies: 4	heavy_data	Bold	25	White
Text	WaveClearText	top center	(0, 0.5)	(-155.3, -106, 0)	317	47	Wave Cleared	heavy_data	Bold	25	White
Text	NewWaveText	top center	(0, 0.5)	(-200, -164, 0)	434	47	New Wave ... Enemies are stronger!	heavy_data	Bold	25	White

After putting in all those values, you need to make a few more adjustments.

First, **center** align the following text GameObjects: **Score**, **WaveClearText**, and **NewWaveText**.

Next, **left justify** the **PickupText** GameObject.

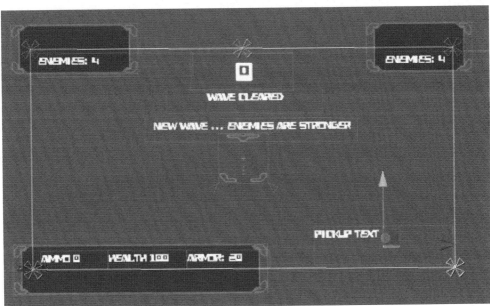

Lastly, disable the Text component on the following GameObjects: **PickupText**, **WaveClearText**, and **NewWaveText**.

Now play your game. Congrats! You have a brand new user interface!

Coding the UI

Open the **GameUI** script in the code editor and add the following variables right below the opening brace of the class:

```
[SerializeField]
private Text ammoText;
[SerializeField]
private Text healthText;
[SerializeField]
private Text armorText;
[SerializeField]
private Text scoreText;
[SerializeField]
private Text pickupText;
[SerializeField]
private Text waveText;
[SerializeField]
private Text enemyText;
[SerializeField]
private Text waveClearText;
[SerializeField]
private Text newWaveText;
[SerializeField]
Player player;
```

These are simply references that correspond to the the UI elements you created above and to the **Player** as well. Save your work and go back to Unity.

Select the **GameUI** and in the Inspector, you'll see all your new fields. Drag all the controls you created to these empty fields. Also, drag the **Player** GameObject to the **Player** field.

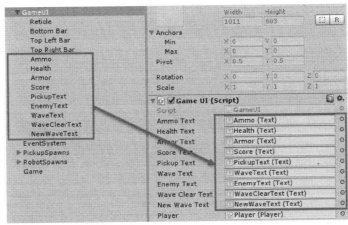

Open the **GameUI** script in the code editor and add the following to the bottom of the class:

```
// 1
void Start() {
   SetArmorText(player.armor);
   SetHealthText(player.health);
}

// 2
public void SetArmorText(int armor) {
   armorText.text = "Armor: " + armor;
}

public void SetHealthText(int health) {
   healthText.text = "Health: " + health;
}

public void SetAmmoText(int ammo) {
   ammoText.text = "Ammo: " + ammo;
}

public void SetScoreText(int score) {
   scoreText.text = "" + score;
}

public void SetWaveText(int time) {
   waveText.text = "Next Wave: " + time;
}

public void SetEnemyText(int enemies) {
```

```
    enemyText.text = "Enemies: " + enemies;
  }
```

Here's what's going on in the code:

1. Initializes the player health and ammo text.

2. This and the rest of the methods are simply setters that set the related text values.

Now to actually update the UI. To do this, you'll use coroutines. Coroutines were covered in the previous chapter so give it a read if you feel unsure of them.

Coroutines are perfect for the UI because you want to show some text for a few seconds and then hide them.

With this in mind, add the following methods to your **GameUI** script:

```
// 1
public void ShowWaveClearBonus() {
  waveClearText.GetComponent<Text>().enabled = true;
  StartCoroutine("hideWaveClearBonus");
}

// 2
IEnumerator hideWaveClearBonus() {
  yield return new WaitForSeconds(4);
  waveClearText.GetComponent<Text>().enabled = false;
}

// 3
public void SetPickUpText(string text) {
  pickupText.GetComponent<Text>().enabled = true;
  pickupText.text = text;
  // Restart the Coroutine so it doesn't end early
  StopCoroutine("hidePickupText");
  StartCoroutine("hidePickupText");
}

// 4
IEnumerator hidePickupText() {
  yield return new WaitForSeconds(4);
  pickupText.GetComponent<Text>().enabled = false;
}

// 5
public void ShowNewWaveText() {
  StartCoroutine("hideNewWaveText");
  newWaveText.GetComponent<Text>().enabled = true;
}

// 6
IEnumerator hideNewWaveText() {
```

```
    yield return new WaitForSeconds(4);
    newWaveText.GetComponent<Text>().enabled = false;
}
```

Taking each commented section in turn:

1. Show the wave clear bonus text by setting its `enabled` state to `true`, then immediately call a coroutine that will hide the text again. You do it this way because you can use the coroutine to pause itself before it actually hides the text.

2. Wait for 4 seconds before setting the `enabled` state to `false` — therefore hiding the text.

3. Enable and set the text for the pickup alert and restart the `hidePickup()` coroutine. This lets the player to pick up two or more pickups in quick succession, without the second pickup's text label displaying before the first pickup's text times out.

4. Wait for 4 seconds before removing the pickup text.

5. Show the new wave text.

6. Wait for 4 seconds before removing the new wave text.

Now that the **GameUI** script has the code necessary to update changes to the UI, you need to add in the code that calls this at the appropriate time.

Save your work and open the **Player** script. In `TakeDamage()`, under the line `armor = effectiveArmor / 2;` add the following:

```
gameUI.SetArmorText(armor);
```

Under the line `armor = 0`, add the line:

```
gameUI.SetArmorText(armor);
```

These lines will update the armor as it takes damage.

Replace the line `Debug.Log("Health is " + health);` with:

```
gameUI.SetHealthText(health);
```

This will update the health as it changes in the UI.

In `pickupHealth()` add the following just above the closing brace:

```
gameUI.SetPickUpText("Health picked up + 50 Health");
gameUI.SetHealthText(health);
```

This shows the pickup text alert and updates the health UI.

In `pickupArmor()`, add the following just above the closing brace:

```
gameUI.SetPickUpText("Armor picked up + 15 armor");
gameUI.SetArmorText(armor);
```

This shows the pickup text alert and updates the armor UI.

In `pickupAssaultRifleAmmo()` add the following just before the closing brace:

```
gameUI.SetPickUpText("Assault rifle ammo picked up + 50 ammo");
if (gunEquipper.GetActiveWeapon().tag == Constants.AssaultRifle)
{
  gameUI.SetAmmoText(ammo.GetAmmo(Constants.AssaultRifle));
}
```

First this alerts the player about the ammo pickup in the UI. Then the code checks to see if the active gun matches the assault rifle before setting the ammo count. If you didn't do this check, then every time you picked up ammo for a different gun it would change the ammo displayed to the wrong type.

Now add the code for the other ammo types.

Before the closing brace of `pickupPistolAmmo()` add:

```
gameUI.SetPickUpText("Pistol ammo picked up + 20 ammo");
if (gunEquipper.GetActiveWeapon().tag == Constants.Pistol) {
  gameUI.SetAmmoText(ammo.GetAmmo(Constants.Pistol));
}
```

Before the closing brace of `pickupShotgunAmmo()` add:

```
gameUI.SetPickUpText("Shotgun ammo picked up + 10 ammo");
if (gunEquipper.GetActiveWeapon().tag == Constants.Shotgun) {
  gameUI.SetAmmoText(ammo.GetAmmo(Constants.Shotgun));
}
```

Save your work. Open the **Ammo** script in the code editor and in `ConsumeAmmo()`, add the following before the closing brace:

```
gameUI.SetAmmoText(tagToAmmo[tag]);
```

This updates the UI each times the user fires his weapon.

Open the **GunEquipper** script in the code editor. Add the following below the other variable declarations:

```
[SerializeField]
Ammo ammo;
```

Now to use this variable. Add the following just before the closing brace in
`loadWeapon();`:

```
gameUI.SetAmmoText(ammo.GetAmmo(activeGun.tag));
```

This will update the ammunition count when the player switches guns. However, `ammo`
hasn't been assigned yet in the editor. Save your work and switch back to Unity.

Select the **Player** GameObject and drag it on top of the **Ammo** field on the
GunEquipper Component:

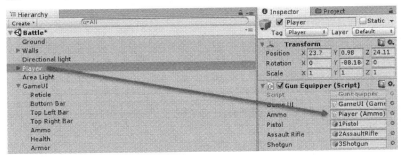

Open the **Game** script in the code editor and add the following variables just after the
opening brace of the class:

```
public GameUI gameUI;
public GameObject player;
public int score;
public int waveCountdown;
public bool isGameOver;
```

These are just some references and counter values you'll be using soon. One variable of
note is `isGameOver` which tracks whether the game has ended. You'll be coding the
Game Over screen a little later, but it's helpful to add this flag now.

Before editing the script further, save your work, go back to Unity, and click the **Game**
GameObject in the inspector.

Drag the **GameUI** GameObject over the **Game UI** field and drag the **Player**
GameObject over the **Player** field.

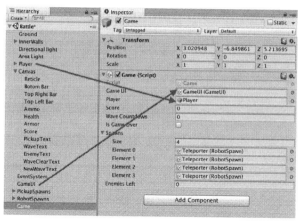

Open the **Game** script in the code editor. Add this import at the top under `using UnityEngine;`:

```
using System.Collections;
```

This import will let you use coroutines. Add this method below the closing brace of `SpawnRobots()`:

```
private IEnumerator updateWaveTimer() {
  while (!isGameOver) {
    yield return new WaitForSeconds(1f);
    waveCountdown--;
    gameUI.SetWaveText(waveCountdown);

    // Spawn next wave and restart count down
    if (waveCountdown == 0) {
      SpawnRobots();
      waveCountdown = 30;
      gameUI.ShowNewWaveText();
    }
  }
}
```

You first check to see if the `isGameOver` flag is set. If it isn't, the script will pause for 1 second before decrementing `waveCountdown` and updating the UI. If the countdown hits 0, you call the spawn robots method, reset the countdown then show the message telling the player that a new wave of robots is on its way!

Now add the following immediately below the method you just added:

```
public static void RemoveEnemy() {
  singleton.enemiesLeft--;
  singleton.gameUI.SetEnemyText(singleton.enemiesLeft);
```

```
    // Give player bonus for clearing the wave before timer is
done
    if (singleton.enemiesLeft == 0) {
        singleton.score += 50;
        singleton.gameUI.ShowWaveClearBonus();
    }
}
```

This will be called when robots are killed. It removes 1 from the enemy count and updates the UI. If there are no enemies left, it alerts the player about the bonus score they earned and adds 50 to their score.

The player should also get points every time they kill a robot. Add the following method just below the last one:

```
public void AddRobotKillToScore() {
    score += 10;
    gameUI.SetScoreText(score);
}
```

This will give the player points when they kill a robot.

The player should also get 1 point for every second they survive. Add the following method below the last one:

```
IEnumerator increaseScoreEachSecond() {
    while (!isGameOver) {
        yield return new WaitForSeconds(1);
        score += 1;
        gameUI.SetScoreText(score);
    }
}
```

This is just a coroutine that updates the score every second.

Start() now needs to be updated to set your new variables up. Add the following after the line containing singleton = this;:

```
StartCoroutine("increaseScoreEachSecond");
isGameOver = false;
Time.timeScale = 1;
waveCountdown = 30;
enemiesLeft = 0;
StartCoroutine("updateWaveTimer");
```

First you start increaseScoreEachSecond, then initialize all the variables to their starting values, before starting updateWaveTimer.

In SpawnRobots() add the following before the closing brace.

```
gameUI.SetEnemyText(enemiesLeft);
```

This sets the enemy count to the latest value after spawning new robots. Save your work and open **Robot.cs** in your code editor:

Here, you need to call the `RemoveEnemy()` method you just created. Add the following immediately after the call to `StartCoroutine("DestroyRobot")`:

```
Game.RemoveEnemy();
```

This will reduce the enemy count by 1 and update the UI. Save your change and switch back to Unity.

Great job getting here! Now you can reap the rewards of your hard labor and Hit Play.

Run around and kill robots and watch the enemies decrease. Notice your ammunition decreases when you fire and updates when you change guns or get a pickup. Also check out the text that notifies the player of the pickup they grabbed. Your health and armor also goes down when you get hit by robots.

You'll also see the new wave text alert, and the bonus you get from killing all the enemies before the wave timer ends. The wave timer will click down every second and spawn new enemies (and reset) when it hits 0.

Adding a Main Menu

You've almost finished the game; this next layer of polish will really make it shine.

First, you are going to add a main menu. In the **Scenes** folder, right-click, select **Create\Scene** and call it **MainMenu**.

Double-click the scene you just created to open it. Drag over the **RobotRampageTitle** Prefab from the **Resources** folder onto the **Hierarchy**.

Set its **Position** to (**15, -61, 538**), its **Rotation** to (**18.07, 180, 0**). This is just a good starting point that was picked when the game was being developed.

Create a **Canvas** like you've done before and name it **MenuUI** — remember how you handled **UI\Canvas** in the Hierarchy.

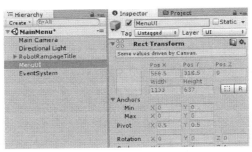

First, create you need to create a button. Right-click in the Hierarchy, select **Create\UI\Button** and rename it to **BeginButton**. Set the **anchor preset** to **bottom center**, **pivot** to (**0.5, 0.5**), **position** to (**0, 165.8, 0**), **width** to **260**, and **height** to **75**.

In the **Image** component, set the **Source Image** to **Pink_Grey_Texture**. In the **Button** component, set the **Transition** to **Sprite Swap**, set the **Highlighted Sprite** to **Pink_Black_Texture** and the **Pressed Sprite** to **Pink_Texture**.

The **Sprite Swap** transition means that different sprite images are used for the button, depending on its state.

The button should look like so:

In the Hierarchy, expand the arrow beside the **BeginButton** to reveal its child **Text** UIGameObject and select it.

Change the **Text** (in the **Text** Component) to **Begin**, set the color to **White**, the **Font Size** to **46**, and the **Font** to **heavy_data**.

Duplicate the previous button by pressing Control-D (or Command-D on the Mac). Call it **ExitButton** and set the **position** to **(0, 82, 0)**.

Expand the arrow beside the **ExitButton** to reveal its child **Text**. Change the **Text** to **Exit**. Your UI should like so:

This is a great looking scene, but it doesn't do anything yet! You will be bringing it to life by adding some callbacks to the buttons so that when they are clicked it either begins or exits the game.

Did you notice that a GameObject was created called **EventSystem** in the Hierarchy after you created the first **Button**?

EventSystem

This is how your UI buttons can be clicked to trigger events. The EventSystem GameObject listens for these click (or hover) events and dispatches them to something that needs to know that they've happened. You don't need to worry about how it dispatches its events, all that matters is how you intercept them.

Create a C# script, name it **Menu** and open it in the code editor. First, add this import line at the top of the script:

```
using UnityEngine.SceneManagement;
```

This allows you to use the **SceneManager** type. This is a class that allows you to manage your scenes such as loading, unloading, or even searching for a scene.

Now add the following methods to the body of the class:

```
// 1
public void StartGame() {
  SceneManager.LoadScene("Battle");
}
```

```
// 2
public void Quit() {
  Application.Quit();
}
```

1. This method will be used when the user clicks the Begin button; it simply loads the **Battle** scene.

2. This method will be used to exit the application. However, note that if you are running the game in Unity (instead of within a standalone build) this won't do anything.

With these methods set up, you can now configure the buttons to actually call them. Save your work and switch back to Unity.

Select the **MenuUI** GameObject and drag over the **Menu** script to it. Now, you must hook up the methods to the buttons.

Select the **BeginButton** GameObject and click the + in the **Button** Component.

This creates a UnityEvent which lets you call another function when this button is clicked. Drag the **MenuUI** UIGameObject over to the field just below the dropdown menu.

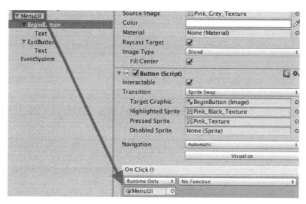

Now the right side dropdown menu will say **No Function**. Click this dropdown and select **Menu\StartGame()**. Now when this button is clicked it will call `StartGame()` in the **Menu** script which will load the battle scene.

Repeat this process for the **ExitButton** except set its callback function to the `Quit()` method.

Hit Play and hit the **Begin** button to load the game. However you might notice the game looks a lot darker. If the lighting looks fine, skip ahead to the Music section.

To fix this lighting issue open the **Battle** scene and open the **Lighting** window. Click the **Lightmaps** tab and, at the bottom, there will be an **Auto** checkbox. Uncheck this and click **Build**.

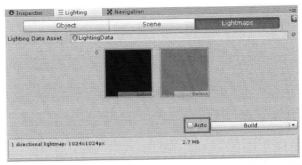

Open the **MainMenu** scene, hit **Play** and see that it loads the battle with the correct lighting.

Music

It would be awesome if this game had a soundtrack — that's what you'll do next.

In the **MainMenu** scene, create an empty GameObject and name it **BackgroundMusic**. Create a C# script, name it **BackgroundMusic** and open it in the code editor. Delete the boilerplate methods and replace them with the following method:

```
void Start() {
   DontDestroyOnLoad(gameObject);
}
```

This simply ensures the GameObject that the script is attached to isn't deleted when changing scenes so the music will keep playing when you switch to the Battle! You'll see this reflected in the Hierarchy when you play your game:

Save your changes. Back in Unity, drag this script over the **BackgroundMusic** GameObject.

Select the **BackgroundMusic** GameObject and add an **Audio Source** component. Set the **Loop** checkbox to **Selected** and set the **AudioClip** to **music**. Now hit Play and hit the Begin button and start killing robots with some epic tunes.

Game over

This game is almost done but it needs a game over screen. Open up the **Battle** scene (by double clicking it in the **Scenes** folder).

First, create a Panel by right-clicking in the **Hierarchy** and selecting **UI\Panel**. Rename it to **GameOverScreen**. Set its **Anchor Preset** to **middle center**, **Pos Y** to **0**, its **Width** to **400**, and its **Height** to **300**. Set the **SourceImage** in the **Image** Component to **Box** and set its **Alpha** to **1** (just click the **Color** box and slide the **A** over to the right.

A panel is just another UI controls which you can use to organize your controls. All subsequent UI controls will be **children** of the **GameOverScreen**.

Create a **Text** UIGameObject, rename it to **GameOverText** and put it under the **GameOverScreen** UIGameObject (by dragging to under it or by having it selected when you create the text). Set the **position** to **(0, 0, 0)**, the **Width** to **400**, the **Height** to **290**.

In the **Text** Component, set the **Text** to **Game Over**, the **Alignment** to **Center**, the **Font** to **heavy_data**, the **Font Size** to **70** and the **Color** to **White**.

The UI should look as follows:

Now create the following buttons.

Note: Once you create your first button, configure the text as explained underneath the table. Then duplicate the button to save yourself some time.

Type	Name	Position	Width	Height	Source Image	Transition	Highlighted Sprite	Pressed Sprite
Button	Restart	(0, 12, 0)	260	60	Pink_Grey_Texture	Sprite swap	Pink_Black_Texture	Pink_Texture
Button	Exit	(0, -34.5, 0)	260	60	Pink_Grey_Texture	Sprite swap	Pink_Black_Texture	Pink_Texture
Button	Menu	(0, -67, 0)	260	60	Pink_Grey_Texture	Sprite swap	Pink_Black_Texture	Pink_Texture

Next, you need to configure the text on all the buttons.

Expand the **Restart** GameObject and select its **Text** child. Change the **Text** to **Restart**, the **Font Size** to **22**, the **Font** to **heavy_data** and the **Color** to **White**.

Do this for both the **Exit** and the **Menu**, changing the actual text to **Exit** and **Menu** respectively.

Your UI will look as follows:

With the layout complete, you just need to hook it up in code.

Open the **Game** script, and before the class declaration add the following:

```
using UnityStandardAssets.Characters.FirstPerson;
using UnityEngine.SceneManagement;
```

You'll need these resources in just a moment. Add the following variable at the top of the script after the opening brace of the class;

```
public GameObject gameOverPanel;
```

Now add these methods to the body of the class:

```
// 1
public void OnGUI() {
  if (isGameOver && Cursor.visible == false) {
    Cursor.visible = true;
    Cursor.lockState = CursorLockMode.None;
  }
```

```
  }

  // 2
  public void GameOver() {
    isGameOver = true;
    Time.timeScale = 0;
    player.GetComponent<FirstPersonController>().enabled = false;
    player.GetComponent<CharacterController>().enabled = false;
    gameOverPanel.SetActive(true);
  }

  // 3
  public void RestartGame() {
    SceneManager.LoadScene(Constants.SceneBattle);
    gameOverPanel.SetActive(true);
  }

  // 4
  public void Exit() {
    Application.Quit();
  }

  // 5
  public void MainMenu() {
    SceneManager.LoadScene(Constants.SceneMenu);
  }
```

Here's the play-by-play:

1. This method frees the mouse cursor when the game is over so the user can select something from the menu.

2. This will be called when the game is over. It sets the `timeScale` to 0 so the robots stop moving. It also disables the controls and displays the Game Over panel you just created.

3. When the user wants to restart the game, this method will be used to reload the scene to start the game again.

4. This will be called when the user selects the Exit button. It quits the application, but only if its being run from a build.

5. You also need a method to go back to the main menu when the user selects the Menu button. This just loads the **Menu** scene.

Save your changes and switch back to Unity. Click the **Game** GameObject and drag over the **GameOverScreen** GameObject to the **Game Over Panel**.

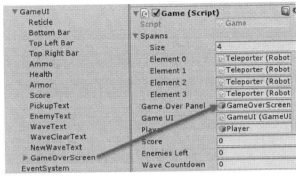

Now deactivate the **GameOverScreen** GameObject. This way, it only appears when the game is over.

Open the **Player** script, and add these variables after the opening brace of the class:

```
public Game game;
public AudioClip playerDead;
```

These are references to the **Game** script, and an **AudioClip** that you'll play when the player dies.

Replace Debug.Log("GameOver") with:

```
GetComponent<AudioSource>().PlayOneShot(playerDead);
game.GameOver();
```

This will play the **playerDead** audio and then call **GameOver** on the **Game** script.

Save your work and switch back to Unity.

Click the **Player** GameObject and drag over the **Game** to the **Game** field.

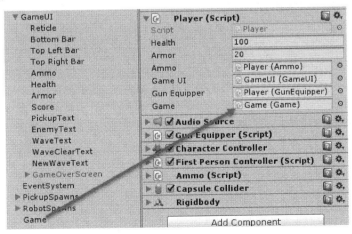

Next set **Player Dead** to the **playerDead** audio file.

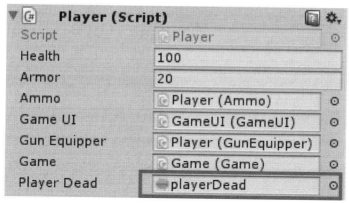

Now when the player's health reaches 0 it calls the game over screen and it plays a death sound.

The last thing to do is configure the button callbacks.

Click the **Restart** GameObject. Add an event by clicking the **+**. Next, drag the **Game** GameObject onto the field, and select **Game\RestartGame()** in the dropdown menu.

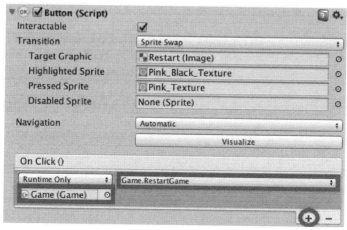

Do this two more times for both the **Exit** and **Menu** GameObjects. When selecting the methods, select **Game\Exit()** for the Exit GameObject, and **Game\MainMenu()** for the Menu GameObject.

Click Play, and blast away until your health reaches 0 to see the game over screen. You should hear the player scream as she dies.

Hit the **Menu** button while the game over screen is up — it's not working! Don't worry, it's simply a matter of adding the MainMenu scene to the build.

Open the **MainMenu** scene, select **File/Build Settings** and click **Add Open Scenes**.

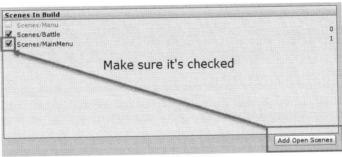

Now go back to the **Battle** scene by double clicking it in the **Scenes** folder, hit **Play**, and die again. With the game over screen open, click **Menu** and you should be taken to the **MainMenu** scene. Clicking **Restart** also should work just fine and reload the battle.

Where to go from here?

Congratulations! You've learned a lot in these last few chapters. From adding weapons and firing logic; to waves of enemies, spawning powerups and flying missiles; to scorekeeping, game over conditions and a full UI, you've created a fantastic and challenging FPS.

You've undoubtedly seen some adjustments you can make to the game. Play around with the map layout; add or change spawn positions, or even give powerups a limited lifespan on the map — you snooze, you lose!

There's a real art to creating FPS games that are intuitive enough to pick up easily, but take some time to master; games that are easy enough in the first few levels to hook players, but take repeated plays to learn the subtle strategy to conquer the game. The most important part of any game is to test-play it with a range of players to find the sweet spot that creates an addictive experience.

Happy blasting!

Section III: 2D Platformers

So far, you've been using Unity to make 3D games. But Unity provides advanced 2D support too, and that's the focus of this section.

Specifically, you'll learn how to use Unity to create a fast-paced 2D platformer where a vulnerable cube of tofu braves a terrifying gauntlet: **Super Soy Boy!**

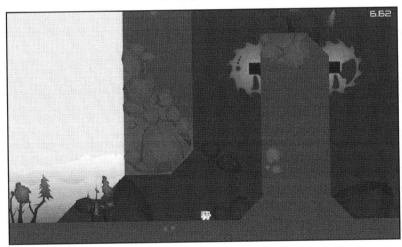

Chapter 12, "Beginning Unity 2D"

Chapter 13, "More Unity 2D"

Chapter 14, "Saving Data"

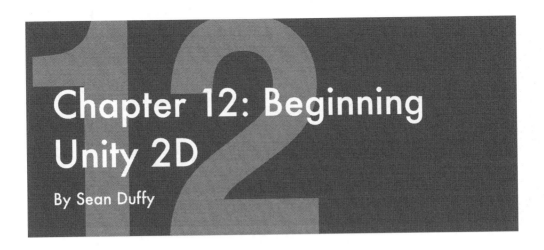

Chapter 12: Beginning Unity 2D

By Sean Duffy

So, you want to learn about creating 2D games with Unity? You're in the right place. In this chapter, you'll learn how to leverage Unity's 2D tools and components to create a game where a vulnerable cube of tofu braves a terrifying gauntlet.

You'll start by learning 2D fundamentals, and then move on to script a really fun platformer. Through it all, you'll learn how to tackle your own 2D projects with confidence!

The game is a **2D platformer** with super-tight controls. You'll navigate Soy Boy around obstacles while running, jumping and wall sliding. He's in a big hurry to reach a steaming bowl of noodles at the end of the level.

Although it's possible to take obstacles slowly and thoughtfully, the most enjoyable gameplay will come from passing levels in one fluid motion. This game is not about taking in the sights or carefully calculating your next move!

Getting started

Unity's extensive list of features and components empower you to create compelling 2D games. Aside from standard components such as sprites, animations and physics colliders, you also get specialized physics, joints and zone effector components. As you create Super Soy Boy, you'll explore the most common and useful 2D components. They generally work hand-in-hand with colliders.

To begin your 2D pilgrimage, open the **Starter** project for this chapter in Unity. It contains all the resources and sprites you'll need to get working. Load the **Game** scene located the **Scenes** sub-folder.

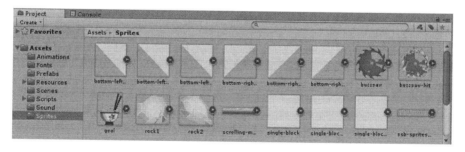

Sprites: building blocks of 2D games

All the sprites you'll need are in the **Assets\Sprites** sub-folder. Locate the **single-block.png** sprite in the Sprites sub-folder then drag and drop it into the **Scene** window.

Congratulations! You've created your first sprite. It's that simple.

Unity automatically created a GameObject, complete with an attached **SpriteRenderer** and assigned sprite texture. Look at the Inspector to confirm that the GameObject was created with a Transform and a SpriteRenderer component.

You might wonder what's up with the white sprites in the Sprites sub-folder. The answer is simple: you can easily color them dynamically in-game, or in the editor with your own color choice, without having to create several sprites for each color.

The single-block sprite will serve as a basic block for the ground — aka platform — that Super Soy Boy runs along. With that in mind, you'll color it brown to represent terrain.

In the Hierarchy, select the **single-block** GameObject and click **Color** in the Inspector to bring up a color picker.

Enter the hex value: **59443CFF** then close the color picker.

Because the sprite's base color is white, the new brown fills it perfectly.

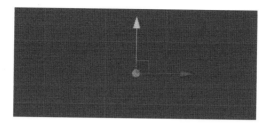

Note: You can manipulate a sprite the same way you manipulate any other GameObject in Unity. For example, you can change its scale, position and rotation using the Transform component and other Unity transform tools in the editor.

Sprites have two different modes: **Single** and **Multiple**.

You saw how to use single sprites when you created the single-block GameObject, but what about multiple mode sprites? They are special sprites that use a **spritesheet**, otherwise known as a **texture atlas**.

- **Single**: A single-image sprite.

- **Multiple**: A sprite with multiple elements. For instance, it might have several versions that you use to create frames — like different pages of a flipbook. Multiples may also comprise different parts, such as arms, legs and a torso.

That brings you to spritesheets. You use them because every image in your game takes up one draw call, which isn't a big deal if you're just working with a few dozen sprites. However, as your game grows in complexity and scope, singles can cause performance issues. With spritesheets, you make just one draw call for multiple sprites, thus reducing the cost to performance.

Super Soy Boy uses a multiple mode sprite so that animation state frames — running, jumping and sliding — are stored in one spritesheet.

Select the **SuperSoyBoySpriteSheet.png** sprite in the **Sprites** sub-folder then switch **Sprite Mode** to **Multiple**. Click **Apply**.

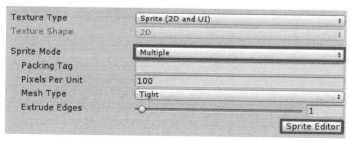

Click the **Sprite Editor** button to open its window. You'll see an enlarged view of the spritesheet.

You have a few options for slicing a spritesheet into individual sub-sprites. For this exercise, you'll use the **Grid By Cell Size** method but you will learn about the others in a few moments. With this method, you enter the pixel size of each "cut-out" sprite as well as offset and padding.

Click the **Slice** drop-down in the top-left of the Sprite editor and change **Type** to **Grid By Cell Size**. Set **Pixel Size** to (**48, 40**) and leave the other options as-is. All Soy Boy animation frames are 48 x 40 pixels. Hence, you're using the same values for grid slicing. Click **Slice** to, well, slice.

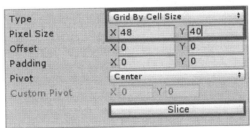

Look at the Sprite editor. You should see bounding boxes around the sprites that show where the grid slice was applied.

There should also be three rows of sprites. The top row contains all the **running** animation sprites, the middle row has **jumping**, and the bottom has a single **sliding** sprite.

Select **each sprite** in the Sprite editor and name accordingly:

- **Top row**: run_0, run_1, run_2, ..., run_14

- **Middle row**: jump_0, jump_1, jump_2, ..., jump_14

- **Bottom row**: slide_0

This naming convention makes it nice and obvious which frames belong to which animations.

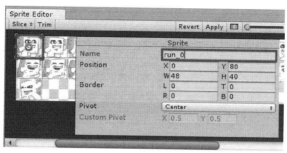

Click **Apply** to commit the slice changes to your sprite. **Close** the Sprite editor.

There are other slice modes that you won't use right now, but they're good to know about:

- **Automatic**: Attempts to locate and cut sprites up automatically by finding their bounding boxes. It's not always accurate when you're slicing complex shapes.

- **Grid By Cell Count**: You split your spritesheets into a defined number of columns and rows.

- **Grid By Cell Size (used above)**: You split based on the width and height of your sprites. As long as they're placed above and next to each other, this technique works well.

> **Note:** Sprites set to Multiple mode give you the option to expand them in the Project Browser and view the sliced sprites they contain.

Select **SuperSoyBoySpriteSheet.png** under the Sprites folder in the **Project Browser**. Click the **expansion triangle** to reveal the sliced sprites.

Click and drag the **run_0** sprite into the **Scene** view to create a new GameObject with the **run_0** sprite. In the Hierarchy, set the **name** to **SoyBoy**. This GameObject is the main character for your game.

Create one more sprite in the scene by dragging the **top-left-corner-small.png** sprite into the Scene view. Enter the hex value **59443CFF** in the color picker.

Position the sprites side-by-side, ensuring they are within the camera's view area in the **Scene** view, and start the game. You'll see the three sprites floating in space — they don't yet interact with the physics engine, so they know no gravity.

You just completed Sprites 101. Well done!

The 2D Orthographic camera

By default, 2D projects use an orthographic camera. Generally, you'll want to stick with it instead of using a perspective camera. Remember: orthographic cameras just render the game view so that objects near and far are the same size — perfect for 2D!

These are the properties of the current Main Camera in the scene.

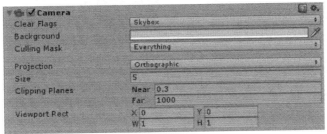

Notice **Projection** is set to **Orthographic** as discussed — you'll learn about the camera's size property in a bit. The other properties will stay at their defaults.

In the Project Browser, select the **single-block.png** sprite under the Sprites sub-folder, then take a look at the Inspector. You'll see that **Pixels Per Unit** is **100**.

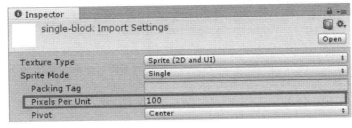

What does 100 really mean?

In Unity, units don't necessarily correspond to pixels on the screen. The convention is to size your objects relative to each other on some arbitrary scale, such as 1 unit = 1 meter.

Then Unity uses Pixels Per Unit to determine sprites' unscaled size in units.

Consider this: an imported sprite is 500 pixels wide. The following table will give you an idea of how the GameObject's width would change on the x-axis with different Pixels Per Unit settings at various x-scales.

Pixels to Units	X-scale	Width Calculation	Width
100	0.5	500 / 100 * 0.5	2.5 units
100	1.0	500 / 100 * 1.0	5.0 units
100	2.0	500 / 100 * 2.0	10.0 units
50	0.5	500 / 50 * 0.5	5.0 units
50	1.0	500 / 50 * 1.0	10.0 units
50	2.0	500 / 50 * 2.0	20.0 units

Now consider an example from your game. The single-block sprite is 100 x 100 px with a Pixels Per Unit value of 100. At a scale of 1 for X and Y, the single-block GameObject would be 1 unit wide and 1 unit tall.

Remember the `Size` property on the Orthographic Camera you saw a moment ago? With the Size set to 5, you would need to stack ten single-block sprites atop each other to reach from the bottom of the camera to the top of the camera's viewport. This is because Unity calculates the Orthographic size from the center of the screen to the top.

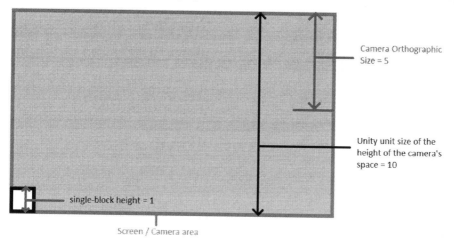

Camera Orthographic Size = 5

Unity unit size of the height of the camera's space = 10

single-block height = 1

Screen / Camera area

Scripting: Smooth camera follow

Scripting is an important part of working in Unity, and you'll start with a simple script that makes the camera follow the player around smoothly. Part of what makes it smooth is that you'll constrain it to a certain plane with X and Y boundaries.

Right-click the **Assets** folder in the Project Browser and select **Create\Folder**. Name the folder **Scripts**. Right-click the new folder and choose **Create\C# Script**. Name the new script **CameraLerpToTransform** then double-click it to open it in your editor.

Remove the empty `Start()` and `Update()` methods in the script template; this script does not require initialization and will use the `FixedUpdate()` method instead of `Update()` to follow the player because the physics engine will move the player.

Place the following code into the now-empty `CameraLerpToTransform` class:

```
// 1
public Transform camTarget;
public float trackingSpeed;
public float minX;
public float minY;
public float maxX;
public float maxY;

// 2
void FixedUpdate() {
  // 3
  if (camTarget != null) {
    // 4
    var newPos = Vector2.Lerp(transform.position,
                   camTarget.position,
                   Time.deltaTime * trackingSpeed);
    var camPosition = new Vector3(newPos.x, newPos.y, -10f);
    var v3 = camPosition;
    var clampX = Mathf.Clamp(v3.x, minX, maxX);
    var clampY = Mathf.Clamp(v3.y, minY, maxY);
    transform.position = new Vector3(clampX, clampY, -10f);
  }
}
```

1. These public variable fields let you specify the target the camera will track, tracking speed and the camera's bounds.

2. `FixedUpdate()` is called with every fixed-framerate frame — it's the best method when dealing with a Rigidbody component of any kind. The result is the camera will track the player, which will have a `RigidBody2D` attached to it.

3. This null check ensures that a valid Transform component was assigned to the `camTarget` field on the script in the editor.

4. `Vector2.Lerp()` performs linear interpolation between two vectors by the third parameter's value (a value between 0 and 1). Normally, you'd usually use this to move between positions over time, but here you actually slow tracking as you near the camera's target (Soy Boy). The rest of the Lerp method ensures that the position calculated is clamped (constrained) to the `MinX`, `MinY`, `MaxX`, and `MaxY` points.

Save the script and return to Unity.

Drag the **CameraLerpToTransform** script to the **Main Camera** GameObject in the Hierarchy.

Select the **Main Camera** in the Hierarchy. Drag the **SoyBoy** GameObject onto the **Cam Target** field on the **CameraLerpToTransform** script component, which is now attached to **Main Camera**.

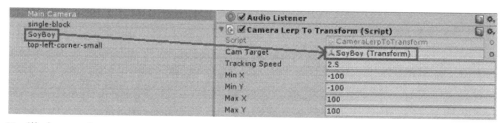

You'll also need to set **MinX**, **MinY**, **MaxX** and **MaxY** to temporary high and low values. You'll reset these constraints when you build a level in Chapter 13, "More Unity 2D".

For now, enter `-100` for **MinX** and **MinY** then `100` for **MaxX** and **MaxY**. Set the **Tracking Speed** to `2.5` — this determines how quickly the camera moves towards its target.

Run the game. Using the **Scene** view along with the move tool, move **SoyBoy** around with the mouse and notice how smoothly the camera follows the sprite. Awesome!

Adding 2D Physics

Right now, your sprites can't interact with the physics engine. They just float in the air. If there were to be a collision, the reaction would make you think you've created a strange alternate universe.

Unity's 2D physics system is similar to the 3D system. The main difference is that you use the 2D versions of each type of component.

These are the physics components you'll use in 2D games to let objects interact with the physics engine:

- **Rigidbody2D**: Puts a sprite or object under the control of the physics engine. You generally need one for every item that uses a collider.

- **BoxCollider2D**: Defines an axis-aligned rectangle collision area around an object.

- **CircleCollider2D**: Creates a circular collision area around an object.

- **PolygonCollider2D**: Makes an arbitrary polygon-shaped collision area around an object that's defined by vertices set up in different positions. They usually have more edges than other colliders, so they also come at a higher cost. Be careful with these!

- **EdgeCollider2D**: Represents an arbitrary set of connected edges defined by vertices.

The following diagram shows an example of each **Collider2D** component. The green lines represent the collision boundaries.

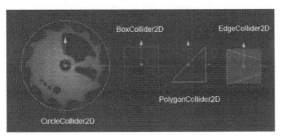

Setting up colliders

Now it's time to get your sprites to play nice with the 2D physics engine. Select the **single-block** GameObject in your scene. In the Inspector, click **Add Component** and choose **Rigidbody 2D** under the **Physics 2D** menu. Enable **Is Kinematic** because Soy Boy won't need to move any terrain — the blocks will be static.

Click **Add Component** again, and under **Physics 2D**, choose **Box Collider 2D**. Unity will add a **BoxCollider2D** component to the sprite and size it to the bounds of your sprite.

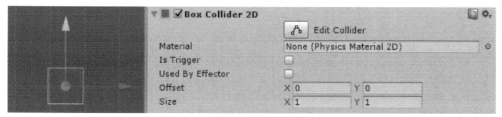

Excellent! Your single-block sprite can now interact with the 2D physics engine.

Note: If you run the game now, the single-block object won't fall with gravity just because you enabled "Is Kinematic". This property effectively locks an object in place, making it useful for static items or items that will be moved by their transform rather than the physics engine. Always enable this property for objects you plan to move without the help of the physics engine.

Select the **SoyBoy** GameObject in your scene then add a **Rigidbody 2D** component and an **Edge Collider 2D** component. *Don't* enable **Is Kinematic** on the rigidbody. Soy Boy will be subject to the forces of physics.

With **SoyBoy** still selected, look in the Scene view for a single green edge that represents the edge collider:

That's not going to cut it. You saw those blades, right?

Unless Soy Boy somehow makes contact with them on that little line — which is difficult given this is a 2D game — he'll avoid the fate of becoming shredded tofu.

Using the Inspector panel, expand the **Points** node on the **Edge Collider 2D** component and change the **Size** to 5 then press **Enter**.

Apply the following to each element's X and Y values:

- **Element 0**: (X:-0.23, Y:0.195)

- **Element 1**: (X:-0.23, Y:-0.192)

- **Element 2**: (X:0.225, Y:-0.192)

- **Element 3**: (X:0.225, Y:0.195)
- **Element 4**: (X:-0.23, Y:0.195)

Soy Boy should now look like this — you might need to select the **SoyBoy** GameObject in the Scene window again.

Polygon Colliders allow more flexibility when defining odd physics shapes, as you'll see in a moment.

There's a triangle block sprite in the starter project that makes a nice building block for levels. You added it to the scene earlier. Now you'll complete it by adding Rigidbody 2D and Polygon Collider 2D components to it.

Select the **top-left-corner-small** GameObject in your scene. As you did for the previous objects, add a **Rigidbody 2D**. These blocks will be part of the static platform and won't move, so enable **Is Kinematic**. Next, click **Add Component**. Under **Physics 2D**, choose **Polygon Collider 2D**.

Select the **top-left-corner-small** GameObject in the Scene view and look at how the collider edges align with the triangular shape.

Unity does a pretty good job with polygons, but sometimes you'll need a little different config. To learn how to adjust them, go to the **Inspector** and click **Edit Collider** on the **Polygon Collider 2D** component. Hover your mouse over the collider shape in the Scene. Drag the points and click the lines to make fine adjustments. When you're done playing, put the lines back on the edges.

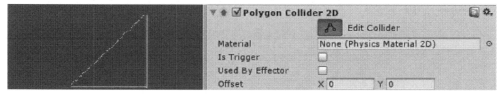

Locate **buzzsaw.png** in the Sprites folder and drag it into the **Scene** view.

Find the new buzzsaw GameObject that was created in the **Hierarchy** window and add a **Rigidbody 2D** and **Circle Collider 2D** component to it. Check **Is Kinematic** on the rigidbody.

Notice how you can change the circle collider's size with the **Radius** property.

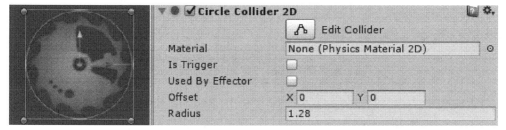

You now have your basic game sprites ready to interact with the Physics engine. Good going!

2D Animation

Sprites come to life with animation. Even a little bit goes a long way! One of Unity's strengths is that animation is fairly simple and flexible.

Creating animations for Soy Boy

The next phase of your Unity 2D journey is learning how to animate sprites, which you'll do by creating Soy Boy's animations — running, jumping and wall sliding!

First, you'll create the animations, and in Chapter 13, you'll write scripts to hook them up with triggers, so they work during gameplay. In this chapter, you'll script the running animation and do some other pre-work for the character controller.

In the Hierarchy, click **SoyBoy** then open the **Animation** editor. You may need to use the **Window\Animation** menu option to display it. Click the **Create** button in the **Animation** editor. You should see the **Create New Animation** dialog.

Make a new subfolder named **Animations** under **Assets** in the Project Browser, then save the animation to the new sub-folder in the dialog. Name it **RunAnimation.anim**.

The Animation editor will switch to a timeline view that has RunAnimation.anim ready for editing. Your task is to make that little cube of tofu run! You'll use the run sprites you sliced up earlier and the **SuperSoyBoySpriteSheet.png** spritesheet.

> **Note:** Unity actually created two files in the Animations folder. `RunAnimation.anim`, the file you're editing, and an Animation Controller called `SoyBoy.controller` that helps control animation states.

With the **SoyBoy** GameObject selected and the Animation window open, navigate to the Sprites folder in the **Project Browser**.

Expand **SuperSoyBoySpriteSheet.png** to reveal the sliced sprites. Select **run_0**, press and hold **Shift** then click **run_14** to select all. Drag and drop the whole lot onto the **RunAnimation** window timeline.

Drag the run sprites and release them here

They should be laid out on the timeline in order, from **run_0** to **run_14**.

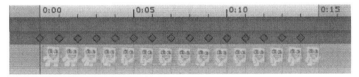

Click the red **stop** button next to the timeline in the Animation window. The animation is complete.

Float the **Animation** editor and position it next to the **Scene** view. Click the **Play** button in the Animation window and watch the **SoyBoy** animation preview. It will loop. Be careful, Soy Boy can lure you in with those doughy eyes!

Click **Play** again to stop the animation.

That's how you make tofu run. Next up is making it jump, slide on walls, and idle.

With the Animation timeline editor still open, click the drop-down that shows the current **RunAnimation**. Click **Create New Clip**.

Save it as **JumpAnimation.anim** in the **Animations** folder. Notice you have the new **JumpAnimation.anim** file, but no new **Animation Controller**. Unity detects the **SoyBoy.controller** and is intelligent enough to realize that an animation controller already exists for this GameObject.

Locate the jump animation sprite frames — **jump_0** to **jump_14** under **SuperSoyBoySpriteSheet.png** in the Project Browser. Drag and drop them into the timeline. Click **record** to end recording.

Two down, two to go. Create another animation clip, but this time, name it **SlideAnimation.anim**. Save it in the **Animations** folder.

Follow the same steps as you did for the previous two animations, by dragging and dropping the only slide sprite into the Animation window. Remember to click **record**.

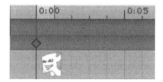

Soy Boy is an active little tofu chunk, so he doesn't stand like a statue when idle. When he's doing nothing, **run_0** will loop constantly.

Create and name the last animation **IdleAnimation.anim** then save it to the **Animations** folder.

Drag and drop *just* **run_0** from the **SuperSoyBoySpriteSheet.png** sprite sheet onto the animation timeline for **IdleAnimation**. Don't forget to click the **Stop** button.

Well done! Soy Boy's animations are all set up.

Open the **Animator** editor — find it under **Window\Animator** from the top menu — and select the **SoyBoy** GameObject in the Hierarchy. This will display the layout of the **SoyBoy.controller** where you'll hook up the animation states shortly, but not yet.

Notice how the four clips are there, as well as a default **Entry** state that moves straight onto the **RunAnimation** clip.

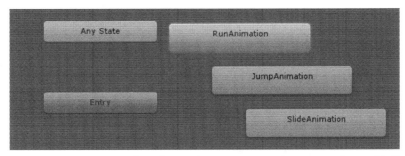

I know you're eager to preview, but first, select **SoyBoy** and temporarily enable **Is Kinematic** on the **Rigidbody 2D** component. If you don't do this, then gravity will drop that little chunk of tofu into the infinite editor void when the game starts!

Play the game in the editor so you can see how Soy Boy runs the moment the game starts. Somebody wants noodles!

Uncheck **Is Kinematic** after previewing the animation.

> **Note:** In Chapter 13, "More Unity 2D", you'll link these three animation states and write code to transition between them based on the player's actions.

Layers and sorting

When arranging sprites on screen in a 2D environment, you don't work with a Z-axis like you do in 3D. Instead, you think in terms of **Sorting Layers** and **Order in Layer**.

Think of this concept as pieces of glass stacked atop each other sprites between each layer. You're viewing the stack from the top, so what's visible and hidden depends on the stack order.

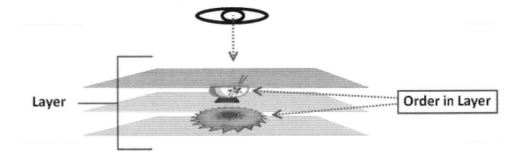

Arranging sprites is also similar to working with layers when you're editing photos.

Unity uses the order to sort sprite visibility first. Then within each layer, it sorts sprites further with an order number such as 0, 1, 2 and so on, with 0 being the very bottom sub-layer.

Unity places new sprites on the **Default** sorting layer with an **Order in Layer** number of 0. If you set a stack of sprites in the same location but don't change this, then you'll get a little rendering dance. Because they're sharing the same layer and order, some sprites might be hidden while others randomly appear and disappear.

It's a best practice to define custom sorting layer names and assign sprites to the right orders as you create them.

Navigate to **Edit\Project Settings\Tags and Layers** to bring up the Tags and Layers editor in the Inspector.

Expand the **Sorting Layers** node. Click the + button three times to add three sorting layers. Name them **Background**, **Hazards** and **Foreground**.

The order in which layers appear in this editor determines their render order. Use the handle icons to the left of each layer to drag and re-order so they match the image below:

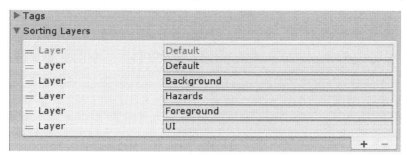

There's a little logic quirk here: The *higher* in the stack, the *lower* it renders on screen. For instance, the **Background** layer will render near the bottom of the stack, and the **UI** layer will render above everything else.

You'd probably like to know what each layer does in the game:

- **Default**: A default layer provided by Unity.

- **Background**: Background sprites, such as mountains, scenery or background blocks that don't obstruct the player's path will go here.

- **Hazards**: Hazards and traps such as the saw blade will go in this layer.

- **Foreground**: Soy Boy will be placed here along with most level objects.

- **UI**: Another default layer that's specifically for rendering UI elements such as buttons and canvases.

As it stands now, your sprites will almost certainly do a funky rendering dance on screen.

But now you know what causes it and probably have some idea of how to fix. In the next few steps, you'll reorganize the sprites with Sorting Layers.

Select the **SoyBoy** GameObject in the scene. In the Inspector, look for the **Sprite Renderer** component. Change the **Sorting Layer** from **Default** to **Foreground** and change the **Order in Layer** to 1.

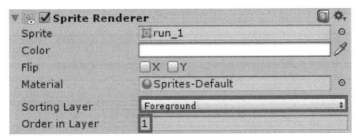

You use a rendering order of 1 for Soy Boy because he'll share the Foreground layer with all the level building blocks — you'll see this when you construct a level. Building blocks will all use an Order in Layer value of 0. Therefore, Soy Boy will always render above the building blocks.

Next, select the **buzzsaw** GameObject in the scene and adjust the **Sprite Renderer** to use the **Hazards Sorting Layer** with an **Order in Layer** value of 1.

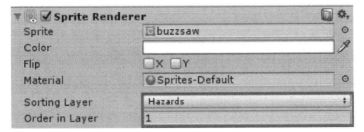

Lastly, select the **single-block** and **top-left-corner-small** GameObjects and change **Sorting Layer** to **Foreground** and **Order in Layer** to 0.

Use the **move** tool to arrange the sprites in the Scene view so they overlap slightly, like below, to check your ordering.

All the sprites appear to be in the correct order. **Foreground** sprites are on top, and the **Hazard** layer is below. The **Order in Layer** setting for Soy Boy renders him in front of the blocks in spite of the fact that they share the **Foreground** layer.

The background layer is not there yet, but you can use it later to add some ornamental scenery to the level. It will sit behind everything else when rendered.

Prefabs and Resources

Prefabs are essential to fluid gameplay. Rather than creating hundreds (thousands?) of sprites during the game, which nibbles away at processing power, Unity can use prefabs as templates to create various GameObjects on demand.

In the case of Super Soy Boy, you'll use prefabs to create levels. They'll consist of multiple copies of a base set of level blocks and shapes. Then you'll just clone these prefabs to make new levels.

Unity has a `Resources` class that lets you access assets in your project via code — any assets placed in a sub-folder of the Assets folder that bears the name `Resources` can be accessed via `Resources.Load()` methods.

You're exploring the resources class now because you'll create your own code for level saving and loading that'll let you save a new level to a special .JSON file. This file will keep references to items used to create the level, e.g., blocks and hazards.

It's impractical to add public fields for every block prefab used in a level. The .JSON file will call the `Resources.Load()` methods to find the referenced objects by name.

A folder named **Resources** is already in the root of the starter project. Find it and create a sub-folder inside named **Prefabs**. Now you'll create the first few prefabs.

One-at-a-time, drag the **single-block**, **top-left-corner-small**, **buzzsaw**, and **SoyBoy** GameObjects from the Hierarcy, and then drop them into the new **Prefabs** folder.

Unity will always include resource items in game builds, whether they end up being used or not. It's important to know because they can sneakily increase your build size.

Scripting basic controls

You're nearing the end of this chapter! But before you get there, you need to dive into scripting so you can implement Soy Boy's animations. He's dying to show you just how nimble a little tofu chunk can be!

Scripting isn't hard, but it's good to ease into it when you're learning. As such, you'll start with some validation for the GameObject, then layer in more script to get him facing the right direction, and then you'll get him running.

Hold on there...does he even have any ground to run on? Not last time you checked. Remember that you had to enable Is Kinematic just to preview his running animation? Before you write one line of code, you need to give Soy Boy some stable footing.

In the **Scene** view, make seven clones of the **single-block** GameObject prefab and set them next to each other in a line.

Select the **single-block** prefab in the Hierarchy by pressing **Control + D** on PC or **Command + D** on Mac then drag the clone left or right in the scene to snap it to one-unit spaces. Move **SoyBoy** above the line of **single-block** GameObjects so that he falls onto them when the game starts.

> **Note:** Matching up the corners of the 2D blocks can be a little tedious. Thankfully, you have vertex snapping to help you out. First select a sprite, hold **V** and select a vertex (a corner of the sprite). Now, drag the sprite, still holding V, and it will snap to any nearby vertex. Pretty convenient!

In the **Project Browser**, right-click the **Scripts** folder and create a new **C# Script**. Name it **SoyBoyController**. Double-click it to open the script in your editor.

At the top of the script, just above the `public class SoyBoyController` definition, add the following:

```
[RequireComponent(typeof(SpriteRenderer), typeof(Rigidbody2D),
typeof(Animator))]
```

This line validates that any GameObject attached to this script has the minimum necessary components required to work — it basically pre-qualifies the components. Your **SoyBoy** GameObject meets the requirement so it will pass with flying colors.

This is a handy script-writing trick that ensures the script only applies to GameObjects that meet the requirements.

Now you need property fields that hold useful values and cache component references for later use. Add the following variables inside the `SoyBoyController` definition but above the `Start()`:

```
public float speed = 14f;
public float accel = 6f;
private Vector2 input;
private SpriteRenderer sr;
private Rigidbody2D rb;
private Animator animator;
```

The `speed` and `accel` floats hold pre-defined values to use when calculating how much force to apply to Soy Boy's rigidbody. You make these public so you can easily tweak them in the editor; for instance, you could use them to change the feel of the controls.

The `Vector2 input` field stores the controller's current input values for x and y at any point in time. Negatives mean the controls are going left (-x) or down (-y), and positives mean right (x) or up (y).

The last three private fields cache references to the SpriteRenderer, Rigidbody2D and Animator components. These prevent you from having to find these references repeatedly during the `Update()` method loop. This approach simply prevents unnecessary variable assignment iterations that could negatively impact performance.

Now you'll create a new method called `Awake()`. Add the following just above the existing `Start()` method.

```
void Awake() {
   sr = GetComponent<SpriteRenderer>();
   animator = GetComponent<Animator>();
   rb = GetComponent<Rigidbody2D>();
}
```

In short, this ensures component references are cached when the game starts.

More specifically, it locates the specified component types on the GameObject upon which **SoyBoyController.cs** sits and assigns them to the three fields. With this, you reap the benefits of using the `RequireComponent()` class attribute.

To bring it full circle, consider this: If you didn't enforce required component types and the GameObject didn't have one or more of these components, then Awake() would fail when it tried to locate the missing component(s)!

Now to make sure Soy Boy knows what direction to face. You'll use Unity's Input class to interpret user input and so you can change the direction Soy Boy's sprite faces.

Add the following code to Update():

```
void Update() {
  // 1
  input.x = Input.GetAxis("Horizontal");
  input.y = Input.GetAxis("Jump");
  // 2
  if (input.x > 0f) {
    sr.flipX = false;
  }
  else if (input.x < 0f) {
    sr.flipX = true;
  }
}
```

1. Input.GetAxis() gets x and y values from the built-in Unity control axes named **Horizontal** and **Jump**. These values will either be −1, 0, or 1, depending on whether the controls are left, right, up, down or neutral. The value is held in the x and y properties of the input variable, which is a Vector2.

2. If input.x is greater than 0 then the player is facing right, so the sprite gets flipped on the X-axis. Otherwise, the player must be facing left, so the sprite is set back to "not flipped".

Save the script and return to Unity.

Add the newly created **SoyBoyController** script to the **SoyBoy** GameObject in your scene, and click the **Apply** button in the Inspector to update the **SoyBoy** prefab.

Run the game and press left or right (or A and D) on the keyboard to see Soy Boy switch directions.

Now to let Soy Boy run around.

Open the script **SoyBoyController.cs** and add the following code:

```
void FixedUpdate() {
  // 1
  var acceleration = accel;
  var xVelocity = 0f;
  // 2
  if (input.x == 0) {
    xVelocity = 0f;
  }
  else {
    xVelocity = rb.velocity.x;
  }
  // 3
  rb.AddForce(new Vector2(((input.x * speed) - rb.velocity.x)
    * acceleration, 0));
  // 4
  rb.velocity = new Vector2(xVelocity, rb.velocity.y);
}
```

1. Assign the value of `accel` — the public float field — to a private variable named `acceleration`. This might seem redundant right now, but later you'll see `acceleration` used to hold ground and air acceleration values, so it's important to define it now.

2. If horizontal axis controls are neutral, then `xVelocity` is set to `0`, otherwise `xVelocity` is set to the current x velocity of the `rb` (aka Rigidbody2D) component.

3. Force is added to `rb` by calculating the current value of the horizontal axis controls multiplied by `speed`, which is in turn multiplied by `acceleration`. Both speed and acceleration values are pre-defined values from the public float fields declared at the top of the script. `0` is used for the y component, as jumping is not yet being taken into account.

4. Velocity is reset on `rb` so it can stop Soy Boy from moving left or right when controls are in a neutral state. Otherwise, velocity is set to exactly what it's currently at. This has the effect of stopping Soy Boy quickly, even from a full run.

Save the script and run the game to try it out!

He's running! But you might notice that when he hits an object or falls far enough, Soy Boy rotates or spins. It happens when force is applied to a collider edge. It adds just enough movement to trigger a spin.

To fix this, you just need to lock the RigidBody's Z-rotation.

Select the **SoyBoy** GameObject, locate the RigidBody2D component and expand the **Constraints** node. Check **Freeze Rotation** for **Z** to lock the RigidBody2D's rotation in 2D. **Apply** the changes to the **SoyBoy** prefab when prompted.

▼ Constraints
    Freeze Position   ☐X ☐Y
    Freeze Rotation   ☑Z

Tweaking the gravity settings

The last tweak will be more noticeable once you've added jumping capabilities, but even now, the current gravity setting is a bit floaty to be considered a "super-tight" character controller.

By default, Unity 2D projects use a gravity setting of (X:0, -9.81) — that means no sideways gravity and a downward force of -9.81. You want a downward gravity force of -30.

Navigate to **Edit\Project Settings\Physics 2D** in the top menu. Change **Y** to **-30**.

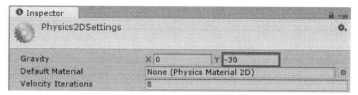

This will make the controls "feel" better, at least they will when you've finished the character controller script in the next chapter.

Finally, select the **SoyBoy** GameObject in the Hierarchy and change the **Collision Detection** on the **RigidBody2D** component to **Continuous**.

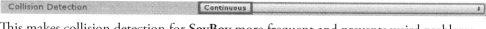

This makes collision detection for **SoyBoy** more frequent and prevents weird problems like getting stuck in the floor when you jump from a very high platform.

Apply the changes to the **SoyBoy** prefab and save the project.

Where to go from here?

Congratulations are in order! You've learned many of the fundamentals for building a solid 2D game in Unity. You've also set up the framework for activity in the next chapter.

So far, you've learned:

• **Sprites**: How to manipulate, edit, animate and arrange them on separate layers.

- **Orthographic camera**: what it is, why use it for 2D games, and how to script it so it follows the action around smoothly.

- **2D Physics**: How to get objects to collide in-game.

- **Resources**: How they can be useful for dynamically loading objects that you may or may not use in-game.

- **Scripting**: You made a basic 2D character controller with left and right movement and oriented the character according to user input

In the following chapter, you'll take things through to completion and finish this 2D platformer game. You'll build out your character controller with jumping, wall jumping, sliding and air control. You'll also hook up those sweet animations you created earlier in this chapter, so they fire off when certain actions are performed in-game.

Chapter 13: More Unity 2D

By Sean Duffy

In the previous chapter you learned some of the basics around the 2D workflow in Unity and began creating the building blocks required to complete your final 2D platformer game.

In this chapter, you will be going into more detail in a variety of different 2D areas the engine offers, including: physics, raycasting, animation controllers, scripting and level creation. These topics will teach you the fundamentals necessary to create your own 2D games.

With that said, you'll now continue your journey of creating the Super Soy Boy game.

Getting started

Open the starter project for this chapter in Unity. Open the **Game.unity** scene located under the **Scenes** folder.

The starter project leaves off exactly where you left things after chapter 11, but with the remaining building block items created for you under the **Resources/Prefabs** folder.

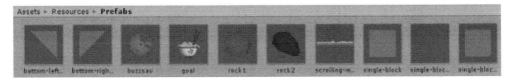

Setting up Physics 2D layers

To get started, you need to setup the layer collion matrix. You can learn more about this matrix in Chapter 4 "Physics".

Configuring the Layer Collision Matrix

Click **Edit\Project Settings\Tags & Layers** to open the **Tags & Layers** Inspector.

Unity provides you with a series of **User Layers** that you can use to define your own custom collision layers, in addition to the default built-in layers.

Use **User Layer 8** and **User Layer 9** to create two new layers called **Player** and **Hazards**.

The player will be placed on the **Player** layer, and the saw blades will use the **Hazards** layer.

Click **Edit\Project Settings\Physics 2D** to open the **Physics2DSettings** Inspector. At the bottom you will see the **Layer Collision Matrix**. Expand it if it is not already shown.

You will see that Unity has added your two new layers (**Player and Hazards**) to the matrix.

Uncheck the boxes where **Hazards** intersects with **Hazards**, and ensure the box is checked for where **Player** intersects with **Hazards**. Make sure the box where **Default** intersects with **Hazards** is also unchecked.

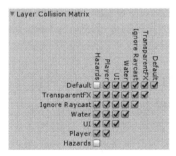

The reasons for these changes are:

- **Hazards intersection with Hazards removed**: This prevents saw blades that are placed close together (or overlapping) from performing collision checks, or hitting each other in the physics engine, and can help increase performance.

- **Player intersection with Hazards enabled**: This ensures that the player can interact with or touch hazards.

- **Default intersection with Hazards removed**: You will be leaving all the level / platform building blocks on the **Default** layer, so you do not want the hazards to be collision checking against these. Usually the saw blades will be "embedded" or placed behind platform blocks, so disabling collisions here will also save on performance.

In the **Game** scene, select **SoyBoy** and change the GameObject layer to the new **Player** physics layer. Click **Apply** to update the prefab instance too.

Completing the 2D character controller

Up until now, Soy Boy has only been able to move left and right and face in those directions. You'll now get to code the meat of the controller to provide the complete range of platformer movement actions.

A note on 2D raycasting

2D raycasting will be used in your character controller to determine when you are touching the ground, jumping, up against a wall, and so on.

Raycasting in 2D is done with the `Physics2D.Raycast()` method. This method returns the **RaycastHit2D** type, which references the first **Collider2D** object that the ray hit. If the ray does not hit anything then the collider reference is null.

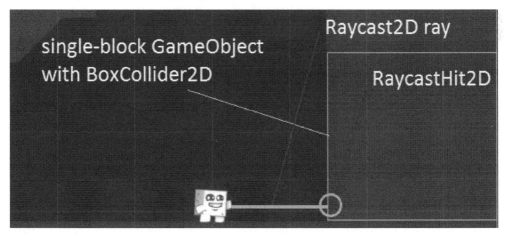

In the example above, a raycast is being performed from Soy Boy, to his right. The ray hits a `Collider2D` object. In code, a `RaycastHit2D` object would be returned, and the `collider` property on this would contain a reference to the object's `BoxCollider2D`.

Scripting the controller for jumping and wall sliding

The first bit of extra functionality you will add is the ability to perform a basic jump.

Open **SoyBoyController.cs** in your code editor, and add the following, new public fields to the top of the script, just below the other existing fields.

```
public bool isJumping;
public float jumpSpeed = 8f;
private float rayCastLengthCheck = 0.005f;
private float width;
private float height;
```

At the bottom of the Awake() method, add the following code:

```
width = GetComponent<Collider2D>().bounds.extents.x + 0.1f;
height = GetComponent<Collider2D>().bounds.extents.y + 0.2f;
```

Here, you grab the width and height of SoyBoy's sprite. In addition to these dimensions, you also add 0.1 and 0.2 to the width and height of the sprite respectively. This just gives a little bit of a buffer, to allow the raycast checks later on to start outside of the sprite, rather than inside the sprite bounds.

Remember that this script is attached to SoyBoy, so the GetComponent calls will search for these components on the SoyBoy GameObject.

You will now perform two checks before allowing the player to actually jump. A check to see if they are not currently jumping, and a check to ensure they are currently touching the ground.

Add the following new method to **SoyBoyController.cs**, just below the existing (empty) Start() method:

```
public bool PlayerIsOnGround() {
  // 1
  bool groundCheck1 = Physics2D.Raycast(new Vector2(
    transform.position.x, transform.position.y - height),
    -Vector2.up, rayCastLengthCheck);
  bool groundCheck2 = Physics2D.Raycast(new Vector2(
    transform.position.x + (width - 0.2f),
    transform.position.y - height), -Vector2.up,
    rayCastLengthCheck);
  bool groundCheck3 = Physics2D.Raycast(new Vector2(
    transform.position.x - (width - 0.2f),
    transform.position.y - height), -Vector2.up,
    rayCastLengthCheck);
  // 2
  if (groundCheck1 || groundCheck2 || groundCheck3) {
    return true;
```

```
    }
  else {
    return false;
  }
}
```

1. The first ground check performs a Raycast directly below the center of the the character (transform.position.x), using a length equal to the value of `rayCastLengthCheck` which is defaulted to `0.005f` — a very short raycast is therefore sent down from the bottom of the `SoyBoy` sprite. The other two ground checks do exactly the same thing, but slightly to the left and right of center. These three raycast checks allow for accurate ground detection.

2. If any of the ground checks come back as true, then this method returns true to the caller. Otherwise it will return false.

Three raycast checks for the ground

Note: RaycastHit2D has an implicit conversion to bool, so you can check if the raycasts done in the code above hit something below the player or not. What this means is that even though `Physics2D.Raycast()` returns a **RaycastHit2D** object, by implicitly checking it like you would a boolean value, you can see if there was a hit or not. The ground check variables will be true or false, depending on whether any of the raycasts hit something or not.

At the bottom of your existing `Update()` method, add the following code:

```
if (PlayerIsOnGround() && isJumping == false) {
  if (input.y > 0f) {
    isJumping = true;
  }
}
```

This code calls the `PlayerIsOnGround()` method to determine if the player is touching the ground or not (true or false). It also checks if the player is not already jumping. If both of these conditions are met, then it performs an inner check to see if there is any input for jumping from the controls (`input.y > 0f`). If so, the `isJumping` boolean variable is set to true.

Before you add force to Soy Boy to allow him to jump, you need a way to control how high he should jump, based on how long the jump button is held on for. This will allow for some very accurate jumps over or around obstacles, depening on how close or far they are spread out.

Add the following new fields to the top of the class:

```
public float jumpDurationThreshold = 0.25f;
private float jumpDuration;
```

At the bottom of the `Update()` method, add the following:

```
if (jumpDuration > jumpDurationThreshold) input.y = 0f;
```

This checks for `jumpDuration` being longer than the `jumpDurationThreshold` (0.25 seconds). If the jump button is held in longer than `0.25` seconds, then the jump is effectively cancelled, meaning the player can only jump up to a certain height.

Now at the bottom of `FixedUpdate()`, add the following:

```
if (isJumping && jumpDuration < jumpDurationThreshold) {
    rb.velocity = new Vector2(rb.velocity.x, jumpSpeed);
}
```

This gives Soy Boy's rigidbody a new velocity if the user has pressed the jump button for less than the `jumpDurationThreshold`. The velocity given in the x direction is the same as his current sideways movement speed but his velocity given in the y direction is set to `jumpSpeed` (which is 8). This equates to upward movement, forming a satisfying, input duration controlled jump!

Don't forget to time the `jumpDuration` though. If you don't time it, Soy Boy will perform the most insane, neverending upward jump, and will never return back to the ground! Your smooth follow camera may even struggle to keep up with him. :]

In the `Update()` method, just below the sprite flipping code, and just above the `PlayerIsOnGround()` check, add the following:

```
if (input.y >= 1f) {
    jumpDuration += Time.deltaTime;
}
else {
    isJumping = false;
    jumpDuration = 0f;
}
```

As long as the jump button is held down, `jumpDuration` is counted up using the time the previous frame took to complete (`Time.deltaTime`). If jump is released, `jumpDuration` is set back to **0** for the next time it needs to be timed, and the `isJumping` boolean flag is set back to false.

Save your code, and run the game to try it out (Tap or hold **Space** to test the different jump heights).

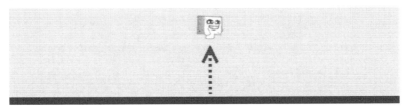

Handling air control

When Soy Boy is in the air, you don't want him to handle as quickly as he normally does when he runs along the ground, so you'll now change the **acceleration** variable value based on whether the player is in the air or not.

Firstly, seeing as you have the `PlayerIsOnGround()` boolean check method available, in the `FixedUpdate()` method, change the `if (input.x == 0)` line to be:

```
if (PlayerIsOnGround() && input.x == 0)
```

This is an extra check to ensure that **xVelocity** is only set to **0f** if the player is on the ground and not using left or right controls.

Add a new variable to the top of the class to hold a value that will be used for air control:

```
public float airAccel = 3f;
```

The value of **3f** for `airAccel` is half the value of the normal `accel` value. You already use `accel` for ground movement, and will now use `airAccel` for air control. This means that air control will no longer be as twitchy as ground control so jumps will not be too difficult or frustrating for players (jump over-compensation).

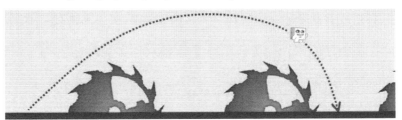

At the top of the `FixedUpdate()` method, replace the line `var acceleration = accel;` with:

```
var acceleration = 0f;
if (PlayerIsOnGround()) {
  acceleration = accel;
}
else {
  acceleration = airAccel;
}
```

This code sets `acceleration` to `0f` to start with (a default, initial value). It then looks to see if the player is on the ground or not, setting `acceleration` to `accel` or `airAccel` respectively.

Further down in the method, the character's rigidbody has force added using the value of `acceleration` as a factor, so this will now dynamically change based on whether the player is in the air or not.

Jumping off walls

Next on the list to implement is wall jumping.

First of all, you need a way of determining if a wall is on the left or the right of the player. This way, when the player jumps off a wall, you know to propel them away from the wall they're on.

In **SoyBoyController.cs**, just below the `PlayerIsOnGround()` method, add the following method:

```
public bool IsWallToLeftOrRight() {
  // 1
  bool wallOnleft = Physics2D.Raycast(new Vector2(
    transform.position.x - width, transform.position.y),
    -Vector2.right, rayCastLengthCheck);
  bool wallOnRight = Physics2D.Raycast(new Vector2(
    transform.position.x + width, transform.position.y),
    Vector2.right, rayCastLengthCheck);
  // 2
  if (wallOnleft || wallOnRight) {
    return true;
  }
  else {
    return false;
  }
}
```

1. Again you're using the implicit bool conversion check of the `Physics2D.Raycast()` method to see if either of two raycasts sent out to the left (`-Vector2.right`) and to the right (`Vector2.right`) of the character sprite hit anything. (Remember that `rayCastLengthCheck` has a small value, so the raycast only goes out a very short distance to the sides of the sprite to check for walls).

2. If either of these raycasts hit anything, the method returns true, otherwise, false.

Now you'll need a way of distinguishing whether the player is touching the ground or a wall. Luckily you already have two methods that do these two different jobs.

In order to know both of these things in one simple method call you'll simply combine them by creating a convenience method that calls both methods and returns true or false.

Add the following variable to the top of the class:

```
public float jump = 14f;
```

Now, just below the `IsWallToLeftOrRight()` method, add the following new method:

```
public bool PlayerIsTouchingGroundOrWall() {
    if (PlayerIsOnGround() || IsWallToLeftOrRight()) {
        return true;
    }
    else {
        return false;
    }
}
```

This method will return true if the character is either on the ground, or has a wall to the left or right of them. If they are against a wall, or on the ground, then you'll know to apply the `jump` value to the character rigidbody's Y velocity. Otherwise, you'll just leave the Y velocity as it currently is.

In the `FixedUpdate()` method, just above the `rb.AddForce(...)` line, add the following:

```
var yVelocity = 0f;
if (PlayerIsTouchingGroundOrWall() && input.y == 1) {
    yVelocity = jump;
}
else {
    yVelocity = rb.velocity.y;
}
```

This ensures that the `yVelocity` value is set to the jump value of `14f` when the character is jumping from the ground, or from a wall. Otherwise, it's set to the current velocity of the rigidbody.

Still in the `FixedUpdate()` method, change the line that reads:

```
rb.velocity = new Vector2(xVelocity, rb.velocity.y);
```

to instead read:

```
rb.velocity = new Vector2(xVelocity, yVelocity);
```

The `yVelocity` is now used to modify the velocity of the character's rigidbody.

At this point, your character can jump up walls, but he will just move straight up next to them when jumping. This definitely doesn't look right. The right way would be to propel him away from walls in the opposite direction when jumping.

Just below the `PlayerIsTouchingGroundOrWall()` method, add another new method:

```
public int GetWallDirection() {
  bool isWallLeft = Physics2D.Raycast(new Vector2(
    transform.position.x - width, transform.position.y),
    -Vector2.right, rayCastLengthCheck);
  bool isWallRight = Physics2D.Raycast(new Vector2(
    transform.position.x + width, transform.position.y),
    Vector2.right, rayCastLengthCheck);
  if (isWallLeft) {
    return -1;
  }
  else if (isWallRight) {
    return 1;
  }
  else {
    return 0;
  }
}
```

This returns an integer based on whether the wall is left (-1), right (1), or neither (0). You'll use the returned value to multiply against the character's X velocity to either make him go left or right (when wall jumping) based on which side the wall is on.

In the `FixedUpdate()` method, just below the line that now reads:

```
rb.velocity = new Vector2(xVelocity, yVelocity);
```

add the following statements:

```
if (IsWallToLeftOrRight() && !PlayerIsOnGround()
  && input.y == 1) {
    rb.velocity = new Vector2(-GetWallDirection()
    * speed * 0.75f, rb.velocity.y);
}
```

This checks to see if there is a wall to the left or right of the player, that they are not on the ground, and that they are currently jumping. If this is the case, the character's rigidbody velocity is set to a new velocity, using the current Y velocity, but with a change to the X (horizontal) velocity.

The change in horizontal velocity is equal to the opposite direction of the wall, multiplied by the speed factor, and then multiplied down by factor of 0.75 (to slightly dampen the horizontal movement a bit).

The opposite direction of the wall is calculated by calling the new GetWallDirection() method and negating its returned value (-1 becomes 1, and 1 becomes -1).

Save your changes and switch back to Unity. Use the **Scene** editor to duplicate some **single-block** prefabs and move the copies up, on top of each other to build some walls. Remember to hold **CTRL** when moving them in the **Scene** editor to keep them snapped to 1 unit size.

Run the game, and jump (**Space**) against the wall. As you land on the wall, jump again, moving in the other direction. With this technique you can now scale walls!

Hooking up character animations

You've completed the character controller with regard to input, and will now complete the animation controller. This will allow you to extend the character controller to control animations! If you need to brush up on Unity's animation, please review Chapter 6, "Animation".

Click the **SoyBoy** GameObject, then open the **Animator** window. Inside this window click the **Parameters** tab.

There are no parameters at the moment. You'll add these next.

In the **Parameters** area of the **Animator** window, click the + (plus) icon three times, each time adding one of the three parameters:

- **Speed** as a Float with value **0.0**.

- **IsJumping** as a Bool, unchecked.

- **IsOnWall** as a Bool, unchecked.

Now to create states. Start by defining a state change from the default **Entry** state to the **IdleAnimation**. Right-click the **Entry** state, select **Make Transition** and then click the **IdleAnimation** block.

An arrow is created from `Entry` pointing to `IdleAnimation`.

Now you need to make the `IdleAnimation` the new default state (indicated by an orange block). Right-click **IdleAnimation** and click **Set as Layer Default State**.

No condition is required to make this transition. It will happen as the game starts.

Now create a transition from **IdleAnimation** to **RunAnimation**, and again from **RunAnimation** back to **IdleAnimation**. You may want to drag the state blocks around in the window to position them better too. This is what you should now have:

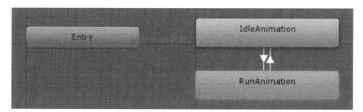

Click the **transition arrow** pointing from **IdleAnimation** to **RunAnimation**. The Inspector window should show you the details of this transition.

Click the + (plus) icon under **Conditions**, and select the **Speed** parameter in the **Condition** drop down. Ensure the check is set to **Greater** than **0**. Uncheck the check box for **Has Exit Time**. This makes sure the animation changes state as soon as the parameter check is met.

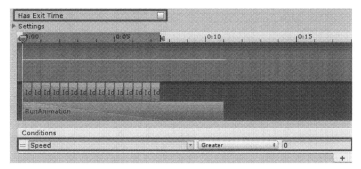

Click the transition arrow pointing from **RunAnimation** back to **IdleAnimation**.

Click the + (plus) icon under **Conditions**, then select the **Speed** parameter in the **Condition** drop down. This time you want to transition from running back to idle, so set the check **Less** than **0.05**. When the player lets go of the horizontal movement controls, speed will go down to 0, and meet this condition.

Don't forget to uncheck the **Has Exit Time** check box, as you want this animation to exit as soon as it can when the condition is met.

Finish creating all the transition arrows you'll need by setting up the transitions as per the image below:

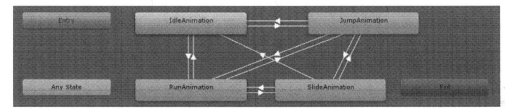

On every transition you make, ensure you uncheck the **Has Exit Time** check box in the **Inspector** for that transition.

There are transitions to and from every state now, except between **SlideAnimation** and **IdleAnimation** where there is only a state change from sliding to idle.

Click each transition arrow in the `Animator` editor and create conditions as specified in the tables below to complete the animation controller.

Idle -> Jump	Jump -> Idle	Run -> Jump	Jump -> Run
IsJumping = true	Speed Less 0.05	IsJumping = true	IsJumping = false
Speed Less 0.5	IsJumping = false		Speed Greater 0
	IsOnWall = false		

Run -> Slide	Slide -> Run	Slide -> Jump	Jump -> Slide	Slide -> Idle
IsOnWall = true	IsOnWall = false	IsJumping = true	IsOnWall = true	IsOnWall = false
	Speed Greater 0	IsOnWall = false	IsJumping = false	Speed Less 0.05

Lastly, select the **RunAnimation** block, and change the speed for the animation from **1** to **2.5**.

Next, you'll change the player controller script to modify your new animation parameters. This will allow the animations to change based on the player's state.

Open **SoyBoyController.cs** in your code editor.

In the Update() method, just below the Input.GetAxis() method calls (right near the top), add the following:

```
animator.SetFloat("Speed", Mathf.Abs(input.x));
```

In the same Update() method, change the block of code that checks for input on the **Y** axis from:

```
if (input.y >= 1f) {
   jumpDuration += Time.deltaTime;
} else {
   isJumping = false;
   jumpDuration = 0f;
}
```

to:

```
if (input.y >= 1f) {
   jumpDuration += Time.deltaTime;
   animator.SetBool("IsJumping", true);
} else {
   isJumping = false;
   animator.SetBool("IsJumping", false);
   jumpDuration = 0f;
}
```

In the Update() method once more, just after the closing brace in the code that says:

```
if (input.y > 0f) {
   isJumping = true;
}
```

add the following:

```
animator.SetBool("IsOnWall", false);
```

Move to the FixedUpdate() method next, and replace this code block:

```
if (IsWallToLeftOrRight() && !PlayerIsOnGround() && input.y ==
1) {
   rb.velocity = new Vector2(-GetWallDirection()
     * speed * 0.75f, rb.velocity.y);
}
```

with this:

```
if (IsWallToLeftOrRight() && !PlayerIsOnGround()  && input.y ==
1) {
   rb.velocity = new Vector2(-GetWallDirection() * speed
     * 0.75f, rb.velocity.y);
   animator.SetBool("IsOnWall", false);
   animator.SetBool("IsJumping", true);
} else if (!IsWallToLeftOrRight()) {
   animator.SetBool("IsOnWall", false);
   animator.SetBool("IsJumping", true);
}
if (IsWallToLeftOrRight() && !PlayerIsOnGround()) {
   animator.SetBool("IsOnWall", true);
}
```

Save your changes and run the game, and try out some basic controls. Soy Boy should transition between all the different states, including sliding down the wall when you're up against a wall and falling. Well done!

Building game hazards

No platformer style game is complete without hazards that can hurt the player. In this section you'll be making a saw blade hazard that has the ability to chop Soy Boy up into minced soy!

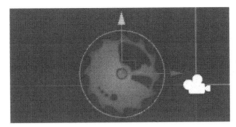

Start by creating a new **C# Script** in the **Scripts** folder and naming it **Hazard**.

Locate the **buzzsaw** sprite GameObject in the Scene view, and **select it**.

Click the **Add Component** button in the Inspector and choose the new **Hazard** script from the **Scripts** list. While you're at it, click **Add Component** again, and add an **Audio Source** component.

Open the **Hazard** script in your code editor.

Add the following fields to the top of the class:

```
public GameObject playerDeathPrefab;
public AudioClip deathClip;
public Sprite hitSprite;
private SpriteRenderer spriteRenderer;
```

These will hold some references to assets that will be used for when the player touches the saw blade and triggers the hazard action.

Add the following, just above the existing Start() method:

```
void Awake() {
  spriteRenderer = GetComponent<SpriteRenderer>();
}
```

This caches a reference to the SpriteRenderer when the script starts.

You will now implement the logic that occurs when the player touches the saw blade.

This is handled using the Unity Physics 2D method called OnCollisionEnter2D(). This method is called automatically when a collision happens between two physics enabled 2D GameObjects. Add the following code:

```
void OnCollisionEnter2D(Collision2D coll) {
  // 1
  if (coll.transform.tag == "Player") {
    // 2
    var audioSource = GetComponent<AudioSource>();
    if (audioSource != null && deathClip != null) {
      audioSource.PlayOneShot(deathClip);
    }
```

```
    // 3
    Instantiate(playerDeathPrefab, coll.contacts[0].point,
      Quaternion.identity);
    spriteRenderer.sprite = hitSprite;
    // 4
    Destroy(coll.gameObject);
  }
}
```

1. First you check to ensure the colliding GameObject has the "Player" tag.

2. Next, determine if an AudioClip has been assigned to the script, and that a valid Audio Source component exists. If so, play the deathClip audio effect.

3. Instantiate the playerDeathPrefab at the collision point, and swap the sprite of the saw blade with the hitSprite version (soy blood covered).

4. Lastly, destroy the colliding object (the player).

Save the script, and go back to Unity to take a look at the **Hazard** script on the **buzzsaw** GameObject.

Drag and drop the **buzzsaw-hit** sprite from the **Sprites** folder, to the **Hit Sprite** field on the **Hazard** script of your **buzzsaw** GameObject.

Do the same to drop the **ssb_death** audio clip from the **Sound** folder to the **Death Clip** field.

The last reference you need to make is for the Player Death Prefab on the Hazard script. This is for the death particle effect that is instantiated when the player touches the hazard. You'll now set up a new prefab with a Particle System component to handle this.

Create a new GameObject in the Scene. Name it **DeathParticleSystem** and add a **Particle System** component to it. Change the **Transform** component's X rotation to **-90**.

Set the main **Particle System** properties up with the following changes:

• **Duration**: 0.15

• **Looping**: Unchecked

• **Start Lifetime**: 2

- **Start Speed**: Random between two constants **10** and **15**

- **Start Size**: 0.15

- **Start Rotation**: Random between two constants **0** and **360**

- **Gravity Modifier**: 3

Enable the **Emission** section on the **Particle System** and set the **Rate** to **300**. Enable the **Shape** section, and set the **Shape** to **Cone**, **Angle** to **35**, and **Radius** to **0.2**. Enable the **Color over Lifetime** section and set the color gradient to go from a solid white color (100% alpha) down to an alpha of 0% value.

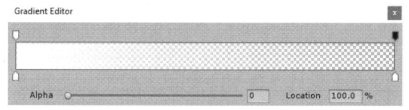

Lastly, expand the **Renderer** section, and change the **Material** to **Sprites-Default** using the selector. Change the **Sorting Layer** to **Foreground**, and the **Order in Layer** value to **10**.

Using the Scene view, with the **DeathParticleSystem** GameObject selected, click the **Simulate** button in the bottom right corner of the editor view. You should see a burst of blood particles spray upward in the air.

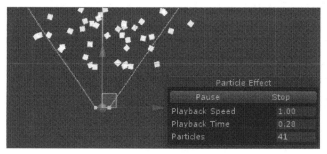

Drag and drop the **DeathParticleSystem** GameObject into the **Assets/Prefabs** folder to turn it into a prefab, then remove it from the Hierarchy window / scene.

Select your **buzzsaw** GameObject in the **Scene** editor, click the **Prefabs** folder in the **Project** window, and then drag and drop a reference from your new **DeathParticleSystem** prefab to the **Player Death Prefab** field on the **Hazard** script.

Click **Apply** at the top of the GameObject in the Inspector window to apply the changes on **buzzsaw** to it's underlying prefab. Your Hazard script should now look like this:

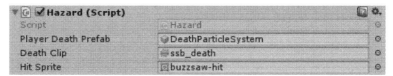

The last thing remaining to add to the saw blade hazard is rotation. You'll do this by adding a simple rotation script.

Create a new C# script called **RotationScript** in the **Scripts** folder and open it in your code editor.

At the top of the class, add the following variable:

```
public float rotationsPerMinute = 640f;
```

In the Update() method, add the following:

```
transform.Rotate(0, 0, rotationsPerMinute * Time.deltaTime,
  Space.Self);
```

This will rotate the GameObject the script is attached to around the Z-axis based on the value of rotationsPerMinute. Save the script, and return to the Unity editor.

Attach the new **RotationScript** to the **buzzsaw** GameObject, then click the **Apply** button in the Inspector to apply the changes you've made to the underlying prefab object.

Select the **SoyBoy** GameObject in the Hierarchy window and set the tag on the GameObject to **Player**. Apply the change to **SoyBoy** prefab.

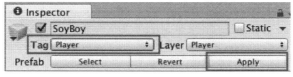

Run the game, and you should see a nice spinning saw blade. Touch the blade and Soy Boy should explode into a spray of soybean particles!

Adding sound to the game

A game featuring relentless running, jumping, and bouncing around off of walls requires a high-energy retro music backing track. Luckily for you, the starter project includes just one of these to get you going!

You'll loop the track to provide level music for Super Soy Boy. Looping a single music track is pretty simple with Unity.

Create a new GameObject called **Music** in the Scene Hierarchy, and add an **Audio Source** component to it.

From the **Sound** folder, drag and drop the **supersoyboy.ogg** audio clip to the **AudioClip** field on the **Music Audio Source** component. Enable the **Loop** property and adjust the **Volume** property down to **0.45**.

Now you'll hook up some SFX to Soy Boy.

Open **SoyBoyController.cs** in your code editor, and at the top of the script, add the following fields:

```
public AudioClip runClip;
public AudioClip jumpClip;
public AudioClip slideClip;
private AudioSource audioSource;
```

You should cache a reference to the `AudioSource` component on start, so in the `Awake()` method, add:

```
audioSource = GetComponent<AudioSource>();
```

When playing sound effects, especially from locations like the game `Update()` method, you'll want to ensure they are not already playing, otherwise you could end up with sound loops playing over each other.

To do this, you'll create a simple method that you can pass the audio clip you wish to be played to.

Add this method to the **SoyBoyController.cs** script:

```
void PlayAudioClip(AudioClip clip) {
   if (audioSource != null && clip != null) {
      if (!audioSource.isPlaying) audioSource.PlayOneShot(clip);
   }
}
```

This checks that the `audioSource` and clip to be played are valid, and also ensures the `Audio Source` component is not already playing a clip before playing the new clip.

In the `Update()` method, change the if statement that checks if the player is on the ground and is not jumping to look like this:

```
if (PlayerIsOnGround() && !isJumping) {
    if (input.y > 0f) {
        isJumping = true;
        PlayAudioClip(jumpClip);
    }
    animator.SetBool("IsOnWall", false);
    if (input.x < 0f || input.x > 0f) {
        PlayAudioClip(runClip);
    }
}
```

Note the addition of two calls to the `PlayAudioClip()` method you added previously. One plays the `jumpClip` and one plays the `runClip`.

Move over to the `FixedUpdate()` method, and locate the section that sets the various boolean parameter values for the animator, right near the bottom.

Modify this section to add two more calls to `PlayAudioClip()` for the jump and slide clips. This is how it should now look:

```
if (IsWallToLeftOrRight() && !PlayerIsOnGround()
    && input.y == 1) {

    rb.velocity = new Vector2(-GetWallDirection() * speed
        * 0.75f, rb.velocity.y);
    animator.SetBool("IsOnWall", false);
    animator.SetBool("IsJumping", true);
    PlayAudioClip(jumpClip);
} else if (!IsWallToLeftOrRight()) {
    animator.SetBool("IsOnWall", false);
    animator.SetBool("IsJumping", true);
}
if (IsWallToLeftOrRight() && !PlayerIsOnGround()) {
    animator.SetBool("IsOnWall", true);
    PlayAudioClip(slideClip);
}
```

Lastly, you'll just need to assign the three new audio clips to the `SoyBoyController` script on `SoyBoy`. Save your changes and switch back to Unity.

Select the **SoyBoy** GameObject in the Hierarchy and, from the **Sounds** folder, drag and drop the **ssb_jump.ogg**, **ssb_run_short.ogg**, and **ssb_slide_loop.ogg** audio clips onto the the three new **AudioClip** fields on the **SoyBoyController** script.

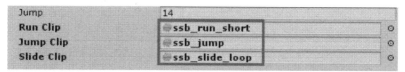

Add an **Audio Source** component to **SoyBoy**, and then apply the changes on **SoyBoy** to the underlying prefab by clicking the **Apply** button in the Inspector.

Run the game, and test that the sound clips now play for music, running, jumping, and wall sliding.

Creating a game manager

You'll now create a game manager that will allow you to manage the win and lose states for the game. To keep things simple, this game manager will just restart the level when you win or lose.

For this purpose, you will create a basic singleton instance script. A singleton is essentially an instance of a class that should only have a single instance at any time.

In the **Scripts** folder, create a new script called **GameManager**. Create a new GameObject in the **Game** scene called **GameManager** and attach the new **GameManager.cs** script to it.

Open **GameManager.cs** in your code editor. At the top of the class, add a new public static field that will hold the instance reference for the **GameManager** singleton:

```
public static GameManager instance;
```

Create the following Awake() method:

```
void Awake() {
  if (instance == null) {
    instance = this;
  } else if (instance != this) {
    Destroy(gameObject);
  }
  DontDestroyOnLoad(gameObject);
}
```

This is the core of the singleton pattern. The first time this script executes Awake(), instance will be null, and so the method will assign the one instance of GameManager to instance. Any other time the method runs, instance will no longer be null.

If another GameManager instance is created elsewhere, then that instance is destroyed, ensuring that there is only ever one instance (the first one that was initialized).

Next, you need a centralised way of telling a level to reload from the GameManager. Add the following using statement to the top of the script, and then two new methods to the class:

```
using UnityEngine.SceneManagement;
```

```
public void RestartLevel(float delay) {
    StartCoroutine(RestartLevelDelay(delay));
}

private IEnumerator RestartLevelDelay(float delay) {
    yield return new WaitForSeconds(delay);
    SceneManager.LoadScene("Game");
}
```

The public method is simply a proxy method — a way of calling the private Coroutine method that actually reloads the Game scene. This method is made public so it is easy to call from the singleton GameManager instance anywhere else in the game code.

Save your changes and open the **Hazard.cs** script.

At the bottom of the OnCollisionEnter2D() method, immediately after the Destroy() call, add the following:

```
GameManager.instance.RestartLevel(1.25f);
```

This will call the GameManager instance's RestartLevel() method, passing in a delay of 1.25 seconds. This will run the coroutine, and restart the level after a 1.25 second delay when called, giving just enough time for the player to see the death particle effect.

Creating the level goal

Create a new C# script in the **Scripts** folder called **Goal**, and open it for editing.

Add the following to the top of the class:

```
public AudioClip goalClip;

void OnCollisionEnter2D(Collision2D coll) {
    if (coll.gameObject.tag == "Player") {
        var audioSource = GetComponent<AudioSource>();
        if (audioSource != null && goalClip != null) {
            audioSource.PlayOneShot(goalClip);
        }
        GameManager.instance.RestartLevel(0.5f);
    }
}
```

Here, you check for player collisions with the `Goal` GameObject. If this happens, the player has reached the goal so you play the `goalClip` audio clip and restart the level after a `0.5` second delay.

Save your changes and head back to Unity. Locate and select the **Goal** prefab in the **Resources/Prefabs** folder using the Project Browser, and add the **Goal.cs** script to this prefab.

Drop a reference from **ssb_goal.ogg** in the **Sound** folder onto the **Goal Clip** field on the **Goal** prefab's **Goal** component.

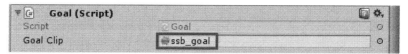

With that, your `GameManager` singleton is complete. It will restart the level when the player dies, and restart the level when the player wins.

Drop a copy of the **Goal** prefab into your **Game** scene and position it on a platform.

Run the game, and run into or jump on to the goal sprite. The level should restart after you hear the goal SFX play.

Adding a simple level timer

Next up, you'll hook up a simple timer script that will time your level runs. The timer will just be used as a reference for how long you take to do level runs. Later on in the Saving Data chapter you'll extend it to add more functionality to the game.

Create a new C# script in the **Scripts** folder, called **Timer**. Open the script for editing.

Add the following using statement to the top of the script:

```
using UnityEngine.UI;
```

Now, replace the `Start()` and `Update()` methods with the following code:

```
private Text timerText;

void Awake() {
```

```
    timerText = GetComponent<Text>();
  }

  void Update () {
    timerText.text =
      System.Math.Round((decimal)Time.timeSinceLevelLoad,
      2).ToString();
  }
```

This code will grab, and cache a reference to the Text component on the same GameObject the script exists on. In the Update() loop, the text will be changed to display the time since the level last reloaded, rounded to two decimal places. Nice and simple!

Save the script, and return to Unity.

Attach the **Timer.cs** script to the **Timer** GameObject, which is nested under the **Canvas** GameObject.

Run the game, and you'll now see the timer ticking over counting the time each time the level starts or restarts.

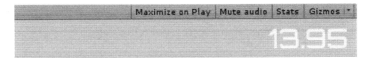

Building your own game level

Instead of providing instructions on where to place every single GameObject to create a level, a couple of pre-built levels have already been included with the **finished** project file for this chapter.

To take a look at these levels, open the **finished** project for this chapter, and then open either the **Level1.scene** or the **Level2.scene** in the Unity editor.

You'll see two examples of fully completed levels, ready to play.

If you take a closer look, you'll see that they are constructed by placing the building block items available in the **Resources/Prefabs** folder into the scene. The level blocks and platform pieces are kept aligned and snapped to the grid by holding down **Ctrl** when moving or placing them.

As the basic building block prefabs are mostly colored white, you can easily change their color on the **Sprite Renderer** component using the color picker to style your levels any way you like.

In order to build your own levels, you'll place a variety of different building block prefabs. These are items like small blocks, large blocks, triangular corner pieces, rocks, trees, and so on. You learned how to create these building blocks in the previous chapter.

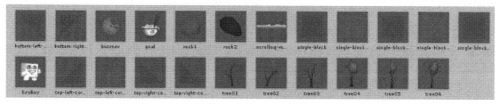

To create a playable level, the level should start off at a certain point (where Soy Boy is located), and require you to then run and wall jump past some saw blade obstacles (that if touched will slice you to bits).

A noodle bowl goal point should be placed at the end of the level that you must reach.

> **Note:** Remember that the `GameManager` will reload the `Game` scene when you die, or hit the goal, so in the case of the `Level1` and `Level2` scenes, you'll be booted into the `Game` scene if you win or lose in these example levels.

Challenge time

As a challenge, you can now use your chapter project to create your own level. To prepare the `Game` scene as a template for building a new level, complete the follow few steps:

Start by removing all the GameObjects from the **Scene Hierarchy**, except for **Main Camera, Canvas, SoyBoy, EventSystem, GameManager** and **Music**.

Create a new GameObject called **Level** in the root of the scene hierarchy. Position this GameObject at **(0, 0, 0)**. This is what your scene hierarchy should now look like:

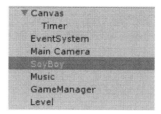

This will leave you with a blank slate that you can start creating your level from. All of your level objects from here on should be placed as children (nested under) the new `Level` GameObject you just created.

As a hint to get you going, the first thing you should generally do, is to decide on a layout for your level, and where hazards should be located.

You'll create the base platform and level structure first. For this you can use the **single-block-large** prefab located under **Resources/Prefabs**. Drag and drop one into the scene view.

Using the hierarchy editor window, select the newly placed **single-block-large** GameObject and hit Ctrl-D on your keyboard to duplicate it as many times as you need to start building platforms and walls to run along and jump up.

Lastly, when creating your own levels, don't forget to place the **SoyBoy** and **Goal** prefabs for the start and goal positions of your level.

Where to go from here?

Congratulations on making it to the end of this chapter! You've come a long way, and learned much about the Unity 2D asset and scripting workflow.

Next you may wish to further familiarize yourself with using and positioning 2D sprites in the editor by attempting the challenge set out above. With this challenge, the idea is to create your own level using what you have created so far.

Chapter 14: Saving Data

By Sean Duffy

Unity provides a multitude of options for saving game data. In this chapter, you'll learn some excellent ways to store and retrieve player data, such as user profiles, level run times, scores and even custom levels for the game.

Getting started

For this chapter, you'll pick up where Chapter 13, "More Unity 2D" left off. Even if you did finish Chapter 13, open the **SuperSoyBoy** starter project for this chapter in the Unity Editor — it has some extras that'll make it easier to get up and running.

There's a new **Menu** scene that includes basic UI to carry you through these exercises in saving data. The other notable change is that the **GameManager** singleton is now in the Menu scene.

Load the **Menu** scene from the **Scenes** folder.

Three ways to work with saved data

This chapter will walk you through three ways to save and load player data in Unity.

- **PlayerPrefs**: The easiest, fastest way to save and load data.

- **Binary Serialization**: A good way to handle sensitive data or accommodate more complex objects than PlayerPrefs.

- **Unity JSON serialization**: Unity introduced the JSONUtility class in version 5.3, which allows you to pack and unpack data with the popular JSON text-based format.

Storing the player's name with PlayerPrefs

PlayerPrefs works by using a system of keys (names) with associated values (data). To save a value, you use one of the `set` methods available in the `PlayerPrefs` class to set the value of a key.

To get a feel for how it works, you'll write code to save the player's name from the main menu. Here's an example of three keys with their corresponding values: a string, an integer and a float.

PlayerPrefs Store		
Key	**Value**	**Type**
PlayerName	Sean	String
Score	1000	Integer
Distance	410.0135	Float

The key is like a bookmark that points to the value you need to store. When you want to find this value again, you use one of PlayerPrefs' `get` methods, such as `PlayerPrefs.GetString("key")`, to retrieve the value, passing in the name of the desired key.

- **PlayerPrefs.SetInt() / GetInt()**: Used to save or load integer values
- **PlayerPrefs.SetFloat() / GetFloat()**: Used to save or load float values
- **PlayerPrefs.SetString() / GetString()**: Used to save or load string values

Open the **GameManager.cs** script. At the top, just above the existing `instance` field, add this:

```
public string playerName;
```

This is a new string field that keeps track of the player's name.

Create a new C# script named **PlayerName** in the **Scripts** folder, and then open it for editing. At the top, but below the other `using` statements, add:

```
using UnityEngine.UI;
```

This is a `using` statement to reference the UnityEngine.UI namespace.

Inside the top of the class, add the following:

```
private InputField input;
```

This variable caches the reference to an `InputField` component.

Modify the remainder of the **PlayerName** script as follows:

```
void Start () {
  // 1
  input = GetComponent<InputField>();
  input.onValueChanged.AddListener(SavePlayerName);
  // 2
  var savedName = PlayerPrefs.GetString("PlayerName");
  if (!string.IsNullOrEmpty(savedName)) {
    input.text = savedName;
    GameManager.instance.playerName = savedName;
  }
}

private void SavePlayerName(string playerName) {
  // 3
  PlayerPrefs.SetString("PlayerName", playerName);
  PlayerPrefs.Save();
  GameManager.instance.playerName = playerName;
}
```

Here's what you're doing in there:

1. Locating and caching the `InputField` component on the GameObject to which the script is attached. You then add a new listener method to the `onValueChanged` event that all InputFields have by default.

   Whenever the input value changes, the `SavePlayerName()` method executes.

2. You then use `PlayerPrefs` to look for and retrieve the value for a key named `PlayerName`. If it exists, then the input field's text is changed to display the player name stored in `PlayerPrefs`.

3. `SavePlayerName()` takes the supplied `playerName` and sets the key named `PlayerName` to this value. `PlayerPrefs.Save()` is then called to persist the state of `PlayerPrefs` to storage.

Save the script and go back to Unity. In the **Menu** scene, locate the **NameInputField** GameObject, which is located under the **Canvas** GameObject.

Attach the new **PlayerName** script to it.

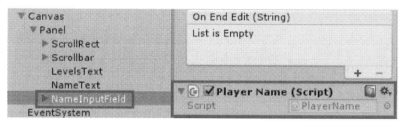

Launch the game from the **Menu** scene. Notice that the default name of Player shows in the InputField — you may need to select **Maximize on Play** at the top of the Game window to see the whole panel. Type your name in the field, and then **stop** the game.

Launch the game again. Your name persisted and reloaded at startup, so it shows in the input field again!

Storing best times with binary serialization

Binary serialization allows you to save and load more complex data structures.

To get familiar with this approach, you'll create a way for players to store their run times. Specifically, you'll make it so that the three best times will show beneath the current level run time after a player completes a level.

Even when the player closes the game, the program stores the times and reloads them when the player reopens the game.

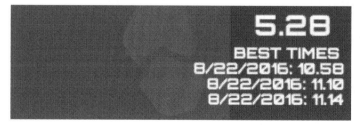

Your first step is to create a new class that will hold two different values in public fields.

You'll use a `DateTime` type field to store the date and time the best run happened, and a `Decimal` type field to store the actual level run time in seconds.

In the **Project** view, open the **Scripts** folder and **right-click** in the empty space. Choose the option to create a new C# script and name it **PlayerTimeEntry**. Open it for editing.

Replace the contents of the default Unity MonoBehaviour script for **PlayerTimeEntry.cs** with the following:

```
using System;

[Serializable]
public class PlayerTimeEntry {
  public DateTime entryDate;
  public decimal time;
}
```

At the top of the class, you'll notice the `Serializable` marker, which allows the binary formatter you'll use next to serialize and deserialize — aka pack and unpack — this data class.

Save your work.

> **Note:** By the way, this script is different from your usual MonoBehaviour script — it won't inherit from MonoBehaviour. You'll use this class with the binary serialization system, and as such, it'll only be used to store data. It doesn't need to know or hold anything else except for the two values that'll be used to store a time entry.

Next, you'll be extending the **GameManager.cs** singleton script to handle saving and loading player level run time entries.

Open the **GameManager.cs** script for editing. Add the following new `using` statements to the top:

```
using UnityEngine.UI;
using System;
using System.Collections.Generic;
using System.IO;
using System.Linq;
using System.Runtime.Serialization.Formatters.Binary;
```

These namespaces allow you to work with some language and library features in the **GameManager.cs** script. `Linq` allows you to use LINQ code to query a list of stored level run times, and `Serialization` allows you to call code that lets you work with binary serialization formatters, which you'll use to save and load data in binary format.

Add the following to the bottom of the **GameManager** class:

```
public List<PlayerTimeEntry> LoadPreviousTimes()
{
  // 1
  try {
    var scoresFile = Application.persistentDataPath +
      "/" + playerName + "_times.dat";
    using (var stream = File.Open(scoresFile, FileMode.Open)) {
      var bin = new BinaryFormatter();
      var times =
(List<PlayerTimeEntry>)bin.Deserialize(stream);
      return times;
    }
  }
  // 2
  catch (IOException ex) {
    Debug.LogWarning("Couldn't load previous times for: " +
      playerName + ". Exception: " + ex.Message);
    return new List<PlayerTimeEntry>();
  }
}

public void SaveTime(decimal time) {
  // 3
  var times = LoadPreviousTimes();
  // 4
  var newTime = new PlayerTimeEntry();
  newTime.entryDate = DateTime.Now;
  newTime.time = time;
  // 5
  var bFormatter = new BinaryFormatter();
  var filePath = Application.persistentDataPath +
              "/" + playerName + "_times.dat";
  using (var file = File.Open(filePath, FileMode.Create)) {
    times.Add(newTime);
    bFormatter.Serialize(file, times);
  }
}
```

That's a lot of new code! Essentially, this code handles saving and loading of times to and from a binary formatted data file kept on local storage.

1. Here, you use a `try...catch` statement to attempt to load saved time entries for the player. You construct the path to the file using a combination of the player's name (stored it in PlayerPrefs), and the `Application.persistentDataPath`.

   The `using` statement opens a file stream to the file path to read in any existing time entries using a binary formatter object. You use the `Deserialize()` method to read — aka unpack — the data in the file by passing in the opened file stream. If the read is successful, it returns a list of player time entries.

2. If deserialization is unsuccessful, the `catch` statement finds the errors. In here, you log an info message and return an empty list back to the caller. This is important because the player might not have logged or saved times, e.g., when playing the first time.

3. When saving a time, you fetch existing times first with the `LoadPreviousTimes()` method.

4. You create an instance of the new `PlayerTimeEntry` object. Then you store the current date and run time, as passed to the method, in the `entryDate` and `time` property fields.

5. You create a binary formatter object to do the magic serialization — aka packing — of the list of player time entries to a file. You create the file path using a combination of the player's name and the `Application.persistentDataPath`. Again, the `using` statement opens the file.

    However, this time it uses the `FileMode.Create` option, which lets you create a new file or overwrite existing files in the same path. Finally, you add the new time entry to the list of pre-existing times before saving them all back into the file.

> **Note:** The `using` statement in the above code is a special statement in C# that you can utilize to deal with objects that implement the **IDisposable** interface. Most file and IO-related operations provided by the framework support this.
>
> It's a good idea to wrap these operations in a `using` statement when supported. Once work on the item inside of the `using` statement finishes, any objects that were created are destroyed.
>
> In the case above, where you're opening and writing to files, you're properly closing off file access when the `using` statement completes. Hence, you shouldn't have locked file issues when writing to the file at a later point.

Now that you've added the structure to save and load run time data, you need a way to display the previous times in the game.

Go back to Unity and open the **Game** scene. On the main **Canvas** GameObject, create a new **Text** GameObject. Name it **PreviousTimes**.

Set the anchor and position of this new UI text component as shown below:

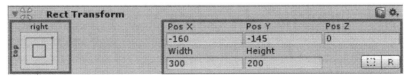

In the **Text** component, set the **Font** to **orbitron-medium**, **Font Size** to 16, **Line Spacing** to 1.2 and text to **right-aligned**. Use the **Best Fit** style with **Max Size** of 16 and set **Color** to **solid white**.

Save the scene. Go back to **GameManager.cs** and add the following to the bottom of the class:

```
public void DisplayPreviousTimes() {
  // 1
  var times = LoadPreviousTimes();
  var topThree = times.OrderBy(time => time.time).Take(3);
  // 2
  var timesLabel = GameObject.Find("PreviousTimes")
    .GetComponent<Text>();
  // 3
  timesLabel.text = "BEST TIMES \n";
  foreach (var time in topThree) {
    timesLabel.text += time.entryDate.ToShortDateString() +
      ": " + time.time + "\n";
  }
}
```

This code will populate time entries in the newly created `PreviousTimes` UI Text component. Here's what it does in more detail:

1. Collects existing times using the `LoadPreviousTimes()` method. `times.OrderBy(time => time.time).Take(3)` is a LINQ query that sorts times from fastest to slowest, and then takes the first three of each.

2. Finds the `PreviousTimes` text component.

3. Changes it to show each time found, separating entries with a line-break using the `"\n"` string.

> **Note:** LINQ stands for Language Integrated Query. It's a querying language that allows you to easily query and manipulate data. There are many useful query expressions, and generally, you can chain them together. Read more about LINQ at: https://en.wikipedia.org/wiki/Language_Integrated_Query

The final piece of the binary serialization puzzle is saving level run times when the player reaches the goal — that steaming bowl of delicious noodles.

Open the **Timer.cs** script and add the following variable declaration:

```
public decimal time;
```

Change the code in Update() to look like this:

```
time = System.Math.Round((decimal) Time.timeSinceLevelLoad, 2);
timerText.text = time.ToString();
```

By storing the game time in the new time variable before updating the timerText value, you're giving other scripts the ability to access the time value.

Open the **Goal.cs** script. At the bottom of the OnCollisionEnter2D() method, inside the if statement that checks for the **Player** tag, add the following:

```
// 1
var timer = FindObjectOfType<Timer>();
// 2
GameManager.instance.SaveTime(timer.time);
```

This saves the time when the player reaches the goal.

1. FindObjectOfType finds the timer script component instance in the level scene. The generic type Timer is indicated here. This Unity method finds the first instance of a script of type Timer. As there is only one Timer script per level, which is used to track level time, this instance is returned.

2. The new SaveTime method you created is called on the GameManager singleton, passing in the current level run time from the Timer script.

Lastly, you need a trigger to display any potential previous run times for the level. In **GameManager.cs**, add the following to the bottom of the GameManager class:

```
private void OnSceneLoaded(Scene scene, LoadSceneMode
loadsceneMode) {
  if (scene.name == "Game") {
    DisplayPreviousTimes();
  }
}
```

The code checks to see if the scene is the `Game` scene, and if so, displays the previous times. Next, add this to the `Start()` method:

```
SceneManager.sceneLoaded += OnSceneLoaded;
```

That line hooks up `OnSceneLoaded()` to a Unity `SceneManager` event named `sceneLoaded` that fires when a scene loads. `OnSceneLoaded()` checks the name of the scene. It calls `DisplayPreviousTimes()` when the result is the Game scene.

Save your changes and run the game.

Play to the end of the level. Now when you dive into that bowl of noodles, aka the goal sprite, you'll trigger the save method.

When the level restarts, the three fastest times show up because the game calls `DisplayPreviousTimes()`, reads the saved times file and feeds the results into the **PreviousTimes** text component. Sucess!!

Basic unity JSON serialization usage

Unity's JSON serialization provides a super-easy way to save and load game data to and from the JSON text format.

JSON stands for JavaScript Object Notation. It's a lightweight data-interchange format, with a nice benefit of being friendly for humans to read and write. It's also amiable to parsing and generating from your code.

Here's an example of some JSON representing a part of a custom Super Soy Boy level.

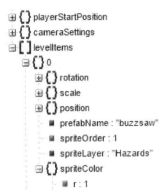

For the rest of this chapter, you'll focus on building a level editor that has a saving and loading system. It'll allow you to save custom level layouts in JSON and load them back to play.

The system you build will prove how easy it is to add modding support to the game or provide players with a way to share custom levels.

Unity support for working with JSON

There are some limitations around what types of objects Unity's JsonUtility system will support.

MonoBehaviours, ScriptableObjects and plain classes/structs with the `[Serializable]` attribute applied are supported.

As a rule of thumb, the utility only supports the public fields of supported types. For example, basic types like integer, string and floats are supported, whereas dictionaries are not. If you want to use arrays, you'll need to wrap them in a class or struct.

Benchmarks show that Unity's JsonUtility outperforms popular .NET JSON solutions. Its speed outweighs the fact that it currently has fewer features than these solutions.

Performance is more important than bells and whistles when it comes to designing games.

Creating a level editor & saving levels

In this section, you'll leverage JSON serialization and deserialization to implement level saving and loading.

You'll be able to construct custom levels in Unity, save them to JSON and share them with anyone else playing Super Soy Boy. Whoever you share it with can place the JSON in the game directory, fire up the game and play the level.

Here's the cool part: You don't have to share any game code or executables!

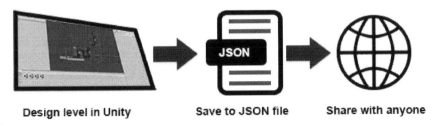

Design level in Unity   Save to JSON file   Share with anyone

Building a custom editor for saving levels

You'll use the Unity editor to design levels and a custom editor script to enumerate all the level pieces in the scene as well as automatically save the layout to a JSON level file. Information about every level piece will be accounted for, including type, position, rotation, sprite color, sprite layer and sprite order in the layer.

Open the **Game** scene in Unity. In the **Project** view, go into the **Scripts** folder and make a new folder named **Editor** (if it doesn't already exist), and then create a new C# script named **LevelEditor**. In the **Scripts** folder, create a new C# script named **Level**.

LevelEditor will look for a GameObject in the scene named **Level** and enumerate all children GameObjects underneath this. It'll save information about each object, as well as information about the starting point for Soy Boy and details about the smooth follow camera to a JSON file.

Look at the **Hierarchy** window to confirm you have a **Level** GameObject that has all the level pieces as its children — the custom editor script will end up enumerating and saving information about these children.

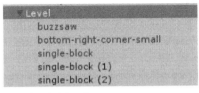

Open **Level.cs** and change it to look like this:

```
using UnityEngine;
using System.Collections;

public class Level : MonoBehaviour {
```

```
        public string levelName;
}
```

The custom level editor script will work on top of this basic MonoBehaviour script, which stores the name of the level you're creating.

Next, open **LevelEditor.cs** and replace its contents with the following:

```
using UnityEngine;
using System.Collections;
using System.Collections.Generic;
using UnityEditor;

[CustomEditor(typeof(Level))]
public class LevelEditor : Editor {
    public override void OnInspectorGUI() {

    }
}
```

The above code changes the script so that it follows the structure of a basic custom editor script.

Back in Unity, attach **Level.cs** to the **Level** GameObject.

Normally, any new public string field — in this case levelName — would appear on the GameObject to which you attached the script. However, Level.cs now has a custom editor — LevelEditor.cs — and nothing was implemented in the `OnInspectorGUI()` method, so nothing changes in the Inspector.

But you need it to show up, so go back to the **LevelEditor.cs** script and add the following to `OnInspectorGUI()`:

```
DrawDefaultInspector();
```

Now Unity can pick up and show LevelName in the Inspector. Save the script and look at **Level** in the Inspector to confirm it's there.

You definitely want a save button in the editor that saves the level in the scene to a JSON file. Add the following to the `OnInspectorGUI()` method:

```
if (GUILayout.Button("Save level")) {
}
```

This adds a custom, clickable GUI button. Save the script then confirm that you see it in the **Level** GameObject.

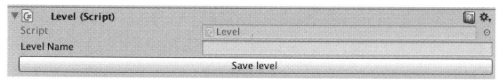

Cool! You're making progress, but nothing will happen if you clicked it now. You'll tackle that shortly.

Hierarchy of a JSON object that defines a level

To serialize and deserialize custom level data, you need to map Unity classes and their associated data to a JSON structure. You'll create three new scripts that will map the data to different parts of the JSON hierarchy that will eventually be a level file.

Create three new scripts in the **Scripts** folder and name them **LevelDataRepresentation.cs**, **LevelItemRepresentation.cs** and **CameraSettingsRepresentation.cs**. Modify each as shown below.

LevelDataRepresentation.cs:

```
using UnityEngine;
using System;

[Serializable]
public class LevelDataRepresentation {
  public Vector2 playerStartPosition;
  public CameraSettingsRepresentation cameraSettings;
  public LevelItemRepresentation[] levelItems;
}
```

LevelItemRepresentation.cs:

```
using UnityEngine;
using System;

[Serializable]
public class LevelItemRepresentation {
  public Vector3 rotation;
  public Vector3 scale;
  public Vector2 position;
  public string prefabName;
  public int spriteOrder;
  public string spriteLayer;
  public Color spriteColor;
}
```

CameraSettingsRepresentation.cs:

```
using System;

[Serializable]
public class CameraSettingsRepresentation {
    public string cameraTrackTarget;
    public float trackingSpeed;
    public float cameraZDepth;
    public float minX;
    public float minY;
    public float maxX;
    public float maxY;
}
```

Each script allows the Unity **JSONUtility** class to serialize and deserialize information that describes levels.

Save your work!

Here's a handy diagram that shows how each class — aka script — maps to the JSON data:

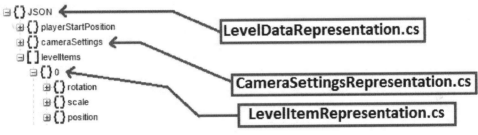

In the mapping diagram above, there's a small section of a saved level file.

Building & nesting data classes for game components

Each level file uses a base **LevelDataRepresentation** object to store the following items in JSON:

- **playerStartPosition**: The position where Soy Boy spawns.

- **cameraSettings**: An object that contains information about how to configure the smooth follow camera, including follow speed and boundaries.

- **levelItems**: An array of level item information. For every object created under the root **Level** GameObject in the level scene, an item will be created in this array that describes what the item is, its location, rotation, sprite color, etc.

By default, Unity's JsonUtility can't serialize camera settings or level item objects because they're not simple types. Hence, they're represented as nested fields in the main **LevelDataRepresentation.cs** class.

In turn, these objects are represented by classes that have simple type fields. Unity's **JSONUtility** will be able to understand them!

For example, look at the **LevelDataRepresentation.cs** class. An instance of the **LevelItemRepresentation.cs** class represents each item stored in the **levelItems** array. The script has these simple type fields:

```
public Vector3 rotation;
public Vector3 scale;
public Vector2 position;
public string prefabName;
public int spriteOrder;
public string spriteLayer;
public Color spriteColor;
```

This nesting of [Serializable] classes is exactly how you make complex objects serialize or deserialize and play nice with JSON.

Parsing a level in the editor & saving it to disk

Open **LevelEditor.cs**. Add the following code just below (GUILayout.Button("Save level")) but above the closing curly bracket:

```
// 1
Level level = (Level)target;
level.transform.position = Vector3.zero;
level.transform.rotation = Quaternion.identity;
// 2
var levelRoot = GameObject.Find("Level");
// 3
var ldr = new LevelDataRepresentation();
var levelItems = new List<LevelItemRepresentation>();
```

1. Grabs a handle on the Level component and sets the Level GameObject's position and rotation to 0, ensuring everything is positioned from the origin point in the scene.

2. Establishes levelRoot as a reference to the Level GameObject, which is the parent of all level items.

3. Creates new instances of LevelDataRepresentation and LevelItemRepresentation.

Add the following just below List<LevelItemRepresentation>(); in the last bit of code:

```
foreach (Transform t in levelRoot.transform) {
    // 4
    var sr = t.GetComponent<SpriteRenderer>();
    var li = new LevelItemRepresentation() {
        position = t.position,
        rotation = t.rotation.eulerAngles,
        scale = t.localScale
    };
    // 5
    if (t.name.Contains(" ")) {
        li.prefabName = t.name.Substring(0, t.name.IndexOf(" "));
    }
    else {
        li.prefabName = t.name;
    }
    // 6
    if (sr != null) {
        li.spriteLayer = sr.sortingLayerName;
        li.spriteColor = sr.color;
        li.spriteOrder = sr.sortingOrder;
    }
    // 7
    levelItems.Add(li);
}
```

Here's what you're doing in there:

4. Loops through every child Transform object of levelRoot. Then it takes a reference to any potential SpriteRenderer component and assigns it to the sr variable. It then creates a new LevelItemRepresentation to hold the position, rotation and scale of each item.

5. This is a bit of a hack to store the name of each level item in the prefabName field. When loading a level later on, your code will need to know which prefabs to use to construct the level based on the name stored in the JSON file. When you design a level, you tend to duplicate or clone multiple items, which adds spaces and numbers in brackets to each cloned item. This hack does its best to trim away spaces and brackets with numbers from the items nested under the Level root. The resulting name will become the name of the prefabs to load later from the Resources/Prefabs folder.

6. Performs a check to ensure that a valid SpriteRenderer was found — because a level item might not have an attached sprite. If the sr variable is not null, then information about the sprite's sorting, order and color stores in the LevelItemRepresentation object.

7. Lastly, the item that has all the collected information is added to the `levelItems` list.

Just below the closing curly bracket of the `foreach` loop you just added, add this code:

```
// 8
ldr.levelItems = levelItems.ToArray();
ldr.playerStartPosition =
  GameObject.Find("SoyBoy").transform.position;
// 9
var currentCamSettings =
FindObjectOfType<CameraLerpToTransform>();
if (currentCamSettings != null) {
  ldr.cameraSettings = new CameraSettingsRepresentation() {
    cameraTrackTarget = currentCamSettings.camTarget.name,
    cameraZDepth = currentCamSettings.cameraZDepth,
    minX = currentCamSettings.minX,
    minY = currentCamSettings.minY,
    maxX = currentCamSettings.maxX,
    maxY = currentCamSettings.maxY,
    trackingSpeed = currentCamSettings.trackingSpeed
  };
}
```

8. Converts the entire list of level items to an array of `LevelItemRepresentation` objects and stores them in the `levelItems` field on the `LevelDataRepresentation` object.

9. Locates the camera script CameraLerpToTransform in the scene. Then it maps its settings against a new `CameraSettingsRepresentation` object and assigns that object to the `LevelDataRepresentation` object's `cameraSettings` field.

You're almost there! Add the following below the last piece of code you just added:

```
var levelDataToJson = JsonUtility.ToJson(ldr);
var savePath = System.IO.Path.Combine(Application.dataPath,
    level.levelName + ".json");
System.IO.File.WriteAllText(savePath, levelDataToJson);
Debug.Log("Level saved to " + savePath);
```

This uses `JsonUtility` to serialize the `LevelDataRepresentation` object, and all of its nested level item fields and values, to a JSON string named `levelDataToJson`.

Then it combines the level name specified in the editor with the game's application data path (pointing to your Assets folder). This path is used to write the JSON string out to a file.

Save your changes. Go to the **Game** scene in Unity, click the **Level** GameObject, type in **my super awesome level** in the name field and click **Save level**.

Look in the **Assets** folder for your shiny new JSON level file.

If you inspect the .JSON file with a text editor, you'll see how all the items that make up the level and their properties were serialized and saved to the file.

Good work!

A menu scene to load levels

Right now, the menu scene has a simple play button that starts the Game scene when clicked. It would suffice if you just wanted some weak little single-level game, but can't handle the stress of multiple levels.

Ideally, the menu scene should parse any .JSON level files stored in the game's directory and display them to the player. When the player clicks a level name, the game should interpret the level's .JSON file then build and load it into the Game scene.

Modifying the menu

The menu scene currently has a UI panel named **LevelItemsPanel** that has a built-in scrolling system. When the panel is full of items, the scroll bar allows the player to scroll through them.

You'll fill the panel with buttons that represent each level file in the directory. As you'd expect, you'll click a button to load the relevant level.

The starter project includes a button prefab in **Assets\Prefabs** that'll be the template for each level's button.

Start by removing the existing **PlayButton** from the **Menu** scene.

Remove the PlayButton

Open **GameManager.cs**. Add these two fields to the top of the class:

```
public GameObject buttonPrefab;
private string selectedLevel;
```

- `buttonPrefab` will hold a reference to the button template each level button will use.

- `selectedLevel` will temporarily hold the path to a level file based on which level button the player clicks.

Now add a new method:

```
private void SetLevelName(string levelFilePath) {
  selectedLevel = levelFilePath;
  SceneManager.LoadScene("Game");
}
```

This sets `selectedLevel` to the path string passed into the method and then loads the Game scene. It'll also come into play later when you add code to load level content based on its value.

Create another new method:

```
private void DiscoverLevels() {
  var levelPanelRectTransform =
    GameObject.Find("LevelItemsPanel")
      .GetComponent<RectTransform>();
  var levelFiles = Directory.GetFiles(Application.dataPath,
    "*.json");
}
```

You guessed it; this method will seek out and discover .JSON level files! First, it locates the UI panel GameObject in the Menu scene and grabs a reference to the `RectTransform` component. It then searches for JSON files — by looking for .json extensions — in the game's `Application.dataPath`.

Still inside `DiscoverLevels()`, add the following below the previous code:

```
var yOffset = 0f;
for (var i = 0; i < levelFiles.Length; i++) {
  if (i == 0) {
    yOffset = -30f;
  }
  else {
    yOffset -= 65f;
  }
  var levelFile = levelFiles[i];
  var levelName = Path.GetFileName(levelFile);
}
```

For a little chunk of code, it's got a lot going on. Here you're looping through the levelFiles array. Each iteration calculates the yOffset, starting at −30f and reducing by 65f decrements. This calculation determines the vertical position of each button on the panel.

levelFile stores the current file from the levelFiles array. Then it determines the file name via Path.GetFileName().

Add the following inside the same method after the previous code you added, inside the for loop just below var levelName = Path.GetFileName(levelFile);.

```
// 1
var levelButtonObj = (GameObject)Instantiate(buttonPrefab,
    Vector2.zero, Quaternion.identity);
// 2
var levelButtonRectTransform = levelButtonObj
    .GetComponent<RectTransform>();
levelButtonRectTransform.SetParent(levelPanelRectTransform,
    true);
// 3
levelButtonRectTransform.anchoredPosition =
    new Vector2(212.5f, yOffset);
// 4
var levelButtonText = levelButtonObj.transform.GetChild(0)
    .GetComponent<Text>();
levelButtonText.text = levelName;
```

1. Instantiates a copy of the button prefab.

2. Gets its transform and makes it a child of **LevelItemsPanel**.

3. Positions it based on a fixed X-position and a variable Y-position, aka yOffset.

4. Sets the button text to the level's name. The GetChild() method finds the Text component. It also passes in an index that refers to the index number of the child transform component. This is a 0 based index, so the first child under the button will be 0.

At this point, you've got a button, a way to find levels and a way to place and name the buttons. Good work! You still need a method that listens for clicks on the button. A handy trick is to add listener methods to the onClick event on a button.

Just beneath the previous code you added, but still inside the for loop, add the following:

```
var levelButton = levelButtonObj.GetComponent<Button>();
levelButton.onClick.AddListener(delegate {
    SetLevelName(levelFile); });
levelPanelRectTransform.sizeDelta =
    new Vector2(levelPanelRectTransform.sizeDelta.x, 60f * i);
```

Remember that private method you added earlier named `SetLevelName()`? Little did you know at the time that you could use that as the listener!

This code passes it into the `AddListener()` method on the `onClick` event with a string parameter that indicates the level file name `levelFile`.

Each iteration of the `for` loop changes the value of `levelFile` because each can point to different .JSON file names. By passing in a delegate that points to `SetLevelName()`, you can dynamically assign different calls to `SetLevelName()` to each instance of a button. Pretty cool! :]

The last trick of the above code is that it expands the vertical size of `LevelItemsPanel` to accommodate all the possible buttons.

Finally, after the `for` loop, but below its closing curly bracket, add the following:

```
levelPanelRectTransform.offsetMax =
  new Vector2(levelPanelRectTransform.offsetMax.x, 0f);
```

This effectively changes the panel's scroll position to ensure it's back at the top after all the level buttons are added.

Now, add the following to the end of the existing `Start()` method:

```
DiscoverLevels();
```

`DiscoverLevels()` is called when the game manager initializes to retrieve any level files from JSON, and populate the menu with buttons for each.

Save your changes and switch back to Unity. In the **Menu** scene, drag and drop the **LevelButton** prefab from the **Prefabs** folder onto the **Button Prefab** reference on the **GameManager** in the scene Inspector.

Now make a bunch of duplicate .JSON level files with different names. Remember you can do this by loading the game scene, selecting the **Level** GameObject, and then clicking **Save level** in the Inspector with different names. Run the game from the **Menu** scene.

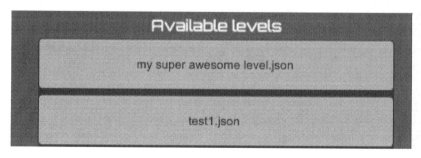

Look at those beautiful, dynamically formed level buttons! In the Hierarchy, you'll see the cloned prefab copies of the button prefab that have been instantiated based on how many level files your script found.

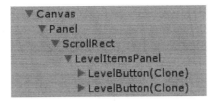

The Game scene will load just fine if you click a level button. However, you won't get any level definition just yet. Only the level you've set up in the Game scene will load. That's the next behavior you'll change.

Scripting logic to load levels

So far, you've implemented the ability to save levels using the Unity editor as a level editor and logic to display those levels in a menu.

You're in the homestretch where you'll write the final bit of code to interpret .JSON level files, and dynamically reconstruct it based whatever level the player chooses.

Open **GameManager.cs** and add the following:

```
private void LoadLevelContent() {
    var existingLevelRoot = GameObject.Find("Level");
    Destroy(existingLevelRoot);
    var levelRoot = new GameObject("Level");
}
```

This code runs when the Game scene loads. It finds the existing `Level` GameObject, destroys it, and then creates a new, "clean" `Level` GameObject.

This might seem a little backward, but there's good reason for it. The Game scene already contains a Level GameObject that has a child level layout, because the scene was used to design and edit the example levels and save them to .JSON.

If you just reconstructed a level with the Game scene, then you would get duplicate objects and a big, sticky mess. When you destroy the Level root GameObject and its children, you tidy up the scene. When the script creates that new root Level GameObject, it's ready to host the loaded level.

Just below the last line of code inside the `LoadLevelContent()` method, add the following:

```
// 1
var levelFileJsonContent = File.ReadAllText(selectedLevel);
```

```
var levelData = JsonUtility.FromJson<LevelDataRepresentation>(
  levelFileJsonContent);
// 2
foreach (var li in levelData.levelItems) {
  // 3
  var pieceResource =
    Resources.Load("Prefabs/" + li.prefabName);
  if (pieceResource == null) {
    Debug.LogError("Cannot find resource: " + li.prefabName);
  }
  // 4
  var piece = (GameObject)Instantiate(pieceResource,
    li.position, Quaternion.identity);
  var pieceSprite = piece.GetComponent<SpriteRenderer>();
  if (pieceSprite != null) {
    pieceSprite.sortingOrder = li.spriteOrder;
    pieceSprite.sortingLayerName = li.spriteLayer;
    pieceSprite.color = li.spriteColor;
  }
  // 5
  piece.transform.parent = levelRoot.transform;
  piece.transform.position = li.position;
  piece.transform.rotation = Quaternion.Euler(
    li.rotation.x, li.rotation.y, li.rotation.z);
  piece.transform.localScale = li.scale;
}
```

Here's what you cooked up in there:

1. Reads the JSON file content of the selected level — selectedLevel is the path where the level resides after the player clicks the corresponding button. JsonUtility is a class that deserializes the JSON content to an instance of LevelDataRepresentation. It also sets all the nested field values, so this object contains all the level hierarchy deserialized in this one object.

2. Makes levelData.levelItems into a fully populated array of LevelItemRepresentation instances.

3. For every item that is looped through in the array, the script locates correct prefab and loads it from the Resources/\Prefabs folder based on the prefabName value.

4. Instantiates a clone of this prefab. When the prefab has a sprite, it's then configured based on sprite data from the .JSON file for that item.

5. Makes the object a child of the Level GameObject then sets and its position, rotation and scale based on the data for that item in the level file.

Find `piece.transform.localScale = li.scale;` at the bottom of the `foreach` loops. Add the following code beneath the closing curly bracket:

```
var SoyBoy = GameObject.Find("SoyBoy");
SoyBoy.transform.position = levelData.playerStartPosition;
Camera.main.transform.position = new Vector3(
  SoyBoy.transform.position.x, SoyBoy.transform.position.y,
    Camera.main.transform.position.z);
```

The Game scene always has a **SoyBoy** GameObject in the Hierarchy. However, when a level loads, it's possible that Soy Boy is in a different starting location — that could be a real problem.

This code locates **SoyBoy** and places him at the `playerStartPosition` location saved in the .JSON file. Next, it positions the camera in line with **SoyBoy**, so the level loads with the view squarely on that little chunk of tofu.

Now you just need some code to set up the camera's smooth follow script settings in accordance with how the level was designed and saved.

Add this code below the last code you added to set the camera's position:

```
// 1
var camSettings = FindObjectOfType<CameraLerpToTransform>();
// 2
if (camSettings != null) {
  camSettings.cameraZDepth =
    levelData.cameraSettings.cameraZDepth;
  camSettings.camTarget = GameObject.Find(
    levelData.cameraSettings.cameraTrackTarget).transform;
  camSettings.maxX = levelData.cameraSettings.maxX;
  camSettings.maxY = levelData.cameraSettings.maxY;
  camSettings.minX = levelData.cameraSettings.minX;
  camSettings.minY = levelData.cameraSettings.minY;
  camSettings.trackingSpeed =
    levelData.cameraSettings.trackingSpeed;
}
```

1. Locates the smooth follow script `CameraLerpToTransform` with the `FindObjectOfType()` method.

2. Checks that the smooth follow script was found, and if so, it populates settings for speed, bounds and tracking target with the values found in the .JSON file.

Now you need to call `LoadLevelContent()` when the Game scene loads.

Replace the existing `OnSceneLoaded()` method in **GameManager.cs** with this:

```
private void OnSceneLoaded(Scene scene,
  LoadSceneMode loadsceneMode) {
```

```
if (!string.IsNullOrEmpty(selectedLevel)
    && scene.name == "Game") {
    Debug.Log("Loading level content for: " + selectedLevel);
    LoadLevelContent();
    DisplayPreviousTimes();
  }
  if (scene.name == "Menu") DiscoverLevels();
}
```

This runs whenever a scene loads that also has the GameManager.cs singleton in it. By checking that the scene name is Game, as well as ensuring selectedLevel is set to something, you ensure that the next bit of code will only run when the Game scene loads and the selectedLevel value has been set.

Finally, the last line of code checks that the scene name is set to Menu before calling DiscoverLevels(). This check ensures that the script did indeed discover all the level files and all those buttons are ready to load the associated level file paths.

Save **GameManager.cs** and run the game from the **Menu** scene.

Choose one of those custom-designed levels saved to .JSON from the **Menu** level selector.

The level is loaded from the file and completely re-constructed.

Congratulations! You now have a fully functional level loader, with the ability to design and save custom levels, as well as display them in the menu's level selector scrolling panel.

Tidying up loose ends

There are a few things to tidy up. Remember those best times you implemented with binary serialization? Well, they only work on one level.

No matter how many different levels you create and play, the same times show up for all of them.

Currently, best times save to a binary file and are concatenated with whatever name you chose to play under and the suffix _times.dat.

It'll work better if you tie the best times to the level names.

Open **GameManager.cs**. In SaveTime(), replace the line that defines the filePath variable with this:

```
var levelName = Path.GetFileName(selectedLevel);
var filePath = Application.persistentDataPath +
   "/" + playerName + "_" + levelName + "_times.dat";
```

With this, you're tacking the level name onto the file name.

Almost done! Now that you changed the naming convention, you broke how the game loads run times — it's still looking for the old naming convention. In the LoadPreviousTimes() method, replace the line that defines the scoresFile variable with this:

```
var levelName = Path.GetFileName(selectedLevel);
var scoresFile = Application.persistentDataPath +
   "/" + playerName + "_" + levelName + "_times.dat";
```

Now the LoadPreviousTimes() method knows to look for scores based on the player and level name. From here on out, run times will be linked to levels by their names. For more polish, you should show the level's name for the scores. Modify DisplayPreviousTimes() as follows:

```
public void DisplayPreviousTimes()
{
  var times = LoadPreviousTimes();
  var levelName = Path.GetFileName(selectedLevel);
  if (levelName != null) {
    levelName = levelName.Replace(".json", "");
  }
  var topThree = times.OrderBy(time => time.time).Take(3);
  var timesLabel = GameObject.Find("PreviousTimes")
    .GetComponent<Text>();
  timesLabel.text = levelName + "\n";
  timesLabel.text += "BEST TIMES \n";
  foreach (var time in topThree) {
    timesLabel.text += time.entryDate.ToShortDateString()
      + ": " + time.time + "\n";
  }
}
```

The only change is that the level name is determined via the `Path.GetFileName()` method on the `selectedLevel` value. You also strip away the .json file extension. Then you create the `timesLabel` text component with the name of the level at the top with the top three times following that.

Save **GameManager.cs** and run the game again from the **Menu** scene. Play two different levels a few times and notice how your run times are specific to each level. Awesome!

If you take another look at the run time score files that are stored, you'll see they're now using the new naming convention as you would expect!

Name	Date modified	Type	Size
John_basic level.json_times.dat	12/09/2016 00:28	DAT File	1 KB
John_my other level.json_times.dat	12/09/2016 00:30	DAT File	1 KB
John_times.dat	11/09/2016 23:20	DAT File	1 KB

Okay, you're at the last bit of scripting, and this is an easy one!

Players should be able to easily return to the **Menu** scene and use the level selection interface.

Add this `Update()` method to **GameManager.cs**:

```
void Update() {
    if (Input.GetKeyDown(KeyCode.Escape)) {
        SceneManager.LoadScene("Menu");
    }
}
```

This checks for an escape keypress and loads the **Menu** scene if detected.

Now it's easy to go back to the level selection UI in the **Menu** scene at any point.

Where to go from here?

You covered a ton of material in this chapter. Here are some of the highlights:

- Three methods to save data: PlayerPrefs, binary serialization and Unity's JSON serialization

- And when and why to use each

- Saving and loading file-specific data for the player to see, scroll and select

- Building custom, shareable game levels

You might have leveled up on your C# skills too.

What does the ability to design and save custom levels allow you to do now? Share them of course! Be sure to post your levels on the http://raywenderlich.com forums for your fellow game designers to download and try out. Let's see how challenging you can make them, and of course, we want to see your best times.

> **Note:** As long as you don't introduce any new prefabs when building the levels, they'll work for everyone else who's working on this game.

Section IV: Blender

In this section, you'll learn how to use Blender — a free 3D modeling and animation tool — to create great-looking assets for your games.

Along the way, you will create a scorpion enemy from scratch: including modeling, texturing, and animating.

Chapter 15, "Modelling with Blender"

Chapter 16, "Texturing with Blender"

Chapter 17, "Animating in Blender"

Chapter 15: Modeling in Blender

By Mike Berg

Blender is a free 3D modeling and animation tool. It is widely used and actively supported, but many game developers are immediately daunted by its unique user interface. Blender is very powerful, though, and more than capable of fulfilling your 3D asset creation needs — once you know the basics!

In this chapter, you'll learn the basics of modeling in Blender as you build this formidable enemy below:

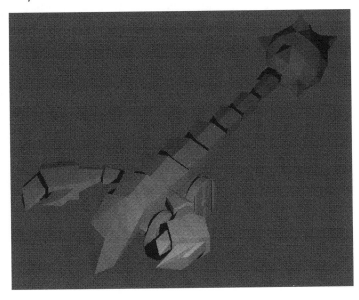

Getting started

Before you dive in, make sure you have a 2-button mouse with a scrollwheel. You should be able to click down on the scrollwheel itself for a middle click. You will need all three of these buttons while using Blender.

Download Blender

Go to the Blender website to download Blender for Windows, Mac or Linux:

https://unite.unity.com/

Setting some defaults

By default, Blender selects object with the right mouse button, and performs actions with the left mouse button. By keeping the selection of an item separated from the action on item, you are less likely to select and move an item by mistake.

This makes Blender very awkward to beginners, but you get used to it in time. That said, you can still change it so the left mouse button both selects and acts on an object, as is common with almost every application on Earth.

Open the preferences by selecting **File\User Preferences**. Click the **Input** tab at the top, then click the **Select With: Left** button. This changes your left mouse button to be your primary selection tool.

Secondly, if you are using a laptop — or any keyboard without a number pad — select the **Emulate Numpad** checkbox. This allows you to change the 3D view using the top row of numbers on your keyboard. you'll learn more about that a bit later.

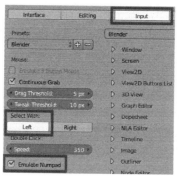

Click the **Save User Settings** button at the bottom, then close the preferences window.

> **Note**: Blender's efficiency relies heavily on keyboard commands. They are even designed to be primarily on the left side of the keyboard, so that you can keep your left hand on the keyboard and your right hand on the mouse (with apologies to you lefties!). You will primarily be using keyboard commands when possible.

Creating your first model

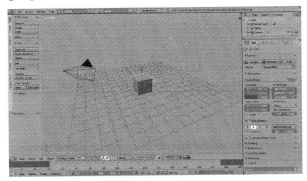

When you first open Blender, there's a cube in your scene. You're going to start with the wheels of the scorpion, so you don't need the cube. The thin white border around an object shows that it is selected, so delete it by pressing... the Delete key?

Nope, not in Blender! Remember, common keyboard commands are on the left side of the keyboard, and the Delete key is *miles* away on the right side of the keyboard.

Press **X** to delete. A confirmation will appear right under your cursor. Click it to delete your object.

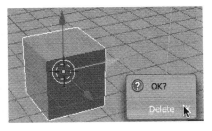

> **Note**: Hotkeys in Blender are specific to the panel your cursor is currently over. If a hotkey doesn't work as expected, move your cursor over the **3D View** in the middle of your screen and try again.

Re-inventing a wheel

Start by creating a cylinder for the wheel. To create a new object, press **Shift-A**.

1. A popup appears under your cursor. Select **Mesh\Cylinder**.

2. Before you do anything else, you'll have to change some settings. At the lower-left of your screen, set the **Vertices** to **20**, and the **Depth** to **0.3**.

3. You should now have a cylinder that looks like this:

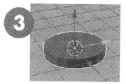

Stand the wheel up on edge by pressing **R** to rotate it. Blender immediately enters a rotation mode; moving your cursor rotates the object freely.

1. Have a look at the small axis indicator at the lower left. You want to rotate the cylinder on the **Y axis**.

2. Press **Y** and your rotation snaps to the y axis (note the green line through your model, indicating this).

3. You can drag your cursor around to rotate it, but for precise rotation simply type **90** and press **Enter** to complete the rotation.

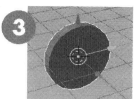

To recap: rotating an object is as simple as quickly typing one command, **R Y 90 Enter**.

> **Note:** This also works for both moving (type **G** for Grab) and scaling (type **S**), where the first command is the type of translation (move, scale or rotate), the second is the axis, and the third is the distance, scale factor, or angle.

The view from here

Before you edit the wheel any further, change the view so that you only see the side of it. Here are the keyboard shortcuts for changing the 3D View:

- **1**: Front View

- **3**: Side View

- **7**: Top View

- **5**: Toggle perspective

Press **3 5** to get a side view, with perspective turned off.

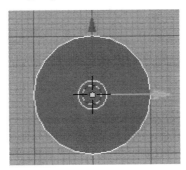

Edit Mode

Now the real fun begins. Get ready to edit some polygons!

Blender has several modes; right now you'll cover **Object Mode** and **Edit Mode**. In Object Mode, you position objects within your scene. In Edit Mode, you edit the polygons of an object. Press **Tab** to toggle between these two modes. You'll see the popup at the bottom of the view change:

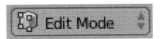

> **Note:** It can be easy to forget which mode you are in while working. Be sure to check the popup above if something isn't working as you expect; you might be trying to do something in Edit Mode that can only be done in Object Mode, and vice versa.

Slice-n-dice with the Knife tool

The **Knife** tool creates a new edge on a face, cutting it in two. Create some boards on the front of the wheel by cutting it into four separate faces:

1. Press **K**, click once on the top-middle vertex, then click on the bottom vertex and press **Enter** to complete the operation. (*Operation!* Polygon surgery... Badum-ching!)

2. Repeat the process for the vertices shown here...

3. ... and here.

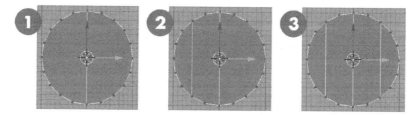

Mesh Select Mode

While in Edit Mode, sometimes you want to work just with points (vertices), sometimes with edges, and sometimes with entire faces. There are three options for working with these elements of your mesh: **Vertex Select**, **Edge Select** and **Face Select**. Switch between them by pressing **Ctrl-Tab**, or by using the toggle buttons at the bottom of the 3D View.

Switch to **Face Select**:

Select the four newly-created faces by clicking one, then holding **Shift** and clicking the others. Selected faces are highlighted.

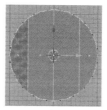

> **Note:** If you make a mistake with a selection, undo works the same for selections as any other action. You can also press **A** to toggle "select all" and "select none".

Orbiting the camera

You need a slightly different view of your model to see the next operation properly. **Middle-click and drag** to orbit the camera around your model.

> **Shift + middle-click + drag** to pan the view, and use your scroll wheel to zoom in and out.

Orbit around your wheel to get a view similar to this:

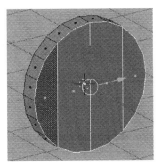

The Inset tool

The **Inset** tool creates a smaller copy of the currently-selected face.

1. Press **I** to invoke the Inset tool. Drag the cursor toward the center of the object and the inset adjusts.

2. You want each individual face to be inset, rather than the whole group of faces. Press **I** again to enter the tool's **Individual** mode.

3. While the Inset tool is still active, you can adjust the height of your inset to create a beveled edge around each of these faces. Hold the **Ctrl** key and drag away from the center of the object to adjust the height. **Left-click** to complete the operation.

4.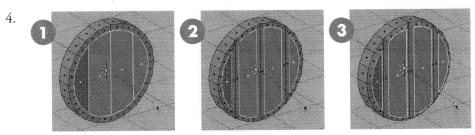

That's it for your wheel! Press **Tab** to return to Object Mode.

> **Note:** Now would be a good time to save. Press **Ctrl-S** to save. You can find a copy of this file in the Resources folder: **Scorpion 01-Wheel.blend**.

Making the axles

Add a cylinder to use as an axle:

1. Press **Shift-A** and select **Mesh > Cylinder**. In the tool options on the left, set the depth to **3**.

2. Type **R Y 90** and press Enter to rotate it.

3. Type **S Shift-X 0.2** to scale the axle. Note that pressing **Shift-X** *excludes* that axis from the scale operation; the object scales only on the Z and Y axes. This works for move and rotate operations, too.

> **Note:** If your new object doesn't appear at the center of the scene, you may have accidentally moved the **3D Cursor** (a dotted red and white circle) by right-clicking in the 3D view. All new objects are aligned with the 3D cursor. Reset it to the center of the scene by pressing **Shift-S** and selecting **Cursor to Center**.

Duplicating the wheel

Click the wheel object to select it.

1. Type **G X 1.2** and press Enter to move the wheel to the end of the axle.

2. Type **Shift-D X -2.4** and press Enter to duplicate the wheel. Adding the axis and distance immediately moves your duplicate along the specified axis. The second wheel is now exactly where it needs to be.

3. Type **R Z 180** to rotate the wheel so that the beveled faces are pointing outward.

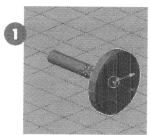  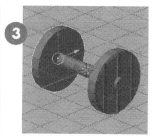

Applying transformations

When modeling for Unity, it's very important to apply the rotation and scale of all objects. After scaling an object to the size you want, applying the transforms will reset the scale values to 1 and the rotation values to zero.

You **will** have scale and rotation problems with your 3D models in Unity, if you don't do this!

1. Click the axle to select it, and press **N** to display the Properties Region. Notice that both the rotation and scale values have been modified.

2. Press **Ctrl-A** and select **Rotation & Scale**.

3. The object doesn't change shape, and all the values are now nice and clean.

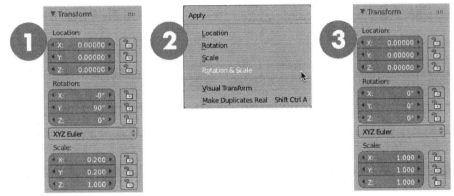

Be sure to **Apply Rotation & Scale** for each of the wheels as well.

Joining objects

Since these three objects are going to be animated as a single object in Unity, it makes them easier to work with if they are combined into a single object.

Click one of the wheels to select it, then hold **Shift**, click the other wheel, then the axle. It's important to select the axle **last**. Press **Ctrl-J** to join them.

Note the dot at the center of the object. This dot is the **origin** of your object. Transformations applied to the object will center around the origin, both in Blender and in Unity. When joining objects, the *last object selected* is the one that keeps its origin.

> **Note:** If you ever need to reset an object's origin, make sure you are in **Object Mode**, then use the menu at the bottom of the 3D View to select **Object\Transform\Origin to Geometry** to snap the origin to the center of its geometry.

Renaming objects

Since you will want to animate this object in Unity, it will be helpful to give it a recognizable name. The top-right panel in Blender is the **Outliner**. Double-click the cylinder object's name to change it to **axle**:

Adding the base

1. Create a new cube by pressing **Shift-A** and selecting **Mesh\Cube**.

2. Scale it twice: type **S Z 0.2** and press Enter, then type **S Y 2** and press Enter.

3. Move it up a bit, so that it's sitting on top of the axle. Type **G Z 0.4** and press Enter.

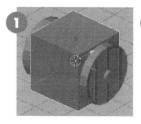 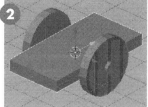 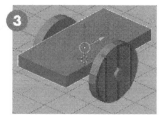

The Bevel tool

The Bevel tool creates a bevelled edge on your object.

1. Select the base and press **Tab** to enter Edit Mode. All the faces of the cube are likely already selected. If not, Press **A** to Select All.

2. Press **Ctrl-B** to invoke the Bevel tool. Drag away from the object's origin to increase the size of the bevel. Notice how the bevel is not evenly applied to all edges. You want a nice 45-degree angle all the way around your base. This is another effect of not using the previously-mentioned **Apply Rotation & Scale** feature.

   Press **Esc** to abort the Bevel operation, then press **Tab** to exit Edit Mode. Press **Ctrl-A** and select **Rotation & Scale**. Press **Tab** to return to Edit Mode.

3. Press **Ctrl-B** and drag to adjust the size of the bevel. Note how the bevel is now applied the way you want it. When you are happy with the bevel size, click to finish the Bevel. Press **Tab** to exit Edit Mode.

> **Note:** While dragging the size of the bevel, try scrolling the scroll wheel on your mouse. This increases the roundness of the bevel. Nice!

Duplicating the axle for the back wheels

Start by moving the existing axle.

1. Click the axle to select it. Move it by typing **G Y 1.3** and pressing Enter.

2. There's another way to duplicate an object called **Duplicate Linked**. This creates a copy of the **object** — which can be moved, rotated and scaled — that shares the same **mesh** as the original. Changes to one mesh will be made to both objects. This will come in handy in the next chapter where you apply color to the mesh; colors applied to one object will be applied to both. Create a linked duplicate, and move the axle by typing **Alt-D Y -2.6** and pressing Enter.

> **Note:** One way to remember the difference between the regular Duplicate (**Shift-D**) and a Linked Duplicate (**Alt-D**) is that "Alt" has the letter "L" in it, for "Linked".

Don't forget to press **Ctrl-S** to save. You can find a copy of this file in the Resources folder: **Scorpion 02-Base.blend**.

Modeling the body

1. You need another cube for the body: create one using **Shift-A**.

2. Scale it: type **S 0.7** and press Enter.

3. Move it up: type **G Z 1** and press Enter. Move it forward: type **G Y -1.3** and press Enter.

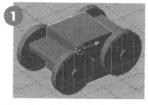  

4. **Middle-click and drag** to orbit around to see the other side of the cube, and press **Tab** to enter Edit Mode.

5. Press **Ctrl-Tab** and ensure you are in **Face Select Mode**. Select the top face of the cube. Remember, press **A** to Select None if there were already faces selected when you entered Edit Mode. Type **S X 1.5** to make that face a bit wider.

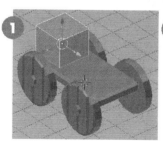 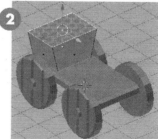

Loop Cut

Making a **Loop Cut** is similar to using the Knife tool, but it makes a cut through the middle of multiple connected faces. You want to create a ridge along the back of the scorpion that sticks up a bit. The Loop Cut tool is perfect for this.

1. Press **Ctrl-R** to invoke the Loop Cut tool. Hover the cursor over an edge and you'll see a line appear, showing a preview of how the loop will be cut. Move your mouse over the edge shown here. **Left-click** once.

2. By default, the loop cut is positioned exactly in the center, and that's what you want. Without moving your mouse, **left-click** again to accept the position and apply the loop cut.

> **Note:** Move your mouse before the second click to move your cut. Scroll the mouse wheel to create multiple cuts. Be aware that loop cuts only work with connected **quads** (faces with four edges). Modeling with only quads is good form.

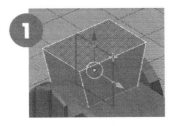
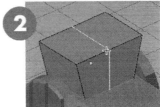

Shaping the body

When you finish a Loop Cut, you'll be automatically switched to **Edge Select Mode**. This is perfect:

1. Click the edge in the middle, on the top.

2. Drag the blue arrow up a bit, or type **G Z 0.3**.

3. Press **Ctrl-Tab** and switch to **Face Select Mode**. Select the back two faces.

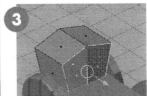

Extrude, scale, repeat

The **Extrude tool** takes your selected faces and extrudes them outward, creating new faces along the sides. This is the primary tool you'll use to create the ridged body.

1. Press **E** to extrude the selected faces. You only need a small extrusion this time, so move the mouse just a bit, then click to complete the extrusion.

2. Press **S** and drag to scale the new face down a bit.

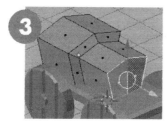
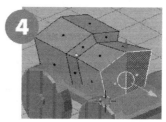

3. Press **E** again and make a larger extrusion; about the same size as the first larger segment.

4. Press **S** and drag to make this end a bit larger.

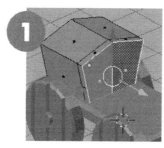
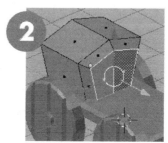

Repeat this process until you have several segments that gradually get smaller and smaller. You might find it easier to press **3** and work in the Side View. Reminder: **Shift + middle-click + drag** to pan the view.

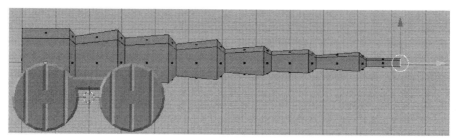

Note: Internally, the Extrude operation is a two-step process. It creates new faces around the edges, then moves the selection. If you start an extrusion, then cancel it with a **right-click** or **Esc** key, you are only canceling the second step. Look closely, and you will see dots along the edges that indicate a face. These extra faces could end up causing problems with your model. To cancel an extrude, press **Esc**, then press **Ctrl-Z**.

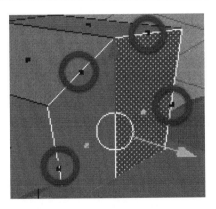

Reminder: Don't forget to save. You can find a copy of this file in the Resources folder: **Scorpion 03-Body.blend**.

Modeling the head

With the body out of the way, it's time to make the head!

1. **Middle-click and drag** to orbit around your model. Select the front two faces of the body mesh.

2. Press **S** and scale down these faces to give it a bit more of a neck.

3. Make a small extrusion (**E drag click**), and scale that up (**S drag click**) to form the back edge of the head.

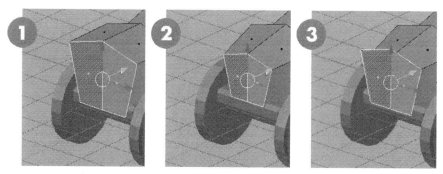

4. Press **3** to switch to the Side View, and extrude the selection to make a shape for the head (**E drag click**).

5. Rotate the selected faces to give the head a wedge shape. Because you are in the Side View, you don't have to worry about locking the rotation to a certain axis. Simply press **R** and drag to rotate.

6. Move the front of the head down a bit. Again, you can move it without locking it to an axis. Press **G** and drag it into place.

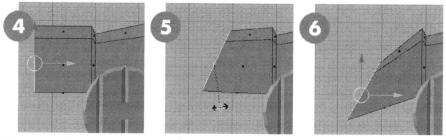

7. Orbit around so you can see the front of the head. Press **Ctrl-Tab** and switch to **Edge Select Mode**. Click the edge in the middle of the head to select it.

8. Press **3** to return to the Side View. Press **G** and move the selected edge down and forward a bit.

9. Now *that* is a nice looking head! Press **Tab** to return to Object Mode.

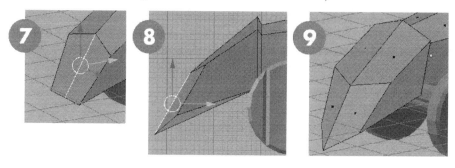

Reminder: Don't forget to save. You can find a copy of this file in the Resources folder: **Scorpion 04-Head.blend.**

Making the claws

1. Press **7** to switch to Top View. Add a new cube (**Shift-A**) and move it (**G**) out to the side.

2. Orbit to to an angled view, and press **S Z 0.5**, then **S X 0.8** to scale the cube a bit. Press **Ctrl-A** to Apply Rotation & Scale.

3. Press **Tab** to enter Edit Mode. Press **Ctrl-R** to create a loop cut, as shown. This time, slide the cut back a bit, instead of centering it.

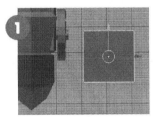  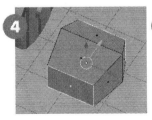

4. Press **Ctrl-Tab** and switch to **Face Select Mode**. Select the front and back faces of the mesh; you'll need to orbit the view around the object to do this. Press **S 0.75** to scale them down a bit.

5. Press **Tab** to return to Object Mode. Press **R Z -45** to rotate the object.

6. Press **Tab** to enter Edit Mode. Select the two faces shown here.

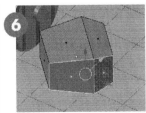  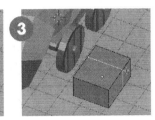

7. Press **I 0.2** to inset.

8. Press **E 1.2** to extrude the selection.

9. Press **Ctrl-Tab** to switch to **Edge Select Mode**, and select the edge shown here.

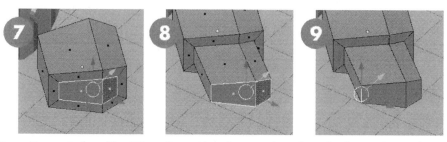

10. Press 7 to switch to Top View. Press **G** and move the selected edge as shown here.

11. Orbit around so you can see the side of the claw again. Press **Ctrl-Tab** and switch to **Face Select Mode**. Select the face shown here.

12. Press 7 to switch to Top View. Press **G** and move the selected face as shown here.

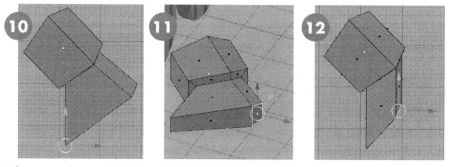

13. Orbit around to see the front of the claw. Select the face on the left.

14. Press **I 0.2** to inset this face the same as the previous inset operation.

15. Press **E 0.7** to extrude it.

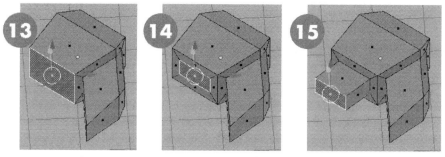

16. Press 7 to switch to Top View. Press **G** and move the selected face as shown here.

17. Orbit around so you can see the ends of both claws. Press **Ctrl-Tab** to switch to **Vertex Select Mode**, and select the vertexes shown here.

18. To merge these two points, press **Alt-M** and select **At Center**. Repeat this process for the tip of the other claw.

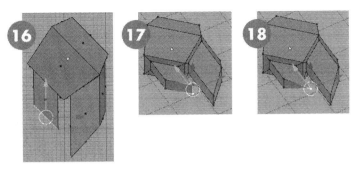

Adding the arm

1. Orbit around so that you can see the faces shown here. Press **Ctrl-Tab** to switch to **Face Select Mode**, and select the faces shown here.

2. Press **I 0.2** to inset.

3. Press 7 to switch to Top View. Press **E 1** to extrude.

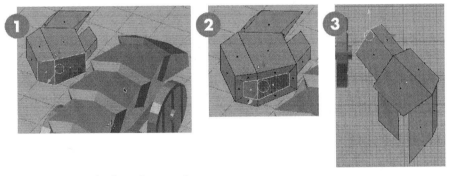

4. Press **S 0.5** to scale the selection down.

5. Ensure you're still in Top View, and press **R -10** to rotate it a bit.

6. Extrude the end a little bit (**E drag click**).

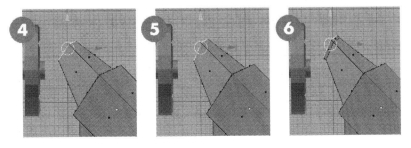

7. Scale the selection: **S 1.5**.

8. Press **E 1** to extrude the next segment.

9. Press **S 0.3** to scale down the end, then press **G** and move the end of the arm so that it's overlapping the body.

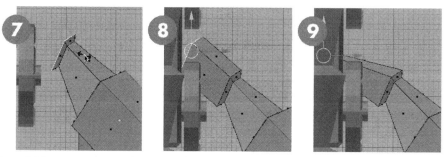

10. Press **Tab** to return to Object Mode. Orbit around to the side of the model. You can see that the arm is sticking out through the wheel!

11. Drag the blue Z Axis arrow upward until the arm is above the wheel.

Duplicate and mirror the arm

Now that you have an arm, it needs to be duplicated, and then flipped for the other side. Before you do that, have a look at the Properties Region (press **N** to toggle it). Remember when you rotated the object: Step 5 of "Making the claws". The object still has a Z-rotation value. This will interfere with the Mirror operation. Press **Ctrl-A** to Apply Rotation & Scale.

Since you're going to be duplicating objects, now is also a good time to revisit the **Outliner** at the top-right of the screen. Keep things organized by double-clicking each of your Cube objects to rename them:

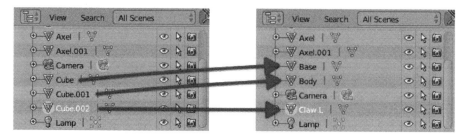

> **Note:** It's good practice to name objects with ".L" and ".R" at the end of their name, for left and right versions of mirrored objects like arms and legs.

That's better! Now it's time to duplicate the arm. Press 7 to switch to Top View.

1. Click on the arm to select it, then press **Alt-D** and immediately press **Enter** to create a linked duplicate of the object and keep it in place. Again, you use Linked Duplicate here to save time when you will color the arms in the next chapter.

2. Press **Ctrl-M** to invoke the Mirror tool. Nothing noticeable changes, but if you look at the bottom of the 3D View, you'll see that the menu bar has changed to a status bar, with the text **Select a mirror axis (X, Y, Z)**.

3. Press **X**, then **Enter** to complete the Mirror operation.

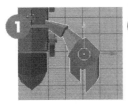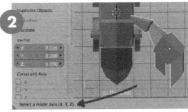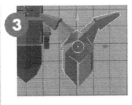

> **Note:** The status bar shows information and options for most tools. It's a good thing to glance at while performing different tasks.

Changing the pivot point

Now, this is mirrored correctly, and you *could* move the object over, but there's a way to mirror and move it in one step. Press **Ctrl-Z** to undo the Mirror operation.

Blender operations are always centered around a **Pivot Point**. So far, you have been using the default pivot point, which is the origin of the current object. There are several other options for the Pivot Point, which you can see in the menu at the bottom of the 3D View:

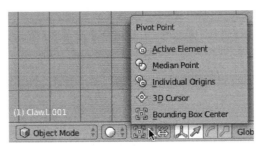

Change the Pivot Point to **3D Cursor**, which is at the center of the scene (remember, press **Shift-S** and select **Cursor to Center** if your cursor has been moved). Now when you mirror the arm, it will not only flip, but flip *over the cursor*.

Give it a try; press **Ctrl-M X** and press Enter to mirror over the X axis.

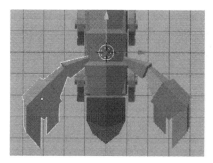

> **Note:** Press **. (period)** to quickly switch the pivot point to **3D Cursor**. Press **, (comma)** to switch it back to **Bounding Box Center**. In this mode, the pivot point is actually the object's origin, which is not always the center of the bounding box.

> **Reminder:** Don't forget to save. You can find a copy of this file in the Resources folder: **Scorpion 05-Arms.blend**.

Modeling the wrecking ball

Next up: adding a sphere for the wrecking ball on the end of the tail. You learned about using the 3D Cursor as a pivot point for the Mirror tool; now use it to change where a new object is created.

1. Orbit around your object so you can see the end of the tail. Select the body object and press **Tab** to enter Edit Mode. Press **Ctrl-Tab** and switch to **Edge Select Mode**. Select the edge in the middle, at the back.

2. Press **Shift-S** and select **Cursor to Selected**.

3. You'll see the cursor snap to the center of the current selection.

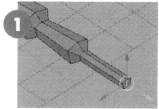

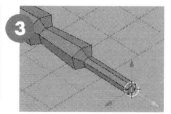

4. Press **Shift-A** and select **Icosphere**. Note that you are adding a new mesh *in Edit Mode*, which is essentially the same as creating two separate objects and combining them, as you did with the wheels and axle. This Icosphere mesh is now part of the Body object.

5. Press **Ctrl-Tab** and switch to **Face Select Mode**. Select one of the faces on the icosphere.

6. Press **E 0.6** to extrude the face.

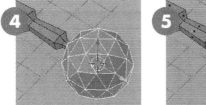
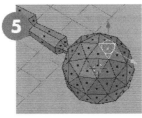
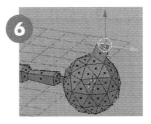

7. Merge the three points of the selected face: press **Alt-M** and select **At Center**.

8. Repeat this process for several faces around the icosphere to create more spikes.

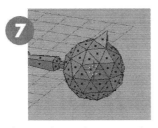
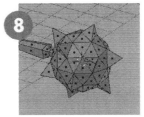

Press **Tab** to exit Edit Mode, and you are done! Press **Shift-Z** to toggle the view to a **Rendered** display. Looking good!

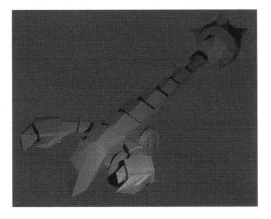

Important: When you finish a model, remember to apply all the transformations on each of your objects before moving on. Select an object in your scene, press **Ctrl-A** and select **Rotation & Scale**. Repeat this for every object.

Where to go from here?

Congratulations! You have mastered some of the mystic arts of modeling in Blender.

So far you've learned several core modeling techniques that could be used to model almost any shape you can imagine. Experiment with what you've learned, and see what other kinds of objects you can create! Hopefully you have become comfortable working with keyboard shortcuts, and can see how they enable to you model efficiently in Blender.

The following page has a list of the keyboard shortcuts you learned, to help you along the way.

In the following chapter, you will learn about UV texturing to add color your model.

Summary of keyboard commands

- **X** - Delete
- **Shift-A** - Create new objects
- **G** - Move
- **R** - Rotate
- **S** - Scale
- **K** - Knife
- **I** - Inset
- **E** - Extrude
- **Ctrl-Tab** - Mesh Selection Mode
- **Shift-D** - Duplicate
- **Alt-D** - Linked Duplicate
- **Ctrl-B** - Bevel
- **Ctrl-A** - Apply (Rotation & Scale)
- **Ctrl-R** - Loop Cut
- **Alt-M** - Merge Points
- **Ctrl-M** - Mirror
- **. (period)** - Move pivot point to 3D Cursor
- **, (comma)** - Move pivot point to current object
- **Shift-Z** - Toggle rendered view

3D View controls:

- **1** - Front View
- **3** - Side View
- **7** - Top View
- **5** - Toggle perspective

Chapter 16: Texturing with Blender

By Mike Berg

In the previous chapter, you just created a sweet model with Blender, but it's a little, uh — *monochrome*. What's next? Giving it some color, of course!

Texturing involves taking 2D artwork and applying it to 3D surfaces.

Note: This chapter builds on the skills learned and the model made in Chapter 15. I recommend you read through that chapter before this one.

Getting started

Texturing a model in Blender can be done in many different ways. You'll be covering the most common method used in video games: **UV Mapping**.

UV Mapping allows you to take each face in your mesh, and "project" part of a 2D image onto it. Typically, this is done by "unwrapping" the mesh so that it can be "laid flat", and arranged onto a 2D image.

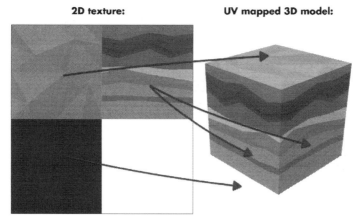

In the above example, each face of a simple cube is mapped to different areas of a single image. Note that UV mapping allows for any area of a texture to be used for multiple faces; in this case, all four sides use the same part of the texture.

To create your 2D texture, you need an image editor. You could use Photoshop, but GIMP is a great alternative. GIMP is an open source image editor that works on all platforms. It's free and it is feature packed. The only thing it truly lacks is a good name, but you can't have everything! :]

The instructions below are for GIMP, but you can use any image editor of your choice. Start by downloading GIMP for Windows, Mac or Linux:

http://www.gimp.org/downloads/

Creating a texture

Launch GIMP. Before you create a new document, set the grid, to make it easier to work with. From the menu bar, select **GIMP\Preferences**. Click **Default Grid**, on the left, and change the **Spacing** to 32×32.

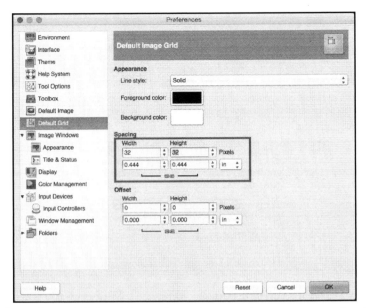

Click **OK**, then select **File\New**. It's good practice to make your texture sizes "power of 2"; 128×128, 256×256, 512×512, and so on. Because we're going to be working with flat colors, we don't need a very big texture; set your new document to 256×256:

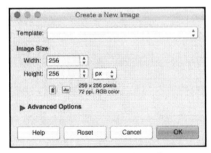

Select **View\Show Grid**, then **View\Snap to Grid**. Before you go any further, select **File\Save As** and save your document into the same folder as your 3D model.

You need some solid, flat colors to use for your model. You can use whatever colors you like, and you'll learn a simple trick for getting some variations on each base color.

1. Start by clicking the **Rectangle Select** tool from the toolbar.

2. Make a selection at the top-left of the document that is 5 grid-squares wide.

3. Click the **Foreground Color** in the toolbar to pick a color.

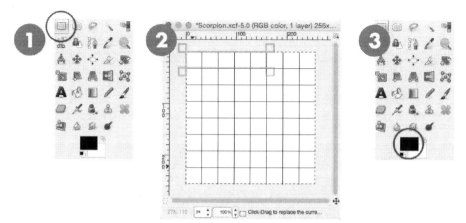

Use the color picker to select one of the colors you want to use on your model. I started with a grey. Enter **707070** in the **HTML notation** field to use the same color, and click **OK**.

4. Select **Edit\Fill with FG Color (Cmd-,)** to fill the selection with the foreground color.

5. Drag the selection down one grid space and select a new color, repeating the process for several colors.

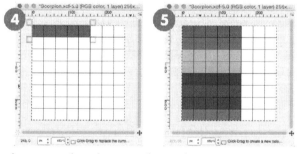

If you want to use the same colors, here are their values: `707070`, `907e52`, `ffd200`, `97b8db`, `933900`, `e23715`, `375f1f`, `438891`.

Select **Select\None (Cmd-Shift-A)**.

Adding shading

While you certainly may want to hand-pick each color, there's a simple trick for adding darker and lighter versions of all of these colors at once — in just a few steps.

1. In the **Layers Palette**, click the **New Layer** button and click **OK** on the resulting dialog to create a new layer.

2. Click the tiny **Foreground/Background** icon in the Tools palette to reset the colors to black and white.

3. Use the **Rectangle Select** tool to select the left-most column in the grid, and press **Cmd-,** to fill it with black.

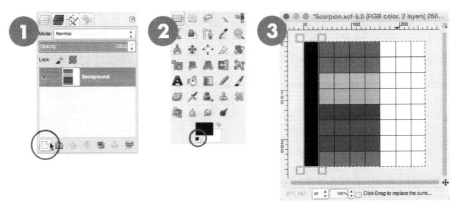

4. Use the **Rectangle Select** tool to select the right-most column in the grid, and press **Cmd-.** to fill it with white.

5. In the **Layers Palette**, change the **Mode** popup to **Overlay**.

6. Your left-most column is now nicely shaded, and your right-most column has a nice highlight.

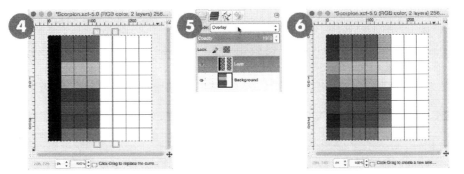

Create another new layer and repeat this process, but this time select the second column and fill it with black. Then select the fourth column and fill it with white.

7. After setting the **Mode** to **Overlay**, set the **Opacity** to **50%**. The opacity setting can be found directly underneath Mode field.

8. Now you have a nice range of colors to work with, and some variation in shading.

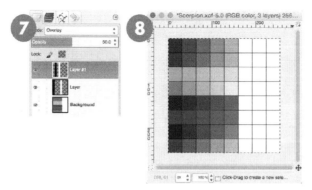

Select **File\Export** and save the PNG into the same folder as your Blender file.

Let's get those colors on your model!

Creating the Material in Blender

When texturing a model in Blender, there are two tabs in the **Properties** panel that you'll need to use: **Material** and **Texture**.

The Material tab

Open your scorpion model or you can open the scorpion starter project included with the resources. Make sure you are in **Object Mode**.

1. Click the body of your model to select it. In the **Properties** panel on the right, click the **Material** tab, then click the **New** button.

2. It's good to get into the habit of naming your material. Do that here.

3. Scroll down to the **Options** section, and select **UV Project**.

The Texture tab

1. In the Properties panel, click the **Texture** tab, then click the **New** button. More options will appear.

2. Ensure that the **Type** popup is set to **Image or Movie**.

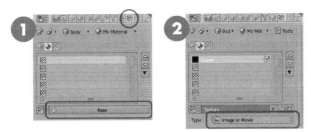

3. Scroll down to **Image** and click **Open**. Select the PNG you just created.

4. Scroll down to **Mapping**, set the **Coordinates** popup to **UV**.

Configuring lighting in your scene

In the **3D View**, switch the **Viewport Shading** to **Material**. This will let you see the material colors you apply, right in the main view.

Not much changes, because you haven't UV mapped your model yet. But notice that with the default lighting in a Blender scene, it can be hard to see your model from all angles.

Orbit around to the bottom of the model and it looks almost completely black. When adding color to your model, you want to be able to see it from any angle.

Select the light in your scene. It looks like this:

> **Note:** You can also select it by clicking the **Lamp** object in the Outliner, at the top-right of your screen.

In the **Properties** panel, click the **Object Data** tab and in the **Lamp** section, change it from **Point** to **Sun**.

This removes falloff, where the light gets dimmer as you get farther from it, and makes the light "parallel", where everything in your scene will be lit the same amount, and from the same angle.

> **Note:** The position of a **Sun** light is irrelevant. Only the rotation angle matters, which is indicated by the dotted line coming out of the light.

Your model is now much brighter, but it's still dark on one side. To solve this, create a **fill light**:

1. Press **1** to switch to front view. Duplicate the light (**Shift-D**) and move the copy down and to the left.

    I know I just said the position doesn't matter, but they will be easier to select if they are not in *exactly* the same place.

2. Press **R** and rotate the angle of the light so that it is pointing in the opposite direction as the first light.

3. In the **Properties** panel, change the **Energy** to **0.6**.

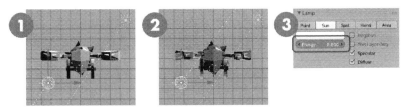

Orbit around your model, and you'll see that it's nicely lit up no matter which angle you're looking from.

UV Mapping your model

Now that you've got your material, texture and lighting set up, it's time to map the texture to the model!

Setting up your workspace

At the top of the Blender window, Switch to the **UV Editing** workspace.

The screen layout now shows two panels, the **UV/Image Editor** on the left, and the **3D View** on the right.

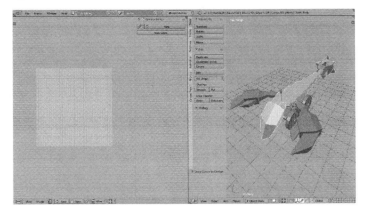

> **Tip:** Move your cursor over the 3D View and press **T** to toggle the Tools panel. With your cursor over the UV/Image Editor, press **N** to toggle the Properties panel. That gives you a bit more screen real estate to work with.

The **Viewport Shading** mode in the UV Editing workspace is controlled independently to the Default workspace, so switch this to **Material** also.

Remember, this will let you see the material colors applied to your model.

Opening the 2D texture

At the bottom of the **UV/Image Editor** panel on the left, click the **Open** button. Open the PNG you made.

Click the **Pin** button at the bottom to prevent Blender from switching away from this image when you select a different object in the **3D View**. You only have one texture for all your objects, so you only want to see that texture.

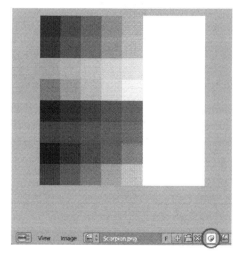

The UV Mapping tool

Now you're ready to "unwrap" your model!

Models are 3D, but each polygon that makes it is actually flat. UV Mapping allows you to "unfold" your model and lay it flat on a 2D texture. If you were doing a hand-painted texture, you'd arrange the faces of your model onto your texture, then paint the texture in your image editor of choice:

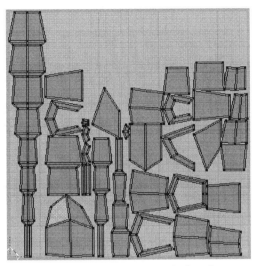

However, this model will be "flat shaded", where each face has a single, flat color. This greatly simplifies things for your UV map.

1. In the 3D View, select the **Body** object. Press **Tab** to switch to Edit Mode. Make sure you are in **Face Select Mode (Ctrl-Tab)**.

2. Start by selecting the faces that make up the body. Pressing **A** for **Select All** doesn't work, since you don't want the spiked ball included. Press **A** to **Select None**, then select one face on the body.

3. Press **L** to **Select Linked**. This selects everything that's attached to the current selection. When you have multiple meshes combined into a single object, this is an *essential* shortcut for selecting them.

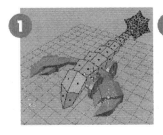
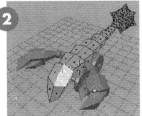
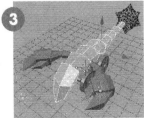

4. Press **1**, then **5** to switch to Front View, no perspective. Press **U** and select **Project From View**.

5. Imagine the mesh getting squashed flat. The flattened mesh is projected onto the image in the **UV/Image Editor** panel on the left.

6. Move the cursor over the **UV/Image Editor** panel and use the same shortcuts for moving and scaling as the 3D View: **G** to move and **S** to scale. Scale it down so that the entire thing fits onto one of the colored squares, then move it onto the darkest green square.

Great! You've got some color on your mesh. But it's a little plain. You can use some of the shaded color variations you made to liven things up a bit.

7. With your cursor in the 3D View, press **7** to switch to Top View. To make the separate segments a slightly different color, you need to select a *loop* of connected faces, that encircle the body. To do this, hold the **Alt** key and click the edge shown directly under the 3D Cursor, here.

8. **Alt-click** performs a **Loop Select** operation. When in Face Select Mode, it selects the quads on either side of the edge, and all connected faces all the way around the model (as long as they are quads). Orbit around your model to verify which faces are selected.

9. Press **7** to return to Top View. **Shift-Alt-click** the segment just forward of the one you have selected, to add it to the selection.

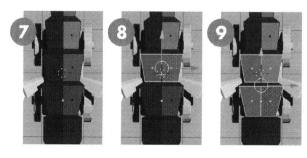

10. The faces you select in the 3D View are now selected in the UV/Image Editor panel. No need to scale them this time! With your cursor in the UV/Image Editor panel, just press **G** to grab them and move them over one square, to the next-lightest shade of green.

11. Repeat the process for each set of two segments, leaving the smaller "folded inward" parts of the model dark. When finished, press **L** to select the whole body again. Your UV Map should look something like this.

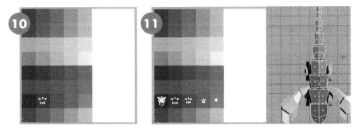

Now the body color has a bit of variation, with some definition along the ridges in each segment.

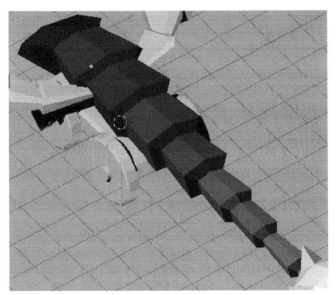

Coloring the head

1. Orbit around to the front, and select the frontmost two faces.

2. Rather than manually selecting each face for the head, use the **Select More/Less** feature. Press **Ctrl + (plus)** to "select more". The faces attached to the current selection are now selected.

3. Orbit around to see the back of the head and press **Ctrl + (plus)** once more. Now all the faces of the head are selected.

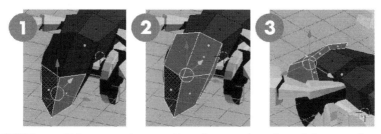

4. In the UV/Image Editor panel, press **G** and move the selected faces to the mid-tone red square.

5. In the 3D View, press **A** to Select None. Reselect the frontmost two faces again, and in the UV/Image Editor panel, move them one color box to the right.

6. Select the top two faces and move their UV coordinates to the lightest red box.

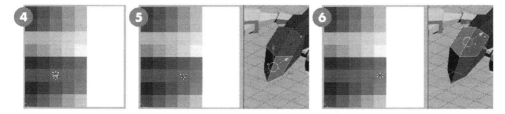

Assigning the material to each object

You're getting the hang of it! To color other objects, you need to assign the material to each one. Use the **Screen Layout** popup at the top of the screen to switch back to the **Default** layout. Press **Tab** to switch back to Object Mode.

1. Click one of the arms to select it.

2. In the **Properties** panel, select the **Material** tab.

3. Click the small **Material popup** beside the **New** button.

4. Select the material you created from the popup, to assign it to the Arm object.

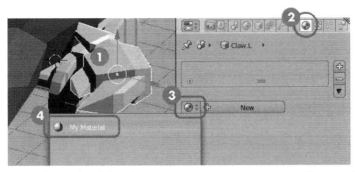

Repeat this process for each of the objects in your scene, to ensure all your objects have the material assigned to them.

Coloring the rest of the model

Switch the Screen Layout back to **UV Editing**, and you're ready to UV map the rest of the model.

1. Select the object.

2. Press **Tab** to enter Edit Mode. Press **Ctrl-Tab** and ensure you are in **Face Select Mode**.

3. Select the faces you want to map. **Alt-click** an edge to **Loop Select**. Press L to select all connected faces/ This will be useful for the spiked ball on the tail, the axels, and wheels.

4. Press **U** and select **Project from View** to project the mesh onto the UV map.

5. In the UV/Image Editor panel, scale and position the mesh onto a color box.

6. In the 3D View, press **A** to Select None, then select some of the faces to add some color variation.

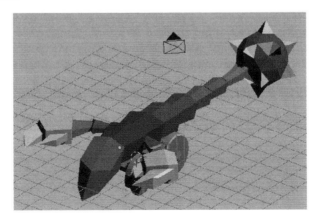

> **Note:** Because you used **Linked Duplicate** when we duplicated the axles and arms in the previous chapter, you only had to UV map one. The second object shares the same mesh, and therefore the UV map, too.

Joining the body parts

Now that the arms are UV mapped, you can **join** them with the body object. If you had joined them *before* UV mapping them, you'd have to UV map each one separately.

Joining these three objects will help in the next chapter, when you'll be animating the entire body. It's easiest if the meshes you are animating are all in one object.

Select one of the arms, then Shift-select the other arm; Shift-select the body last. The order of selection matters! The last object selected is the one that the other objects are merged into, and it is the one that keeps its origin point.

Press **Ctrl-J** to Join the three objects.

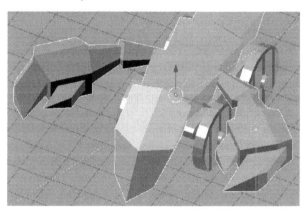

A sneaky, hidden problem

Something has happened here that is not obvious, but *will* cause problems later on.

Switch the **Viewport Shading** to **Solid** to see one indication of the problem. See how the arm that was flipped is a darker grey?

When you flipped the object, Blender did so by using a scale transformation for the X axis of -1. When that object was joined with other objects that did not have that scale factor, that flipped the *faces* inside out.

In a game engine, a polygon will only display when you look at it from one side. The direction a polygon is facing is called its **Normal**. When the geometry was mirrored, the normals got flipped, too.

This is an easy one to miss because it's not always immediately obvious — until you get the model into Unity, where it looks like this:

It's a bit hard to see unless you can actually rotate around it, but what you're seeing here is the *inside* of the mesh faces on that arm.

Back in Blender, there's an easy way to check the normals on a model.

In the 3D View, press **Tab** to enter Edit Mode, then press **N** to toggle the Properties shelf, if it's not already open.

Scroll down to the **Mesh Display** section, and click the **Display face normals as lines** button. Increase the **Size** to 0.4, to make the lines more noticeable.

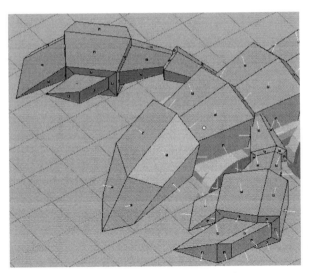

As you can see, toggling the display of the face normals makes it easy to tell which ones are facing the right way.

Fortunately, it's easy to fix. Select one of the culprit faces and press **L** to Select Linked. In the menu bar at the bottom of the 3D View, select **Mesh\Normals\Flip Normals**. Press **Tab** to return to Object Mode.

> **Reminder:** Don't forget to save (**Ctrl-S**).

Rendering your model

Your model is really starting to shine. To get an even better look at it, change the **Viewport Shading** popup to **Rendered**.

> **Tip:** Press **Shift-Z** to toggle **Viewport Shading** to **Rendered**; press it again and the shading will revert to **Solid**. Use the popup to set it back to **Material**, if you still want to see your colors.

Ambient occlusion

Your render looks nice, but there's a quick way to make it look even better. In the **Screen Layouts** popup at the top, make sure you are in the **Default** layout.

1. While in **Rendered** view, go to the **Properties** panel and click the **World** tab.

2. Scroll down and check the **Ambient Occlusion** checkbox. Much nicer!

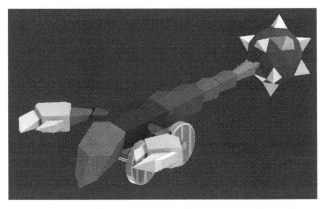

Ambient occlusion does a much better job of calculating ambient light and shadows in a scene, and will almost always make your renders look better. Simple and effective!

Exporting a rendered image

Unless a simple screenshot is good enough for you, you'll want to save a rendered image. To do that, you need to work with Blender's camera to fully set up a render. You've probably noticed the camera in the scene; it looks like this:

Adjusting the camera angle

Before you start adjusting the camera itself, there's one setting that will make things easier. Select **File\User Preferences** and click the **Interface** tab at the top. Select the **Rotate Around Selection** checkbox, then click **Save User Settings**, and close the window:

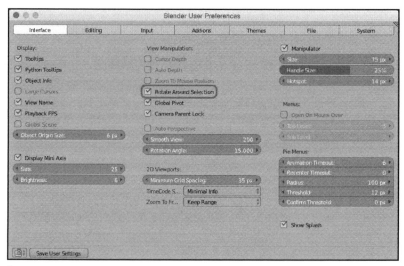

Back in the 3D View, press **0** (**zero**) to switch to the Camera's view. Note that if you orbit or zoom the view, it jumps out of the Camera view. To control the camera's position with the regular view controls, press **N** to open the Properties panel. Under **View**, select **Lock Camera to View**.

Select the body object in the scene, so that the **Rotate Around Selection** feature knows what to rotate around. Now when you orbit (**Middle-click and drag**), pan (**Shift-middle-click and drag**) or zoom (**scroll wheel**), the camera moves right along with you.

Adjust the camera angle until you have a nice view of your model.

Adjusting the camera settings

In the **Properties** panel, click the **Render** tab. There are several important settings here.

1. **Resolution** set the width (X) and height (Y) of your render. Note that the % slider in that section is applied to those dimensions. If your render is set to 1920 x 1080, and the slider is set to 50%, your final render will be 960 x 540.

2. To create a transparent PNG, scroll down to the **Shading** section and change the **Alpha** popup to **Transparent**.

3. Scroll down to the **Output** section and change the File Format to **PNG\RGBA**.

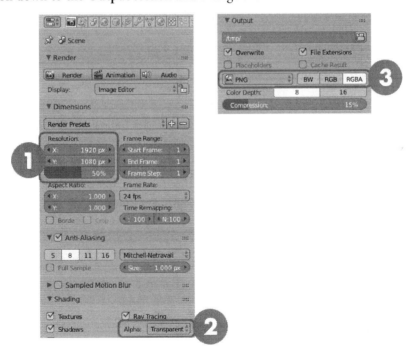

Rendering and saving an image

1. Press **F12** to render the scene using the camera. This replaces the entire 3D View with a UV/Image Editor panel, displaying your shiny new render.

2. In the menu bar at the bottom of the window, select **Image\Save as Image** (or press **F3**). Choose a place on your computer to save it, and you're done!

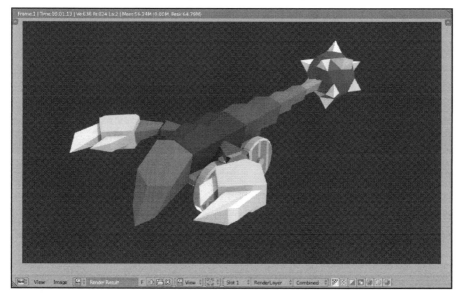

Press **Esc** to return to the 3D View.

Where to go from here?

Congratulations! You have taken plain grey geometry and given it a vibrant splash of color. As you experiment with Blender more and more, try adding different graphics or "decals" to parts of your texture, then mapping those to different faces of your model to further customize its look.

So far you've learned:

• **How to create a 2D texture** in GIMP.

• **How to set up basic lighting** for your scene.

• **The basics of texturing models** using UV Maps and 2D textures.

• **How to configure the camera** and render beautiful images of your creation.

In the following chapter, you will learn how to rig and animate your model.

Summary of keyboard commands

L - Select Linked

Alt-click - (on an edge in Edit Mode) Loop Select

U - UV Unwrap selected faces

Ctrl + - Select More

Ctrl - - Select Less

Ctrl-J - Join Objects

Shift-Z - Toggle rendered view

N - Toggle Properties panel

T - Toggle Tools panel

0 (zero) - Switch to camera view

F12 - Render

F3 - Save image

Chapter 17: Animating in Blender

By Mike Berg

The journey of bringing your model to life is almost over. The only thing left? Animation! Nothing makes a character feel more alive than animation.

> **Note:** This chapter builds on the skills learned and the model made in Chapters 15 and 16. I recommend you read through those chapters before this one.

Getting started

Like many animation tools, Blender uses something called a **Rig** to create animation. Rigs are made up of (among other things) an **Armature**, which consists of one or more **Bones**. A mesh is then applied to a rig, and when the bones move, the mesh moves with it. Think of bones in Blender just like bones in your body; they give you joints and define where and how you can move.

Here's what the armature for your scorpion will look like:

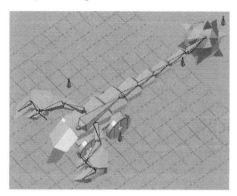

Creating the rig

Start by selecting the Body object, pressing **Shift-S**, and selecting **Cursor to Selected**. The 3D Cursor snaps to the origin of the Body object. This is a good starting point for your armature.

Adding the first bone

1. Press **Shift-A** and select **Armature\Single Bone** to create your first bone.

2. Press **3** to switch to Side View, and press **Tab** to enter **Edit Mode**.

3. It's a bit tough to see because most of the bone is inside the body geometry. In the **Properties** panel, click the **Armature** tab and select the **X-Ray** checkbox, so that you can see your bones even when they are inside an object.

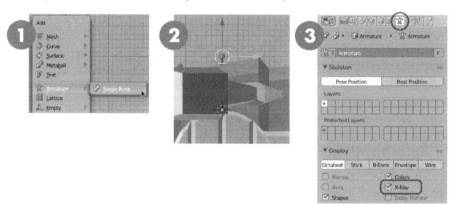

Edit Mode for bones is slightly different from editing meshes. A bone can be selected by clicking on the middle part of the bone. Each bone also has two **ends**, that appear as spheres at the end of each bone. These ends can be selected and moved independently by clicking on one and pressing **G** to Grab (move) it.

> **Note:** When you have an armature selected, the "Object Mode / Edit Mode" popup has a new item in it: **Pose Mode**. Be careful not to accidentally enter Pose Mode when you need to be in Edit Mode. In Pose Mode, the bones display with a light blue outline.

Select the top end of the bone and press **G** to move it to the right. Line it up with the end of the segment — and closer to the top than the bottom — as shown here:

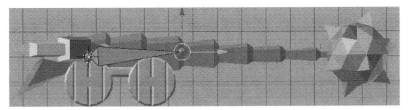

Using 'Extrude' to create more bones

Press **E** and drag your mouse to the right to **Extrude** the bone's end, creating a whole new bone. Click when you are happy with the new bone's position.

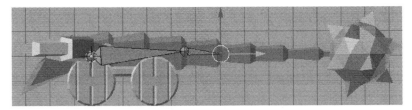

Repeat the extrude step to create a bone for each segment of the tail. The curve of the tail should be slightly concave; this will help us out later, when you curl the tail upward.

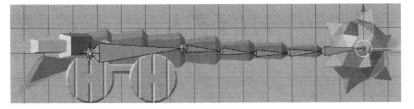

Attaching the mesh to the armature

Press **Tab** to return to Object Mode. Press **A** to Select None. Click the Body object to select it, then hold **Shift** and click the armature, so they are both selected. This can be hard to do in the 3D View, because the armature is inside the body. If so, use the **Outliner**, at the top-right, to make the selection.

> **Note:** Selection order matters. Make sure you select the armature **last**.

1. Press **Ctrl-P** and select **Set Parent To Armature Deform\With Automatic Weights**.

2. Nothing will appear to change, but if you look in the **Outliner**, you'll see that the Body is now a child of the Armature.

Pose Mode

Here's where the real fun begins. Click the **Object Mode** popup at the bottom of the screen and select **Pose Mode**. Click the second bone in the armature and press **R** to rotate it. The tail moves with it!

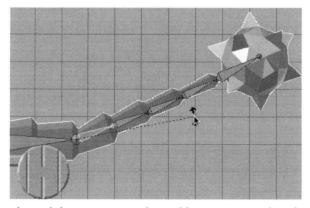

Now, that's definitely cool, but animating this tail by rotating each individual joint would be a pain. Thankfully, there's an easier way...

Inverse Kinematics

The animation style just described (rotating each tail bone one at a time, until you get to the end of the tail) is known as **Forward Kinematics**. **Inverse Kinematics** uses a target bone that the entire chain aims at. Moving the **IK Target** automatically adjusts the rotation of each of the bones in the chain. This way, you only have to animate one object.

1. Switch back to **Edit Mode**, and right-click to the right of the spiked ball to move the 3D Cursor there.

2. Press **Shift-A** to add a new bone. Press **A**, then click the body of the bone, to select the entire thing.

3. In the **Properties** panel, click the **Bone** tab and change the name of the bone to **Tail IK**. It's a good idea to name all your bones, especially the ones you plan to animate; you will identify them later by their names in the animation window.

4. Near the bottom of the **Bone Properties** panel, deselect the **Deform** checkbox. You do not want this bone to deform the mesh.

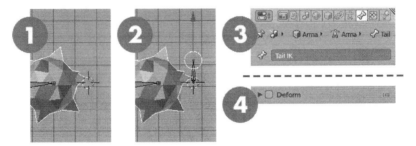

Creating the IK Target

1. Switch to **Pose Mode**. Select the IK bone first, then Shift-select the last bone in the tail.

2. Press **Shift-Ctrl-C** to open the **Add Constraint (with Targets)** menu. Under **Tracking**, select **Inverse Kinematics**.

1. Select the last bone in the tail (it is now highlighted yellow). In the **Properties** panel, click the **Bone Constraints** tab and look for the **Chain Length**. The tail has 5 bones, so change the **Chain Length** to 5. This limits the number of bones that are affected by the IK target.

2. Select the **Tail IK** bone and press **G** to move it up over the body of the model. Now *that* is magic!

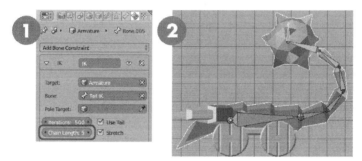

Creating a Pole Target for the tail

This rig is working very well, but it can be even better. If you were to animate it now, the spiked ball would *always* lead the way, and the tail would follow. It would look a bit like the head of a snake moving around. That might look cool, but it would also have the effect of making that big spiked ball look very light weight.

Think of a pitcher throwing a baseball. They draw their elbow back first, then their forearm and the ball *follow* the elbow.

To make your spiked ball look heavy and feel real, you need to be able to move the tail a bit, separately, so that it can lead and the ball can follow. To do this, use something called a **Pole Target**.

1. Switch to **Edit Mode**. Notice how the pose you made in Pose Mode is not shown; the model snaps back to its "Rest Position". Don't worry, your pose is still saved. **Right-click** below the tail to move the 3D Cursor, as shown.

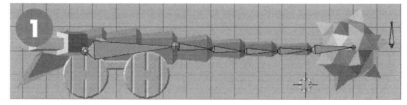

2. Press **Shift-A** to add a bone. Press **A** to Select None, then click on the middle of the bone to select it.

3. In the **Properties** panel, switch to the **Bone** tab and rename the bone to **Tail Pole Target**. Don't forget to deselect the **Deform** checkbox.

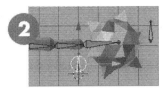 

4. Switch back to **Pose Mode** and select the yellow bone at the end of the tail. In the **Properties** panel, click the **Bone Constraints** tab, click the **Pole Target** field, and select **Armature**. Another field appears below that lets you choose the specific bone. Select the **Tail Pole Target** bone.

5. Press **1** to switch to Front View. It doesn't look quite right... the tail is pointed to the side, instead of at the Pole Target!

6. Back in the **Bone Constraints** tab, find the **Pole Angle** field. Click and drag side-to-side to adjust this number and see how the changes affect your model in real time. In this case, a value of **-90 degrees** works perfectly.

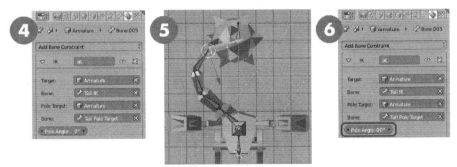

Press **3** to go back to Side View, then select the **Tail Pole Target** bone and press **1** again to switch back to Front View. Move the bone left and right (**G** to grab) to see how it affects the tail.

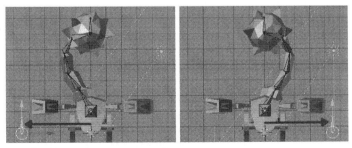

Fantastic! The rig for the tail is now complete.

Adding the arm bones

Select the existing armature and enter Edit Mode. You'll use the same armature for the arm bones.

1. Start in Top View, set your 3D Cursor to the spot where the left arm meets the body. Press **Shift-A** to create the first bone.

2. Press **1** to switch to front view, as your first bone is created in an upright position. Click the middle portion of the bone to select the whole bone. Drag the blue arrow up until its base is in line with the center of the arm.

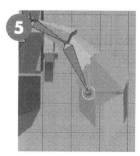
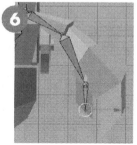

3. Press **A** to deselect, then select the end of the bone, and press **G** to grab it and move it approximately to the elbow.

4. Press **7** to switch to top view. Drag the green arrow to move the end of the bone forward to align it in this view too.

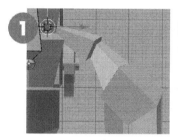
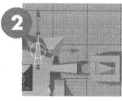

5. Stay in top view and press **E** to extrude a new bone to the midpoint of where the "thumb" meets the "hand", shown here.

6. Press **E** again to extrude a "thumb" bone.

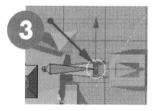
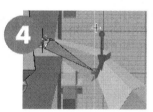

7. Click the end of the **2nd bone** and press **E** to extrude a bone to the midpoint of where the large claw meets the "hand".

8. Press **E** to extrude the bone for the large claw.

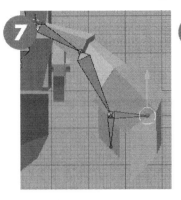
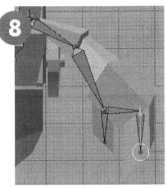

> **Note:** Name each bone, and be sure to use ".L" at the end of each name. In the **Properties\Armature** tab, select the **Names** checkbox to see bone names right in the 3D View.

Adding the arm IK Target

Another way to create an IK Target is to extrude it right from the joint you want to have pointing at it. You want the "hand" to point at the IK Target to control the arm, but not the claws, which will be animated separately.

1. Select the sphere at the intersection of the arm and "thumb" bones.

2. Press **E** and extrude a bone out to the left.

3. Press **A** to Select None, and click the bone itself. Press **Alt-P** and select **Clear Parent**. This takes the bone out of the hierarchy, but it's still part of the same armature.

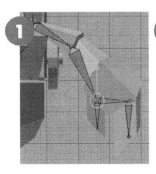
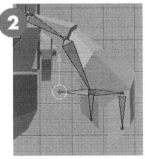
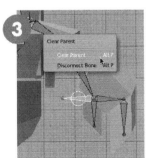

4. In the **Properties** panel, under the **Bone** tab, rename the bone **Arm IK Target.L**. Don't forget to scroll down and deselect the **Deform** checkbox.

5. Switch to **Pose Mode**, select the **Arm IK Target.L** bone first, then Shift-select the "forearm" bone. Press **Shift-Ctrl-C** and select **Inverse Kinematics**. The forearm turns yellow.

6. Select the forearm. For the purposes of IK, this arm has two bones. In the **Properties\Bone Constraints** tab, set the **Chain Length** to 2.

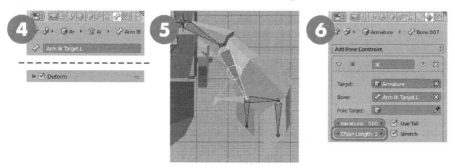

Adding the Pole Target for the elbow

1. Switch to **Edit Mode**. Select the sphere at the "elbow" of the arm.

2. Press **1** to switch to Front View, and press **E** to extrude the arm upward.

3. Press **A** to Select None, then select the bone, press **Alt-P** and select **Clear Parent**. Press 7 to switch to Top View, press **G** and drag the bone away from the arm a bit.

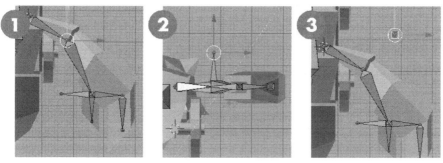

4. Don't forget to go to **Properties\Bone** to name the bone **Elbow.L**, and deselect the **Deform** checkbox.

5. Switch to **Pose Mode** and select the forearm bone. Go to **Properties\Bone Constraints**, click the **Pole Target** field, and select **Armature**. Below that, select the **Elbow.L** bone.

6. Orbit around your model to ensure the elbow is pointed at the Pole Target. If it's not, adjust the **Pole Angle** until it looks right. **-90** worked for me.

Note: In Blender, input fields that have arrows on the left and right side can be adjusted by clicking on them and dragging left and right.

Flipping the arm bones for the other arm

1. Remember when you flipped the arm geometry in the modeling chapter? Flipping the bones is the same: First, make sure you're in **Edit Mode**, then press **Shift-S** to snap the 3D Cursor to the center. Press **. (period)** to transform around the cursor. Select all the arm bones, including the IK and Pole Targets, and press **Shift-D** then **Enter** to duplicate. **Ctrl-M X** then **Enter** to mirror over the X axis.

2. In the menu at the bottom of the 3D View, select **Armature\Flip Names** to automatically rename bones with **.L** to **.R**, for the right arm.

3. Switch to **Object Mode**. You've created new bones, but they have not had their Automatic Weights set up for the mesh. Select the mesh, then **Shift-click** the armature. Press **Ctrl-P** and select **Set Parent To Armature Deform\With Automatic Weights** again. The mesh is already parented to the armature, so now it just recalculates the automatic weights; this time for all the new bones, too.

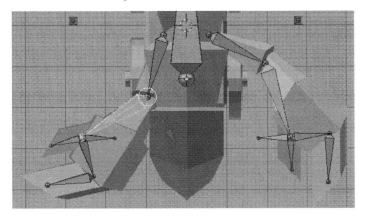

4. What happened to the right arm? When the bones got flipped, the **Pole Angle** for the elbow stayed the same. Switch to **Pose Mode** and select the yellow-highlighted bone in the right arm. In the **Properties** panel, click the **Bone Constraints** tab, and change the **Pole Angle** to **90**.

Your rig is now complete! Time for some movement...

> **Note:** Don't forget to save. If you want to look at the rig I made, open **02-Scorpion-Rigged.blend** in the Resources folder.

Animation

Creating animation in Blender is similar to most other animation applications; it uses **keyframes** and **tweening**.

A keyframe is a point in the **timeline** where you have specified the position, for example, of an object. Then you set another keyframe at a different point in time, with the object in a different position.

When you play the animation, the object will move smoothly from the position set by the first keyframe, to the position set by the second keyframe. This automatically-generated motion between keyframes is called **tweening**.

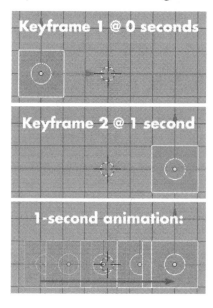

At the top of the screen, switch to the **Animation** workspace. There are some new panels here:

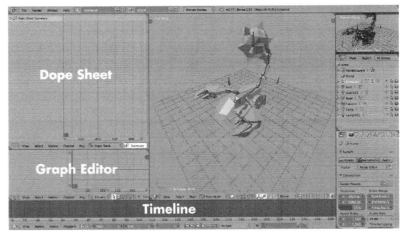

- The **Dope Sheet** shows you an overview of everything that is animated, in your scene. Every property that you animate will show up as a channel in the left column, with its keyframes displayed in the timeline column on the right.

- The **Graph Editor** displays a motion graph for selected keyframes. This lets you fine-tune the speed of each tween; slowing down or speeding up an animation on either side of a keyframe. This is called **easing**.

- The **Timeline** shows a simplified overview of your entire timeline, along with playback controls.

> **Note:** To move the playhead in any timeline view, **Right-click & drag**. Zoom and Pan controls are almost the same as in the 3D View: **Scrollwheel** to zoom, and **Middle-click & drag** to pan. Holding Shift to pan is not necessary in a 2D panel.

Creating an Action for the tail animation

Blender allows you to create multiple animations for a single armature, which can be triggered independently in Unity. Each animation is called an **Action**. You'll use Actions to create a looping animation for a swaying tail, and a separate, non-looping animation for a swinging claw.

> **Note:** For more information on how to trigger these animations in Unity, see Chapter 5, "Animations".

1. At the bottom of the Dope Sheet panel, click the **Dope Sheet** popup and select **Action Editor**.

2. Click the **New** button to create a new Action.

3. Click the **Action** name field and change the name to **Tail Sway**.

4. **Important**: Click the **F** button next to the name. This gives the Action something called a Fake User, and forces Blender to save your action, even if it is unlinked. I won't go into detail on this, except to note that your Action may not be saved if you do not press this button!

Creating keyframes

First up, you'll create a looping animation for the tail, so that it bobs back and forth as the minion trundles along its path. In the 3D View, press **1** to switch to Front View, then **5** to turn off perspective. Press **N** to turn on the **Properties** shelf.

You'll animate the **Tail IK** bone to move along a path like this:

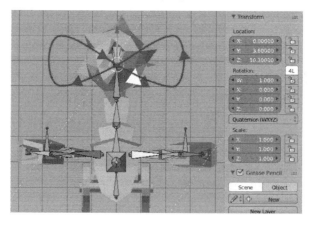

> **Note:** I'll be giving you exact coordinates for each keyframe, but feel free to eyeball it and use what looks right to you. The values you use may also be slightly different, since they are relative to where the **Tail IK** bone was first created.

1. Make sure you are in **Pose Mode**, and select the **Tail IK** bone. In the Properties shelf, set the **Location** coordinates to: **X 0, Y 3.6, Z 10.3** (as shown at the top-right of the screenshot above).

2. Make sure the playhead is on frame zero, then **right-click** on the X field (the one you just set to zero) and select **Insert Single Keyframe**. Do the same for the Y field. *The fields turn yellow to show that they have been keyed.*

3. Look in the Dope Sheet; a new channel appears for each of the values you have keyed, with the name of the value — **X Location** — followed by the name of the object in brackets — **(Tail IK)**. The keyframe itself displays as a diamond on the Dope Sheet's timeline.

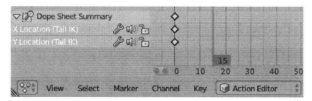

Great, you've created your first keyframes! There's nothing moving yet, since this is just a starting position. Create some more keyframes to see some action:

4. **Right-click** and drag on the timeline to move the playhead to frame 15. Remember that you can use the scroll wheel to zoom in; middle-click to pan/scroll around.

5. Make sure the **Tail IK** bone is still selected, and change the location values to: **X -1.3, Y 3.3** (you won't be animating the Z value at all, so leave that one alone). Right-click on each field after you change it and select **Insert Single Keyframe**.

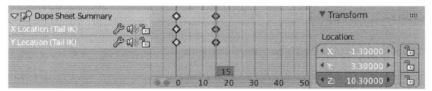

6. At the bottom of the Blender window, in the Timeline panel, set the **End** field to **80**. This gives your animation a duration of 80 frames. Press the **Play** button to preview your animation.

> **Tip:** Press **Alt-A** to play/pause the playhead at any time. You can orbit the 3D View while the animation is playing, to get a good view of it from any angle.

Here are the frame numbers and the coordinates for the rest of the keyframes. Don't forget to right-click and select **Insert Single Keyframe** after you make each change, *before* you move the playhead, or your changes won't be keyed.

- **Frame 25** - X -1.3, Y 3.9
- **Frame 40** - X 0, Y 3.6
- **Frame 55** - X 1.3 Y 3.3
- **Frame 65** - X 1.3 Y 3.9
- **Frame 80** - X 0 Y 3.6

Your Dope Sheet should look like this:

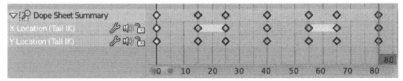

Press **Alt-A** to preview your animation. It's getting there, but the motion feels a bit wooden; it doesn't flow as naturally as it could. To fix that, shift your attention to the **Graph Editor**.

The Graph Editor

At this point, your Graph Editor panel should look like this:

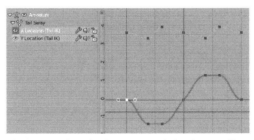

Feel free to zoom in to see more detail, if your graph looks small. Note also that you can drag the panel edges to resize any panel.

The Graph Editor charts a curved line for each animated channel. The **horizontal** axis represents **time**; the **vertical** axis represents the **value of the channel**. The **points** on the line represent **keyframes** that you've set.

Using the Graph Editor to create smooth motion

Click the first point on the **X Location** curve. Once selected, each point has handles on either side that control the strength and direction of the curve. Drag the handle on the right so that it is approximately 45 degrees:

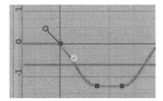

This will create a smoother looping motion, when the animation goes from frame 80 back to frame 1.

Smooth out the curves on all the points, so that your path looks more like this:

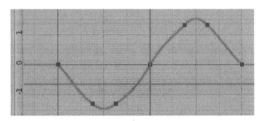

> **Note:** When editing the points on a curve, you need to click and drag a bit to get the handle moving, then **release** the mouse button. The handle will still be active, and moving the mouse will reposition it. **Click** again, to finish the adjustment.

Press **Alt-A** to preview the animation. Much better already! But it can be a bit better, still.

Look at the Graph Editor; see how the valley and peak of your loop don't look quite right? They're not quite as smooth as they could be. The two keyframes on either side are a bit too close together.

To fix this, you'll use a familiar tool (Scale), and one new one: **Box Select**. You *could* Shift-select the two points you want to adjust, but there's an easier way.

1. Press **A** to Select None, then press **B** to invoke the **Box Select** tool.

2. Click and drag around the objects you want to select.

3. The objects are selected.

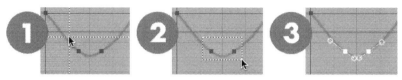

> **Note: Box Select** can be used in almost any panel in Blender.

Now that you have your keyframes selected simply press **S**, then drag your mouse to scale them. Pull the keyframes away from each other nicely, until you have a nice rounded curve. Repeat this for the keyframes at frames 55 and 65, so that your graph looks like the screenshot below. You may need to tweak the handles on your points a bit, after scaling them.

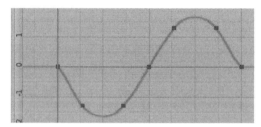

Have a look at the Dope Sheet. Note how the keyframes for the **X Location** channel have moved; this is simply reflecting the changes you made in the Graph Editor.

> **Note:** Select a point and type **G Y** to move it vertically in the Graph Editor. If the playhead is on the same frame as the keyframe, you will see your change reflected in the 3D View. This is a quick way to visually edit keyframes in a motion curve.

Don't forget to save!

Animating the Pole Target

The tail animation is looking good, but remember when I talked about that big heavy spiked ball looking light-weight? It's time to animate the Pole Target to make the tail lead the ball a bit, to make it look like it's pulling it along.

Make sure you are still in Pose Mode. Select the **Tail Pole Target** bone. This object will only slide from side to side, so you'll only need to animate the **X Location** value.

Here are the keyframes to set:

- **Frame 0** - X 0

- **Frame 20** - X -1.5

- **Frame 40** - X 0

- **Frame 60** - X 1.5

- **Frame 80** - X 0

In the Graph Editor, tweak the points so that they are nice and smooth, giving you a curve like this:

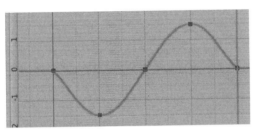

Preview the animation now, and it will look almost exactly the same as it did before! That's because the Pole Target is moving in sync with the tail. To get it to *lead* the tail a bit, you need to adjust the timing.

In the Dope Sheet, press **B** and Box Select all the keyframes in the **X Location (Tail Pole Target)** channel.

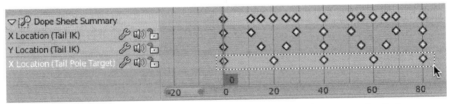

Press **G -20**, then **Enter** to move the selected keyframes 20 frames to the left.

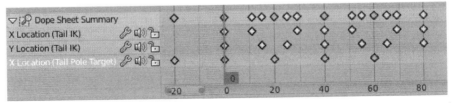

Preview the animation now, and you'll see that the tail is leading the way. Nice! But the animation no longer loops correctly. In the Dope Sheet, press **A** to Select None, and click on the keyframe at frame 0 to select it.

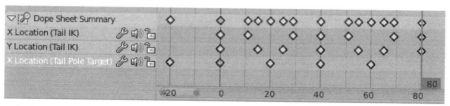

Press **Shift-D** to duplicate. Drag the duplicate keyframe all the way across the timeline and **left-click** when it's on frame 80.

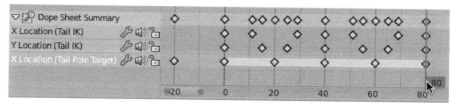

Now press **Alt-A** to preview your animation. Orbit around your scene a bit, while it's playing, to get a good look at how your Pole Target is affecting the tail.

That's it for the tail animation. Great work! Time to create a new Action for the arms.

Don't forget to save.

Creating an Action for the claw animation

The tail sway is complete; now you need a new **Action** to store the next animation.

1. At the bottom of the Dope Sheet, click the + button next to the **Tail Sway** action name to create a new Action.

2. Blender actually duplicates the current action; rename the new Action **Claw Attack.L**. Don't forget to click the **F** button.

3. Now the keyframes need to be deleted. Move your cursor over the Dope Sheet and press **A** to Select All, then **X**, followed by **Delete Keyframes** to delete them.

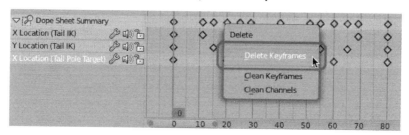

Animating the claw

Start by animating the IK Target for the left arm; **Arm IK Target.L**.

1. Make sure you are still in Pose Mode, and select that bone.

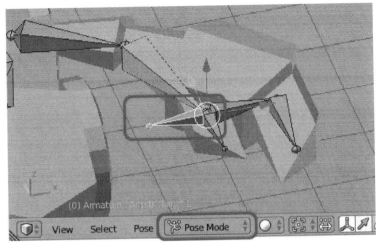

2. Right-click on any of the axes in the **Location** section of the Properties shelf. This time, you'll create a keyframe for all three axes at once by selecting **Insert Keyframes**. All three fields turn yellow; your starting keyframes for this bone are now set.

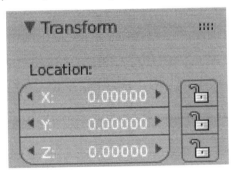

> **Note:** Only keyframe all three axes if you know the object will be moving in all three directions. Creating keyframes only for the axes you are animating keeps your Dope Sheet nice and clean. This becomes more important as your animations get more complex.

3. Continue creating the following keyframes for the **Arm IK Target.L** bone.

Frame 20:

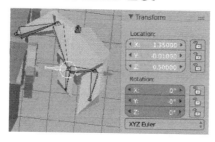

Frame 40:   Frame 65:

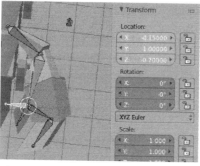   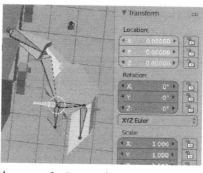

Now you have the basic movement keyed for a claw attack. Press **Alt-A** to preview your animation. It's coming along, but it's definitely not quite right yet. This time, the tweened animation is *too smooth*. Remember, adjusting the tweening involves the Graph Editor.

Creating sharp, sudden movement with the Graph Editor

Right now, the claw attack looks more like a friendly wave. You want the claw to quickly dart forward, hit whatever it's attacking, and bounce off. At this point, the Graph Editor should look like this:

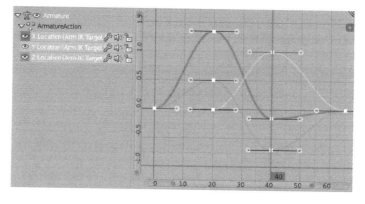

Note: See the small dots at the ends of each scroll bar? Try dragging them to adjust the vertical or horizontal scale of the graph.

The tip of the attack animation is at frame 40. Making a sudden change in direction involves changing the curves at this frame to a sharp angle. However, simply dragging a handle doesn't create a sharp angle, it only adjusts the curve:

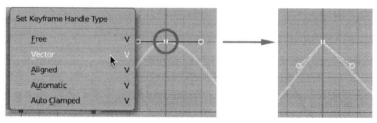

To create a sharp angle, you need to change the **Keyframe Handle Type**. Select the keyframe itself — the dot in the middle, not one of the handles on either side — press **V** to open the **Set Keyframe Handle Type** menu, and select **Vector**.

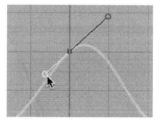

Convert all three keyframes at frame 40 to **Vector**, and adjust their handles to look like this:

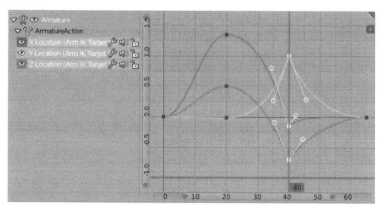

Press **Alt-A** to preview your animation. Much better! The elbow draws back, has a short pause, then strikes forward swiftly. One thing that could use some adjustment is the animation *after* the strike. Right now, it doesn't look like it bounces off, or recoils, after hitting its target.

Move the playhead to frame 50 and set the following keyframe:

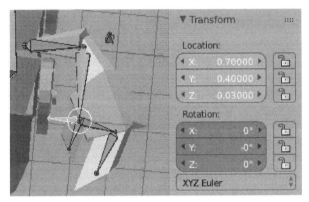

Press **Alt-A** to preview. Now the animation feels much more natural.

> **Note:** This is a good method for creating an animation. Start by keying the basic outline of the animation first, then add keyframes where necessary, to add extra movement details.

Adjusting the Pole Target to raise the elbow

The claw attack animation is almost complete. Using the Pole Target will allow you to raise the elbow, so that the arm comes up, and strikes down from above. Select the **Elbow.L** pole target bone.

1. Move the playhead to **frame zero**. The Pole Target will only move up and down, so right-click the **Location: Y** field and select **Insert Single Keyframe**.

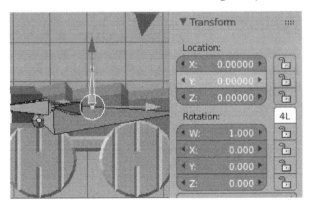

2. Move the playhead to **frame 20**. Change the **Location: Y** field to **1.5**, right-click it, and select **Insert Single Keyframe**.

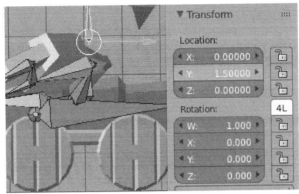

3. Move the playhead to **frame 65** and create a keyframe setting the **Y** value back to zero.

Preview the animation and orbit around it while it's playing. Now the elbow comes up nicely, as the arm is pulled back.

Opening the claws using Forward Kinematics

For the claws, instead of moving an object that they are aimed at, simply rotate them. This is called Forward Kinematics.

1. Move the playhead to frame 0 then select the **Thumb.L** bone. Look in the Properties shelf, ensure the **Rotation Mode** popup is set to **XYZ Euler**, then right-click the **Z** value and create a single keyframe of **0**.

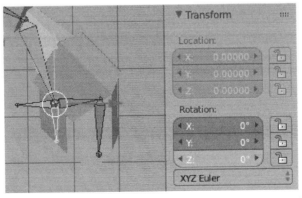

2. Move the playhead to frame **20** and change the **Z Rotation** to **-50**. Don't forget to right-click and select **Insert Single Keyframe**.

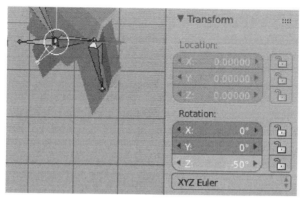

3. Move the playhead to frame **40** and set a keyframe with the **Z Rotation** back to **0** (remember that you could also duplicate the keyframe at frame zero in the Dope Sheet and move it to frame 40).

Repeat this process for the **Claw** bone. At frame **20** for this bone, set the **Z Rotation** to **30**:

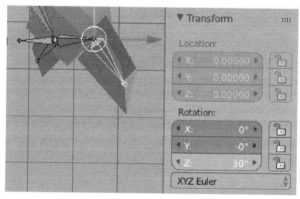

Preview your animation; the claw animation is nearly complete. The keyframes are all set; the only thing that could be better is the speed. The animation feels a bit slow right now.

Scaling keyframes in the Dope Sheet

Selecting some keyframes and squashing or stretching them on the timeline is very simple, using the **Scale** tool. One important thing to note is that the point in time that it *scales from* is the playhead position.

1. Move your playhead to frame zero and press **A** to Select All. Press **S** to **Scale**:

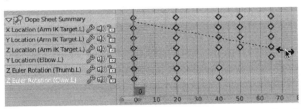

2. Drag your cursor toward the playhead to compress the timing for the selected keyframes. Scale it until the last keyframes are on frame **40**, and **left-click** when you're finished.

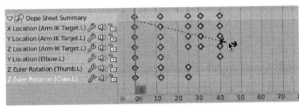

This is a very easy way to speed up or slow down the timing of multiple keyframes. Just remember to move the playhead to the keyframe that should remain unchanged, before scaling.

Copying the animation to the other arm

If you want your scorpion to be able to give the ol' one-two punch, the animation you just created needs to be copied to the right arm.

1. In the **Dope Sheet**, make sure the **Claw Attack.L** action is selected, and press the **+** button next to the action name to duplicate it. Rename the new one **Claw Attack.R.** Don't forget to click the **F** button.

2. In the **3D View**, select the **Arm IK Target.L** bone.

3. In the **Graph Editor**, if your points aren't selected, press **A** to Select All.

4. With the cursor over the Graph Editor, press **Ctrl-C** to copy the animation curves.

5. In the **3D View**, select the **Arm IK Target.R** bone.

6. Make sure the playhead is at frame 0, then, in the **Properties** panel, right-click one of the **Location** fields and select **Insert Keyframes**. The X, Y and Z Location channels will appear in the graph editor for the **Arm IK Target.R** object.

7. In the **GraphEditor**, press **Ctrl-V** to paste the animation data.

> **Note:** In my experience, the animation does not always look exactly mirrored, so you may need to play with the keyframes a bit if you want them to be exactly the same. When animating a living creature, it's OK if each arm is not exactly the same.

This process will need to be repeated for each object. Take note of the channel(s) you are animating, and create an empty keyframe in that channel, so that you have somewhere to paste the animation.

Don't forget to double-check the **XYZ Rotation Order** popup when doing the Thumb and Claw bones – they need to be set to **XYZ Euler**. Once you paste the rotation values for the thumb, you'll see that it's rotating in the opposite direction to how it should be. To fix this:

1. Move the playhead to the frame with the appropriate keyframe (if you scaled this animation the same as I did, it should be frame 12).

2. Select the **Thumb.R** bone in the 3D View. In the Properties panel, change the **Z Rotation** value from **-50** to **50**.

3. **Right-click** on the field and select **Replace Single Keyframe**.

> **Note:** Any time you change a keyed value, you *need* to use **Replace Single Keyframe** to update the keyframe itself. If you do not, your change will be removed as soon as you move the playhead.

Once you have the animation working for the right arm, be sure to use **B** to **Box Select** all the keyframes for the left arm, and press **X**, followed by **Delete Keyframes** in the Dope Sheet to remove them from the Claw Attack.R action.

> **Note:** Don't forget to save. If you'd like to see Blender file at this point, find **03-Scorpion-Animated.blend** in the Resources folder.

Where to go from here?

Congratulations! You've learned how to rig a character and create animations in Blender. I hope you had fun, and can see the potential for all kinds of character animations and object movement that you can use in your games.

So far you've learned:

- **How to rig a model** using bones.

- **How to apply a mesh to a rig** so that it moves when the bones move.

- **How to use Inverse Kinematics** to make animations easier and more natural.

- **How to use Pole Targets** to aim a bone at specified object.

- **How to animate an armature** using keyframes and the Dope Sheet

- **How to adjust animation tweens** to create smooth or sharp animations using the Graph Editor.

- **How to create multiple animations** for a single armature using Actions, for use in Unity.

Try creating a separate **Tail Smash** Action, where the tail takes a swing and smashes to the ground; or a **Victory Dance** Action using the arms.

Once you've completed the scorpion, read the chapters on creating a tower defense game, then import the scorpion into the game. You can do this by simply dragging the blender file into Unity. Once in Unity, you may have to texture it.

This involves creating a new material, assigning the **scorpion.png** to the **Albedo** property, and adding the material to various parts of the model. For a refresher on this, read "Chapter 2: GameObjects" and look under the **Fixing the Models** section.

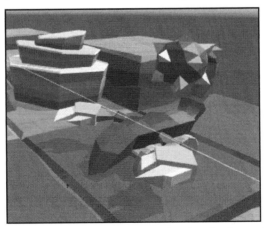

3D animation is a lot of fun; I hope you can use what you've learned to add life to your games in ways you couldn't before.

Summary of keyboard commands

- **Ctrl-P** - Set Parent
- **Alt-P** - Clear Parent
- **Shift-Ctrl-C** - Add Constraint (with Targets)\Tracking\Inverse Kinematics *(you must be in Pose Mode for this)*
- **Alt-A** - Play animation
- **B** - Box Select

Section V: Tower Defense Games

In this section, you'll use everything you've learned so far to create one final game. In addition, you'll learn how bring it into the 21st century and make it ready for Virtual Reality hardware, and how to package and publish your games for multiple targets, including Android, iOS, and WebGL.

In the process, you'll create a 3D tower defense game called **Runestrife**, including multiple waves, multiple tower types, and multiple enemies.

Chapter 18, "Making a Tower Defense Game"

Chapter 19, "Making Towers"

Chapter 20, "Virtual Reality"

Chapter 21, "Publishing Your Game"

Chapter 18: Making A Tower Defense Game

By Eric Van de Kerckhove

In a **tower defense** game, you build up defenses to protect yourself from advancing waves of enemies. To do this, you build and upgrade towers or other defensive elements that either damage or slow down the enemies as they pass by.

Some of the earliest examples of this genre are a game from 1990 called *Rampart* where you placed cannons that would automatically attack incoming enemies. In the Fort Condor minigame from the 1997 classic *Final Fantasy VII*, the player had to put down units to defend the fort. With the release of the popular custom maps for *Warcraft III*, the genre became extremely popular with lots of modern titles in all kinds of flavors coming out on all platforms.

Now you know what a tower defense game is, you're ready to create one yourself!

In this chapter you'll learn how to:

- Use manager classes to do all sorts of stuff

- Use utility scripts to make your life easier

- Get enemies to spawn and move around on a path

At the end of this project you will have a fully functional tower defense game called **Runestrife!**

Getting started

Open up the starter project in Unity and take a look at the Project Browser. The assets for this project are arranged in several sub-folders. Here's a quick rundown of what each sub-folder contains:

- **Materials**: Materials needed to for the tiles, towers and enemies

- **Models**: Meshes

- **Music**: Background music

- **Prefabs**: Particles, level tiles, enemies, towers and the tower projectiles

- **Scenes**: Title and Game scenes

- **Scripts**: This is where your scripts should go

- **Sound FX**: Sound effects including shoot sounds and enemy hits

- **Textures**: Textures for the models and UI elements

Now that the project overview is out of the way, it's time to get down to business!

Before setting up your project, it's best to set the aspect ratio. Use the drop down menu at the top of the **Game** window. Depending on your project type, it may default to **Free Aspect**. Change it to **16:9** to get consistent results.

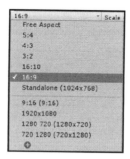

Preparing the Game scene

Open up the **Game** scene and take a look at what's inside.

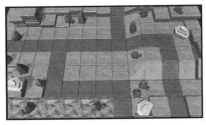

What a view! This map is the perfect base for the rest of this project.

It would be a good idea to disable automatic lighting, since the Unity editor has a small bug that makes the whole scene look dark when it gets loaded by another scene:

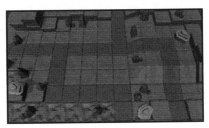

This bug won't be present in a build — it's only in the editor that Unity behaves like this. However, you'll be spending a lot of time in the editor, and it's nice to be able to test out the whole game from start to finish with proper lighting. To fix this, you have to uncheck the **Auto checkbox** in the **Lighting** window (**Window\Lighting**). Then press the **Build** button to manually bake the lightning in this scene.

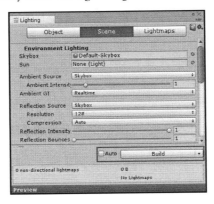

Making a path

To prepare the map for enemies moving about, you'll need to make a simple **waypoint system** so they can go from point to point. This is one of the easiest way of doing primitive pathfinding.

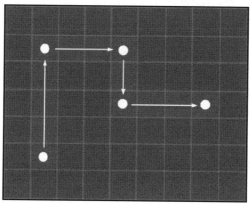

To start off, create a new empty GameObject in the root of the Hierarchy and name it **EnemyPaths**. Select the object. Then reset its **Transform** by clicking on the settings icon in the Inspector panel. In the drop-down click on **Reset**.

Now make another empty GameObject and name it **Path 0**. In the Hierarchy panel, drag **Path 0** on to **EnemyPaths** to make it a child game object.

There will be two paths that the enemies can traverse; this is the first one. It's named **0** because it will be used later in a **zero-based array**.

Create a new **Sphere (Create\3D Object\Sphere)**, set its **scale** to (**0.3, 0.3, 0.3**) and name it **Waypoint (1)**. Set its **position** to (**2, 0, -5**) and parent it to **Path 0**. This is the starting point of the path and also the spawning point of any enemies that will use this path. Now duplicate **Waypoint (1)** by right-clicking on it and selecting **Duplicate** from the context menu. Set its position to (**2, 0, 4**).

Keep duplicating and moving waypoints to follow this path below. Make sure you use snapping by holding **Control** (or **Command**) while moving around the waypoints.

This is what the result looks like when viewed in the Scene view:

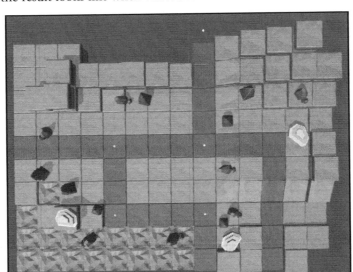

Here are the positions for you, in case something went wrong:

- Waypoint (1): (2, 0, -5)

- Waypoint (2): (2, 0, 4)

- Waypoint (3): (-10, 0, 4)

- Waypoint (4): (-10, 0, 13)

- Waypoint (5): (2, 0, 13)

- Waypoint (6): (2, 0, 28)

Now that you have a series of waypoints, you can store their positions in an array. The array will form a path used by enemies to decide how they should move.

In the Broject Browser, inside the **Scripts\Game\Enemy** folder, create a sub-folder named **Waypoints**. Inside the **Waypoints** folder, create a new **C# Script** and name it **WayPointManager**. Replace the contents with this code:

```
using UnityEngine;
using System.Collections.Generic;

public class WayPointManager : MonoBehaviour {
  //1
  public static WayPointManager Instance;
  //2
  public List<Path> Paths = new List<Path>();
```

```
  void Awake() {
    //3
    Instance = this;
  }
  //4
  public Vector3 GetSpawnPosition(int pathIndex) {
    return Paths[pathIndex].WayPoints[0].position;
  }
}
//5
[System.Serializable]
public class Path {
  public List<Transform> WayPoints = new List<Transform>();
}
```

This script stores the paths and its waypoints. Here's a detailed explanation of the different parts:

1. A static variable that holds a reference to this script. Static values can be accessed from all classes without the need for linking components in the editor or by way of scripting. This is a simplified version of the Singleton pattern, which allows easy access to a manager-type class from anywhere. All manager scripts will use this pattern and it'll soon become clear why this is so handy.

2. The list of stored paths. Path is a custom class that's defined in entry 5 of this list. Essentially it's a list of lists: several paths that each contain several waypoints.

3. Sets the value explained in **entry 1**. The keyword this refers to the class it's written in; in this case, WayPointManager.

4. Returns the position of the enemy spawn point based on what path they will take. It does this by taking the first waypoint (index 0) of the chosen path and returning that position.

5. Path is defined here as a class containing a list of waypoints which are stored as Transforms. [System.Serializable] makes the class serializable, meaning you can edit it in the Inspector.

Save the script and return to the Unity editor. It's time for the waypoint manager to show its worth. **Create a new empty GameObject** in the Hierarchy and name it **Managers**. This will be a **folder object** as it will contain all the different managers nice and neat.

Create another empty GameObject and parent it to **Managers**. Name it **Waypoint Manager**. Drag the **WayPointManager** script from the **Project** panel on to the object.

This is what it looks like in the Inspector:

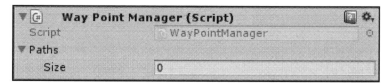

Set the **Size** of **Paths** to **1** to create a new path. This will correspond to **Path 0** you made earlier.

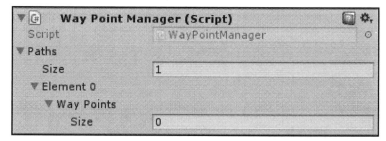

The waypoints you made earlier will need to be dragged to the Way Points field. By default, it's quite hard to drag them all in at once, as the focus in the Inspector will change to the waypoints instead of the Waypoint Manager. The solution here is to lock the Inspector view so Waypoint Manager stays visible at all times.

Press the small **lock icon** at the top left of the Inspector to lock the view:

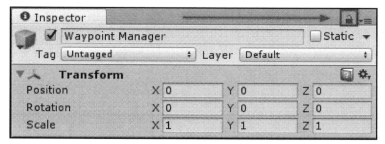

In the Hierarchy, expand **EnemyPaths\Path 0** to see all the waypoints. Select all of them and drag them to Waypoint Manager's **Way Points** field.

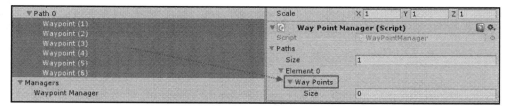

This should fill up the Way Points field with a list of all waypoints. Press the lock icon again to unlock the Inspector. You now have the first set of waypoints stored away for later use.

To make things more interesting, there will be two paths the enemies can take.

Create a new empty GameObject, name it **Path 1** and parent it to **EnemyPaths** in the Hierarchy. Now reset its **Transform**.

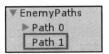

Duplicate **Waypoint (1)** of **Path 0** and drag it unto **Path 1** to parent it. Name it **Waypoint (1)** and set its position to (-25, 0, 13). Also disable **Path 0** in the Inspector (uncheck the checkbox next to its name) so it won't get in your way. This will be the starting point of the second path, which has to look like this:

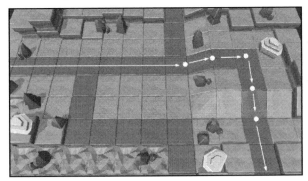

Notice the slopes at the top right. These need extra waypoints at the start and end of them to make sure enemies ascend and descend them properly. Without these, they would either appear to be floating or moving through the ground.

Add the necessary waypoints to make this path by duplicating **WayPoint (1)** and moving the copies around the map. Here's the list of positions to check after you're done:

- Waypoint (1): (-25, 0, 13)

- Waypoint (2): (3.5, 0, 13)

- Waypoint (3): (6.5, 1.5, 13)

- Waypoint (4): (11, 1.5, 13)

- Waypoint (5): (11, 1.5, 8.5)

- Waypoint (6): (11, 0, 5.5)

- Waypoint (7): (11, 0, -6.5)

Now increase the size of **Paths** in the Waypoint Manager to **2**. Set the **Size** of **Way Points** to **0** and drag in your new waypoints like you did before. Now disable **EnemyPaths**. You don't need the visualization of the path to progress.

And that's how you make a waypoint system. They're pretty easy to use too as we'll see in the next part about enemies!

Enemies

Enemies, often called minions or creeps in tower defense games, are the cannon fodder for the towers as they try to reach the exit of the map.

In Runestrife there are three kinds of enemies: a normal one (**Knight**), a fast one (**Airship**) and a sturdy one (**Ram**). Each of these has different speeds and amount of health but in essence they're the same, they all try to reach the exit before they get killed.

These enemies are located in the **Prefabs\Enemy** folder. Drag the **Fast Enemy** to the Hierarchy and set its **Position** to (2, 0, -5). Press the play button to see what happens.

He's just standing there right now. That's no good! To make him move, you'll have to edit the **Enemy** script so it uses the **Way Point Manager** that you made earlier. Open up the **Enemy** script in the **Scripts\Game\Enemy** folder and add these methods underneath Die():

```
void Update() {
  //1
  if (wayPointIndex <
WayPointManager.Instance.Paths[pathIndex].WayPoints.Count) {
    UpdateMovement();
  } else { // 2
    OnGotToLastWayPoint();
  }
}

private void UpdateMovement() {
  //3
  Vector3 targetPosition =
    WayPointManager.Instance.Paths[pathIndex]
    .WayPoints[wayPointIndex].position;
  //4
  transform.position = Vector3.MoveTowards(
    transform.position, targetPosition,
    moveSpeed * Time.deltaTime);
  //5
  transform.LookAt(targetPosition);
  //6
  if (Vector3.Distance(transform.position, targetPosition) < .
1f) {
    wayPointIndex++;
  }
}
```

Taking each commented section in turn:

1. While there's still waypoints left, update the movement.

2. No more waypoints, so call OnGotToLastWayPoint().

3. The next waypoint is the target position.

4. Move towards the target position.

5. Look at the target.

6. If the enemy is very close to the target waypoint, set the next waypoint as the target. You can't just use if(transform.position == targetPosition) because that will often fails due to floating point error. Floats are not accurate enough to do exact comparisons.

Save this script and return to the editor. Save and play the scene and behold: The enemy moves along the path you made!

Adding some utility

When working with Unity, there are often actions that you use in several different scripts across your game. Some examples:

- Moving an item up and down like it's floating

- Constantly rotating an object

- Scaling an object up and down

- Making objects look at other objects

Instead of adding these functions to each script that might need it, you can write small utility scripts that you can reference and use instead. The utility scripts you'll be writing here can be useful for just about any game. It's like a toolbelt for Unity!

First up is a script that constantly rotates the GameObject it's attached to. This will be handy for the enemies as two of them have wheels and one of them has a rotor.

In the Project Browser, create a new **C# Script** in the **Scripts\Utility** folder named **LoopRotate** and open it in your code editor. Remove the `Start()` method completely and put this line right under the class declaration:

```
public Vector3 rotation;
```

This is the desired rotation of the GameObject that this script will attach to.

Inside the `Update()` method, add this line:

```
transform.Rotate(rotation * Time.deltaTime);
```

This will make the object rotate every frame by the rotation specified in `rotation`. Pretty simple, right? It will help tremendously though!

Save this script return to the Unity editor.

You should still have the **FastEnemy** in your Hierarchy. If not, drag it in from the **Enemy** prefabs folder. Expand **FastEnemy** and **Airship** to see the children named **Airship** and **Prop**.

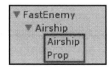

Select **Prop** and take a closer look at it (**press Shift-F and zoom in using the scroll-wheel**).

This seems like a perfect candidate to test the out the rotator script on.

Add the **Loop Rotate** component on **Prop** and set the **Rotation** value on that to (**1000, 0, 0**). In the **Prefab** section near the top of the Inspector click the **Apply** button. This will apply changes to the prefab that the GameObject was based on.

Press the play button to see the effect. Looks pretty neat! Time to give Knight and Ram some rotation too.

Delete **FastEnemy** and drop **NormalEnemy** into the scene from the **Prefabs\Enemy** folder. Set its **Position** to (2, 0, -5). Fully expand it to see all of its children.

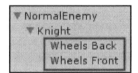

Select both wheels and add the **Loop Rotate** component to them. Set the **Rotation** to (0, -360, 0). See if it works by going into play mode.

Select **Normal Enemy** in the Hierarchy. Update its prefab settings by pressing the **Prefab\Apply button** in the Inspector.

Delete **NormalEnemy** and drag and drop **TankyEnemy** to the Hierarchy from the **Prefabs\Enemies** folder. Set its **Position** to (2, 0, -5). Fully expand it and select **Wheels**

Back. Add the **Loop Rotate** component to it and set the **Rotation** to (0, -300, 0). Select **Wheels Front**, add a **Loop Rotate** component and set its **Rotation** to (0, -180, 0).

The reason why these wheels need different rotation speeds is because they have different sizes:

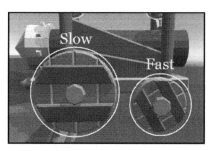

Apply the **Tanky Enemy** prefab settings and see check out the result in play mode.

Sweet. On to the next utility: **Auto Scaler**! This is a utility component that's quite handy for making things grow or shrink continuously at a set rate. Make a new **C# Script** inside the **Scripts\Utility** folder and name it **AutoScaler**. Open it up in a code editor.

Delete the whole `Start()` method and add this line right under the class declaration:

```
public float scaleSpeed;
```

This simple variable controls both the speed of scaling and if the GameObject should shrink or grow. Negative values makes the object shrink, positive ones — you guessed it — makes them grow.

Add this line inside `Update()`:

```
transform.localScale += (new Vector3(scaleSpeed, scaleSpeed,
    scaleSpeed) * Time.deltaTime);
```

This is what actually does the scaling. It adds the `scaleSpeed` to all three axes every frame. There's no use case for this just yet. But stay tuned as there pretty soon will be!

Save this script and open up the **UtilityMethods** script inside the **Scripts\Utility** folder.

This script is actually a simple class, not a MonoBehaviour. It holds static helper methods that can easily be called from all scripts.

You'll be adding a very useful method named `SmoothlyLook`, which allows GameObjects to rotate and look at a certain position smoothly by using interpolation.

Add this method underneath `MoveUiElementToWorldPosition()`:

```
// 1
public static Quaternion SmoothlyLook(Transform fromTransform,
  Vector3 toVector3) {

  //2
  if (fromTransform.position == toVector3) {
    return fromTransform.localRotation;
  }

  //3
  Quaternion currentRotation = fromTransform.localRotation;
  Quaternion targetRotation = Quaternion.LookRotation(toVector3
  -
    fromTransform.position);

  //4
  return Quaternion.Slerp(currentRotation, targetRotation,
    Time.deltaTime * 10f);
}
```

Here's what each part does:

1. `SmoothlyLook()` takes two parameters: the `Transform` which has to be rotated and the position where it wants to look. It returns a `Quaternion`, which is the new local rotation for the `Transform`. It's also `static`, which means that — as you may remember — it can be called from any class without having to have a reference to it beforehand.

2. This check makes sure that the method stops executing if the origin point and destination are the same, which would create a zero-length vector. The `LookRotation()` method doesn't like that so that's why this check is in place.

3. This blocks stores the current rotation and creates the target rotation for the `Transform` by using the `LookRotation()` method.

4. This is the actual method that makes the rotation interpolate, `Slerp()`. It might sound like some sort of frozen beverage. But in reality it's a handy way of getting a value between two other values (also called **tweening**) with a distinct beginning and end.

The `SmoothlyLook()` method can be used to replace the popping rotation of the enemies with a nice turn.

Save this script, open up the **Enemy** script again and remove this line from the `UpdateMovement()` method:

```
transform.LookAt(targetPosition);
```

Put this in its place:

```
transform.localRotation = UtilityMethods.
  SmoothlyLook(transform, targetPosition);
```

Now save the **Enemy** script and return to the editor. Make sure you have at least one enemy in the scene and press the play button. You should now see the enemy turning smoothly at turns and ledges. Finally, delete any enemies left in the Hierarchy.

That's it! Three handy utilities for Runestrife — and for your own games if you like.

Waves of enemies

In the current state of the game, there isn't anything happening without you dragging an **Enemy** prefab to the scene. You want waves of enemies to spawn onto the map in intervals.

To do that, you'll first need to think about what an enemy wave actually is:

- A group of enemies...

- That spawn on a certain path...

- With a delay between each spawn.

With this info you can make a class that represents this data.

Enemy waves and the Wave Manager

Create a new folder in the **Scripts\Game\Enemy** folder and name it **Wave**.

Inside the **Wave** folder, create a new **C# Script** and name it **EnemyWave**. Open it in your favorite code editor. Delete everything that's in there and replace it with this code:

```
using System;
using System.Collections.Generic;
using UnityEngine;
```

```
//1
[Serializable]
public class EnemyWave {
  //2
  public int pathIndex;
  //3
  public float startSpawnTimeInSeconds;
  //4
  public float timeBetweenSpawnsInSeconds = 1f;
  //5
  public List<GameObject> listOfEnemies = new
List<GameObject>();
}
```

This is a simple class that'll be used as data container to make it easy to add waves in the Unity editor. Here's what's happening inside:

1. The [Serializable] attribute makes sure this class is serialized so it can be seen and edited in the editor when used by a MonoBehaviour.

2. The index of the path this wave should take.

3. Time in seconds before this wave starts.

4. Delay in seconds between each spawn.

5. The list of enemies in this wave.

Now that you have a representation of a wave in code, you can make a manager script that will use this data to actually spawn the enemies in the world.

Save the **EnemyWave** script and return to the editor. In the same folder as **EnemyWave**, make a new **C# Script** and name it **WaveManager**. Open it in a code editor and remove both the Start() and Update() methods completely.

The full script is quite large, but bear with me, I'll explain it all in parts. At the very top of the file, right under using UnityEngine;, add this line:

```
using System.Collections.Generic;
```

This makes sure you can make **List<>** objects without errors.

Under the class declaration add these variable declarations:

```
//1
public static WaveManager Instance;
//2
public List<EnemyWave> enemyWaves = new List<EnemyWave>();
//3
private float elapsedTime = 0f;
//4
```

```
private EnemyWave activeWave;
//5
private float spawnCounter = 0f;
//6
private List<EnemyWave> activatedWaves = new List<EnemyWave>();
```

Here's the play-by-play:

1. Just like the **WayPointManager**, this class also uses the Singleton pattern to make itself available everywhere using this variable.

2. The list of enemy waves that'll be spawned by this class.

3. This variable keeps track of how much time has passed since the level started in seconds.

4. The wave that's currently spawning enemies.

5. This keeps track of when the last spawn happened. It gets reset to 0 with every spawn, and is incremented in every frame while a wave is spawning.

6. A list of waves that were already started. Any waves in here won't be started again.

Under the variable declarations you just added, add these methods:

```
//1
void Awake() {
  Instance = this;
}
//2
void Update() {
  elapsedTime += Time.deltaTime;

  SearchForWave();
  UpdateActiveWave();
}
private void SearchForWave() {
  //3
  foreach (EnemyWave enemyWave in enemyWaves) {
    //4
    if (!activatedWaves.Contains(enemyWave)
      && enemyWave.startSpawnTimeInSeconds <= elapsedTime) {

      //5
      activeWave = enemyWave;
      activatedWaves.Add(enemyWave);
      spawnCounter = 0f;
      //6
      break;
    }
  }
}
```

```
//7
private void UpdateActiveWave() {

}
```

Here's what these methods do:

1. Sets the `Instance` variable to script itself.

2. Add to `elapsedTime`. Check if a new wave has to be started and update the wave that's active every frame.

3. Iterate over the `enemyWaves` list.

4. Check that a wave wasn't already started before, and the time spent in the level is past the start time of that wave.

5. If so, make the enemy wave the active one. Add it to the list of already activated waves and reset the spawn counter.

6. Break out of the list iteration as a suitable wave has been found.

7. An empty method up until now. This is filled in the next part.

Now for the actual spawning of enemies. Add this code inside `UpdateActiveWave()`:

```
//1
if (activeWave != null) {
  spawnCounter += Time.deltaTime;

  //2
  if (spawnCounter >= activeWave.timeBetweenSpawnsInSeconds) {
    spawnCounter = 0f;

    //3
    if (activeWave.listOfEnemies.Count != 0) {
      //4
      GameObject enemy = (GameObject)Instantiate(
        activeWave.listOfEnemies[0], WayPointManager.Instance.
        GetSpawnPosition(activeWave.pathIndex),
Quaternion.identity);
      //5
      enemy.GetComponent<Enemy>().pathIndex =
activeWave.pathIndex;
      //6
      activeWave.listOfEnemies.RemoveAt(0);
    } else {
      //7
      activeWave = null;
      //8
      if (activatedWaves.Count == enemyWaves.Count) {
        // All waves are over
```

```
            }
          }
        }
      }
```

Here's what's happening:

1. Only continue if there's an active wave.

2. If the spawn counter is higher than the active wave's `timeBetweenSpawnsInSeconds` variable, there's an enemy that needs to be spawned. Also reset the spawn counter in this case.

3. Check if there's still enemies in the current wave.

4. Spawn the first entry in the enemy list at the position of the first waypoint of the wave's path.

5. Set the new enemy's `pathIndex` so it knows where it should move.

6. Remove the first entry in the list of enemies.

7. If the check in `//2` fails, there are no more enemies in the current wave. Empty the `activeWave` variable by giving it a `null` value.

8. If the number of total waves equals the number if waves that were already activated that means all waves are over.

These parts combined give the **WaveManager** all needed functionality to start spawning enemies!

There's still one small method that needs to be added so the spawning can be stopped completely if necessary. Add this under `UpdateActiveWave()`:

```
public void StopSpawning() {
    elapsedTime = 0;
    spawnCounter = 0;
    activeWave = null;
    activatedWaves.Clear();
    enabled = false;
}
```

This resets all variables that hold time values and clears both the active wave and the list of waves that were already activated. Finally, it disables the **WaveManager** script completely.

Save this script and return to the Unity editor. In the Hierarchy, make a new empty GameObject named **Wave Manager** and parent it to **Managers**. Add the **WaveManager** component you just made to it (**Scripts\Wave Manager**).

You can now make waves from inside the editor. Set the **Size** of **Enemy Waves** to **1** to create the first one. Fully expand all field to see expose all variables:

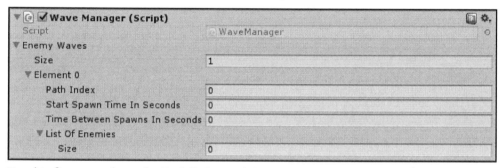

For this first wave, leave the **Path Index** and **Start Spawn Time In Seconds** at **0** and set **Time Between Spawns In Seconds** to **2**.

To add the actual enemies, open the **Prefabs\Enemy** folder in the Project Browser and select the **Wave Manager** again in the Hierarchy. Now drag and drop the enemy prefabs onto the **List Of Enemies** field to add them to the list.

The prefabs will be spawned top to bottom:

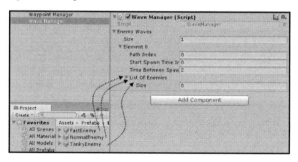

Fill up the list with mostly **NormalEnemy** and sprinkle a few of the others around. Don't add more than 8 enemies to this first wave. Mine looks like this:

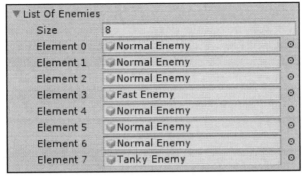

Now it's time to see this bad boy in action. Save your scene and press the play button to see what happens:

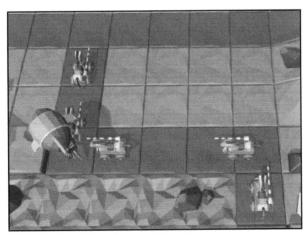

The enemies appear one by one and follow the path! Exactly what you needed to blow some life into the game.

The Enemy Manager

Now that you have a bunch of enemies moving about, it's wise to think about a way of managing them so you can find them again when needed. At the moment, there are no references to them saved anywhere. They get spawned and that's it.

To fix this, you can make an **Enemy Manager** that will let enemies register themselves as they spawn and unregister as they die.

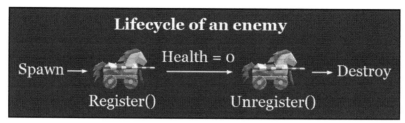

Make a new **C# Script** in the **Scripts\Game\Enemy** folder and name it **EnemyManager**. Open it in a code editor. Remove the `Start()` and `Update()` methods and add these two lines to the top of the file:

```
using System.Collections.Generic;
using System.Linq;
```

Now insert these properties and methods into the class definition:

```
//1
public static EnemyManager Instance;
//2
public List<Enemy> Enemies = new List<Enemy>();
//3
void Awake() {
  Instance = this;
}
//4
public void RegisterEnemy(Enemy enemy) {
  Enemies.Add(enemy);
}
//5
public void UnRegister(Enemy enemy) {
  Enemies.Remove(enemy);
}
//6
public List<Enemy> GetEnemiesInRange(Vector3 position, float
range) {
  return Enemies.Where(enemy => Vector3.Distance(position,
enemy.transform.position) <= range).ToList();
}
//7
public void DestroyAllEnemies() {
  foreach (Enemy enemy in Enemies) {
    Destroy(enemy.gameObject);
  }
  Enemies.Clear();
}
```

Here's the explanation:

1. This is another Singleton. Store this script in the `Instance` variable for global access.

2. The list with registered enemies.

3. Sets the `Instance` to this script.

4. Register an enemy by adding it to the `Enemies` list.

5. Unregister an enemy by removing it from the `Enemies` list.

6. This is a helper method. It returns a list of all enemies withing a certain `range` from the `position` given. This single line statement is a LINQ (Language-Integrated Query) that lets you write C# code in a SQL-like manner to get data out of lists and arrays.

7. Iterate through the whole `Enemies` list and destroy all of them. The list also has to be cleared of any references by calling `Clear()` on it.

Save this script and return to the editor.

Make a new empty GameObject, name it **Enemy Manager** and parent it to **Managers**. Add the **EnemyManager** script to it.

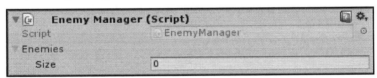

Unlike the other managers, this one doesn't need any setup. The **Enemy** script does need some additions to make the system work like it should.

Open up the **Enemy** script (**Scripts\Enemy**) and add this method right above `OnGotToLastWayPoint()`:

```
void Start() {
    EnemyManager.Instance.RegisterEnemy(this);
}
```

This will make the enemy register itself to the **EnemyManager** once it spawns.

Replace the contents of the `Die()` method with this:

```
if (gameObject != null) {
    //1
    EnemyManager.Instance.UnRegister(this);
    //2
    gameObject.AddComponent<AutoScaler>().scaleSpeed = -2;
    //3
    enabled = false;
```

```
    //4
    Destroy(gameObject, 0.3f);
}
```

This method is pretty straightforward:

1. Unregister this enemy.

2. Add the **AutoScaler** component and set it to shrink rapidly as a visual dying effect.

3. Disable the enemy script.

4. Destroy itself after 0.3 seconds to let the scaling effect show.

Save the script and return to the editor. Play the scene to and look at **Enemy Manager's** Inspector to see the list fill up with enemies:

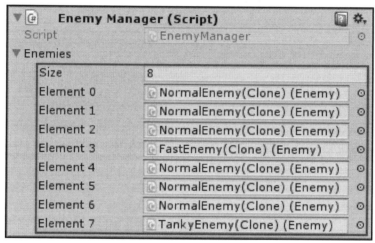

When enemies die, they'll shrink:

Pretty cool, right? It'll look even better when they do that after a fatal blast from a tower!

The Game Manager

There are a few variables and functionality that don't fit into any specific script but need to be accessed from many other scripts. A **Game Manager** fits perfectly in this situation. It stores all sorts of global information such as the amount of gold the player has, or the number of enemies that have escaped. It also contains some methods for things like restarting the game and returning to the title screen.

Create a new **C# Script** in the **Scripts\Game** folder and name it **GameManager**. Open it in a code editor. Remove the Start() and Update() methods completely. Put this below the other using statements at the top of the file:

```
using UnityEngine.SceneManagement;
```

Insert these variable declarations into the class definition:

```
//1
public static GameManager Instance;
//2
public int gold;
//3
public int waveNumber;
//4
public int escapedEnemies;
//5
public int maxAllowedEscapedEnemies = 5;
//6
public bool enemySpawningOver;
//7
public AudioClip gameWinSound;
public AudioClip gameLoseSound;
//8
private bool gameOver;
```

Here's the role of each:

1. The static variable for global access.

2. The amount of gold the player has.

3. Number of the wave that's currently being spawned.

4. Amount of enemies that made it to the exit.

5. Number of escaped enemies before you lose the game.

6. This is set to true when all enemies have been spawned and is used to help check if the player wins.

7. The Audio Clip references for the win and lose states.

8. Set to `true` when the game is over. It doesn't matter if the player won or lost.

Now add these methods under the variable declarations you just added:

```
//1
void Awake() {
  Instance = this;
}

void Update() {
  //2
  if (!gameOver && enemySpawningOver) {
    // Check if no enemies left, if so win game
    //3
    if (EnemyManager.Instance.Enemies.Count == 0) {
      OnGameWin();
    }
  }

  // When ESC is pressed, quit to the title screen
  //4
  if (Input.GetKeyDown(KeyCode.Escape)) {
    QuitToTitleScreen();
  }
}

//5
private void OnGameWin() {
  AudioSource.PlayClipAtPoint(gameWinSound,
    Camera.main.transform.position);
  gameOver = true;
}
//6
public void QuitToTitleScreen() {
  SceneManager.LoadScene("TitleScreen");
}
```

Taking each section in turn:

1. Sets `Instance` to the current script.

2. Checks if the game isn't over yet, but the enemies have all been spawned.

3. If there are no more enemies, the player has won, so call `OnGameWin()`.

4. When the Escape key is pressed, call `QuitToTitleScreen()`.

5. When the player wins, play the win audio clip and set `gameOver` to true.

6. Return to the TitleScreen scene.

Now add these methods below the other ones:

```
//1
public void OnEnemyEscape() {
  escapedEnemies++;

  if (escapedEnemies == maxAllowedEscapedEnemies) {
    // Too many enemies escaped, you lose the game
    OnGameLose();
  }
}

//2
private void OnGameLose() {
  gameOver = true;

  AudioSource.PlayClipAtPoint(gameLoseSound,
    Camera.main.transform.position);
  EnemyManager.Instance.DestroyAllEnemies();
  WaveManager.Instance.StopSpawning();
}

//3
public void RetryLevel() {
  SceneManager.LoadScene("Game");
}
```

Quite simply:

1. If the amount of enemies that have escaped surpasses the amount allowed, call `OnGameLose`.

2. Set `gameOver` to `true`, destroy all enemies that are still on the map and tell the **Wave Manager** to stop spawning new enemies.

3. Reload the **Game** scene.

That's it for the **GameManager** script! Save the script and return to the editor.

Create a new empty GameObject, name it **Game Manager** and parent it to **Managers**. Add the **Game Manager** script to it:

There are just two fields here that need some setup: **Game Win Sound** and **Game Lose Sound**. In the **Project** view, open up the **Sound FX** folder to see all the sound effects present in the project:

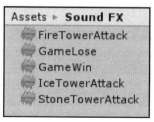

Drag **GameWin** to the **Game Win Sound** field and drag **GameLose** to **Game Lose Sound**.

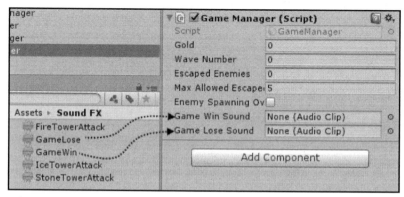

Now that the **Game Manager** is in place, there are a few scripts that need to be modified to use its features. Open up the **WaveManager** script (**Scripts\Game\Enemy\Wave**) and add this inside the `SearchForWave()` method, right under `spawnCounter = 0f;`:

```
GameManager.Instance.waveNumber++;
```

This will notify the GameManager that a new wave started.

Add this line to the `UpdateActiveWave()` method, right under `if (activatedWaves.Count == enemyWaves.Count) {`:

```
GameManager.Instance.enemySpawningOver = true;
```

This is to tell GameManager that the WaveManager has stopped spawning enemies.

Save the **WaveManager** script and open the **Enemy** script (**Scripts\Game\Enemy folder**). Add this to line to `OnGotToLastWayPoint()`, right above `Die()`:

`GameManager.Instance.OnEnemyEscape();`

That will notify the GameManager that this enemy got to the exit.

Now add the following method under `TakeDamage()`:

```
void DropGold() {
    GameManager.Instance.gold += goldDrop;
}
```

Also place a call to the above method in `TakeDamage()`, right above `Die()`:

```
DropGold();
```

Now the enemy will give the player some gold when it dies of an attack.

Save the script and return to the editor. Press the play button and look at the Game Manager in the Inspector. Each time an enemy escapes the Escaped Enemies variable will go up:

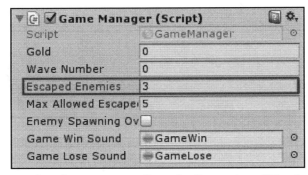

Once the number reaches the maximum allowed, all enemies will be destroyed and the lose sound will play.

That concludes the GameManager; all the global values are now stored neatly in that class.

Where to go from here?

Congratulations on finishing this chapter! You have the foundation of game! In this chapter you've learned how to:

- Use manager classes to do all sorts of stuff

- Use utility scripts to make your life easier

- Get enemies to spawn and move around on a path

In the next chapter, you'll how to make towers and how to link the UI system to the rest of the game.

Chapter 19: Making Towers

By Eric Van de Kerckhove

In the previous chapter, you learned how to create some paths and spawn your enemies to follow those paths. But that's not much of a game. To even the playing field a little, you need some killer towers to lob stones, ice and even fire at your invaders!

In this chapter you'll create all the missing pieces to make the final game. In the process, you'll learn how to:

- Create waves of enemies.
- Make towers that shoot projectiles.
- Craft a UI that binds everything together.
- Make winning and losing logic.

You can continue from where you left off in the previous chapter, but if you want to start fresh, open up the starter project in Unity. Open the **Game** scene and prepare for making some awesome scripts!

First up: creating a tower.

Creating your first tower

Before creating any towers, you need a **TowerSlot** to place them on. Drag the **TowerSlot** prefab from the **Prefabs\Tower** folder into the Hierarchy. Set its position to (-4, 0, 10).

This a quad with a texture on it and a **Box Collider** to allow interaction with it by clicking. Notice that there's an **Event Trigger** component attached. This handles all the events for when the player's cursor enters and exits, and when a click happens as well.

Stone tower

The first of the towers is the affordable and reliable **Stone Tower**.

Drag the **Stone Tower** prefab from the **Prefabs\Tower** folder into the Hierarchy and change its position to (-1, 0, 10) so you can still see the **TowerSlot**.

Create a new folder named **Tower** inside the **Scripts\Game** folder. Then create a new **C# Script** named **Tower** and open it in a code editor. At this point, you may be thinking "Wait a minute, I'm making the script for a **Stone Tower** here. Shouldn't the script be called **StoneTower**?"

The answer is "no". While there's going to be a Stone Tower script as well, it will derive from this common Tower script. That means all logic shared between towers is going into **Tower** and the other tower scripts inherit its properties and functionality while still having to ability to add their own.

Back to the script, delete everything that's in there, then add these lines:

```
using UnityEngine;
using System.Collections.Generic;
```

These `using` make sure you can access Unity classes and use lists. Now add this snippet:

```
public enum TowerType {
    Stone, Fire, Ice
}
```

This small `enum` will be used throughout several classes so they know what type of tower they're dealing with. It contains the three types of towers you'll be adding to the project.

Add this code block right underneath:

```
public class Tower : MonoBehaviour {

}
```

This is the actual class declaration where you can insert these variables:

```
//1
public float attackPower = 3f;
//2
public float timeBetweenAttacksInSeconds = 1f;
//3
public float aggroRadius = 15f;
//4
public int towerLevel = 1;
//5
public TowerType type;
//6
public AudioClip shootSound;
//7
public Transform towerPieceToAim;
//8
public Enemy targetEnemy = null;
//9
private float attackCounter;
```

Here's what these variables are for:

1. The amount of damage the tower inflicts to enemies.

2. Cooldown between shots.

3. The minimum distance between the tower and the enemy before the tower starts targeting the enemy.

4. Level of the tower which can be increased with an upgrade.

5. The type of tower.

6. The sound effect that plays when this tower shoots.

7. The Transform that should be aimed at the enemy (the Head, for example).

8. Enemy that this tower is currently targeting.

9. This counter will decrement every frame. When it hits 0, the tower is allowed to shoot.

Quite a lot of useful variables! Next up is looking and attacking. Add these methods under the variable declarations:

```
private void SmoothlyLookAtTarget(Vector3 target) {
  towerPieceToAim.localRotation = UtilityMethods.
    SmoothlyLook(towerPieceToAim, target);
}

protected virtual void AttackEnemy() {
  GetComponent<AudioSource>().PlayOneShot(shootSound, .15f);
}
```

`SmoothlyLookAtTarget()` uses the `SmoothlyLook` utility method to look at the enemy target. `AttackEnemy()` simply plays the shoot sound effect. This is because each tower will implement its own way of attacking. Notice the `virtual` keyword. This means any classes derived from Tower can use this method as-is, add to it, or override it completely.

The towers need a way to detect enemies close by and select the nearest one as a target. Add the following methods:

```
//1
public List<Enemy> GetEnemiesInAggroRange() {
  List<Enemy> enemiesInRange = new List<Enemy>();
  //2
  foreach (Enemy enemy in EnemyManager.Instance.Enemies) {
    if (Vector3.Distance(transform.position,
enemy.transform.position)
      <= aggroRadius) {
```

```
         enemiesInRange.Add(enemy);
      }
   }
   //3
   return enemiesInRange;
}

//4
public Enemy GetNearestEnemyInRange() {
   Enemy nearestEnemy = null;
   float smallestDistance = float.PositiveInfinity;
   //5
   foreach (Enemy enemy in GetEnemiesInAggroRange()) {
      if (Vector3.Distance(transform.position,
enemy.transform.position)
         < smallestDistance) {

         smallestDistance = Vector3.Distance(transform.position,
            enemy.transform.position);
         nearestEnemy = enemy;
      }
   }
   //6
   return nearestEnemy;
}
```

Here's what's going on above:

1. `GetEnemiesInAggroRange()` returns a list of all enemies withing this tower's aggro radius.

2. Iterate through all enemies and add enemies that are within range to the `enemiesInRange` list.

3. Return the list.

4. `GetNearestEnemyInRange()` returns the enemy that's closest to this tower.

5. Iterate through all enemies within range and keep storing the enemy that's the most close by. When the whole list has been iterated, the `NearestEnemy` will be the one that's closest.

6. Return the nearest enemy.

The biggest and most important method of Tower is `Update()`; it handles the rotation, targeting and attacking. Add this below the other methods:

```
public virtual void Update() {
   //1
   attackCounter -= Time.deltaTime;
   //2
```

```
   if (targetEnemy == null) {
     //3
     if (towerPieceToAim) {
       SmoothlyLookAtTarget(towerPieceToAim.transform.position -
         new Vector3(0, 0, 1));
     }
     //4
     if (GetNearestEnemyInRange() != null && Vector3.Distance
         (transform.position,
   GetNearestEnemyInRange().transform.position)
         <= aggroRadius) {

       targetEnemy = GetNearestEnemyInRange();
     }
   } else { // 5
     //6
     if (towerPieceToAim) {
       SmoothlyLookAtTarget(targetEnemy.transform.position);
     }
     //7
     if (attackCounter <= 0f) {
       // Attack
       AttackEnemy();
       // Reset attack counter
       attackCounter = timeBetweenAttacksInSeconds;
     }

     //8
     if (Vector3.Distance(transform.position,
       targetEnemy.transform.position) > aggroRadius) {

       targetEnemy = null;
     }
   }
}
```

This chunk of code does quite a lot for you:

1. Decrement the `attackCounter`.

2. Check if there's currently no enemy targeted.

3. If there's a transform to rotate, look at a neutral position. This is the tower's idle state.

4. Attempt to find a new new target enemy.

5. Check if there's a target enemy assigned.

6. If so, look at the target enemy.

7. If `attackCounter` is equal or below zero, call `AttackEnemy()` and reset the counter.

8. If the target enemy moves out of aggro range, set the `targetEnemy` to nothing.

Almost done! Add this last method to complete the **Tower** script:

```
public void LevelUp() {
    towerLevel++;

    //Calculate new stats for this tower
    attackPower *= 2;
    timeBetweenAttacksInSeconds *= 0.7f;
    aggroRadius *= 1.20f;
}
```

This levels up the tower: it adds a level and increases the tower's attack power, shooting cooldown and aggro radius by multiplying the values. This ensures an upgraded tower is more powerful than a new level 1 variant.

Save this script and return to the editor to make a script for the Stone Tower. Create a new **C# Script** in the **Scripts\Game\Tower** folder named **StoneTower** and open it up. Remove the `Start()` and `Update()` methods completely and replace this line:

```
public class StoneTower : MonoBehaviour {
```

with:

```
public class StoneTower : Tower {
```

This makes sure this class inherits from Tower.

Next, add this code right under the line you replaced:

```
//1
public GameObject stonePrefab;
//2
protected override void AttackEnemy() {
    base.AttackEnemy();
    //3
    GameObject stone = (GameObject)Instantiate(stonePrefab,
        towerPieceToAim.position, Quaternion.identity);
}
```

A straightforward method:

1. The projectile this tower will shoot.

2. Override `AttackEnemy()` and call `base.AttackEnemy()` so the parent code gets executed first.

3. Spawn a new stone projectile.

Save the script and return to the editor. Add the **StoneTower** script to the **StoneTower** GameObject in the Hierarchy. Change **Attack Power** to **15**, **Time Between Attacks** to **2** and **Aggro Radius** to **8**.

Also set the **Shoot Sound** to **StoneTowerAttack** drag the **StoneTower**'s child **Head** to the **Tower Piece To Aim** field.

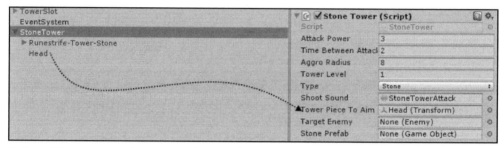

Before this tower can shoot it needs something to use as ammo — that's where the stone prefab and its projectile script come in.

Projectiles

This simple script will follow an enemy around until it hits it target, damaging it in the process!

Make a new folder in **Scripts\Game\Tower** named **Weapons** and create a new **C# Script** in there named **FollowingProjectile**. Open it in a code editor and remove the `Start()` and `Update()` methods.

This class will be another abstract class as the actual scripts you'll be putting on the projectiles will be derived from it. This makes it easy to add new types of projectiles. Add the `abstract` keyword between `public` and `class` to make it into an abstract class.

```
public abstract class FollowingProjectile : MonoBehaviour {
```

An abstract is meant to be subclassed, but can still provides behavior that subclasses can inherit. Now add this underneath the line you edited:

```
//1
public Enemy enemyToFollow;
//2
public float moveSpeed = 15;

private void Update() {
  //3
  if (enemyToFollow == null) {
```

```
      Destroy(gameObject);
    } else { //4
      transform.LookAt(enemyToFollow.transform);
      GetComponent<Rigidbody>().velocity = transform.forward *
moveSpeed;
    }
  }

  //5
  public void OnTriggerEnter(Collider other) {
    if (other.GetComponent<Enemy>() == enemyToFollow) {
      OnHitEnemy();
    }
  }

  //6
  protected abstract void OnHitEnemy();
```

Here's the play-by-play:

1. The Enemy this projectile needs to follow.

2. Speed at which this projectile moves in units per second.

3. If the enemy this projectile is following doesn't exist anymore, it should destroy itself.

4. As long as there's still a target enemy, look at the target and move towards it.

5. If this projectile hits an object, and it's the enemy it's following, then call OnHitEnemy().

6. OnHitEnemy() is an abstract method that needs to be implemented by the derived class. It's also protected which is the same as private except that it can be called from derived classes.

Save the script and return to the editor to make another script. This time, it's the unique script for the StoneProjectile that needs coding. Make a new **C# Script** in **Scripts\Tower\Weapons** named **Stone** and open it up.

Remove the Start() and Update() methods and replace MonoBehaviour with FollowingProjectile, as that's what this class is deriving from. At this point, you'll probably get an error saying this class doesn't implement OnHitEnemy() yet. Ignore this and add this snippet where you removed the methods:

```
//1
public float damage;

//2
protected override void OnHitEnemy() {
  //3
```

```
    enemyToFollow.TakeDamage(damage);
    Destroy(gameObject);
  }
```

Taking each numbered comment in turn:

1. The amount of damage that gets inflicted to the enemy on impact.

2. Override `Followingprojectile`'s `OnHitEnemy()` method.

3. Deal damage to the enemy and destroy the projectile.

Save this script and return to the editor. Time to link things up!

Select the **StoneProjectile** prefab in the **Prefabs\Tower\Weapons** folder and add the **Stone** script to it. You can do that by first selecting the prefab. Then in its Inspector panel, click the **Add Component** button at the bottom. Then search for "Stone" and select the script:

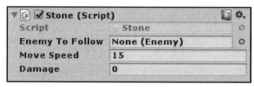

Now drag the **StoneProjectile** prefab to **StoneTower**'s **Stone Prefab** field:

Now the **StoneTower** script needs a little addition before the projectile will work as it should. Open up the **StoneTower** script (**Scripts\Game\Tower** folder) and add these lines right under the `Instantiate` line:

```
    stone.GetComponent<Stone>().enemyToFollow = targetEnemy;
    stone.GetComponent<Stone>().damage = attackPower;
```

These give the stone projectile an enemy to follow and an amount of damage to deal to enemies.

Save the script and return to the editor; StoneTower is ready to go. Press the **Apply** button to save the changes back into the prefab.

Save the scene and prepare for awesomeness! **Duplicate the StoneTower in the Hierarchy a few times and move them around, using snapping to get them right on the center of the tiles.**

Press the play button to see the towers looking at enemies and shooting them down! Now delete the StoneTower and its duplicates from the scene and save the scene again.

Tower Manager

The **TowerManager** handles creating new towers and holds the prices for the different towers.

Create a new **C# Script** named **TowerManager** inside the **Scripts\Game\Tower** folder and open it in a code editor. Completely remove the `Start()` and `Update()` methods and add these lines under the other `using` statements:

```
using System;
using System.Collections.Generic;
using System.Linq;
```

Add the following struct right above `public class TowerManager : MonoBehaviour {`:

```
[Serializable]
public struct TowerCost {
  public TowerType TowerType;
  public int Cost;
}
```

This will let the script use an external, easy editable list of prices.

Now under the class declaration, add this code:

```
//1
public static TowerManager Instance;

//2
public GameObject stoneTowerPrefab;
public GameObject fireTowerPrefab;
public GameObject iceTowerPrefab;
```

```
//3
public List<TowerCost> TowerCosts = new List<TowerCost>();

//4
void Awake() {
  Instance = this;
}

//5
public void CreateNewTower(GameObject slotToFill, TowerType
towerType) {
  switch (towerType) {
    case TowerType.Stone:
      Instantiate(stoneTowerPrefab,
slotToFill.transform.position,
        Quaternion.identity);
      slotToFill.gameObject.SetActive(false);
      break;
    case TowerType.Fire:
      Instantiate(fireTowerPrefab,
slotToFill.transform.position,
        Quaternion.identity);
      slotToFill.gameObject.SetActive(false);
      break;
    case TowerType.Ice:
      Instantiate(iceTowerPrefab,
slotToFill.transform.position,
        Quaternion.identity);
      slotToFill.gameObject.SetActive(false);
      break;
  }
}

//6
public int GetTowerPrice(TowerType towerType) {
  return (from towerCost in TowerCosts where
towerCost.TowerType
    == towerType select towerCost.Cost).FirstOrDefault();
}
```

Here's how it works:

1. As this is another Singleton, a static reference to this script is stored away in `Instance`.

2. References to the tower prefabs, needed to spawn new instances.

3. Store the cost of each type of tower in a list.

4. Sets the `Instance` variable to this script.

5. Accepts a tower slot and a type of tower as parameters, and create a new copy of the chosen tower at the position of the tower slot. It also disables the tower slot so you can't place two towers on one slot.

6. A LINQ utility method to easily get the price of a tower type.

Now save the script and hop back into the editor.

In the Hierarchy, create a new empty GameObject. Name it **Tower Manager** and parent it to **Managers**. Add the **TowerManager** script to it using the **Add Component** button in the Inspector panel and searching for it.

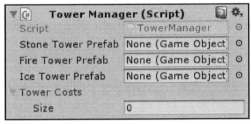

Drag the **StoneTower** prefab from the **Prefabs\Tower** folder onto the **Stone Tower Prefab** field.

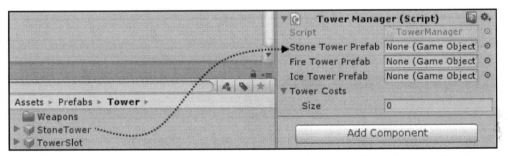

The other towers aren't ready yet, so ignore the two other tower fields for now. Set the **Tower Costs Size** to **3**:

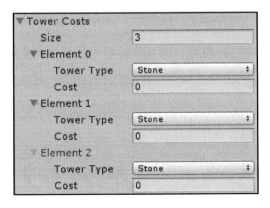

Change the list as follows:

- Leave the first entry's **Tower Type** set to **Stone** and adjust its **Cost** to **100**.

- Set the second **Tower Type** to **Fire** and change its **Cost** to **200**.

- Change the last **Tower Type** to **Ice** and set the **Cost** to **150**.

The Tower Manager is now ready for use! Before you can buy new towers though, **Screen Canvas'** child **AddTowerWindow** needs a script to link its **UI** to to **TowerManager**.

Linking the UI

Create a new **C# Script** named **AddTowerWindow** inside the **Scripts\Game\UI** folder. Open the script and add this line to the top of the file:

```
using System;
```

Now remove the `Start()` and `Update()` methods and insert the following block of code in their place:

```
//1
public GameObject towerSlotToAddTowerTo;

//2
public void AddTower(string towerTypeAsString) {
  //3
  TowerType type = (TowerType)Enum.Parse(typeof(TowerType),
    towerTypeAsString, true);
  //4
  if (TowerManager.Instance.GetTowerPrice(type) <=
    GameManager.Instance.gold) {

    //5
    GameManager.Instance.gold -= TowerManager.Instance
      .GetTowerPrice(type);
    //6
    TowerManager.Instance.CreateNewTower(towerSlotToAddTowerTo,
type);
    gameObject.SetActive(false);
  }
}
```

Here's what each comment references:

1. The reference to the tower slot where the tower should be built.

2. The `AddTower()` method takes a single `string` parameter: the tower's type.

3. Convert the `string` parameter that was passed into the **TowerType** enum. The reason why the method doesn't simply accept the TowerType enum as a parameter is because enums aren't supported for Event Triggers.

4. Check that the player has enough gold to afford the chosen tower.

5. Subtract the tower's price from the player's gold.

6. Call `CreateNewTower()` on the TowerManager and disable the **AddTowerWindow**.

That's it for the **AddTowerWindow** script. Save it and return to the editor.

In the Hierarchy, select and enable **AddTowerWindow** which is a child GameObject under **Screen Canvas**. Add the **AddTowerWindow** script to it by using the **Add Component** button in the Inspector panel and searching for it or dragging it from the **Project** panel.

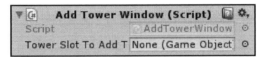

Drag **TowerSlot** from the **Hierachy** to the **TowerSlotToAddTo** field in the Inspector panel.

Time to link up the buttons to allow the creation of towers in the future:

In the Hierarchy, expand the GameObject **AddTowerWindow**, then expand its child GameObect **HorizontalLayout**. Select its child **BtnStoneTower** and drag the **AddTowerWindow** GameObject from the Hierarchy to the **On Click () Object** field.

Click the method dropdown — that is, the dropdown where **No Function** is currently selected. Select **AddTowerWindow.AddTower(string)** in the method dropdown. In the parameter field under the dropdown, insert **Stone** if it isn't inserted automatically.

Select **BtnFireTower**. Do the same as you did for stone, but insert **Fire** in the parameter field under the dropdown.

Finally, select **BtnIceTower**. Do the same as you did for stone and fire, but this time insert **Ice** in the parameter field.

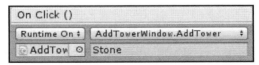

The buttons are all set to go now. Disable the AddTowerWindow GameObject and move on to the next part so you can actually buy some towers!

UI Manager

For the UI Manager, create a new **C# Script** named **UIManager** in the **Scripts\Game\UI** folder and open it in a code editor, then remove the `Start()` method.

Append `using UnityEngine.UI;` to the list of `using` statements at top of the file.

Under the class declaration, add these variables:

```
//1
public static UIManager Instance;
//2
public GameObject addTowerWindow;
//3
public Text txtGold;
public Text txtWave;
public Text txtEscapedEnemies;
```

Here's the purpose of each:

1. The static reference to the UIManager.

2. Reference to the AddTowerWindow component.

3. References to the Text components of the TopBar.

Add the following methods underneath the variable declarations:

```
//1
void Awake() {
  Instance = this;
}

//2
private void UpdateTopBar() {
  txtGold.text = GameManager.Instance.gold.ToString();
  txtWave.text = "Wave " + GameManager.Instance.waveNumber + " /
" +
    WaveManager.Instance.enemyWaves.Count;
  txtEscapedEnemies.text = "Escaped Enemies " +
    GameManager.Instance.escapedEnemies + " / " +
    GameManager.Instance.maxAllowedEscapedEnemies;
}

//3
public void ShowAddTowerWindow(GameObject towerSlot) {
  addTowerWindow.SetActive(true);
  addTowerWindow.GetComponent<AddTowerWindow>().
    towerSlotToAddTowerTo = towerSlot;

  UtilityMethods.MoveUiElementToWorldPosition(addTowerWindow.
```

```
    GetComponent<RectTransform>(),
towerSlot.transform.position);
}
```

Here's what the code above does:

1. Set `Instance` to the `UIManager` script.

2. Update the gold, wave and escaped enemies **Text** values.

3. Takes a Tower Slot as a parameter, passes it along to the Add Tower Window and shows it at the position of the slot using the utility method `MoveUiElementToWorldPosition()`.

Finally, add this method call inside the `Update()` method:

```
UpdateTopBar();
```

This updates the text in the TopBar every frame.

Now save the script and return to the editor to link up the parts.

In the Hierarchy, add a new empty GameObject, name it **UI Manager** and parent it to **Managers**.

Add the **UIManager** script to it by either using the **Add Component** button in the Inspector panel or dragging it from the **Project** panel.

Drag **AddTowerWindow** to the **Add Tower Window** field. Then do the same for **Screen Canvas\TopBar**'s children **TxtGold**, **TxtWave**, **TxtEscapedEnemies** and the **Txt Gold, Txt Wave** and **Txt Escaped Enemies** fields respectively.

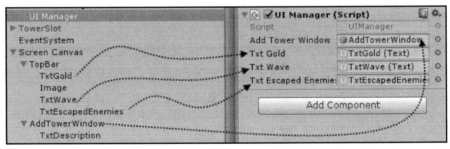

Now for the actual tower buying when clicking a tower slot.

Select **TowerSlot** in the Hierarchy, drag **UIManager** to its **Pointer Click** event's **Object** slot and select **UIManager\ShowAddTowerWindow(GameObject)** from the method dropdown. Finally, drag **TowerSlot** to the parameter field underneath to pass along the slot itself. Press the prefab **Apply** button to save the changes you made to **TowerSlot** to its prefab.

Select **Game Manager** and set the amount of **Gold** to **400**. This will be the starting gold so players can buy towers from the start. It would be a pretty pointless game if you started off with 0! :]

Press the play button and test out the tower slot. When you click on it, the AddTowerWindow should appear and when you click on the Stone Tower icon, a tower should be built in that spot!

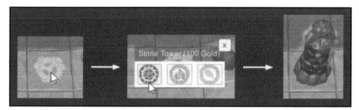

With that working, it's a good idea to make all the tower slots and organize them. In the Hierarchy, create a new **empty GameObject** and name it **TowerSlots**. Reset its **Transform** and drag **TowerSlot** to **TowerSlots** in the Hierarchy to make it a child GameObject.

Now keep duplicating **TowerSlot** and move the copies around using snapping (hold **Control** or **Command**) until you've got all these positions covered:

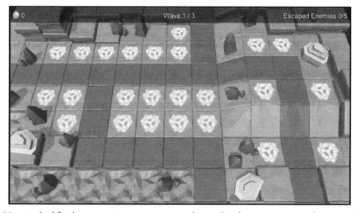

You can use **Y-axis** half-tile snapping to get to those higher parts on the top right of the map. Now save the scene, run the it again and buy some stone towers to kill all enemies. You should hear the win sound effect when you cleared off the wave of enemies.

Tower Info Window and upgrading

The **Tower Info Window** lets players check the level of a tower is and upgrade it if they can afford it.

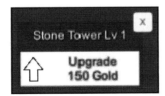

You can find it the window in the scene as a child of the **Screen Canvas**; it's simply a window without any functionality at the moment. To add that, create a new **C# Script** named **TowerInfoWindow** in the **Scripts\Game\UI** folder and open it in your code editor. Remove both the `Start()` and `Update()` methods completely and add this line under the other `using` statments:

```
using UnityEngine.UI;
```

Add these variables right under the class declaration:

```
//1
public Tower tower;
//2
public Text txtInfo;
public Text txtUpgradeCost;
//3
private int upgradePrice;
//4
private GameObject btnUpgrade;
```

Here's what these variables are for:

1. Reference to the tower that can be upgraded.

2. The Text components for the info and the text on the button.

3. The gold cost to upgrade the tower.

4. Reference to the upgrade button.

Now add these methods underneath:

```
//1
void Awake() {
  btnUpgrade = txtUpgradeCost.transform.parent.gameObject;
}
```

```
//2
void OnEnable() {
  UpdateInfo();
}

private void UpdateInfo() {
  // Calculate new price for upgrade
  //3
  upgradePrice = Mathf.CeilToInt(TowerManager.Instance.
    GetTowerPrice(tower.type) * 1.5f * tower.towerLevel);

  //4
  txtInfo.text = tower.type + " Tower Lv " + tower.towerLevel;
  //5
  if (tower.towerLevel < 3) {
    btnUpgrade.SetActive(true);
    txtUpgradeCost.text = "Upgrade\n" + upgradePrice + " Gold";
  } else {
    btnUpgrade.SetActive(false);
  }
}

//6
public void UpgradeTower() {
  if (GameManager.Instance.gold >= upgradePrice) {
    GameManager.Instance.gold -= upgradePrice;
    tower.LevelUp();
    gameObject.SetActive(false);
  }
}
```

Taking each comment in turn:

1. Find the upgrade button.

2. When the window opens, call `UpdateInfo()`.

3. Calculate the price to upgrade the tower.

4. Set the info text to reflect the tower's level.

5. If the tower level is less than 3, show the upgrade button. If not, hide it.

6. When upgrading the tower, check if the player has enough gold, then subtract the amount of gold that's need to upgrade. Finally, disable the TowerInfoWindow GameObject.

Now save the script, open up the **UIManager** script and add this line right underneath `public GameObject addTowerWindow;`:

```
public GameObject towerInfoWindow;
```

This is the reference to the Tower Info Window.

Add this method underneath `Update()`:

```
public void ShowTowerInfoWindow(Tower tower) {
    towerInfoWindow.GetComponent<TowerInfoWindow>().tower = tower;
    towerInfoWindow.SetActive(true);

    UtilityMethods.MoveUiElementToWorldPosition(towerInfoWindow.
        GetComponent<RectTransform>(), tower.transform.position);
}
```

This method accepts a Tower to see info about and/or upgrade. It opens up the TowerInfoWindow and moves it to the tower's position.

The last script that needs editing for the upgrade system to work is the **Tower** script. Open it up in a code editor and add this method underneath `LevelUp()`:

```
public void ShowTowerInfo() {
    UIManager.Instance.ShowTowerInfoWindow(this);
}
```

This method calls **UIManager**'s `ShowTowerInfoWindow()` method and passes the selected tower. Save this script and return to the editor.

Select and fully expand TowerInfoWindow and add the **TowerInfoWindow** script to it using either the **Add Component** button in the Inspector panel or dragging it from the **Project** panel. You can find it in the **Project** panel under **Scripts\Game\UI**.

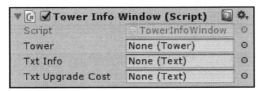

Drag **TxtInfo** to the **Txt Info** field and drag **BtnUpgradeTower**'s child **TxtUpgradeCost** to the **Txt Upgrade Cost** field.

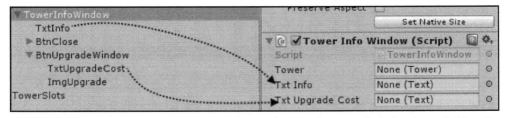

Select **BtnUpgradeTower**, drag **TowerInfoWindow** to the **On Click () Object** field and select **TowerInfoWindow\UpgradeTower** in the method dropdown.

That's it for the Tower Info Window. Now drag an instance of the **StoneTower** prefab into the scene from the **Prefabs\Tower** folder. Select the **StoneTower** and drag **StoneTower** onto the **Pointer Click Event**'s **Object** field and select **StoneTower\ShowTowerInfo** in the method dropdown. Press the **Apply** button to save the prefab then delete **StoneTower** from the Hierarchy.

The UIManager still needs a reference to the Tower Info Window in order to do be able to show it. Select **UIManager** and drag **TowerInfoWindow** to its **Tower Info Window** field.

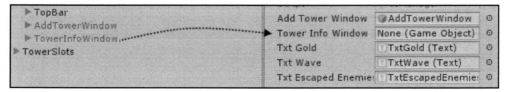

Save the scene and test out the new changes by pressing the play button. Buy a new tower and try to upgrade it by clicking on the tower and pressing the upgrade button in the Tower Info Window.

Win and Lose Windows

These are the windows that appear when the player wins or loses the game:

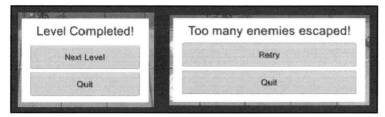

To make the windows appear, there are some adjustments needed in both GameManager and UIManager. Open up the **UIManager** script and add these lines under `public GameObject towerInfoWindow;` :

```
public GameObject winGameWindow;
public GameObject loseGameWindow;
public GameObject blackBackground;
```

These will hold the references to the windows and the background.

Now add these methods underneath `ShowTowerInfoWindow()`:

```
public void ShowWinScreen() {
  blackBackground.SetActive(true);
  winGameWindow.SetActive(true);
}

public void ShowLoseScreen() {
  blackBackground.SetActive(true);
  loseGameWindow.SetActive(true);
}
```

Each of these methods opens the corresponding window and enables the black background to block the player from clicking the towers and tower slots after the game is over.

Save this script and open up the **GameManager** script, which is in the **Scripts\Game** folder. Add this line to the bottom of `OnGameWin()`:

```
UIManager.Instance.ShowWinScreen();
```

Also add this line to the bottom of the `OnGameLose()` method:

```
UIManager.Instance.ShowLoseScreen();
```

These will ensure the windows show up when the player wins or loses. Save this script and return to the editor. Select **UI Manager**, drag **Screen Canvas\WinWindow** and **LoseWindow** to the **Win Game Window** field and **Lose Game Window** fields respectively. Finally, drag the **Black Background** GameObject to the **Black Background** field.

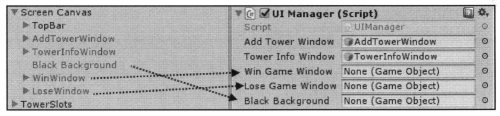

Now add the events on both the Win and Lose Windows. Select **WinWindow**'s child **BtnNextLevel** and drag **GameManager** to the **On Click ()** Object field. Then select **GameManager\Retrylevel** in the dropdown.

Now select **BtnQuit**, drag **GameManager** to its **Object** field and select **GameManager\QuitToTitleScreen** in the method dropdown.

Finally, do the same for LoseWindow's children, **BtnRetry** and **BtnQuit**.

Save your scene and press the play button to test the game. Either kill off the enemies or lose the game. You should now be presented with either the win or lose window!

Enemy health bars

Right now there's no way of knowing how much health an enemy has left. This can be fixed by adding health bars to the enemies:

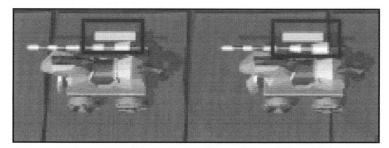

The **Health Bar** prefab is located in the **Prefabs\UI** folder. In order for it to work, the UI Manager and Enemy Manager need some additions to their scripts. Open the **UIManager** script and add these variables underneath `public Text txtEscapedEnemies;` :

```
public Transform enemyHealthBars;
public GameObject enemyHealthBarPrefab;
```

The variable `enemyHealthBars` holds a reference to the parent **EnemyHealthBars** and `enemyHealthBarPrefab` stores a reference to the Health Bar prefab so new ones can be spawned.

Now add this method underneath `ShowLoseScreen()` for the actual making of the health bar:

```
//1
public void CreateHealthBarForEnemy(Enemy enemy) {
  //2
  GameObject healthBar = Instantiate(enemyHealthBarPrefab);
  //3
  healthBar.transform.SetParent(enemyHealthBars, false);
  //4
  healthBar.GetComponent<EnemyHealthBar>().enemy = enemy;
}
```

Going over the above method:

1. `CreateHealthBarForEnemy` accepts the enemy that needs a health bar as its sole parameter.

2. Create a new health bar.

3. Parent the new health bar to EnemyHealthBars.

4. Pass the enemy reference to the health bar.

Save this script and open up the **EnemyManager** script located in the **Scripts\Game\Enemy** folder. Add this line to the bottom of the `RegisterEnemy()` method:

`UIManager.Instance.CreateHealthBarForEnemy(enemy);`

This will create a new health bar for each enemy that spawns. Save this script and return to the editor.

Select the **UIManager** and drag **Screen Canvas\EnemyHealthBars** from the Hierarchy to the **Enemy Health Bars** field. Then drag the **Prefab\UI\Health Bar** from the **Project** panel to the **Enemy Health Bar Prefab** field.

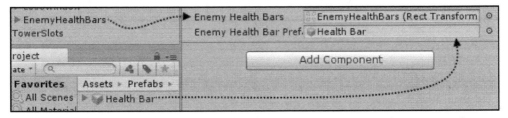

Save the scene and run the game. You'll notice the enemies entering the map now have small health bars above their bodies!

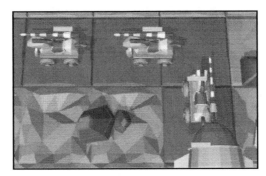

Center Window

The Center Window is used to notify the player a new wave of enemies is coming:

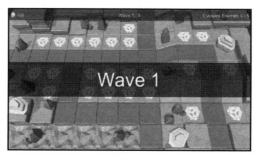

Open up the **UIManager** script and add this variable underneath `public GameObject blackBackground;`:

```
public GameObject centerWindow;
```

This holds the reference to the Center Window. Now add this method and co-routine under the `CreateHealthBarForEnemy()` method:

```
//1
public void ShowCenterWindow(string text) {

centerWindow.transform.FindChild("TxtWave").GetComponent<Text>()
.
    text = text;
  StartCoroutine(EnableAndDisableCenterWindow());
}

//2
private IEnumerator EnableAndDisableCenterWindow() {
  for (int i = 0; i < 3; i++) {
    yield return new WaitForSeconds(.4f);
    centerWindow.SetActive(true);

    yield return new WaitForSeconds(.4f);
    centerWindow.SetActive(false);
  }
}
```

Here's what each section does:

1. Set the text of the Center Window to the `string` value set for the parameter. Then start the `EnableAndDisableCenterWindow()` co-routine.

2. This enables and disables the Center Window every 0.4 seconds three times so it flickers to demand the player's attention.

Save this script and open up the **WaveManager** script located in the **Scripts\Game\Enemy\Wave** folder. Add this line inside the `SearchForWave()` method, right above `break;`:

```
UIManager.Instance.ShowCenterWindow("Wave " + GameManager.
    Instance.waveNumber);
```

Since the WaveManager is the class responsible for making new waves, it's the perfect place to let the UI Manager know when to show the Center Window. It does this by calling `ShowCenterWindow()` on UIManager.

Save this script and return to the editor. Time to wire things up. Select **UI Manager** in the Hierarchy and drag **CenterWindow** to its **Center Window** field.

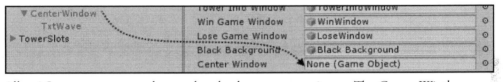

All set! Save your scene and press the play button to test it out. The Center Window should flicker three times at the start of the enemy wave.

Damage Canvas

Now open up the **UIManager** script for the last time to show the **Damage Canvas**. It's a red border to indicate an enemy has escaped. Add this variable underneath `public GameObject centerWindow;`:

```
public GameObject damageCanvas;
```

This is a reference to the Damage Canvas. Now add this method and co-routine combo under the other methods:

```
//1
public void ShowDamage() {
    StartCoroutine(DoDamageAnimation());
}

//2
private IEnumerator DoDamageAnimation() {
    for (int i = 0; i < 3; i++) {
        yield return new WaitForSeconds(.1f);
        damageCanvas.SetActive(true);

        yield return new WaitForSeconds(.1f);
```

```
        damageCanvas.SetActive(false);
    }
}
```

Very quickly:

1. When `ShowDamage()` is called, start the damage animation.

2. Quickly flicker the DamageCanvas three times by disabling and enabling it in quick succession.

Save this script and switch over to the **GameManager** script. Inside the `OnEnemyEscape()` method, add this line right under `escapedEnemies++;`:

```
`UIManager.Instance.ShowDamage();`
```

Save this script as well and return to the editor for the final UI linking. Select **UIManager** and drag **Screen Canvas\DamageCanvas** onto the **Damage Canvas** field.

Now save your scene and play it to test out the effect. Let a few enemies pass through to the exit and you'll see the red border blinking away!

Fire Tower

The time has come to create the **Fire Tower** — a hugely overpowering weapon of mass destruction — that will obliterate your foes en masse.

Before being able to set up the Fire Tower, you'll need to fix up its particles. Select the **Fire Tower Particles** prefab inside the **Prefabs\Particles** folder and notice this component with its script missing at the bottom of the Inspector. Press the **selection button** next to **Missing (Mono Script)** and select **AutoScaler**. This should re-link the component to its script.

Note: This happened because this prefab was created with the original copy of **AutoScaler.cs**. But that was deleted so you could rebuild it in the previous chapter. So now you need to associate your new version with it. Whenever you find yourself with a missing script like this, remember you can just re-link it like you did here — as long as you remember which script was un-linked.

Moving on, the Fire Tower needs a unique script to make it work. Create a new **C# Script** named **FireTower** inside the **Scripts\Game\Tower** folder and open it in a code editor. To derive it from the Tower class, replace this line:

```
public class FireTower : MonoBehaviour {
```

with:

```
public class FireTower : Tower {
```

Now remove both the `Start()` and `Update()` methods and add this code in their place:

```
//1
public GameObject fireParticlesPrefab;
//2
protected override void AttackEnemy() {
  //3
  base.AttackEnemy();
  //4
  GameObject particles =
(GameObject)Instantiate(fireParticlesPrefab,
    transform.position + new Vector3(0, .5f),
    fireParticlesPrefab.transform.rotation);

  //5
  // Scale fire particle radius with the aggro radius
  particles.transform.localScale *= aggroRadius / 10f;
  //6
  foreach (Enemy enemy in
EnemyManager.Instance.GetEnemiesInRange(
    transform.position, aggroRadius)) {

    enemy.TakeDamage(attackPower);
  }
}
```

Here's what you have above:

1. A reference to the fire particles that will spread out from the tower each time it attacks.

2. Override the `AttackEnemy()` method from the `Tower` class to expand on it.

3. Call the `Tower` class `AttackEnemy()` method.

4. Spawn new fire particles.

5. Change the particle range depending on this tower's aggro radius.

6. Damage all enemies in this tower's range. This is often referred to as an AOE (Area Of Effect) attack in games.

Save this script and return to the editor. Select **FireTower** in the **Prefabs\Tower** folder and add the **FireTower** script to it.

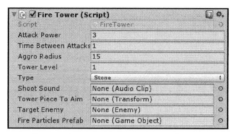

Set its **Attack Power** to **12**, adjust **Time Between Attacks In Seconds** to **3** and change **Aggro Radius** to **8**.

Now change its **Type** to **Fire** and choose **FireTowerAttack** as the **Shoot Sound**.

Finally, drag **Fire Tower Particles** from the **Prefabs\Particles** folder to the **Fire Particles Prefab** field.

Set up the **Event Trigger** by dragging the **FireTower** prefab to the **Object** field and select **FireTower.ShowTowerInfo** in the method dropdown.

To make the fire tower available for buying, select **TowerManager** and drag the **FireTower** prefab to the **Fire Tower Prefab** field.

Save your scene and press the play button to test out the Fire Tower. Enjoy its fiery wrath!

Ice Tower

The last of the towers is the subtle **Ice Tower**, which aids the other towers with its ice-cold icicles that freeze enemies to the core and makes them move much slower!

Before the Ice Tower can shoot, it needs an icy projectile! There's one in the **Prefabs\Tower\Weapons** folder ready to be used, except for its logic. For that, you'll need to adjust the **Enemy** class and create a new projectile script.

Open up the **Enemy** script (**Scripts\Game\Enemy folder**) and add these variables under wayPointIndex:

```
//1
public float timeEnemyStaysFrozenInSeconds = 2f;
//2
public bool frozen;
//3
private float freezeTimer;
```

These variables are going to be used for the enemies to keep track of their freezing state caused by the **Ice Towers**:

1. The duration in seconds this enemy stays frozen.

2. Is this enemy frozen or not?

3. This timer counts up while the enemy is frozen. When it reaches the timeEnemyStaysFrozenInSeconds duration, the enemy defrosts.

Add these methods under Die():

```
//1
public void Freeze() {
  if (!frozen) {
    //2
    frozen = true;
    moveSpeed /= 2;
  }
}

//3
```

```
void Defrost() {
    freezeTimer = 0f;
    frozen = false;
    moveSpeed *= 2;
}
```

Here's what this code does:

1. Freezes the enemy if it wasn't already.

2. Set the `frozen` flag and halve this enemy's speed.

3. Defrost the enemy by resetting the timer, unsetting the `frozen` flag and restoring the enemy's speed.

Now add this code to `Update()`, under the existing `if..else` statement:

```
//1
if (frozen) {
  //2
  freezeTimer += Time.deltaTime;
  //3
  if (freezeTimer >= timeEnemyStaysFrozenInSeconds) {
    Defrost();
  }
}
```

Some simple logic here:

1. Check if the enemy is frozen.

2. If so, increment the freeze timer.

3. If the freeze times equals or exceeds the time the enemy should stay frozen, call `Defrost()`.

Next up is the **ice projectile** script. Save this script and create a new **C# Script** named **Ice** inside the **Scripts\Game\Tower\Weapons** folder. Open it in your trusty code editor and remove both the `Start()` and `Update()` methods.

Replace the following line:

```
public class Ice : MonoBehaviour {
```

with:

```
public class Ice : FollowingProjectile {
```

This makes the `Ice` class derive from `FollowingProjectile`.

Now add the following method under the class declaration:

```
protected override void OnHitEnemy() {
  enemyToFollow.Freeze();
  Destroy(gameObject);
}
```

This method overrides `FollowingProjectile` and adds its own logic. When the Ice Projectile hits the enemy, the enemy should freeze and the projectile destroy itself.

Save this script and return to the editor. Select **Prefabs\Tower\Weapons\IceProjectile** and add an **Ice** component in the Inspector panel using the **Add Component** button and searching for it.

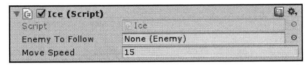

The last script that needs to be added for the Ice Tower to work is the **Ice Tower** script itself! Create a new **C# Script** named **IceTower** inside the **Scripts\Game\Tower** folder. Open it up and remove both the `Start()` and `Update()` methods.

Now replace this line:

```
public class IceTower : GameObject {
```

with:

```
public class IceTower : Tower {
```

Next, add this variable under the class declaration:

```
public GameObject icePrefab;
```

This variable holds a reference to the Ice Projectile prefab.

Add these methods underneath:

```
//1
private void GetNonFrozenTarget() {
  foreach (Enemy enemy in GetEnemiesInAggroRange()) {
    if (!enemy.frozen) {
      targetEnemy = enemy;
      break;
    }
  }
}
```

```
//2
protected override void AttackEnemy() {
  base.AttackEnemy();
  //3
  GameObject ice = (GameObject)Instantiate(icePrefab,
    towerPieceToAim.position, Quaternion.identity);
  ice.GetComponent<FollowingProjectile>().enemyToFollow =
targetEnemy;
}
```

Taking each section in turn:

1. Iterate over all enemies inside this tower's aggro range and find one that isn't frozen. Set that one as the target enemy.

2. Override `Tower`'s `AttackEnemy()` method and add custom functionality.

3. Create a new ice projectile and set its enemy to follow to the target enemy.

Finally, add this method:

```
public override void Update() {
  base.Update();
  GetNonFrozenTarget();
}
```

This makes sure the IceTower always has a target enemy.

Save this script and return to the editor once again.

Select **Prefabs\Tower\IceTower** and add the **IceTower** script to it. Use the **Add Component** button in the Inspector panel and search for it.

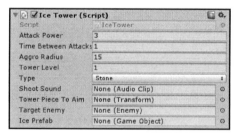

Set **Time Between Attacks** to 1, change **Aggro Radius** to 5 , set **Type** to **Ice** and set **IceTowerAttack** as the **Shoot Sound**.

Drag the **IceProjectile** prefab from the **Prefabs\Tower\Weapons** folder to the **Ice Prefab** field. Drag **IceTower**'s child **Head** to the **Tower Piece To Aim** field.

Finally, set up its **Event Trigger** by dragging the **Ice Tower** prefab to the **Object** slot and selecting **IceTower\ShowTowerInfo** in the method dropdown.

Now select the **TowerManager** in the Hierarchy and drag the **IceTower** prefab from the **Prefabs\Tower** folder onto the **Ice Tower Prefab** field.

Phew — that's it for the last of the towers!

Save the scene, press the play button and test out the Ice Towers. They should slow down the enemies and make it a lot easier for the other towers to get some more hits in.

Tweaks

Now that the game is fully up and running, there are a few tweaks that will make it a bit more enjoyable. One of these is creating more waves! Currently there's only one lonely wave that follow the first path. Time to add some more.

Select **Wave Manager** in the Hierarchy, collapse **Element 0** and set the **Size** of **Enemy Waves** to 5.

Configure the waves as follows:

- **Element 1**: Set **Path Index** to **1**, **Start Spawn Time** to **30** and **Time Between Spawns** to **1.9**. Drag a **Tanky Enemy** prefab to the **List Of Enemies** from the **Prefabs\Enemy** folder.

- **Element 2**: Set **Path Index** to **0**, **Start Spawn Time** to **60** and **Time Between Spawns** to **1.6**. Drag **3 Fast Enemy** prefabs into the **List Of Enemies**.

- **Element 3**: Set **Path Index** to **1**, **Start Spawn Time** to **110** and **Time Between Spawns** to **1.5**. Drag **4 Fast Enemy** prefabs into the **List Of Enemies**.

- **Element 4**: Set **Path Index** to **0**, **Start Spawn Time** to **130** and **Time Between Spawns** to **1.4**. Drag **4 Tanky Enemy** prefabs into the **List Of Enemies**.

That should certainly up the ante. Test the game out with these new settings and see how you do. Be sure to upgrade your towers as often as you can!

Where to go from here?

Congratulations on completing this project!

In this chapter you've learned how to:

- Link the UI to the gameplay
- Create towers
- Make winning and losing logic
- Make tweaks to improve gameplay

The fun isn't over just yet though. In the next chapter, I'll explain how you can take Runestrife into the magical realm of VR using Google VR and the Oculus Rift. Exciting, isn't it?

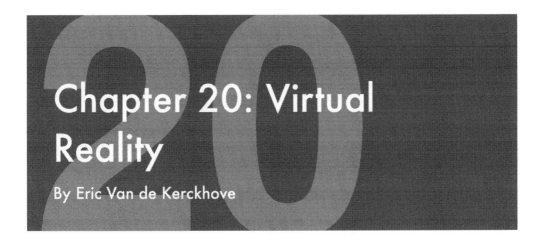

Chapter 20: Virtual Reality

By Eric Van de Kerckhove

For centuries, humans have been fascinated by the idea of virtual worlds they could step into: an escape from reality where anything is possible. From panoramic paintings that were so large they gave the illusion of actually stepping into them, to stereoscopic viewers, primitive head mounted displays and Nintendo's Virtual Boy, people have been searching for a portal to the land of endless imagination for a long time.

Virtual reality has become an accessible technology in the last few years. Individuals can be transported into virtual worlds and interact with its inhabitants from the comfort of their homes using modern state-of-the-art head mounted displays and unique technologies to accept user input. Two especially popular devices are the Oculus Rift and the HTC Vive, both offering experiences never seen before.

In this chapter, you'll learn how to use this bleeding edge tech in Runestrife, which will get you ready to use it in your own projects. You'll transform Runestrife into a VR game, and learn how to use the Oculus Rift and HTC Vive with Unity.

> **Note**: Everyone has a different reaction to movement and rotation while wearing a head-mounted display, or HMD. If it's your first time, be sure to take it easy and take a break if you feel nauseous or uncomfortable. Most people get used to VR quite quickly. So don't fret if you're not feeling well the first few times — the feeling will probably pass.

You can jump straight to the section that matches your VR device of choice. There is a bit of overlap between the two, but they're different enough that each warrants its own section!

Getting started with the Oculus Rift

If you don't have an Oculus Rift yet, you can order one from their website (www.oculus.com). Make sure your PC meets the recommended requirements. Once you've got it by your side, set up the hardware and install the newest software and drivers.

Now open up the Oculus application and click on the **Settings** button:

Click on the text on the left that says **General** to open the **General** settings. Make sure that **Unknown Sources** is enabled:

This will permit games that haven't been reviewed by Oculus (like Runestrife) to run on their hardware. It's necessary to enable this before you can do any development.

With that out of the way, open up the **Oculus** starter project in Unity. Open the **Game** scene and take a look around in the **Scene** view.

If you try out the game, you'll notice it's impossible to add any towers as the AddTowerWindow isn't showing up on-screen. This is because the Screen Space Canvas has been replaced by a **World Space Canvas**. This means the elements are free to be placed, scaled and rotated in the game world instead of being locked to the screen.

Also take a look at the giant floating UI elements around the camera. These have been placed along a curved mesh.

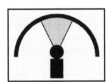

This lets the UI stay at a relatively constant size without being squished. Try looking at a poster or a TV screen from a sharp angle, and you'll immediately know what I'm talking about.

That concludes the tour of the scene. On to making cool stuff!

In order to use the Oculus Rift and its remote in Unity, you'll need to download the newest version of the **Oculus Utilities For Unity 5** found here: (https://developer3.oculus.com/downloads)[https://developer3.oculus.com/downloads].

Once you've downloaded the utilities, **unzip** the file and double click the **unitypackage**. Open the **Import Package** window. Press the **Import** button at the bottom right to import the whole package into Unity. Now take a look at the **Project** view. A new folder called **OVR** has been added to the **Assets** folder.

This folder includes several prefabs and scripts to help with the development progress.

Before using these though, there are some things that need to be set up inside Unity in order for the Oculus Rift to work correctly.

Setting up Unity for the Oculus Rift

Unity has had built-in support for the Oculus Rift since version 5.4, so it's quite easy to start using it!

Select **File\Build Settings...** to open the **Build Settings** window and click the **Player Settings...** button. This opens up the **PlayerSettings** in the Inspector.

Now check the **Virtual Reality Supported** checkbox to enable the Rift support.

This list will now appear, showing all detected and enabled built-in VR SDKs:

Make sure your Rift is turned on, then save and play the Game scene.

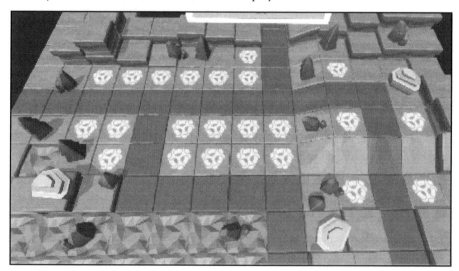

If you pick up the Rift and gently sway around, the display will echo that movement and rotation. Don't put on the HMD just yet though, as the camera isn't set up properly just yet.

Disable **Main Camera** and drag the **OVRCameraRig** prefab from the **OVR\Prefabs** folder into the Hierarchy.

Select **OVRCameraRig** and set its **Position** to (-1, 7.3, 1.54). This will position the camera correctly. Position yourself correctly and get the **HMD** ready, now run the scene and put the **Rift** on.

Look around at the UI and at the incoming enemies. Everything should work as expected — until you try to take a closer look at the scenery or the enemies. When you do, you'll notice you can hardly move around, only look. This is because the default scale of the OVRCameraRig is set to be realistic. If you move a bit in the real world, the camera will move approximately the same amount in the scene.

To counter this, you're going to turn into a giant! Select OVRCameraRig and set its scale to (**12, 12, 12**). Now stand up with your HMD ready, make some room so you can crouch, and press the play button to test your new-found powers. Now try looking and moving around, and crouch to look at the enemies and scenery up close.

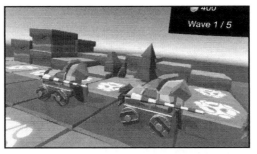

Pretty cool, right? The next step is to get some interaction going. Right now the enemies keep coming, but there's no way to use the tower slots to put down new towers.

Interacting with the world

First of all, the OVR camera needs a **Physics Raycaster** to fire raycasts into the scene where the player is looking. Select **OVRCameraRig\TrackingSpace\CenterAyeAnchor** in the Hierarchy and add a **Physics Raycaster** component. You can do this in the Inspector panel by clicking the **Add Component** button and searching for **Physics Raycaster.**

The next thing to add is a way to point at and select objects in the world and on the UI. For that, you'll need a new Input Module, namely a **Gaze Input Module**.

Gaze input means that there's a 3D pointer in the middle of the player's view that lets them easily focus on objects.

Traditionally you'd select things by staring (or gazing) at the object. But in the case of the Oculus, you have the remote that can be used to quickly confirm your actions. Unfortunately this isn't a built-in **Input Module** in Unity, nor is it supplied by Oculus. No worries though, it's easy to make one from scratch.

In the **Project** panel, find the **Scripts** folder and create a new sub-folder called **VR**. Create a new **C# Script** in there named **OcculusGazeInputModule**. Open it up in your favorite code editor and remove both the Start() and Update() methods completely. Add these two lines to the other using statements at the top of the file:

```
using System.Collections.Generic;
using UnityEngine.EventSystems;
```

Now replace this line:

```
public class OcculusGazeInputModule : MonoBehaviour {
```scratch

with this:
```cs
public class OcculusGazeInputModule : PointerInputModule {
```

This turns this class into an input module. At this point, you may get an error saying this class does not implement an inherited member. Ignore this. You'll be adding the appropriate method in a bit.

Add these variables underneath the class declaration:

```
//1
public GameObject reticle;
//2
public Transform centerEyeTransform;
//3
public float reticleSizeMultiplier = 0.02f;
//4
```

```
private PointerEventData pointerEventData;
//5
private RaycastResult currentRaycast;
//6
private GameObject currentLookAtHandler;
```

Here's what they are for:

1. This holds a reference to the `reticle` GameObject, which will be a small sphere that gets positioned over any object the player is looking at.

2. A reference to the center eye camera of the OVRCameraRig.

3. This reticle will get scaled based on this value. This is the size the reticle will be when it is exactly one unit away from the center eye camera.

4. Stores all events that will happen with the virtual pointer.

5. Stores the result of the raycasts into the scene from the center camera.

6. This holds the **IPointerClick** events that should happen when the player presses the remote's **Select** button.

Now add this empty method to get rid of the error:

```
public override void Process() {

}
```

Add the `HandleLook()` method under `Process()`:

```
void HandleLook() {
  //1
  if (pointerEventData == null) {
    pointerEventData = new PointerEventData(eventSystem);
  }
  //2
  pointerEventData.position = Camera.main.ViewportToScreenPoint
    (new Vector3(.5f, .5f));
  //3
  List<RaycastResult> raycastResults =
    new List<RaycastResult>();
  //4
  eventSystem.RaycastAll(pointerEventData, raycastResults);
  //5
  currentRaycast = pointerEventData.pointerCurrentRaycast =
    FindFirstRaycast(raycastResults);
  //6
  reticle.transform.position = centerEyeTransform.position +
    (centerEyeTransform.forward * currentRaycast.distance);
  //7
```

```
    float reticleSize = currentRaycast.distance *
      reticleSizeMultiplier;
    reticle.transform.localScale =
      new Vector3(reticleSize, reticleSize, reticleSize);
    //8
    ProcessMove(pointerEventData);
  }
```

Taking each commented section in turn:

1. If there's no PointerEventData yet for the current Event System, create a new one.

2. Set the position of a virtual pointer to the center of the screen.

3. Create a list to hold the results of the raycasts shot into the scene.

4. Do a raycast for every enabled raycaster in the scene for the UI and 3D colliders.

5. Get the first hit of any raycast and save it in both currentRaycast and the PointerEventData's raycast data. The current raycast will be used to move the reticle while the one inside the event data will be used for processing input.

6. Move the reticle to the point where the raycast hit.

7. Resize the reticle based on the distance from the center eye camera and the reticleSizeMultiplier. This will ensure the reticle always appears to have the same size.

8. Pass the pointer data to the Event System so the entering and exiting of objects is handled correctly.

Add this method to handle player input:

```
void HandleSelection() {
  //1
  if (pointerEventData.pointerEnter != null) {
    //2
    currentLookAtHandler = ExecuteEvents.GetEventHandler
      <IPointerClickHandler>(pointerEventData.pointerEnter);
    //3
    if (currentLookAtHandler != null &&
      OVRInput.GetDown(OVRInput.Button.One)) {

      //4
      ExecuteEvents.ExecuteHierarchy(currentLookAtHandler,
        pointerEventData, ExecuteEvents.pointerClickHandler);
    }
  } else { //5
    currentLookAtHandler = null;
  }
}
```

This one is pretty straightforward:

1. Continue only if the pointer has entered an object to interact with.

2. Get the `OnPointerClick()` event of the entered object.

3. Check that there's still something to click on and the player has pressed the Select button on their remote.

4. Execute the object's `OnPointerClick()` event.

5. No object to interact with, reset the `currentLookAtHandler`.

Finally, inside the `Process()` method, add these calls to the methods you just made:

```
HandleLook();
HandleSelection();
```

That's it for the input module. Save the script and return to the editor to start using it. In the Hierarchy, select **EventSystem** and add the **Occulus Gaze Input Module** script. You can do that in the Inspector panel by using the **Add Component** button and searching for it.

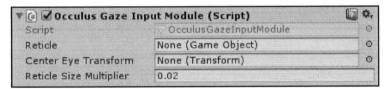

Now disable the **StandaloneInputModule**, as it will fight with the gaze input over the object selection.

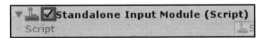

Create a new **Sphere** (**3D Object\Sphere**) in the scene, name it **Reticle** and reset its **Transform**. Now change its **Scale** to (**0.2, 0.2, 0.2**) and remove the **Sphere Collider**.

Finally, set its **Material** to **Reticle**, a simple gray material to keep some contrast with the white tower slots and UI elements.

You could use any shape you want for this and add dynamic animations when a clickable object is found, but for the purpose of this chapter you're going to keep it simple and go with a static sphere.

Make a new folder inside the **Prefabs** folder named **VR** and drag the **Reticle** into it to make it into a prefab.

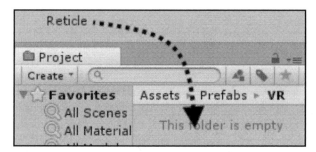

Select **EventSystem** again and drag the **Reticle** from the Hierarchy to the **Reticle** field.

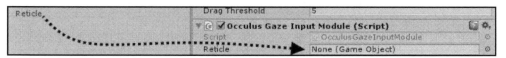

Now fully expand **OVRCameraRig** and drag **CenterEyeAnchor** to the **Center Eye Transform** field.

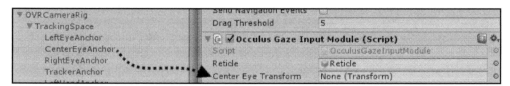

Now save the scene and press the play button to test out the new input module and its reticle. Put on your HMD, take the remote in your hand and look around.

You should be able to see the reticle when you look at the tower slots.

Press the **Select** button on your remote to open up the **AddTowerWindow**. But it won't be where you'd expect. It'll appear underneath the board where it shows your gold and the wave number!

While you can actually buy towers this way, it's far from practical. You also might have noticed the enemies' health bars are nowhere to be seen. Time to tackle both of these problems with some scripting magic.

Automatically positioning and scaling world UI

There are some tweaks that need to be made to the **UIManager** script for the windows to come into view when you click either the tower slots or the towers.

Open up the **UIManager** script (**Scripts\Game\UI folder**) and add this variable under `txtEscapedEnemies` at the top of the script:

```
public static float vrUiScaleDivider = 12;
```

This will be used to automatically scale UI elements based on their distance to the player.

Now add this method call at the end of `ShowAddTowerWindow()`:

```
UtilityMethods.MoveUiElementToWorldPosition(addTowerWindow
    .GetComponent<RectTransform>(), towerSlot.transform.position);
```

Also add this at the end of `ShowTowerInfoWindow()`

```
UtilityMethods.MoveUiElementToWorldPosition(towerInfoWindow
  .GetComponent<RectTransform>(), tower.transform.position);
```

Both of these do the same thing: They'll make sure the window will get moved and resized to the position of either the tower slot or the tower that was selected.

`MoveUiElementToWorldPosition()` needs to be updated for this new functionality. You'll do that once the UIManager is complete.

Add this to the beginning of both of those `Show...` methods:

```
if (GameManager.Instance.gameOver) {
  return;
}
```

This ensures that the windows won't open up if the game is over.

In both `ShowWinScreen()` and `ShowLoseScreen()`, remove this line:

```
blackBackground.SetActive(true);
```

Because you can fully see the world at any time, the background doesn't make much sense and would just distract the player.

Save this script. Open the **UtilityMethods** script (**Scripts\Utility** folder) and add this method to it:

```
//1
private static void ScaleRectTransformBasedOnDistanceFromCamera
  (RectTransform rectTransform) {

  //2
  float distance = Vector3.Distance(Camera.main.transform.
    position, rectTransform.position);
  //3
  rectTransform.localScale = new Vector3(distance /
    UIManager.vrUiScaleDivider, distance /
    UIManager.vrUiScaleDivider);
}
```

Going over this quickly:

1. Get the `RectTransform` that needs to be scaled as a parameter.

2. Calculate the distance between the camera and the Rect Transform.

3. Set the Rect Transform's Scale to the distance divided by UIManager's `vrUiScaleDivider`. This make the UI appear the same relative size at any distance.

Objects that are further away are scaled up, while objects that are right in the player's face are scaled down, making everything appear the same size regardless of actual distance. This increases the readability tremendously.

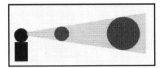

Now remove the contents of the `MoveUiElementToWorldPosition()` method and replace it with these lines:

```
//1
rectTransform.position = worldPosition + new Vector3(0, 3);
//2
// Needed to rotate UI the right way
rectTransform.LookAt(Camera.main.transform.position +
    Camera.main.transform.forward * 10000);
//3
ScaleRectTransformBasedOnDistanceFromCamera(rectTransform);
```

Here's what the code above does:

1. Adds a small offset so objects don't appear inside other objects.

2. Makes the object look at the player.

3. Calls `ScaleRectTransformBasedOnDistanceFromCamera()` to scale the Rect Transform.

Save this script and return to the editor. Now stand up with both the HMD and the remote, and play the scene. Try buying and creating new towers and upgrading them. The windows will now appear around the spot where you make your selections.

Nice! That's it for the Game scene already. Now open the **TitleScreen** scene to make that work in VR as well.

Modifying the title screen

Start off by disabling the **Main Camera**. Now drag the **OVRCameraRig** prefab from the **OVR\Prefabs** folder into the Hierarchy.

Select **EventSystem** and disable the **Standalone Input Module**. Add the **Occulus Gaze Input Module** script to it instead. You can do that through the Inspector panel by clicking the **Add Component** button and searching for it.

Now drag the **Reticle** prefab from the **Prefabs\VR** folder into the scene and drag the new copy into the **Reticle** field of **Occulus Gaze Input Module**. Next, fully expand **OVRCameraRig** and drag **CenterEyeAnchor** onto the **Center Eye Transform** field.

Finally, select **OVRCameraRig**'s grandchild **CenterEyeAnchor**. Set its **Clear Flags** to **Solid Color** and change the **Background** color to pure black (**00000000**).

Now try out the changes by playing the scene with the HMD on and the remote in your hand. You should be able to press the **Start** button to start the game.

That's it for the Oculus Rift. Congratulations on finishing this section of the chapter!

In the next section, you'll learn how to get similar results with the HTC Vive.

Getting started with the HTC Vive

If you're not already a proud owner of a HTC Vive, you can buy one on their website (https://www.htcvive.com) or (depending on where you live) in a store near you. Be sure your PC meets at least the minimum requirements. Once it's in your possession, download and install the software and set up the hardware. Also update the firmware on all devices if there are updates available.

Open up the **HTC Vive** starter project in Unity and open the **Game** scene:

If you try out the game, you'll notice it's impossible to add any towers as the AddTowerWindow isn't showing up on-screen. This is because the Screen Space Canvas has been replaced by a **World Space Canvas**. This means the elements are free to be placed, scaled and rotated in the game world instead of being locked to the screen.

Also take a look at the giant floating UI elements around the camera. These have been placed along a curved mesh.

This lets the UI stay at a relatively constant size without being squished. Try looking at a poster or a TV screen from a sharp angle, and you'll immediately know what I'm talking about.

To use the **Vive** in Unity, you'll need to download and import the newest version of the **SteamVR** Plugin from the **Asset Store**.

Click **Window\Asset Store** to open the **Asset Store**. Now type in **SteamVR** in side the search box at the top and press **Enter**. Scroll down to the results and find the **SteamVR Plugin**. It should be the first entry:

Click on the SteamVR icon to open the store page and click the **Download** button:

Once the plugin has finished downloading it will open an **Asset Import** dialog window. Click the **Import** button at the bottom right to add it to the project:

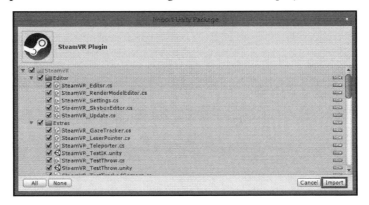

If a window pops up asking you to make recommended changes for **SteamVR**, accept them all — except if it asks for the color space to be **Linear** instead of **Gamma**. The project will become dark if you'd do that, as all lightning is configured for gamma space coloring.

You can now close the **Asset Store**; you won't be needing that any further for this project.

Take a look at the **Project** view. There's a new folder named **SteamVR**:

This folder is filled with all kinds of scrips, prefabs and examples to help you on the way. You'll be using a few of these in the next part as it's time to get the actual **Vive** setup working in Unity!

Setting up Unity for the HTC Vive

In the Hierarchy, disable the **Main Camera** and drag in [**CameraRig**] from the **SteamVR\Prefabs** folder to the scene:

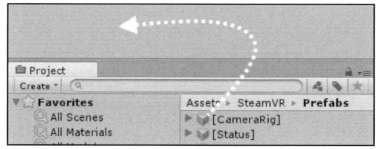

Rename it to **ViveRig**, and set its **position** to (**0, 0, 10**).

Now take a look at it in the **Scene** view:

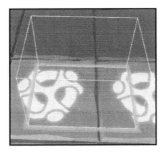

The blue border represents the player's room. Right now it's tiny compared to the world as it uses real world units. Get your Vive and its controllers ready and run the scene. Put on the HMD and look and walk around a bit. The enemies are huge!

To fix this, change the scale of the **ViveRig** to (**10, 10, 10**) to make the room a lot bigger:

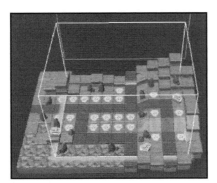

Try playing the scene again with the **Vive** on and you'll notice the difference:

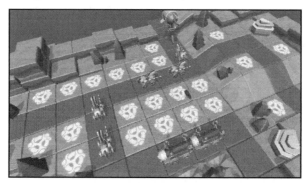

You're now a giant walking on the map! Walk around a bit and crouch to look up close at the enemies.

The next step is adding interaction with the world by putting down towers.

Interacting with the world

There are several ways of handling input in VR. But for Runestrife you'll be using one of the controllers to point at the world and the UI to interact with it. The SteamVR plugin doesn't come with such a system out of the box, so you'll have to add it yourself.

Start off by by expanding the **ViveRig** in the Hierarchy so you can see its children. Select **Controller (right)**. Right click it, and select **Camera** to create a new camera as a child. Name it **ControllerCamera**.

This camera won't be used to actually see through. It's going to be used purely to fire raycasts into the scene so you can select and interact with colliders and UI elements.

Change the camera's **Clear Flags** to **Solid Color**, set its **Depth** to -5 and adjust its **Target Eye** to **None (Main Display)**. Next, remove the **Flare Layer**, **GUI Layer** and **Audio Listener** components. This camera won't be used for rendering anything. It doesn't need to listen to sounds or music either, so those components aren't necessary.

Finally, add a **Physics Raycaster** component so it can send raycasts to 3D colliders. You can do that in the Inspector panel by clicking **Add Component** and searching for it by name.

Create a new folder named **VR** in the **Prefabs** folder and drag the ViveRig into it to make it into a prefab.

The next thing to add is a method to know where the controller is pointing. You'll do this through a combination of a 3D reticle and a laser to make it easy for the player:

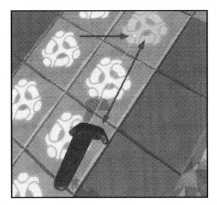

First up — the reticle in the Hierarchy. Create a new **Sphere (3D Object\Sphere)** and name it **Reticle**. Now reset its **Transform**, set its scale to **(0.1, 0.1, 0.1)** and remove the **Sphere Collider** component. Finally, drag the **Reticle** to the **Prefabs\VR** folder to make it into a prefab.

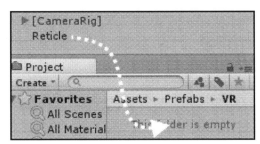

For the laser, create a new **Cube (3D Object\Cube)** and name it **Laser**. Reset its **Transform** and adjust its **scale** to **(0.01, 0.01, 1)**. Remove its **Box Collider** and set its **Material** to **LaserMaterial**, which is simply an unlit white material.

Drag the Laser to the VR prefabs folder as well:

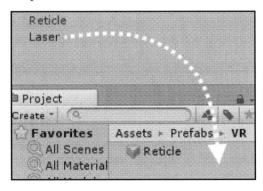

You might be wondering why the "laser" is just a long rectangular prism, instead of a cylinder or a line renderer:

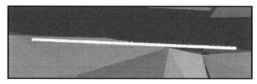

Coupled with the **Unlit** material, the cube has all the properties you want from a good laser. It always has a consistent width no matter which angle you view it, and the caps won't be visible either, so the player won't even notice it's not a line!

Select **EventSystem** and disable its **Standalone Input Module**. You're going to write your own input module for the controller, so you don't want the mouse cursor fighting over the selection.

In the **Project** view, create a new folder named **VR** in the **Scripts** folder. Create a new **C# Script** in there named **ViveControllerLookModule**. Open it up in your favorite code editor and remove both the Start() and Update() methods. Add these two lines to the other using statements at the top of the file:

```
using System.Collections.Generic;
using UnityEngine.EventSystems;
using Valve.VR;
```

Now replace this line:

```
public class OcculusGazeInputModule : MonoBehaviour {
```

with this:

```
public class OcculusGazeInputModule : PointerInputModule {`
```

This turns this class into an input module. At this point, you may get an error saying this class does not implement an inherited member. Ignore this; you'll be adding the appropriate method in a bit.

Add these variables underneath the class declaration:

```
//1
public Camera ControllerCamera;
//2
public SteamVR_TrackedObject RightController;
//3
public GameObject reticle;
//4
public Transform laserTransform;
```

```
//5
private Transform rightControllerTransform;
//6
// The size of the reticle will get scaled with this value
public float reticleSizeMultiplier = 0.02f;
//7
private PointerEventData pointerEventData;
//8
private RaycastResult currentRaycast;
//9
private GameObject currentLookAtHandler;
```

This is what these variables are for:

1. A reference to the camera attached to the right controller.

2. This holds a reference to the right controller itself, to be able to get its input.

3. Reference to the Reticle.

4. A reference to the Laser.

5. This holds the right controller's Transform so it can be used to get its position and rotation.

6. The reticle will get scaled based on this value. This is the size the reticle will be when it's exactly one unit away from the controller.

7. This stores all events that will happen with the virtual pointer.

8. Stores the result of the raycasts into the scene from the controller camera.

9. This holds the IPointerClick events that should happen when the player presses the controller's trigger button.

Now add this empty method to get rid of the error:

```
public override void Process() {

}
```

Next, add the Awake() method:

```
void Awake() {
    rightControllerTransform = RightController.transform;
}
```

This gets the Transform component out of the Right Controller.

Add the `HandleLook()` method under `Process()`:

```
void HandleLook() {
  //1
  if (pointerEventData == null) {
    pointerEventData = new PointerEventData(eventSystem);
  }
  //2
  pointerEventData.position = ControllerCamera.
    ViewportToScreenPoint(new Vector3(.5f, .5f));
  //3
  List<RaycastResult> raycastResults = new
    List<RaycastResult>();
  //4
  eventSystem.RaycastAll(pointerEventData, raycastResults);
  //5
  currentRaycast = pointerEventData.pointerCurrentRaycast =
    FindFirstRaycast(raycastResults);
  //6
  // Move reticle
  reticle.transform.position = rightControllerTransform.position
    + (rightControllerTransform.forward
    * currentRaycast.distance);
  //7
  laserTransform.position = Vector3.Lerp(
    rightControllerTransform.position, reticle.transform.
    position, .5f);
  //8
  laserTransform.LookAt(reticle.transform);
  //9
  laserTransform.localScale = new Vector3(
    laserTransform.localScale.x, laserTransform.localScale.y,
    currentRaycast.distance);
  //10
  float reticleSize = currentRaycast.distance *
    reticleSizeMultiplier;
  //Scale reticle so it's always the same size

  reticle.transform.localScale = new Vector3(reticleSize,
    reticleSize, reticleSize);
  //11
  // Pass the pointer data to the event system so entering and
  // exiting of objects is detected
  ProcessMove(pointerEventData);
}
```

There's quite a bit going on here:

1. If there's no PointerEventData yet for the current Event System, create a new one.

2. Sets the position of the virtual pointer to the center of the screen.

3. Create a list to hold the results of the raycasts shot into the scene.

4. Do a raycast for every enabled raycaster in the scene (both for the UI and 3D colliders).

5. Get the first hit of any raycast and save it in both `currentRaycast` and the PointerEventData's raycast data. The current raycast will be used to move the reticle while the one inside the event data will be used for processing input.

6. Move the reticle to the point where the raycast hit.

7. Move the laser right between the controller and the reticle.

8. Let the laser look at the reticle.

9. Size the laser's Z-scale by the distance between the controller and the reticle.

10. Resize the reticle based on the distance from the controller and the reticleSizeMultiplier.

11. Pass the pointer data to the Event System so the entering and exiting of objects are handled correctly.

This method will make sure both the reticle and the laser get positioned and scaled correctly.

Add the `IsTriggerPressed()` method to check if the player pressed the Trigger button on their controller:

```
private bool IsTriggerPressed() {
  return SteamVR_Controller.Input((int)
    RightController.index).GetPressDown(
    EVRButtonId.k_EButton_SteamVR_Trigger);
}
```

Now add the following to use the player's input:

```
void HandleSelection() {
  //1
  if (pointerEventData.pointerEnter != null) {
    //2
    currentLookAtHandler = ExecuteEvents.GetEventHandler
      <IPointerClickHandler>(pointerEventData.pointerEnter);
    //3
    if (currentLookAtHandler != null && IsTriggerPressed()) {
      //4
      ExecuteEvents.ExecuteHierarchy(currentLookAtHandler,
        pointerEventData, ExecuteEvents.pointerClickHandler);
    }
  } else { //5
    currentLookAtHandler = null;
  }
}
```

Here's what's going on above:

1. Continue only if the pointer has entered an object to interact with.

2. Get the `OnPointerClick()` event of the entered object.

3. Check that there's still something to click on and the player has pressed the Trigger button on their controller.

4. Execute the object's `OnPointerClick()` event.

5. If there's no object to interact with, reset the `currentLookAtHandler`.

Finally, inside the `Process()` method, add these calls to the methods you just made:

```
HandleLook();
HandleSelection();
```

That's it for the input module. Save the script and return to the editor to start using it.

In the Hierarchy, select **EventSystem** and add the **ViveControllerLookModule** script. In the Inspector panel, press the **Add Component** button and search for it or drag it from the **Project** panel.

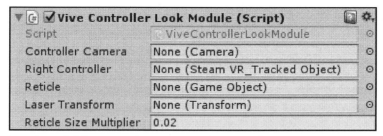

Time to fill up these fields! Expand **ViveRig** and **Controller** (**right**) to expose the **ControllerCamera**. Drag this to the **Controller Camera** field. Also drag **Controller** (**right**) to the **Right Controller** field.

Now drag the **Reticle** and **Laser** to the **Reticle** and **Laser Transform** fields respectively.

Select **World Canvas** and drag the **ControllerCamera** onto the **Event Camera** field of the **Canvas** component:

This ensures the controller can access the UI elements in the World Canvas.

Now save the scene, prepare the HMD and the controllers, and press the play button. Try pointing the right controller at the tower slot. It should turn yellow and the laser and reticle should be clearly visible:

Press the Trigger button on your controller to open up the AddTowerWindow — and once again, it's underneath the board.

Automatically Positioning and scaling world UI

Open the **UIManager** script (**Scripts\Game\UI folder**) and add the following variable under `txtEscapedEnemies` at the top of the script:

```
public static float vrUiScaleDivider = 12;
```

This will be used to automatically scale UI elements based on the distance to the player, similarly to the reticle.

Now add this method call at the end of `ShowAddTowerWindow()`:

```
UtilityMethods.MoveUiElementToWorldPosition(addTowerWindow.
   GetComponent<RectTransform>(), towerSlot.transform.position);
```

Also add this at the end of `ShowTowerInfoWindow()`:

```
UtilityMethods.MoveUiElementToWorldPosition(towerInfoWindow.
   GetComponent<RectTransform>(), tower.transform.position);
```

Both of these do the same: they'll make sure the window is moved and resized to the position of either the tower slot or the tower that was selected. `MoveUiElementToWorldPosition()` needs to be updated for this new functionality; you'll do that once the UIManager is complete.

Also add this code to the beginning of both `Show...Window()` methods:

```
if (GameManager.Instance.gameOver) {
  return;
}
```

This ensures that the windows won't open up if the game is over. In both `ShowWinScreen()` and `ShowLoseScreen()`, remove this line:

```
`blackBackground.SetActive(true);`
```

Because you can fully see the world at any time, the background doesn't make much sense and would just distract the player.

Save this script and open up the **UtilityMethods** script (**Scripts\Utility folder**). Add the following method to it:

```
//1
private static void ScaleRectTransformBasedOnDistanceFromCamera
  (RectTransform rectTransform) {

  //2
  float distance = Vector3.Distance(Camera.main.transform.
    position, rectTransform.position);
  //3
  rectTransform.localScale = new Vector3(distance /
    UIManager.vrUiScaleDivider, distance
    / UIManager.vrUiScaleDivider);
}
```

Briefly:

1. Get the RectTransform that needs to be scaled as a parameter.

2. Calculate the distance between the camera and the Rect Transform.

3. Set the Rect Transform's scale to the distance divided by UIManager's `vrUiScaleDivider`. This make the UI seem to be the same relative size at any distance.

Objects that are further away are scaled up, while objects that are close by are scaled down, just as before.

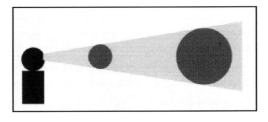

Now remove the contents of the `MoveUiElementToWorldPosition()` method and replace it with these lines:

```
//1
rectTransform.position = worldPosition + new Vector3(0, 3);
//2
// Needed to rotate UI the right way
rectTransform.LookAt(Camera.main.transform.position +
  Camera.main.transform.forward * 10000);
//3
ScaleRectTransformBasedOnDistanceFromCamera(rectTransform);
```

Here's what's going on in the code above:

1. Add a small offset so objects don't appear inside other objects the player selected.

2. Make the object look at the player.

3. Call `ScaleRectTransformBasedOnDistanceFromCamera()` to scale the Rect Transform.

Save this script and return to the editor. Now stand up with both the HMD and the right controller and play the scene. Try buying and creating new towers and upgrading them. The windows will now appear around the spot where you make your selections.

Nice job! That's it for the Game scene. Open up the **TitleScreen** scene to make that work in VR as well.

Modifying the title screen

Start off by disabling the **Main Camera**. Now drag the **ViveRig** prefab from the **Prefabs\VR** folder into the Hierarchy and set its position to (**0, -10, -8**). Select **EventSystem** and disable the **Standalone Input Module**. Add the **Vive Controller Look Module** script to it instead. You can do this in the Inspector panel by clicking the **Add Component** button and searching for it.

Now drag the **Reticle** and **Laser** prefabs from the **Prefabs\VR** folder into the scene and drag them into the **Reticle** and **Laser Transform** fields of **Vive Controller Look Module**.

Next, fully expand **ViveRig** and its child **Controller (right)**. Drag **ControllerCamera** and **Controller (right)** onto the **Controller Camera** and **Right Controller** fields.

Next, select **Title Canvas** and drag the **ControllerCamera** to the **Canvas** component's **Event Camera** field.

Finally, select **Camera (head)**'s child **Camera (eye)**. Set its **Clear Flags** to **Solid Color** and change the **Background** color to pure black (**00000000**).

Now try out the changes by playing the scene with the HMD on your head on and the right controller in your hand. You should be able to select the **Start** button and start the game now.

That concludes the HTC Vive section!

Where to go from here?

Congratulations on taking the first steps inside the virtual world!

VR is still in an early stage in life, so there is a lot to discover about how to make use of this new technology. Make sure you experiment a lot and share your findings, or some new best practices with the rest of us game developers!

Chapter 21: Publishing Your game

By Eric Van de Kerckhove and Brian Moakley

Making a game can be rewarding in its own right, but getting it out there for people to play and getting awesome feedback is a whole other level of gratification. Unity currently supports **24 platforms** — and the list is still growing! It's easy to make one game and export it to multiple platforms with minor adjustments.

In this chapter, you'll learn how how to create builds for the most common platforms:

- Standalone (Windows, Mac OSX & Linux)

- WebGL

- Android

- iOS

Since the process to submit to stores such Apple iTunes and Google Play is rather involved and changes frequently, we've supplied links to tutorials which cover the store submission process in depth.

This chapter assumes you have selected the above platforms in the **Download Assistant**. If you haven't, download the newest version of Unity and select these platforms when installing:

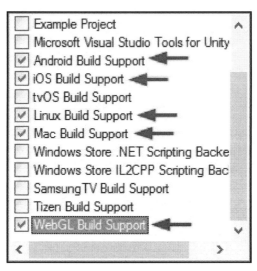

Getting started

Open the starter project in Unity and make sure everything works correctly by playing the game. This is the finished project from Chapter 19 with two extra files added to the Textures folder — the icon:

And the banner:

To make sure the icon is used for builds, select **File\Build Settings...** and click **Player Settings...** to open the **Player Settings view** in the **Inspector**. It's best to get familiar with opening this view as you'll be doing it a lot throughout this chapter.

Click **Select** next to **Default Icon** and choose **Icon** in the list. This will make sure that this icon is used across platforms.

Next, expand the **Splash Image** module. Click **Select** next to **Config Dialog Banner** and select **Runestrife-Banner**.

Also set up the **Company Name** and **Product Name**:

This can be your real name, a pseudonym or the name of your company. Keep the **Product Name** as it is for now.

Now on to the specifics of building for each platform. Standalone is up first.

Standalone

Windows, Mac OSX and Linux are considered **standalone** platforms. The builds have both the executable and the data in a folder you can easily share.

Open up **Player Settings** and expand the **Resolution and Presentation** module:

These are some of the most important settings when exporting for standalone. Most of the defaults are just fine. The common ones are:

- **Default Is Full Screen**: Enables full screen mode by default when the game starts.

- **Run In Background**: Keep the game running when it is out of focus. This is especially handy for networked games as the connection might be lost otherwise.

- **Display Resolution Dialog**: When enabled, pops up the resolution configuration dialog at the start of the game. It can also be set to **Hidden By Default**, which means the dialog will only show up when the players holds down **Alt** (or **Option**) while starting up the game.

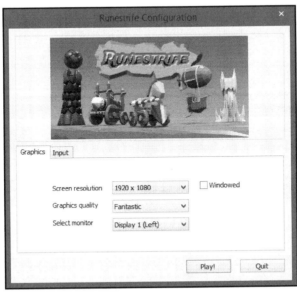

- **Supported Aspect Ratios**: These checkboxes decide which aspect ratios can be selected in the resolution dialog at startup if they are supported by the player's montior. Uncheck all checkboxes here except for **16:9**. Runestrife only supports this aspect ratio, as anything less wide will cause some tower slots to be cut off from the screen. You can try it out for yourself by changing the aspect in the **Game** view's control bar:

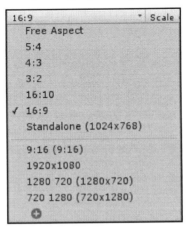

Everything is now ready for you to create some builds!

Select **File\Build Settings...** to open the **Build Settings** window. Here you can choose what platform to build for in the **Target Platform** dropdown:

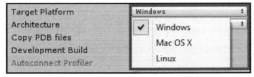

You can also choose the architecture, which means either **32-bit**, **64-bit** or both (for **Mac OSX** and **Linux**). Almost all computers since around 2006 have 64-bit processors, so it's safe to always built for this architecture. You can build for 32-bit if you like to be safe. In the case of Mac OSX and Linux, always select the universal architecture as that covers both.

Select **Windows** and **x86_64** in their respective dropdowns and click **Build** in the the bottom right. Choose a folder to store the build and create a new folder at that location named **Runestrife-Windows**. Choose the new folder as the location, then click **Save**. Unity will now compile the project into a build. The time it takes to build depends on the size of the project; Runestrife shouldn't take more than a minute or so.

When the build is done, the folder containing the build will open. If you're on Windows, double-click the .EXE file to try it out.

Now follow the same process to create **Mac OSX** and **Linux** builds. Create a **Runestrife-MacOSX** and a **Runestrife-Linux** folder for the builds. If you're on either one of these platforms, try out the build to see if everything is working correctly.

You can now submit your builds to websites like itch.io and Game Jolt or share them with your friends and family to play.

Next up: creating a **WebGL** build.

WebGL

WebGL lets you to incorporate your game directly into a webpage — no plugins needed! This build option was first introduced in Unity 5.0, but was hardly usable at that point due to several limitations and bugs. The build sizes were also huge so people had to wait a long time for the game page to load.

As of Unity 5.4, WebGL is now a respected platform to target. Most of the limitations have been removed, and the builds are now compressed to avoid large downloads.

To start using WebGL, open the **Build Settings** window, select **WebGL** and click **Switch Platform**.

The editor will now take a while to recompile all assets for the chosen platform. When it's done, open up the **Player Settings** view.

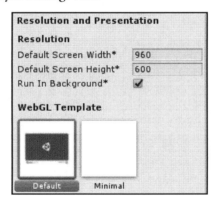

Notice that things look quite different from the standalone settings. Here are the most important settings in the **Resolution And Presentation** module:

- **Default Screen Width & Height**: These control the dimensions of the WebGL canvas on the webpage. Make sure these are the aspect ratio that your game supports. The default is **960×600**, which has an aspect ratio of **16:10**. Change this to **960x540** to make it **16:9**.

- **Run In Background**: As with the standalone player, this allows the game to continue running even when it's out of focus.

- **WebGL Template**: All of the project's WebGL templates will show up here. By default these are simply example templates provided by Unity. You can add your own by creating a **WebGLTemplates** folder in your project and dropping the necessary HTML, JS and CSS files in there. For more details, check out Unity's documentation on WebGL templates: https://docs.unity3d.com/Manual/webgl-templates.html.

Now open the **Publishing Settings** module:

Publishing Settings	
WebGL Memory Size	256
Enable Exceptions	None
Compression Format	Gzip
Data caching	✔
Debug Symbols	☐

These three settings are extremely important when making WebGL builds:

WebGL memory size

This is the amount of memory in megabytes available to the WebGL runtime. This is a huge potential pitfall of WebGL development. Instead of being able to dynamically increase the size of the heap like other platforms, WebGL needs to know *beforehand* how much memory it needs to set aside when loading the game. If this value is too low, you'll get out-of-memory errors. If it's too high, some browsers and platforms will not have enough and either fail to load the game or crash. A sticky situation indeed.

It's recommended you play the game and stress test the worst-case scenarios using the **Profiler** to see how much memory it's actually using. Then give it that amount of memory plus a bit extra for overhead. For more information, see this page: https://docs.unity3d.com/Manual/webgl-memory.html. Just leave it at **256** for now. **Runestrife** doesn't require much memory.

Enable exceptions

This setting has three options:

- **None**: Maximum performance and minimal file size. When an exception occurs, the game reports the error and stops running.

- **Explicitly Thrown Exceptions Only**: Decent performance and build size. Only exceptions with a `throw` statement will get caught and cause the `finally` blocks to work.

- **Full**: Worst performance and file size. Every exception is thrown, even Null References. Only use this for tracking down unique **WebGL** bugs, this setting will bring down your game to its knees.

Set **Enable Exceptions** to **None**. You know your game runs fine so there's no need to sacrifice any performance.

Data caching

With data caching enabled, the player only has to download the assets for your project on the first load. Subsequent visits will load the data from an **IndexedDB**. If the game has been updated, the cache is cleared and the player has to do a full re-download. Enable this for Runestrife by checking the checkbox.

That concludes the WebGL player settings. Time to make a build!

Open up the **Build Settings** and click **Build And Run** this time. Unity creates a small local webserver when you use **Build And Run**; if you simply build, you can open the generated **index.html** file in a web browser. If you use Google Chrome, start it up with the `--allow-running-insecure-content` switch and open the **index.html** file.

Set up another folder named **Runestrife-WebGL** and create a build there. The build times for WebGL are huge, so get something to drink while you wait.

When the building is done, it should automatically open up a webpage pointing to `localhost` with the game's HTML page loaded.

If it doesn't load correctly for some reason, try restarting the browser or try it with another one. Firefox currently has the best support for WebGL, but other browsers should work as well.

Take a look at the build folder:

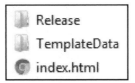

The **index.html** file is the webpage, the **Release** folder contains all game data and **TemplateData** contains other files like JSS and CSS.

You can upload the game on Game Jolt or on your own webserver to share it with others.

Time to look at publishing to Android!

Android

Unlike the previous platforms, Android builds have more steps. To build for Android, you'll need the following:

- Get and install the latest **Android SDK** (and optionally, **Android Studio**) here: https://developer.android.com/studio/index.html

- Sign up for a **Google Play** publisher account. Get the instructions here: https://developer.android.com/distribute/googleplay/start.html

These are optional steps, but I recommend them so you can test your games on your phone:

- Enable **USB debugging** on your Android device.

- Connect your device to the SDK. You might need additional drivers if you're using Windows.

Restart Unity, and it should automatically detect the Android SDK. You can check this by opening the **Unity Preferences** window, then opening the **External Tools** tab. The **SDK path** should be filled in:

Android			
SDK	D:/Android/android-sdk	Browse	Download
JDK	C:\Program Files\Java\jdk1.8.0_05	Browse	Download
NDK		Browse	Download

If it isn't, you can click **Browse** to select the **SDK** folder manually.

Now open the **Build Settings** window, select **Android** and click **Switch Platform**:

The editor will now re-import all assets to optimize them for Android. Open up the **Build Settings** window again and click **Player Settings...** to open the **Player Settings** view in the **Inspector**.

Open the **Resolution and Presentation** module:

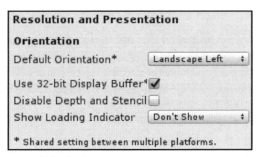

- **Default Orientation**: By default this is set to **Auto Rotation**, which means it will always render the game at the device's orientation and size, whether it's in landscape or portrait.

  This is not usually what you want. Most mobile game developers design the game and UI around one particular orientation, which is also the case with Runestrife. It will only look correct in landscape — unless, that is, you want to nail that "peeking through a keyhole" feel.

Be sure that **Default Orientation** is set to **Landscape Left** for this project. This fixes the orientation so the top of your device goes left while the bottom goes right.

- **Use 32-bit Display Buffer**: Use 32-bit colors instead of 16-bit. When this is off, you may see color banding on gradients and textures using soft alpha blends. Keep this on unless you really need the memory benefit of turning this off.

- **Show Loading Indicator**: Show Android's native loading indicator in the corner. Always set this to **Don't Show**. The loading indicator looks unprofessional and doesn't add any value.

Moving on to **Other Settings** and the **Identification** section:

Identification	
Bundle Identifier	com.raywenderlich.runestrife
Version*	1.0
Bundle Version Code	1
Minimum API Level	Android 4.4 'Kit Kat' (API level 1'‡

These settings are **extremely** important for publishing and updating Android games:

- **Bundle Identifier**: The string used to uniquely identify your game. You set this up once per game, then never change it again. Otherwise, it would be considered a different game. The format of this string is: **com.[DEVELOPER].[GAME NAME]**.

- **Version**: The version of the game. This could be **1.0**, **2.4.0.1** or **Unicorn Rainbow** — it's your choice.

- **Bundle Version Code**: This is the number you have to increment every time you build a new version of your game for publication.

- **Minimum API Level**: The lowest version of Android the game will run on. You'll need to download the SDK version of the version you choose here. Most devices have version 4.4 or higher, so it's a good idea to leave it at 4.4. If you need specific functionality from the Android system that requires a higher version, be sure to adjust this value.

Open the **Publishing Settings** module:

Here's where you choose or create a **keystore**. The keystore is used to authenticate your applications and games. It's a certificate to prove that you are the developer. If you already created a key, simply click **Browse Keystore** to find your **keystore** file, then enter the password.

Now select or create the **Alias** you want to use, enter its password and you're good to go!

If you don't have a keystore yet, select **Create new Keystore**, click **Browse Keystore** and choose a location to save the keystore. Now choose a password for the keystore and create an alias and its password.

You're now ready to make an Android build!

Open the **Build Settings** window and either click **Build And Run**, if you have an Android device attached to test the build immediately, or click **Build** to simply create an **APK (Android Application Package)**. Either way, you'll have to choose a name and location to put the resulting APK.

Once you do, the editor will building and compile all assets into an Android package, and copy and install it if you chose **Build And Run**. Be sure to remember where you chose to put the **APK** as you'll need it soon.

Congratulations — your Unity game is now available to be published on the Google Play. To learn more about the process of submitting your app to Google Play, check out Google's guide, Developer Console Help Guide.

iOS

Publishing your app to the iOS App store is an easy process in some respects, but the actual app submission process can be very complicated. The process requires you to have a Mac, the latest version of Xcode (version 8 at the time of this writing) and an Apple Developer Account. The developer account costs $99 USD per year, but you'll be making millions off your game soon...right?

To enroll in the Apple Developer Program, head to https://developer.apple.com/programs/.

Open the **Build Settings** window, select **iOS** and click **Switch Platform**.

One of the nice things about switching to the iOS platform is that the Game view will update with all the device sizes. This makes it easy to test on a device screen size without pushing to a device.

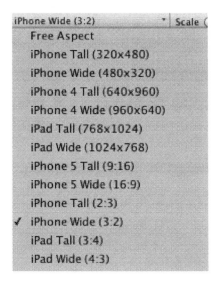

Open the **Player Settings** and make sure iOS is selected. First you must choose a company name and a product name. The product name is what the game will be called on the device.

At this point, you can change specific iOS settings. Here's the breakdown:

- **Resolution and Presentation**: Lets you to set the starting orientation, whether you'd like the status bar to display, and full screen support.

- **Icon**: The icons used in the app. Unity populates the icons based on your default icon, but you can override the icon for certain devices.

- **Splash Image** is the first image the user sees when the game is launched. Ideally, this should be a static screenshot of the first screen in your game.

- **Debugging and Crash Reporting**: Lets you turn profiling on and determine how the app will behave when it encounters an unhandled exception.

- **Other Settings**: Configure build settings, and specific device settings.

Expand the **Resolution and Presentation** and set the **Default Orientation** to **Auto Rotation**. You will see a series of orientations for your game. **Uncheck** the **Portrait** and **Portrait Upside Down**.

Now to customize the launching of your game in iOS. In iOS, Apple recommends you provide a screenshot of your first screen. When the user taps your launch icon, iOS shows this screenshot, which gives the feeling that the app launches right away even though it is still loading.

By default, Unity will provide a **Made with Unity** screen. If you have the Pro version of Unity, you can disable this splash screen. For now, leave it enabled so you can see how it looks.

> **Note**: In later versions of Unity, you will be able to customize the Made with Unity screen.

Finally, expand the **Other Settings** section and change the **Bundle Indentifier** to match your company name. This is very important, as every app must have a unique identifier. The format of this string is: **com.[DEVELOPER].[GAME NAME]**. When configuring your app in iTunes Connect, you'll need to use this identifier.

Now to make your build. Open **File\Build Settings** and click **Build**. You will be prompted for a location to save the build. Select your **Desktop**, call it **Runestrife**, and click **Save**.

Unity will take a bit of time to generate the Xcode project which contains your iOS port of your game. All that's left to do is submit it to the App Store.

The Xcode project contains everything necessary to build and test your game on a device, and publish the game to the App Store. Apple will permit you to test the game on a device without a paid developer account, but you must have a paid developer account to submit to the App Store.

To learn more about creating a developer account, running your app on a device, and submitting your game to the App Store, check out our tutorial How to Submit An App to Apple: From No Account to App Store.

Where to go from here?

Congratulations on finishing this chapter! You're now ready to make awesome games and share them with the world on the platform of your choice. Go out there, create some beautiful games and make us proud!

Section VI: Appendices

In this section, we've collected an assortment of handy reference chapters that will serve you well on your development journey with Unity.

Chapter 22, "C# Crash Course"

Chapter 23, "The Unity API"

Chapter 24, "Unity Code Editors"

Chapter 22: C# Crash Course

Brian Moakley

Playing games is fun, but making your own games is divine!

With Unity's powerful visual editor, you can do a lot without writing any code at all. You can place objects, lay out levels, configure behavior, and more.

However, you can only go so far without coding. To get the full power of Unity, you need to write some scripts for your game logic.

Unity provides two languages to do this: C# and UnityScript. UnityScript is often referred to as JavaScript, but this is a misnomer. The two languages are very different from each other, and while you may be able to leverage some of your JavaScript skills into UnityScript, the differences are great enough to warrant a time investment into learning the language.

The other downside is that UnityScript isn't used outside of Unity. If you ever decide to stop producing games or switch to another game engine, the language won't travel with you.

This is why we recommend that you learn C#. C# is a modern object oriented programming language. Granted, for the non-programmer, it will take time to fully understand the language and how to use it, but those skills can be directly transferred to other languages and/or applications.

Unfortunately, if you have no programming experience whatsoever, this chapter is not going to help you. In fact, all it will probably do is confuse you. Thankfully, we offer a free C# video course over at www.raywenderlich.com which will teach you the basics of the language one step at a time, so we recommend you watch that instead.

If you already know a programming language, then getting up to speed should be relatively easy; that's what this chapter is for. In particular, if you have any Java experience, then you will be right at home as C# and Java are very similar.

Getting started

An easy way to get the know the language is to fire up Unity and do some scripting. But for this quick crash course, it's even easier to write your code online and have it parsed in real time.

Head over to http://rextester.com. You'll see a window much like this:

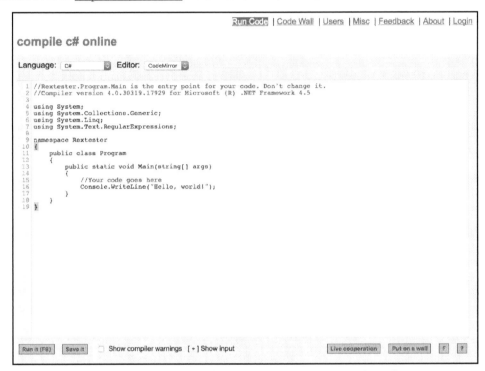

This is both a simple editor and a way for you to run some C# without having to worry about code editors or compiling anything. This site will do it all for you.

> **Note:** Compiling is the process of taking human understandable code and converting it into a language that the computer can understand.

Click the **Run it** button and you should see `Hello, world!` printed to the console.

All of the appropriate C# code is run in `Main()`. This is the the method called at the start of all C# programs and in this case, the program simply prints a message to the console. In Unity, you won't need to create `Main()` since Unity does it for you.

The basics

C# is a strongly typed language. This means, you must define your variable types before you use them. The more common types are: `int`, `float`, `double`, `string`, and `bool`.

Inside of `Main()`, add the following before the closing brace:

```
int meaningOfLife = 42;
float smallPi = 3.14f;
double bigPi = 3.14159265359;
string vaporWare = "Half Life 3";
bool likesPizza = true;
```

Your code should look as follows:

```
1  //Rextester.Program.Main is the entry point for your code. Don't change it.
2  //Compiler version 4.0.30319.17929 for Microsoft (R) .NET Framework 4.5
3
4  using System;
5  using System.Collections.Generic;
6  using System.Linq;
7  using System.Text.RegularExpressions;
8
9  namespace Rextester
10 {
11     public class Program
12     {
13         public static void Main(string[] args)
14         {
15             //Your code goes here
16             Console.WriteLine("Hello, world!");
17
18             int meaningOfLife = 42;
19             float smallPi = 3.14f;
20             double bigPi = 3.14159265359;
21             string vaporWare = "Half Life 3";
22             bool likesPizza = true;
23         }
24     }
25 }
```

The variables just hold the data. `int` holds integer data. `float` and `double` hold numbers with decimal points, otherwise known as floating point data.

A `double` uses twice as much memory to store as a `float`, so it can hold a much larger range of values.

`strings` are meant to hold text and a `bool` can only be set to `true` or `false`. This is important when making decisions in your code.

Notice that the value for `smallPi` is `3.14f`. The `f` indicates that the number is a float. By default, all floating point numbers are considered doubles, so you must indicate that you mean to use a float.

Delete the `f` and click the **Run it** button. You'll see the following:

```
Run it (F8)    Save it    ☐ Show compiler warnings  [ + ] Show input
Compilation time: 0,12 s


Error(s):
(19:29) Literal of type double cannot be implicitly converted to type 'float'; use an 'F' suffix to create a literal of this type
```

C# thinks you are assigning a `double` to a `float` — and there isn't enough room to store a `double` in a `float`.

Unity uses floats all over the place so you'll often run into this issue.

Add the **f** back to **3.14**.

You'll also notice that each line concludes with a semicolon. In C#, this is the same as a period at the end of a sentence. It lets the compiler know that a statement is concluded. If you forget to add a semicolon, you'll experience a compile error. That is, C# will not be able to determine the intent of your code, and it will stop compiling.

C# can also infer the type of a variable. Change the variables to the following:

```
var meaningOfLife = 42;
var smallPi = 3.14;
var bigPi = 3.14159265359;
var vaporWare = "Half Life 3";
var likesPizza = true;
```

By using the `var` keyword, C# is able to determine the type based on the value being assigned to it. This is a nice feature to save time. If you are new to the language, then defer to declaring your types so you can get used to thinking in types.

Often times, you'll want your variables to be immutable. Add the keyword `const` before `likesPizza` like so:

```
const var likesPizza = true;
```

Now try and change it. Add the following code underneath the previous statement:

```
likesPizza = false;
```

Click the **Run it** button. You'll now get two errors.

```
Error(s):

(22:19) Implicitly-typed local variables cannot be constant
(23:13) The left-hand side of an assignment must be a variable, property or indexer
```

First, you cannot use a constant with an inferred type. This means you should replace var with bool. Second, you are trying to change something that you've defined as a constant.

Update the definition of likesPizza like so:

```
const bool likesPizza = true;
```

and **delete**:

```
likesPizza = false;
```

Click the **Run it** button and your code will run.

Arrays

Arrays are constructs that hold multiple values. Add the following:

```
string[] writers = { "Brian", "Anthony", "Sean", "Eric" };
```

This creates a list of writers, all accessible from the variable called writers. If you don't know the values that you are using, you can just define the the number of values you think you'll need, like so:

```
string[] editors = new string[5];
```

This creates an array with a capacity of five elements. Notice the new keyword. This creates an instance of the array of strings. This keyword becomes important when working with objects.

Add the following:

```
Console.WriteLine(writers[1]);
```

Click the **Run it** button and you'll see Anthony's name printed to the console.

```
Hello, world!
Anthony
```

C# starts counting with zero, so the second element of the array is accessed by 1. You can replace a value in the array.

Add the following:

```
writers[0] = "Ray";
```

This replaces the first string in the array with another string. Now, when you access the first element, it will read: Ray instead of Brian.

Unfortunately, you can't remove indexes. Once you define an array with four elements, it will always contain four elements. If you want to copy the array to another array, you'll need to create a new array and copy all the values.

Control flow

When writing your programs, you'll need to control how the code flows based on certain values. The if statement will get you started. Add the following underneath the previous code:

```
if (likesPizza == false) {
    Console.WriteLine("You monster!");
}
```

Like other languages, the statement is evaluated and the code is run in between the braces. When assigning variables, C# also contains a ternary operator. Add the following:

```
bool isMonster = (likesPizza == true) ? false : true;
```

This is just a shorthand way of assigning a value. You can think of it as a condensed if statement.

Like other languages, you also have a bevy of loops at your disposal. The first loop is the traditional for loop.

Add the following:

```
for (int i=0; i < 10; i++) {
    Console.WriteLine("C# Rocks!");
}
```

The loop works to initialize a variable named i, then loops ten times, all the while incrementing i after each iteration.

Click the **Run it** button and you'll see that C# really does rock.

```
C# Rocks!
C# Rocks!
C# Rocks!
C# Rocks!
C# Rocks!
C# Rocks!
C# Rocks!
C# Rocks!
C# Rocks!
C# Rocks!
```

Loops work great with arrays. The array has a Length property which tells you how many elements are in the array.

Add the following:

```
for (int i=0; i < writers.Length; i++) {
   string writer = writers[i];
   Console.WriteLine(writer);
}
```

This loops through all the elements of the array and prints each element to the console. Click the **Run it** button and you'll see all the names.

```
Ray
Anthony
Sean
Eric
```

Another option is the foreach loop. This is great when working with collections like arrays. Replace the previous loop with the following:

```
foreach (string writer in writers) {
   Console.WriteLine(writer);
}
```

Click the **Run it** button and you'll see the same names.

What's nice about the foreach loop is that you don't have to worry about initializing variables and checking conditions.

Variable scope

Like other C-based languages, variables exist in a scope. This determines how they can be accessed. When a variable is outside of scope, it is no longer accessible and you will encounter a compile time error if you attempt to access it.

Add the following code:

```
if (meaningOfLife == 42) {
    bool inScope = true;
}
```

In this case, you've created an if-block and defined a new variable inside of the braces. The braces define the scope. It is only within the braces that you can access inScope.

Add the following after the brace:

```
inScope = false;
```

Click the **Run it** button and you'll see a new error.

```
Error(s):

(43:13) The name 'inScope' does not exist in the current context
```

This is what happens when you try to access an error out scope. You can only access the variable inside of the braces. The same goes for loops as well.

Delete the last line so the code compiles.

Classes and structures

There are two different ways to organize your data in C#: Structures and Classes. Let's take a look at both and explore what the differences are.

Structures

To define a structure, put the following after the last brace of Program.

```
struct Point2D {

}
```

This defines a new object type called Point2D. This isn't an object itself, but rather, a template of one. It doesn't do much, so add the following between the braces:

```
public int X;
public int Y;
```

The structure now defines a 2D point that contains two properties, an X and a Y location. public indicates that the properties can be changed from **outside** the object. If you only wanted to be able to change the properties from within the object itself, you would mark them as `private`.

In C#, the convention is to capitalize public variables. In Unity, when the variable is only intended to be used in the Inspector, then the variable is lowercased.

Now to create a new `Point2D` object. In `Main()`, before the closing brace, add the following code:

```
Point2D myPoint = new Point2D();
```

This creates a new `Point2D` struct object. Now, you need to set up the properties of the `Point2D`. Add the following code:

```
myPoint.X = 10;
myPoint.Y = 20;
```

The way to access the properties is through the dot operator followed by the property name, after which you can simply assign a value. Now that you've defined the state of the structure, you need to define the behavior. You do this by creating some methods.

Add the following to `Point2D`, after the property definitions:

```
public void AddPoint(Point2D anotherPoint) {

}
```

This is a method. `void` indicates the return type of the method, which is literally nothing. If you wanted the method to return a value instead, you'd specify the type of the value it is returning. Next is the name of the method. The parenthesis contains any parameters being passed into the method.

This method is meant to add two different points together. To do this add the following between the braces:

```
this.X = this.X + anotherPoint.X;
this.Y = this.Y + anotherPoint.Y;
```

`this` refers to the current object. In this case, you're increasing the current object's X and Y variables with the equivalent X and Y variables from another `Point2D` object, named `anotherPoint`, that has been passed into the method.

To see this in action, you need to create another `Point2D` object. In `Main()`, add the following before the closing brace:

```
Point2D anotherPoint = new Point2D();
anotherPoint.X = 5;
```

```
anotherPoint.Y = 15;
```

Now, call AddPoint() with the following:

```
myPoint.AddPoint(anotherPoint);
```

Like accessing variables, method are also accessed using the dot operator. To see the results of the method, do the following:

```
Console.WriteLine(myPoint.X);
Console.WriteLine(myPoint.Y);
```

Click the **Run it** button and you'll see the following results:

```
15
35
```

Aren't structures awesome?

Classes

So far, you've seen structures in action, but you also have something called classes.

Underneath Point2D, add the following:

```
class Point2DRef {
    public int X;
    public int Y;

    public void AddPoint(Point2DRef anotherPoint) {
        this.X = this.X + anotherPoint.X;
        this.Y = this.Y + anotherPoint.Y;
    }
}
```

Besides the name of the class, you'll notice the definition is exactly the same as a struct. The big difference between a structure and a class is how they are handled in memory. A structure is a **value** type, whereas a class is a **reference** type. A value type exists in the stack whereas a reference type exists in the heap.

The stack is short term memory whereas the heap is designed for long term memory. Ultimately, your structures are meant to handle short-lived objects that represent a value such as a leaderboard entry. A class is meant to exist for larger stretches of your program and tend to be unique, such as a player character.

These types also behave differently.

Add the following in `Main()` before the closing brace:

```
Point2D yetAnotherPoint = myPoint;
yetAnotherPoint.X = 100;
```

Here you created a new `Point2D` object by assigning an existing `Point2D` object to a variable. Then you changed the X property of the new object. When you changed the X property, what do you think happened to the original value?

Add the following to find out:

```
Console.WriteLine(myPoint.X);
Console.WriteLine(yetAnotherPoint.X);
```

Click the **Run it** button and you'll see the following results:

```
15
100
```

This is exactly as you would expect. Each new assignment to a variable copies an instance of the struct. Now add the following:

```
Point2DRef pointRef = new Point2DRef();
pointRef.X = 20;
Point2DRef anotherRef = pointRef;
anotherRef.X = 25;
```

This code creates an instance of the `Point2DRef` object, then assigns a value to its X property. Next the reference is assigned to another reference, and its X property is changed to 25. Now print out both values by adding the following:

```
Console.WriteLine(pointRef.X);
Console.WriteLine(anotherRef.X);
```

Click the **Run it** button and you'll see the following results:

```
25
25
```

As you can see, the values of the properties in each object are the same. Instead of two individual objects, you have two references to the same object. When you change a property on one reference, the change will be reflected in the other.

Memory management

The difference between classes and structs really show up in how memory is collected. For structs, memory is reclaimed when a variable goes out of scope.

This isn't true with classes. Class objects are collected when there is no more references to them. This is done through the use of `null`. By assigning `null` to a variable, the object is no longer accessible.

Add the following under the previous code:

```
pointRef = null;
```

The object is still in memory because there is another reference to it. This means the object is still accessible. Add the following:

```
anotherRef.X = 125;
Console.WriteLine(anotherRef.X);
```

Click the **Run it** button and you'll see the following result:

```
125
```

Now, set the reference to null by adding the following:

```
anotherRef = null;
```

Now that the object has no more references, it is considered eligible for **garbage collection**. This is an process that runs at indeterminate times, scanning the current application memory. If the garbage collector finds any objects without references to them, it removes those objects from memory.

Inheritance

With classes, C# employs single parent inheritance. This means objects can inherit methods and properties from their parent classes. This allows you to create general purpose classes and then specialize them based on their use.

Underneath the `Point2DRef` class, add the following:

```
class Person {
  public string Name;
  public virtual void SayHello() {
    Console.WriteLine("Hello");
  }
}
```

This creates a class named `Person` that contains a `Name` as well as a method named `SayHello()`. The method is marked `virtual` because a sub-class will override it; that is, reimplement the method to provide specialized behavior.

Underneath `Person`, add the following:

```
class RenFairePerson : Person {
  public override void SayHello() {
    Console.Write("Huzzah!");
  }
}
```

There's a couple of things happening here. First, `RenFairePerson` extends `Person`. The classname after the colon indicates the super class. Next, the class implements `SayHello`. It indicates that it is overriding the parent method by the keyword `override`.

Add the following to the bottom of `Main()`:

```
RenFairePerson person = new RenFairePerson();
person.Name = "Igor the Ratcatcher";
person.SayHello();
```

Click the **Run it** button and you'll see the following results:

```
Huzzah!
```

First, you set the name of the person. This property is obtained from the parent class. Next, you override `SayHello()`. Instead of saying `"Hello"`, the object says `"Huzzah"` instead.

At times, you may want to call the parent method. In `RenFairePerson`, add the following to the top of `SayHello()`:

```
base.SayHello();
```

Click the **Run it** button and you'll see the following results:

```
Hello
Huzzah!
```

This calls the parent method, which prints out `"Hello"` and then prints out `"Huzzah"`.

Where to go from here?

As this point, you should have enough knowledge of C# to make your way through the book. This chapter is by no means comprehensive, but it gives you a good overview of the language. As you work through the book, the text will explain the purpose of each block and what it is attempting to achieve. To learn more about C#, watch our free online C# series and reach out on our forums if you have any questions about the code. Good luck!

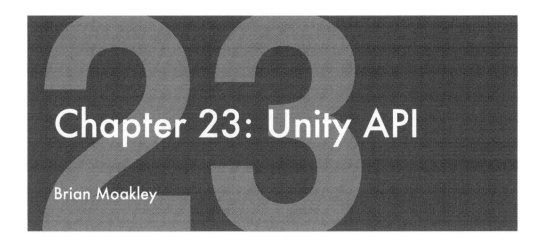

Chapter 23: Unity API

Brian Moakley

Unity is a complicated piece of software. Not only does it need to render high quality games in a variety of resolutions, but it also needs to run on dozens of platforms: from mobile to high-end PCs.

This book covered the basics of creating games with Unity, but as you can imagine, the underlying Unity API goes very deep. Understanding this API is critical to writing good games in Unity.

Unlike other chapters, this chapter is not written in the style of a tutorial, nor is it meant to be comprehensive. Rather, this is meant to give you a brief tour of the various sub systems used throughout this book so you can get a deeper idea of how and why it is being used.

So sit back, grab your self a nice drink, and enjoy this tour of the Unity API!

Vector3

Throughout your games, you will use lots of `Vector3` objects. You use them to represent two things: points, and directions.

First, you can use vectors to represent the (x,y,z) position of a GameObject in space. For example, you may set the position of a GameObject to be (100, 100, 100).

> **Note:** Unity contains other Vector objects. The `3` in `Vector3` indicates three coordinates. When working with 2D, you use `Vector2` objects and there is even a `Vector4` object. For the sake of simplicity, this section will just focus just on `Vector3` objects.

Second, you can use vectors to represent the direction and magnitude of an object. For example, when applying force to an object, you provide a `Vector3` object to indicate in what direction to apply the force, and how strong it can be. The big question: how does Unity extract that information from a single value?

Well, think back to math class when you did some charting. A vector consists of an origin (start point), an end point, a magnitude, and a direction. The origin is the start of the vector, the direction is where the vector is pointing from the start point to the end point and the magnitude is the length of the line itself.

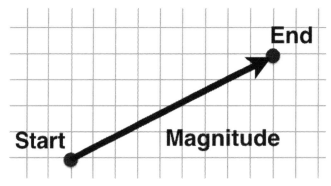

The same holds true with Unity. Take this example:

```
Vector3 myVector = new Vector3(10, 20, 10);
```

When you use a vector to indicate magnitude and direction, you are actually setting the end point of the vector. You didn't set the origin, because it's implied that the origin is zero. From this information, you can now determine both the direction and the magnitude.

Directions

You'll be using vectors a lot when setting directions. In fact, they are used so much that vectors have a bunch of static methods to help you out. There are directions for up, down, left, and right. There's also static properties for forward and back. You access them like so:

```
Vector3.forward
```

These calls return normalized coordinates (which is a fancy way of saying "vectors of length 1") referenced in global space, pointing in the appropriate directions.

For example, the forward property will return you the coordinates (0, 0, 1) whereas the back property will return: (0, 0, -1). These values will never change since they are in global space.

This is useful when working in global space; for instance, if you were moving a GameObject in a global forward direction, you would multiply the speed of the movement by the direction.

> **Note:** If you want to use local coordinates, try using transform.forward, transform.up, and transform.right instead. You'll learn more about this later in this chapter.

The positive value means the GameObject moves forward, whereas the negative value would send it in reverse. A zero, indicating no direction, means the GameObject wouldn't move at all.

Moving

Most GameObjects move. It's simply a fact of life.

In some cases, GameObjects move at a predetermined rate. For instance, you may have a spaceship in the middle of the screen that fires a bullet towards the edge of the screen.

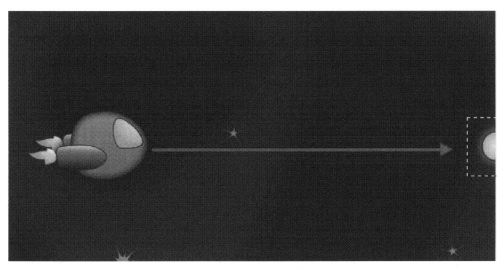

The bullet's start position and the edge of screen can be represented by vectors. All that's missing is a time component. By stating that it takes one second for the bullet to travel between the two points, you can determine the location of the bullet along a timeline.

When 0 seconds have passed, the bullet is located at the start point. At 1 second, the bullet can be found at its end point. When half a second has passed, the bullet can be found exactly between the two points.

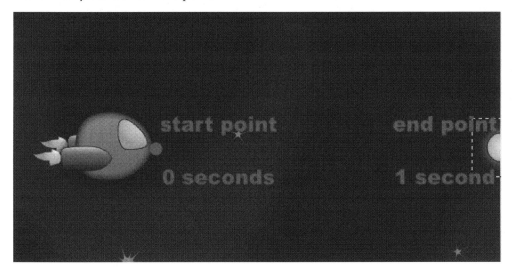

The method of finding the location based on time is called `Lerp()`. This is a function that you'll use all the time in Unity to move objects across the screen. Here's an example of `Lerp()`:

```
Vector3 result = Vector3.Lerp(start, end, .5f);
```

Both `start` and `end` represent `Vector3` objects. The last argument is the position along the timeline between the start and end points, and ranges between `0` and `1`. The value of `0` represents the start position and `1` represents the end position. `0.5` is the exact midpoint between those two points.

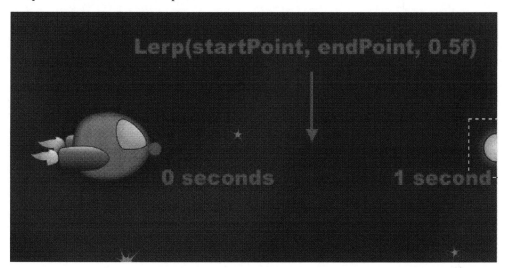

Typically, you'll call this every frame and update the GameObject's position from the result of `Lerp()`. You store the accumulated time from the start of the movement by way of `Time.deltaTime`. `deltaTime` is how much time has passed since the last frame.

```
float timePasssed += Time.deltaTime;
```

Then, you divide the total accumulated time by the length of the animation.

```
float currentTime = timePassed / 1.0f;
```

Since the total length of the animation is one second, you divide `timePassed` by 1. The result of this division is passed into `Lerp()`.

```
bullet.position = Vector3.Lerp(startPosition, endPosition,
    currentTime)
```

This will animate the bullet to the edge of the screen.

`Lerp()` moves in a straight line. If you want to move a GameObject along a curve, you use `Slerp()` instead which takes the magnitudes of the `Vector3` objects into account.

Operators

Vectors also come with overloaded operators, which makes it easy to work between vectors. For instance, when adding two vectors, you may be tempted to do this:

```
Vector forward = Vector3.forward;
Vector down = Vector3.down;
Vector3 result = new Vector3(forward.X + down.X, forward.Y +
down.Y,
    forward.Z + down.Z);
```

Instead, you can just add them together like so:

```
Vector forward = Vector3.forward;
Vector down = Vector3.down;
Vector3 result = forward + down;
```

You can also multiply, divide, and subtract vectors as well. This makes the intent more clear, with less chance of error.

Transform

If there's one property all GameObjects share, it's that they all come with Transform components. The transform provides three things: the position, the scale, and the rotation.

The `position` property is simply a Vector3 indicating the location of the GameObject. To set the scale, you use the `localScale` property, which is relative to the parent GameObject. To set the rotation, you have two options: `localRotation` and `rotation`. `localRotation` is the rotation of the GameObject relative to the parent object, whereas `rotation` is relative to the world.

When rotating your objects, you use an object called a "quaternion". You'll learn about quaternions in the next section.

Direction

When working with GameObjects, it's critical to understand its concept of direction; that is, where is the front, and where is the back? For instance, if your GameObject is a spaceship, you may want to move the ship in a forward direction. Unity provides a couple of properties to help you out.

`transform.forward` gives you the forward direction of the GameObject, `transform.right` determines the right hand side, and `transform.up` give you the up direction relative to your GameObject.

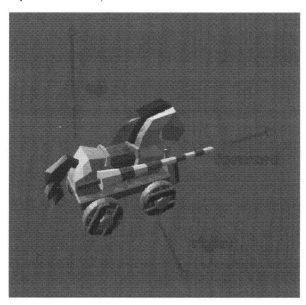

Notice that there is no left, down, or backwards properties. To get these values, you multiply the transform direction by −1 like so:

```
Vector3 left = transform.right * −1;
```

It's an extra step, but not too tricky to figure out.

Relationships

Transform (like all other components) derives from the **Component** class. One handy property it inherits is **gameObject**, which lets you get a reference to the GameObject that the component is attached to.

Transform itself also comes with some handy properties and methods. For example, there are times when you need to access the parent GameObject. For this, use the **parent** property on **Transform**:

- If there isn't a parent GameObject, then the property will return a null value.

- If you want to set a parent, you use **SetParent()**.

- Setting the parent to **null** will remove the GameObject from the parent GameObject.

```
transform.parent = null;
```

Transforms also allow you to search for any child GameObjects by name. To do this, you use `Find()`. The problem with `Find()` is that it's slow, so if you need to use it in a loop or in a repeating method like `Update()`, store the results of `Find()` in a variable.

```
transform enemy = transform.Find("enemy");
```

And of course, to get rid of all those children, you use `DetachChildren()`. This doesn't destroy the GameObjects. It simply moves them out of the current hierarchy.

```
enemy.DetachChildren();
```

Transforms contain a lot of additional methods to allow you to do things such as face a GameObject towards another, change the name or tags, or even move GameObjects by way of `Translate()`. In short, when you need to manipulate a GameObject in 3D space, check with the transform first. Chances are, it has a method to do what you need.

Quaternions

A quaternion is an object that represents the rotation of an object. At its heart, a quaternion a complex mathematical construct that will keep you up nights questioning your existence. All jokes aside, although quaternions may seem complex at first, they aren't too difficult to work with in practice.

A quaternion represents an x, y, z, and w coordinate. The x, y, and z coordinates represent the coordinate of the rotation, while w indicates the cosine of half the rotation angle. Unity recommends that you never directly adjust any of these coordinates unless "you know what you are doing". If you don't understand the math behind the quaternion, let the `Quaternion` class handle it for you.

When setting up an object, you'll often need to set up its default rotation. To provide a quaternion without any rotation, you use the identity property like so:

```
Quaternion.identity;
```

When working with rotation in the Inspector, you'll use what are known as **Euler angles**. These make it easy to understand the rotation in terms we're used to thinking about (i.e. "90 degrees along the X-axis"). You can use Euler angles to set the rotation of quaternion like so:

```
Quaternion objectRotation = Quaternion.identity;
objectRotation.eulerAngles = new Vector3(90, 0, 0);
```

This rotates the quaternion by 90 degrees along the x-axis, which you can then assign back to the transform.

Quaternions also give you lots of other functions as well such as `RotateTowards()`, `Slerp()`, and `Inverse()`. Finally, if you have two different quaternions, you can multiply them together to combine the rotations.

```
Quaternion combined = horizontalRotation * verticalRotation;
```

GameObjects

GameObjects are the bread and butter of Unity. You use them all over the place to account for all the various objects in your game. Every GameObject can be accessed any of its components like so:

```
transform.gameObject
```

You'll frequently need to access the components of GameObjects. For instance, you may want to change the color of a lighting component. To do so, you call `GetComponent()` like so:

```
Light pointLight = GetComponent<Light>();
```

You must pass in the type of the component using generic syntax. If there is no light attached to the GameObject, then the return value will be `null`. While not an expensive method to use, a common pattern is to cache the results in a variable to avoid making lots of lookup calls.

There are also methods to get components in children, in parents, or just get a listing of components on the current GameObject. In short, you have a variety of options to access components of the current GameObject and any related GameObjects.

Disabling GameObjects

You may not need a GameObject in a particular scene, but still need it on hand for later in the game. To disable a GameObject, you call `SetActive()` like so:

```
gameObject.SetActive(false);
```

This means the GameObject will simply disappear from the scene, but it will still be present in the Hierarchy. All of its components will be deactivated and it won't interact with any of the current GameObjects.

MonoBehaviour

`MonoBehaviour` is the base class every script derives from. It has a lot of handy methods you can use: for example, `MonoBehaviours` can create GameObjects with `Instantiate()` and can delete objects with `Destroy()`.

In addition, you can override certain methods on `MonoBehavior` to be notified upon certain events, which correspond to various phases in the lifecycle of the object the script is attached to.

The following phases occur in the order listed.

Initialization phase

These are events that correspond when the `MonoBehaviour` is first initialized or re-enabled.

- **Awake**: Occurs only once when the script is called, after all the objects are initialized. This means you can access other GameObjects without having to worry if they've been instantiated or not.

- **OnEnable**: Called when the current script has either been re-enabled or started for the first time. This means `OnEnable()` will be called, at least once, for every GameObject.

- **Start**: Called immediately before the first `Update()`, but only if the script has been enabled.

Physics phase

These events may occur more than once per frame to calculate the physics of the particular GameObject.

- **FixedUpdate**: Occurs at fixed points in time in conjunction with the physics engine, regardless of the frame rate. Any changes in regards to physics should occur in this event.

- **OnTriggerEnter**: Called when a GameObject with a collider crosses a trigger.

- **OnCollisionEnter**: Resembles `OnTriggerEnter()`, except it's called when two objects collide with each other.

Input events phase

These events occur when the user interacts with the mouse in some fashion.

- **OnMouseDown**: Occurs when the user presses the mouse button over a collider or GUIElement.

- **OnMouseUp**: Called when the user releases the mouse button.

- **OnMouseOver**: Called when the mouse is over a collider or GUIElement.

- **OnMouseEnter**: Called when the mouse enters a collider or GUIElement.

- **OnMouseExit**: Called when the mouse exits a collider or GUIElement.

- **OnMouseDrag**: Called when the mouse button is clicked and held over a collider or GUIElement.

- **OnMouseUpAsButton**: Occurs when a mouse is over a collider or GUIElement and the mouse button is pressed and released.

Game logic

These are prime logic events inside your game.

- **Update**: Occurs once per frame and is where your general game logic occurs.

- **LateUpdate**: Called after all the calculations have completed in Update(). This is handy when you need to make additional calculations based on the results of Update().

Scene rendering

These events occur with the rendering of all the graphics in the current scene.

- **OnPreCull**: Called before the camera determines which GameObjects can be seen. This event occurs before the culling process.

- **OnWillRenderObject**: Called for each camera that can see a GameObject.

- **OnBecameVisible**: Occurs when a renderer becomes visible to any camera.

- **OnBecameInvisible**: Occurs when a renderer is no longer visible to any camera.

- **OnPreRender**: Called just before the scene is rendered by the camera.

- **OnPostRender**: Called when the camera has finished rendering the scene and is meant to be associated with an enabled camera component.

- **OnRenderObject**: Called right after the camera has completed rendering the scene.

This is very similar to `OnPostRender` except it will work with GameObjects.

- **OnRenderImage**: Called after rendering is complete to create an image. This allows you to add effect in the post-processing pass, such as turning a color image black and white.

Pausing, disabling and decommissioning

This final batch of events occur when you pause, disable, and decommission GameObjects.

- **OnDisable**: Occurs when a component becomes disabled or inactive.

- **OnApplicationQuit**: Occurs when the application is about to end or if you are exiting playmode.

- **OnDestroy**: Called before the `MonoBehaviour` is going to be destroyed. If you need to do any clean up, this is a good time to do it.

The `MonoBehaviour` contains a lot of events; we haven't covered them all here. Check out the Unity documentation to see what more events are available to you.

Unity attributes

Unity attributes are special declarations you can use throughout your code. These attributes perform a variety of functions on your GameObjects.

One of the great things about attributes is that you can use them to extend the editor. By default, all code runs in Play mode, but with an attribute, you can make it run in the editor as well.

Here are a few attributes available to you:

RequireComponent

You'll often write scripts that depend on a variety of components. Use `RequireComponent` to ensure that a component is always present:

```
[RequireComponent (typeof (Text))]
```

This line of code enforces that a `Text` component must be available. Unity will automatically add the component, and it will prevent you from removing it so long as the attribute is there.

SerializeField

You can use this attribute when you want a field to be accessible in the Inspector, but not accessible from other scripts.

```
[SerializeField]
private bool isAlive = true;
```

Using the above code, you can now set the value of isAlive in the Inspector, but not from other scripts.

HideInInspector

You also can hide public values in the Inspector as well.

```
[HideInInspector]
public int Score
```

Here the variable is exposed to other scripts but will not appear in the Inspector.

Setting a range

Instead of using a text field to set a number, you can use a slider instead. This means that a value will never be outside any give range.

```
[Range (1,100)]
public int secretNumber;
```

The field will now look like this in the Inspector:

Special folders

Throughout the book, you've organized the Project Browser according to the assets used. Placing assets in these folders alters the behavior of the editor. Typically, you do this to tweak the editor to your needs, but you can also create a plugin for the editor as well.

Editor

Any assets placed in the Editor folder will be treated as editor augmentations. These scripts allow you extend the editor and add additional functionality. When you build a game, these assets are removed and not included with the final game.

Gizmos

Gizmos are graphics used in the Scene view to help you annotate the scene. For instance, you can use them to denote invisible spawn points.

Plugins

The plugin folder contains any code that can also extend Unity. These plugin files can be DLLs written in C or C++ that you incorporate directly into Unity.

Resources

Resources are additional files you can include with your game that can be loaded on-demand. For instance, you may want to use XML to store some of your game variables. You would include those XML files inside the Resources folder, and then load them on demand.

Standard Assets

If you import any of the packages from Unity's standard assets, these assets will be included in this folder.

Streaming Assets

These are assets that are streamed from the file system to the player. For instance, if you were to include a movie with your game, you'd place the movie file inside this folder.

Where to go from here?

As you can see, the Unity API goes very deep.

By going through this book and this chapter, you now have some practical experience making games with Unity, and a firm overview of the Unity API. From here on out, we recommend you just dive into making your own game!

Just be sure to keep the Unity API documentation available for reference as you go:

• https://docs.unity3d.com/ScriptReference

We look forward to seeing some great games from you! :]

Chapter 24: Code Editors

By Brian Moakley

One thing to love about Unity is that you can use any code editor you like to write Unity scripts. This chapter will introduce you to two popular editors: MonoDevelop and Visual Studio.

Each section will cover some of the more common operations, such as setting up tabs and code preferences, as well as walk you through the basics of using the debuggers. You'll also learn about some of their benefits and caveats.

On their own, each of the integrated developer environments (IDE) are quite expansive. Once you pick an environment, you should research and learn its ins and outs to the best of your ability to make the most of the toolset.

MonoDevelop vs Visual Studio

Unity ships with MonoDevelop to provide a cohesive development experience across all platforms.

MonoDevelop is an open source IDE that was first released on Linux for C# development. It was designed to work with Mono runtime, which is the open source implementation of the .NET runtime.

MonoDevelop does everything you'd expect from a reliable IDE. There's syntax highlighting to visually differentiate variables from keywords. It has code completion that saves you precious typing time — not to mention typos — while also providing an easy means of discovering unknown methods and properties. It even packs an integrated debugger that lets you find issues in your code before compiling and running.

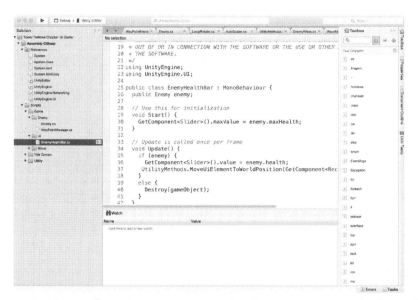

Unfortunately, it's not all good news. MonoDevelop has some annoying little quirks. In the past few years, the environment has become a bit of a sore spot due to core features acting strangely or just not working. Nothing is worse than having your code completion stop working on the eve of a deadline, or opening a file only to discover your code space settings mysteriously reset themselves.

The other complaint about MonoDevelop is that Unity packages its own version with the noble intent of providing smoother integration with the engine. The unfortunate result is that if you find a bug, you have to wait for the MonoDevelop team to fix it, and then keep your cool while the Unity team picks up and rolls the fix into their own version.

Thankfully, things have improved with each release of MonoDevelop. Unity has apparently listened to developers and designed Unity so that MonoDevelop isn't the only game in town. In Unity's general settings (**Edit\Preferences** on PC, **Unity\Preferences** on Mac), you'll notice that you have the ability to change your editor settings.

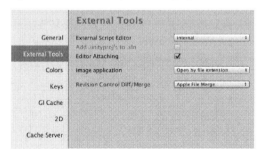

From here, you can switch to an editor that suits your preferences. For Windows users, this means you can leverage a real powerhouse of an editor: Visual Studio.

Visual Studio is not just one tool, rather, it's a series of tools produced by Microsoft for developing applications for its ecosystem. The suite is mature, powerful and well supported. Not too long ago, acquiring Visual Studio meant paying a hefty fee; however, Microsoft recently released "community editions" that will do everything you need, but for the low, low price of free!

Of course, there are criteria for using the community version (much like the free version of Unity), and if you don't fit these criteria, you'll have to open your wallet and get the pro version.

A note on IDEs and Unity

IDEs will often integrate a compiler so that you can easily compile code. Instead of having to save your code and run the compiler from the command line, you simply click a button, and voila, your project builds!

This is not the case with Unity where the engine itself compiles your code. While the IDE does this for you too, Unity disregards the result of that compilation and recompiles it on its own. This is an automatic process. Whenever you return to Unity, it checks your code. If it finds an update, it will recompile the code without any input from you.

This feature provides a unique advantage, as Unity will recompile your code even when you're playing your game. It allows you to make code changes and instantly see the results in your game. In other environments, you need to restart the game after each change and then recreate the state where you found the issue. Ugh.

In Unity, it's all automatic — automagic, even.

There's a downside, unfortunately. There may be times when Unity and the IDE are out of sync, and in turn, you get inconsistent error messages. This usually only happens with MonoDevelop. Essentially, MonoDevelop builds your code and for some reason, reports a successful compilation. Then, upon returning to Unity, you'll get a list of errors.

Always defer to Unity. In these cases, the chances are that the IDE is using some cached code. To break out of the madness, you have to perform a clean operation to rebuild everything rather than just capturing the changes. Alternatively, you can just restart the IDE.

Getting started with MonoDevelop

If you've already downloaded Unity, congratulations — you've also downloaded MonoDevelop.

If you choose to stick with it, you'll be spending a lot of time inside of MonoDevelop, so it helps to learn the lay of the land.

MonoDevelop, like Unity, is composed of a series of views. Each view is intended to help you with a certain task. The editor is broken down like so:

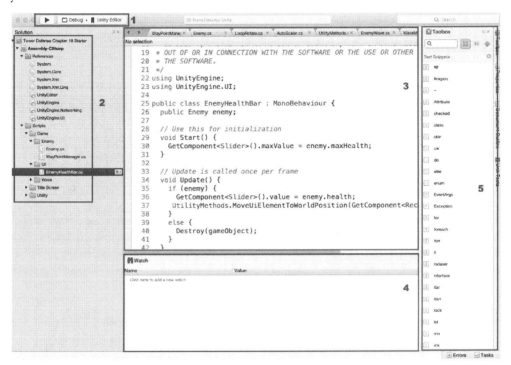

1. This is the current target of the IDE which should be Unity Editor. When debugging, you can also set this to a game in progress — more on this later.

2. This section contains all the files in your current assembly. It provides a nice way of switching files without leaving the editor.

3. This is the code editors and where you'll spend the majority of your time. I often use this as my only view.

4. This view is used for debugging scripts in real-time.

5. This view contains a bunch of utilities to assist with the writing of your code. For instance, the Toolbox has boilerplate code that you can copy into your project.

Some views will pop-out then disappear, whereas others will remain fixed in place. You can customize this behavior from the view itself. Each view contains two buttons in the upper-right corner.

Pressing the square will either keep the view in place or make it visible for the limited time you need it. The **x** will remove it entirely. If you wish to recover a view, you can display it from the **View** menu.

Spaces or tabs

Developers tend to either use spaces or tabs to indent their code. As you probably know, which one is best can be a rather contentious issue. MonoDevelop doesn't care; in fact, it's easy to change this setting.

Open the MonoDevelop preferences (**Tools\Options** on Windows and **MonoDevelop\Preferences** on Mac). You'll see a window with a ton of configuration options. Look for the section called **Source Code**, expand **Code Formatting** and select **C# source code**.

The **Whitespace** section contains all the options needed to match your preferences. Keep in mind that these settings only affect new projects versus your current projects. For this reason, it's a good idea to set up the editor **first** before you start using it.

MonoDevelop also has the concept of policies, which are simply sets of predefined behaviors. For instance, if you prefer spacing to match K&R Style, you can select the K&R policy from the **Policy** dropdown.

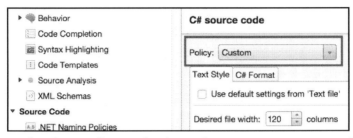

These changes only affect C# files. Under the Code Formatting section, you'll notice other file types such as **Text file** and **XML file**. If you want those files to behave in a similar manner, you'll have to configure them as well.

Braces

Braces, like tabs and spaces, are another source of controversy between developers. Everyone has their preferences, and it's terribly obnoxious when an IDE forces the matter. Thankfully, MonoDevelop allows you to reconfigure how braces are formatted as well.

To configure your braces, select the **C# Format** tab in the **C# Source code** page. You'll then see a panel with some sample code.

```
Text Style  C# Format

Edit
Preview:

using System;

namespace Example
{
  public class Test
  {
    public static void Main (string[] args)
    {
      for (int i = 0; i < 10; i++) {
        Console.WriteLine ("{0}: Test", i);
      }
    }
  }
}
```

The code window shows the current brace style. To change the styling, click the **Edit** button to reveal a list of options. In here, you can configure all aspects of C# formatting.

From the Category option, select **Braces**.

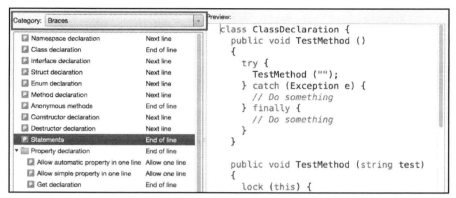

At this point, you can configure how braces will behave throughout MonoDevelop. If you were particularly mischievous, you could reconfigure a friend's environment according to your preferences the same way.

Project templates

You'll quickly discover that even though you've configured your MonoDevelop settings, new C# files created inside of Unity won't reflect these changes. This is because Unity uses templates to generate `MonoBehaviour` classes — yes, the International English spelling is correct syntax.

You have to modify the project templates so all new files will acquire them. On Windows, you access them from **C:\Program Files\Unity\Editor\Data\Resources\ScriptTemplates**. On a Mac, you need to open the Applications folder in Finder, then right-click the **Unity.app** bundle and select **Show Package Contents**. Inside the bundle, you can access the templates in **Contents/Resources/ScriptTemplates/**.

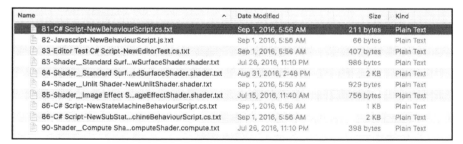

Only after that will your changes be applied to newly generated scripts inside of Unity. Make sure to **restart Unity** after your changes. Be advised that new versions of Unity may go ahead and overwrite your precious templates, so do yourself a solid and keep a separate copy of them somewhere safe, perhaps even in a safe deposit box.

Debugging

When working with Unity, the easiest way to diagnose bugs is to print a message to the console like so:

```
Debug.Log("Hello!");
```

This is a basic way of approaching a problem that's also known as **caveman debugging**. While it's useful to see certain values in the console, it fills your log with messages. For repeating methods like Update(), finding the important messages is very much like searching for a needle in a haystack.

Thankfully, Unity comes with an integrated debugger that empowers you to solve problems in a more sophisticated manner.

To get started with debugging, you need to create a breakpoint. A **breakpoint** is an indication to the debugger where the code should pause its execution. In MonoDevelop, you specify a breakpoint by clicking the gutter on the left-hand side of the editor. Doing so produces a red dot and highlights the selected line in red.

```
1 using UnityEngine;
2 using System.Collections.Generic;
3 public class WayPointManager : MonoBehaviour {
4     //1
5     public static WayPointManager Instance;
6     //2
7     public List<Path> Paths = new List<Path>();
8     void Awake() {
9         //3
10        Instance = this;
11    }
```

This won't stop your code — yet. You must start the debugger. To do that, press the **play** button, making sure the Unity Editor is the current target.

Once you start the debugger, it will attach itself to the Unity editor. At this point, when you play your game, the editor will pause at the breakpoint, giving you an opportunity to inspect any variables.

You can do this with the Locals view found in the debug area.

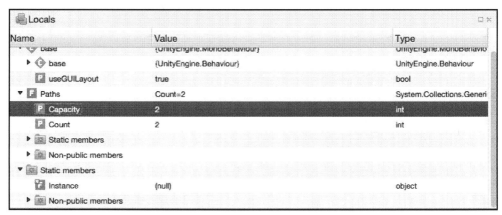

This view allows you to inspect variables in real-time without having to bother with writing log statements. Of course, you can also move through your code, line by line. Near the debugger play button, you'll notice a series of controls.

These controls allow you to resume execution of the program, skip a line, or step in and out of a certain method.

As you develop games, you'll discover that the debugger is indispensable.

Getting started with Visual Studio

As mentioned before, Unity comes bundled with MonoDevelop. While it does provide a consistent coding environment on all platforms, its quirks are bound to drive you to pulling your hair out — eventually.

Thankfully, on Windows, installing Visual Studio is easy. You might be tempted to head over to Microsoft's download center, but stop right there.

Unity requires additional software to integrate with Visual Studio. It's finicky like that. The right way to get Visual Studio is by downloading it via the Unity installer.

If you deleted the installer, just download it again from Unity's website.

When you start the installer, select the option, **Microsoft Visual Studio Community 2015**.

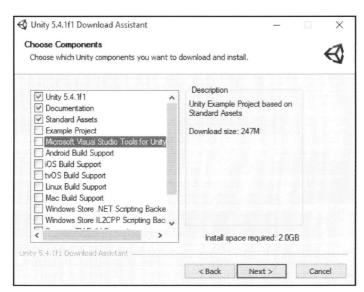

You'll be prompted to accept some EULAs, and then it's a just a matter of sitting back and waiting for the IDE to install.

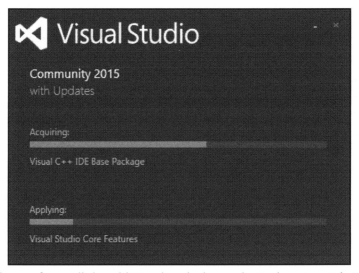

Unity will also configure all the additional tools that make it play nice with Unity. The installation will take a while, but it's worth the wait.

Getting used to Visual Studio

Visual Studio can be intimidating, but it's not so bad once you get to know it. Like Unity, it's composed of a series of views you can arrange into custom layouts. You can save your layouts and reuse them for certain tasks and workflows.

Here's a breakdown of the editor:

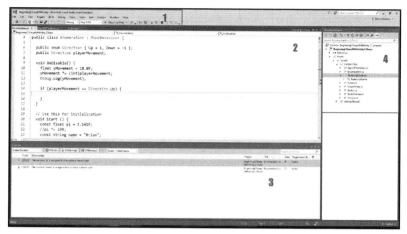

1. This is your standard menubar and toolbar to assist with various tasks. An important button is the **Attach to Unity** button, which you'll use to start debugging.

2. This your code editor. I tend to keep just this view open when working on projects, as it helps me avoid the distraction that comes from visual noise.

3. Some views will appear underneath the editor. Typically, this is where you manage your debugger and learn of errors in your project.

4. The right-hand column provides another location for tools such as the Solution Explorer which allows you to not only see all your script files, but expand them to see all their methods and properties at a glance.

Like Unity, views can be added, removed and docked. By clicking the **View** option from the menubar, you'll see that you have a plethora of views at your disposal, complete with hotkeys to activate them without the hassle of using your mouse.

<>	Code	F7
↪	Open	
	Open With...	
▣	Solution Explorer	Ctrl+Alt+L
◉	Unity Project Explorer	Shift+Alt+E
▥	Team Explorer	Ctrl+\, Ctrl+M
▤	Server Explorer	Ctrl+Alt+S
▭	Bookmark Window	Ctrl+K, Ctrl+W
⋰	Call Hierarchy	Ctrl+Alt+K
◈	Class View	Ctrl+Shift+C
▢	Code Definition Window	Ctrl+\, D
▦	Object Browser	Ctrl+Alt+J
▣	Error List	Ctrl+\, E

WTF is CR LF?

When you first open a script in Unity, you may encounter a weird dialog that looks like the following:

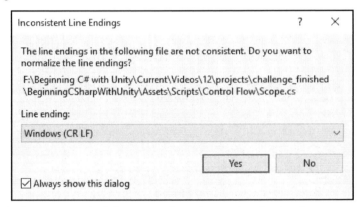

No warning is fun, never mind those warnings that make absolutely no sense. This pesky warning relates to the line endings of the generated script files.

That's right, the cause of the problem is the *file itself*.

Whoever created the file did it in a Unix-based system, whereas you're using a Windows-based system. Unix manages line endings differently than Windows, so this error is Visual Studio way of asking how to handle these mysterious line endings.

Simply click **OK** and Visual Studio will politely convert the line endings for you.

"But wait", you say, "I get this even when I create a new file! What gives?"

Unity creates new scripts based on templates, and those templates are the cause of the line ending issues. To fix the issue, you must change the templates. What is it with IDEs and their funky templates?

First, open Visual Studio. Click **File\Open\File** and then head over to the following location: **C:\Program Files\Unity\Editor\Data\Resources\ScriptTemplates**.

This directory contains a list of templates that Unity uses to create your scripts. For fixing the C# templates, open **81-C# Script-NewBehaviourScript.cs.txt**.

Next, click **File\Advanced Save**. Here you'll see a familiar dialog. Set the line endings to **Windows (CR LF)** and click **OK**.

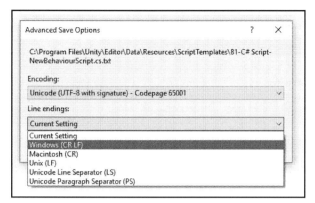

Now you'll no longer get that message. When working with a source control program such as `git`, the Windows line endings will be stripped — don't be surprised when you encounter the message again.

Braces and spaces

If you ever want to start a fight at a developer conference, pick a packed table at lunch, declare "tabs for life", then get out of there before the lasagna starts flying so you can livestream the fiasco. Developers have their preferences and can be quasi-religious about them.

Thankfully, Visual Studio is amiable. It won't scold you for inserting tabs nor will it scoff at you for tapping the space bar. To customize formatting, select **Tools\Options**. When the window opens, you'll see a *ton* of things to configure. Thankfully, the options contain a search bar to make it easier to find the setting(s) you seek.

To change your indent style, you can find the options under **Text Editor\C#\Tabs** like the following:

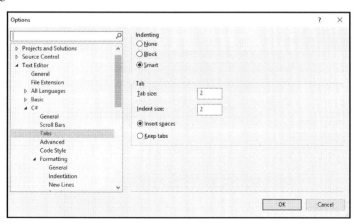

To change your brace style, you can find the options under **Text Editor\C#\Formatting\New Lines** like so:

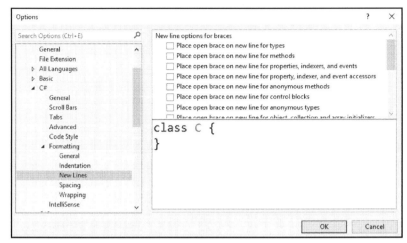

You can set up your braces by reviewing the options and checking the conditions for when the brace should be on a new line.

Keep in mind that any changes that you make to brace options in Visual Studio won't be reflected in any new Unity script files. This is because Unity creates new scripts based on — you guessed it — templates as covered in the previous section. To change the styling, you'll need to change the template files as outlined in the last section. Restart Unity after making your changes.

These changes will only affect new scripts. For existing scripts, you'll have to change things manually.

Debugging

Being a top-level IDE, Visual Studio also comes with a top-level debugger. Debuggers allow you to pause your game in motion and inspect the state of the variables.

> **Note:** This section matches the previous debugging section for MonoDevelop with the instructions for Visual Studio instead.

To get started with debugging, you first need to create a breakpoint. A breakpoint is an indicator to the debugger that it should pause its execution at that point. Just as you do with MonoDevelop, you create a breakpoint by clicking on the gutter in the left-hand side of the editor. Doing so will produce a red dot and highlight the line in red.

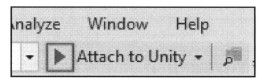

```
 8    void OnDisable() {
 9        int value = 36;
10        int additionalValue = 0;
11        if (shouldProceed) {
12            additionalValue = 6;
13        }
```

This won't stop your code — yet. To start the debugger, press the **play** button and make sure the Unity Editor is the current target.

Once you start the debugger, it will attach itself to the Unity editor. When you play the game, the editor will pause at the breakpoint so that you can inspect any variables in your game. You can do this with the Autos view.

This view allows you to inspect your variables in real-time without writing bothersome log statements. Of course, you can also move through your code line by line. You'll notice a series of controls near the debugger play button.

These controls allow you to resume execution of the program, skip a line, and step freely in and out of methods.

As you develop games, you'll discover the debugger is an indispensable tool.

Expiration

After 30 days, you may log in and get a rude awakening about how the evaluation period has ended. Once you cross that threshold, there's no turning back. You won't be able to use the software until you appease the makers — you must register it with your Microsoft account.

Have no fear! If you're using the community edition, you still don't have to pay to play. All you need do is create a free Microsoft account (or use your existing) and then answer some questions. After that, it's business as usual.

To register your copy of Visual Studio, simply go to **Help\Register Product**. It's better to do it early in the process rather than waiting until the trial ends. You know how Murphy's law works, right? You'll get that message at the worst possible time. Doing it early means you won't have worry about jumping through hoops when your internet has crashed, and you have a deadline staring you in the face. :]

Where to go from here?

IDEs are meant to assist with your pursuit of being a faster and more productive coder. If you find yourself changing your development habits to match the workflow of the editor, then you should reconsider the relationship and investigate alternatives.

Ultimately, choose what works best for you and your team. Once you select your tool, make sure to keep learning about it; these programs are feature-rich and can take a while to master. The more you understand your IDE, the less time you spend figuring out how the thing works and the more time you spend making amazing games!

Conclusion

We hope you've enjoyed this book as much as we enjoyed making it! Unity is an amazing platform for building games that look incredible and are a joy to play. We can't wait to see what you'll produce on your own, now that you're armed with all the information you covered in this book.

If you have any questions or comments as you continue to develop with Unity, please stop by our forums at http://www.raywenderlich.com/forums and share your thoughts.

We thank you sincerely for purchasing this book. Your continued support is what makes the tutorials, books, videos, conferences and everything else we do at raywenderlich.com possible — we truly appreciate it!

Wishing you all the best, wherever your Unity gaming adventures take you,

– Mike, Sean, Brian, Eric, and Anthony

The *Unity Games by Tutorials* team

Made in the USA
Middletown, DE
15 June 2017